THE ENGLISH REPUBLICAN EXILES IN EUROPE DURING THE RESTORATION

The Restoration of the Stuart monarchy in 1660 changed the lives of English republicans for good. Despite the Declaration of Breda, where Charles II promised to forgive those who had acted against his father and the monarchy during the Civil War and Interregnum, opponents of the Stuart regime felt unsafe, and many were actively persecuted. Nevertheless, their ideas lived on in the political underground of England and in the exile networks they created abroad. While much of the historiography of English republicanism has focused on the British Isles and the legacy of the English Revolution in the American colonies, this study traces the lives, ideas and networks of three seventeenth-century English republicans who left England for the European Continent after the Restoration. On the basis of sources from a range of English and continental European archives, Gaby Mahlberg explores the lived experiences of these three exiles – Edmund Ludlow in Switzerland, Henry Neville in Italy and Algernon Sidney – for a truly transnational perspective on early modern English republicanism.

GABY MAHLBERG is Honorary Associate Professor at the University of Warwick and the author of *Henry Neville and English Republican Culture in the Seventeenth Century* (2009). With Dirk Wiemann, she is co-editor of *European Contexts for English Republicanism* (2013) and *Perspectives on English Revolutionary Republicanism* (2014).

T0382462

IDEAS IN CONTEXT

Edited by
David Armitage, Richard Bourke and Jennifer Pitts

The books in this series will discuss the emergence of intellectual traditions and of related new disciplines. The procedures, aims and vocabularies that were generated will be set in the context of the alternatives available within the contemporary frameworks of ideas and institutions. Through detailed studies of the evolution of such traditions, and their modification by different audiences, it is hoped that a new picture will form of the development of ideas in their concrete contexts. By this means, artificial distinctions between the history of philosophy, of the various sciences, of society and politics, and of literature may be seen to dissolve.

The series is published with the support of the Exxon Foundation.

A full list of titles in the series can be found at: www.cambridge.org/IdeasContext

THE ENGLISH REPUBLICAN EXILES IN EUROPE DURING THE RESTORATION

GABY MAHLBERG

University of Warwick

CAMBRIDGE
UNIVERSITY PRESS

CAMBRIDGE
UNIVERSITY PRESS

Shaftesbury Road, Cambridge CB2 8EA, United Kingdom

One Liberty Plaza, 20th Floor, New York, NY 10006, USA

477 Williamstown Road, Port Melbourne, VIC 3207, Australia

314–321, 3rd Floor, Plot 3, Splendor Forum, Jasola District Centre, New Delhi – 110025, India

103 Penang Road, #05–06/07, Visioncrest Commercial, Singapore 238467

Cambridge University Press is part of Cambridge University Press & Assessment,
a department of the University of Cambridge.

We share the University's mission to contribute to society through the pursuit of
education, learning and research at the highest international levels of excellence.

www.cambridge.org
Information on this title: www.cambridge.org/9781108794985

DOI: 10.1017/9781108894463

First published 2020
First paperback edition 2024

A catalogue record for this publication is available from the British Library

Library of Congress Cataloging-in-Publication data
NAMES: Mahlberg, Gaby, author.
TITLE: The English republican exiles in Europe during the Restoration / Gaby Mahlberg.
DESCRIPTION: New York : Cambridge University Press, 2020. | Series: Ideas in context |
Includes bibliographical references and index.
IDENTIFIERS: LCCN 2020015208 (print) | LCCN 2020015209 (ebook) |
ISBN 9781108841627 (hardback) | ISBN 9781108794985 (paperback) |
ISBN 9781108894463 (epub)
SUBJECTS: LCSH: Great Britain–History–Charles II, 1660-1685–Biography. |
Republicanism–England–History–17th century. | Republicanism–Europe–History. |
Neville, Henry, 1620-1694–Influence. | Sidney, Algernon, 1623-1683–Influence. |
Ludlow, Edmund, 1617?-1692–Influence.
CLASSIFICATION: LCC DA447.A3 M34 2020 (print) | LCC DA447.A3 (ebook) |
DDC 942.06/209224–dc23
LC record available at https://lccn.loc.gov/2020015208
LC ebook record available at https://lccn.loc.gov/2020015209

ISBN   978-1-108-84162-7   Hardback
ISBN   978-1-108-79498-5   Paperback

*For exiles, expats, émigrés and refugees escaping
and missing their home*

Contents

Figures

Acknowledgements

This is my very own Brexit book, which in many ways reflects on the relationship of early modern England with the European Continent. The bulk of it was written following my move to Berlin in 2015 after having lived in the United Kingdom on and off for the best part of fifteen years and just as the government was gearing up to the fateful referendum. As I am writing these lines, the UK is about to break with the European Union. Yet the idea for this book goes back a lot further. It was first conceived in the early 2000s when I was doing my PhD at the University of East Anglia. While undertaking research on the English republican Henry Neville, I noticed how little secondary literature there was on his Italian exile, and I soon came to realise that there was a similar dearth of material on other republican thinkers of the period who had spent time abroad. There simply had not been much interest in the continental European connections of seventeenth-century English republicans. Two decades later this has changed somewhat, but there is still a lot of scope to explore the multiple ways in which the British Isles and Europe were entangled with each other through geography, culture, politics, faith and, most of all, personal connections, especially now that the UK is redefining its relationship with Europe and the European Union.

The initial research for this book was made possible by a Small Grant of the British Academy which I received shortly after starting a new post at Northumbria University in Newcastle upon Tyne in 2011. This grant allowed me to travel and follow my three English republican exiles across Europe, while a period of research leave also helped with the writing. I also benefited from two short-term fellowships at the Research Center for Social and Cultural Studies in Gotha, and at the Herzog August Bibliothek in Wolfenbüttel. Alas, I soon felt compelled to leave my friends and colleagues in Newcastle behind, disappointed by the way the academic world was changing and shocked by the destructive effects the market-isation of higher education was leaving on staff and students alike.

I returned to Germany and to journalism, and it was here among my colleagues at the German Press Agency dpa that I recovered my energy and my love of writing. While I had initially only planned to stay for a six-month work secondment, my work on the news front seemed ever more relevant to my academic research. I was writing a book on exile and migration just as hundreds of thousands of refugees were making their way across the Mediterranean to Europe from Syria and a range of northern African countries in the late summer of 2015. So I decided to stay for the time being and see where this new journey would take me.

Now that the book is done I have incurred many debts, and I would like to thank all the people who contributed with their ideas, advice and enthusiasm to bringing this project to fruition. Some of them helped with practical and linguistic queries, others with research questions, yet others through interesting conversations or simply their friendship and support. Foremost among them are Tom Ashby Luc Borot, John Brewer, Peter Burschel, the late Justin Champion, Cesare Cuttica, J. C. Davis, Delphine Doucet, Myriam-Isabelle Ducrocq, Markus Egg, Anja-Silvia Göing, Christophe Guillotel-Nothmann, Rachel Hammersley, André Holenstein, Thérèse-Maria Jallais, Mark Knights, Vivienne Larminie, Juan Andrés León, Andrew McKenzie-McHarg, Thomas Munck, Neil Murphy, Andreas Pečar, Markku Peltonen, Sabrina Pietrobono, Alasdair Raffe, Jonathan Scott, Mark Somos, Liam Temple and Howard Wickes.

I would also like to thank various colleagues and institutions who invited me to give papers and the audiences who patiently listened to them and made useful comments and suggestions. Ideas for my book were presented among others at the Franco-British History Seminar at the Sorbonne in Paris, the Cambridge Seminar in Political Thought and Intellectual History, the Herzog August Bibliothek in Wolfenbüttel, the Université Paul Valéry Montpellier 3, the Université de Toulouse II-Le Mirail, the Academy of Finland in Helsinki, the Folger Institute in Washington, several workshops at Northumbria University, Sunderland University, Newcastle University and the city's Lit&Phil, and the History Research Seminar at the Martin-Luther-Universität Halle-Wittenberg.

The staff of all the libraries and archives I used are too numerous to name individually, and many names of those who helped me I never learnt. But I am eternally grateful for their expertise, patience and good-will. I would also like to thank the History Department at the University of Warwick, who generously made me Honorary Associate Professor and granted me access to their library and online resources during the crucial writing-up stages of this book. At Cambridge University Press, my greatest thanks go to Liz Friend-Smith for the patient competence with which she steered the book towards publication and to Atifa Jiwa and Stephanie Taylor for their practical assistance throughout the process. They are named here as representatives of the whole team at CUP. I would also like to thank my copyeditor Fiona Little and the anonymous readers at the Press whose intense scrutiny of the manuscript and many helpful suggestions probably made this a better book.

I also benefited from the support of my academic friends and colleagues, who continued to believe in me and my work even after I had deviated from the prescribed academic path. In particular, the Translating Cultures Group at Wolfenbüttel has revived my faith in collegial collaboration and will hopefully remain part of my European network for a long time to come. I am also grateful to my wonderful colleagues at dpa, whose discipline and joy of writing along with the buzz of the Berlin newsroom honed my own writing routine.

Finally, special thanks go to Cesare Cuttica, Rachel Hammersley and Juan Andrés León, who all read a full draft of the manuscript before it went to press. The responsibility for any remaining errors is my own.

Berlin, July 2020

Note on the Text

Chapters 1 and 5 use parts of my article '*Les juges jugez, se justifiants* (1663) and Edmund Ludlow's Protestant Network in Seventeenth-Century Switzerland', *Historical Journal*, 57 (2014), 369–96. © The Historical Journal. Reprinted with permission.

Abbreviations and Conventions

ACV	Archives Cantonales et Vaudoises, Lausanne
AD	Archives Départementales
AE	Centre des Archives Diplomatiques du Ministère des Affaires Étrangères, Paris
AEG	Archives d'État, Geneva
AN	Archives Nationales, Paris
ASFi	Archivio di Stato, Florence
BNF	Bibliothèque Nationale de France, Paris
BRO	Berkshire Record Office
CSPD	*Calendars of State Papers, Domestic Series*
DBI	*Dizionario biografico degli Italiani*, www.treccani.it/biografico/index.html
HLS	*Historisches Lexikon der Schweiz*, https://hls-dhs-dss.ch/de/
NA	National Archives, London
ODNB	*Oxford Dictionary of National Biography*, www.oxforddnb.com
SP	State Papers, available at www.gale.com/intl/primary-sources/state-papers-online
STAB	Staarsarchiv, Bern

The spelling of original early modern quotations has been normalised with 'u' turning into 'v' and 'i' into 'j' for ease of reading, while other linguistic quirks have been retained as far as possible to reflect the fact that contemporary spelling and grammar had not been standardised.

For practical purposes, the numerous foreign-language quotations included in this book have been translated into English by the author, unless otherwise stated. The footnotes guide the reader to the original version.

All dates are given either in Old Style or Old Style and New Style, depending on the context. The year is presumed to begin on 1 January.

Introduction

Exiles cross borders, break barriers of thought and experience.

Edward Said, *Reflections on Exile*[1]

The English Republican Exiles in Europe

This book traces the lives, ideas and political activism of three English republican exiles, who were forced by circumstance to spend time abroad after the Restoration of the Stuart monarchy in 1660: Edmund Ludlow in Switzerland, Henry Neville in Italy and Algernon Sidney, who travelled widely on the Continent before eventually settling in the south of France. However, this study aims to be more than a work of comparative biography and political thought. Its purpose is to gain a better understanding of the transnational networks that enabled the exiles to escape from England and survive in relative security on the European continent for lengthy periods of time – more than thirty years in the case of Ludlow – and the role these networks played in the development and dissemination of English republican thought. More often than not, these support networks were of a religious nature, with Reformed Protestants playing a significant role in assisting English republicans on their migrant journey. By exploring the exiles' political thought alongside their lived experience this book thus provides a fresh approach to the history of early modern republicanism. Besides these three key figures, whose political lives and published writings created a reputation for them beyond the confines of the British Isles and who therefore will form the basis of three entwining case studies, the present volume will also touch on the lives of a number of other, often lesser-known republican exiles who belonged to the same networks as Ludlow, Neville and Sidney, but neither were

---

[1] Edward W. Said, 'Reflections on Exile', in *Reflections on Exile and Other Literary and Cultural Essays* (London: Granta, 2012), pp. 173–86, at p. 185.

I

necessarily authors and politicians of the same stature nor would attract a similar European audience.

The experiences of the exiles suggest that they must have been able to tap into pre-existing communities as well as developing their own net-works based on personal, political and religious connections.[2] This book will argue that in order to understand the survival and relatively wide dissemination of republican ideas from the English Civil War and Interregnum period into the Restoration and beyond, we need to look, among others, at the English republican exiles, their networks and their intellectual environment in their new chosen context. I hope to show that English republicanism in the seventeenth century was transnational or (if we want to avoid the anachronism for a period before the nation state) transterritorial or transcultural in nature and was shaped to a significant extent by personal, political and religious networks, even though the nature and confessional make-up of these religious networks might at times be unexpected, with Catholic contacts frequently featuring alongside fellow Protestant dissenters. This cosmopolitan and multi-confessional context of English republicanism also goes some way to explain the international outlook of early modern political thinkers, who, far from being patriots in a narrow parochial sense, always considered themselves part of a bigger transterritorial project either as Protestants belonging to God's invisible church around the world or, increasingly, as citizens of the world, who not only strove to transform government in England, but ultimately sought to apply their principles of religious and political liberty to countries around the globe.[3]

Like English royalism in the 1640s and 1650s, English republicanism after 1660 became an exile movement depending on continental support.[4] As republicans had lost their power base in England with the return of the Stuart dynasty, they had to rely on help from abroad for their survival and

---

[2] Jason Peacey hints at the existence of such networks in '"The good old cause for which I suffer": The Life of a Regicide in Exile', in Philip Major (ed.), *Literatures of Exile in the English Revolution and Its Aftermath 1640–1690* (Farnham: Ashgate, 2010), pp. 167–80, at p. 168.

[3] On the Puritan view of the 'true Church' of Christ as international, see Anthony Milton, 'Puritanism and the Continental Reformed Churches', in John Coffey and Paul C. H. Lim (eds), *The Cambridge Companion to Puritanism* (Cambridge, UK: Cambridge University Press, 2008), pp. 109–26, at p. 111. See also Steven Pincus's observation that 'Though there can be no doubt that Englishmen and women from the accession of Elizabeth were certain they were part of *an* elected nation, that elect nation was only a part of the wider elect nation of European Protestant believers', in his *Protestantism and Patriotism: Ideologies and the Making of English Foreign Policy, 1650–1668* (Cambridge, UK: Cambridge University Press, 1996), p. 450.

[4] Helmer J. Helmers, *The Royalist Republic: Literature, Politics, and Religion in the Anglo-Dutch Public Sphere, 1639–1660* (Cambridge, UK: Cambridge University Press, 2015), p. 9.

protection. This help would come not just from their allies in the American colonies, but also from countries and regions on the Continent that shared their Protestant faith and their broader political outlook, although strategic interests also played a role and diplomatic pressures meant that even those perceived as natural allies sometimes found it hard to offer the support the republicans hoped for. Where prominent English royalists had sought help at courts in The Hague, Brussels and Paris (Fontainebleau) and in Cologne, English republicans turned to members of the continental Reformed churches and to Dutch and Swiss republicans as well as former French Frondeurs.[5] English Puritans felt a close affinity to the Reformed churches, even though they might not agree on all particulars.[6] Most importantly, however, continental Reformed Protestants shared the experience of being a persecuted minority, which helped to forge closer links between groups and communities across borders that sought to provide mutual support.[7] Therefore, the history of the English republican exiles also connects to the history of religious migration in the post-Reformation period.[8]

For the major part, the exiles' destinations were located within the Protestant regions of Europe, where they had existing contacts and could expect to live in relative safety. This included the Protestant cantons of the Old Swiss Confederacy as well as the city of Geneva, which at the time still was 'an allied neighbor rather than a canton'.[9] The majority of cantons, with the exception of the principality of Neuchâtel, were also governed as republics, although de facto rule in individual places was increasingly confined to a select number of wealthy families.[10] Geneva, where Jean Calvin had started his reformation experiment, became Ludlow's first target destination. From there he moved on to Lausanne and Vevey in

---

[5] Geoffrey Smith, *The Cavaliers in Exile, 1640–1660* (Basingstoke: Palgrave Macmillan, 2003), pp. 6–7.

[6] Helmers, *The Royalist Republic*, p. 68; Milton, 'Puritanism and the Continental Reformed Churches'.

[7] Ole Peter Grell, *Brethren in Christ: A Calvinist Network in Reformation Europe* (Cambridge, UK: Cambridge University Press, 2011).

[8] See in particular Nicholas Terpstra, *Religious Refugees in the Early Modern World: An Alternative History of the Reformation* (Cambridge, UK: Cambridge University Press, 2015); and Yosef Kaplan (ed.), *Early Modern Ethnic and Religious Communities in Exile* (Newcastle upon Tyne: Cambridge Scholars Publishing, 2017).

[9] Richard Whatmore, *Against War and Empire: Geneva, Britain and France in the Eighteenth Century* (New Haven, CT, and London: Yale University Press, 2012), p. xiii. The Old Swiss Confederacy had gained legal independence from the Holy Roman Empire only in 1648.

[10] This restriction of power to a small aristocracy or oligarchy in the republican cantons would become even more pronounced over the course of the eighteenth century. Neuchâtel was governed as a principality until 1848.

the Pays de Vaud, which had been annexed by the Protestant canton of
Bern during the Reformation and would become the home of many
displaced Huguenots during the Refuge following the revocation of the
Edict of Nantes in 1685.[11] As we will see below, Ludlow was attracted to
the country by the Swiss love of freedom and the prospect of living there in
peace, able to worship according to his own faith until the Lord would set
him on a new path.

Sidney travelled around the Holy Roman Empire, which he would
praise in his *Discourses* as a loose association of independent territories
held together by an elective ruler limited by the law, even though he did
not take to its unrefined inhabitants.[12] The places where he made longer
stays included key Protestant locations such as Hanau, Frankfurt and
Augsburg, where other refugees from England had settled, while he also
spent significant time in the United Provinces, primarily at Rotterdam,
which had large English and Scottish merchant communities and through
its close links to England and Scotland would become a centre for
republican and dissenting conspirators in 1665–6.[13] In between, Sidney
settled in the Huguenot south and south-west of France associated with
the Fronde, where he benefited from long-standing friendships with
former Frondeurs.[14] Exceptions to the pattern of Protestant countries as
places of refuge for the English republican exiles were Rome and Florence.
Catholic Italy, however, became a destination for more strategic political
reasons, and both Sidney and Neville kept a close eye on the connections
between a Catholic interest among Charles II's subjects and the papacy in
the immediate aftermath of the Restoration. Rome was also 'one of the
main nodes of the network through which political information spread

---

[11] Marie-Jeanne Ducommin and Dominique Quadroni, *Le refuge protestant dans le pays de Vaud (fin XVIIe – début XVIIIe s.): aspects d'une migration* (Geneva: Droz, 1991).

[12] Algernon Sidney, *Discourses Concerning Government*, ed. Thomas G. West (Indianapolis, IN: Liberty Fund, 1996), pp. 166–7, 504, 508; I will be quoting from this modern edition of Sidney's 1698 text throughout. See also Algernon Sidney, Frankfurt am Main, to Robert, Earl of Leicester, 8 September 1660, in Arthur Collins (ed.), *Letters and Memorials of State in the Reigns of Queen Mary, Queen Elizabeth, King James, King Charles the First, Part of the Reign of King Charles the Second, and Oliver's Usurpation*, 2 vols (London: Printed for T. Osborne, in Gray's-Inn, 1746), ii, pp. 695–8, at p. 698.

[13] See Chapters 2 and 4; and Richard L. Greaves, *Deliver Us from Evil: The Radical Underground in Britain, 1660–1663* (Oxford: Oxford University Press, 1986), pp. 91–5, 203–4; Douglas Catterall, *Community without Borders: Scots Migrants and the Changing Face of Power in the Dutch Republic, c. 1600–1700* (Leiden: Brill, 2002), p. 25; and Douglas Catterall, 'Fortress Rotterdam? Rotterdam's Scots Community and the Covenanter Cause, 1638–1688', in David Worthington (ed.), *British and Irish Emigrants and Exiles in Europe, 1603–1688* (Leiden and Boston: Brill, 2010), pp. 87–105.

[14] Jonathan Scott, *Algernon Sidney and the English Republic* (Cambridge, UK: Cambridge University Press, 1988), pp. 181–5, 222–49.

throughout the other European countries'. Thus it was invaluable to have good contacts there.[15] The fact that Neville could spent considerable time in Florence in relative safety was certainly due to the fact that Tuscany was ruled by the anglophile Medici dukes and had strong commercial ties to England. There was a large English merchant community in Livorno under the protection of Ferdinando II that might have been exposed to persecution officially, but was tacitly left undisturbed as long as the 'heretical' guests behaved appropriately in public. Problems arose only occasionally when Protestants openly flouted the rules.[16]

Since strategic concerns played a major role in the choice of exile, other Catholic countries, such as Spain, had little to offer to a Protestant republican on the run. While Spain might have recognised the Commonwealth early on, Philip IV had offered sanctuary to Charles II during the 1650s as well as a formal treaty, and the murder of the Commonwealth diplomat Anthony Ascham by royalist assassins on Habsburg territory was still within recent memory.[17] Besides, Spain's location on the periphery of Europe meant it would have been harder for exiles to keep their hand in any political business.

Yet even within the territories and communities that welcomed the English republican refugees, diplomatic considerations might limit the extent of support they would receive. Two factors played a major role in limiting this support: the republicans' Independent leanings and their association with the regicide. The Protestant Reformed churches on the Continent tended to have a synodal government, following the structure first established by Calvin in opposition to a Catholic Church led by an apostolic succession of bishops, deacons and priests. The English republican exiles meanwhile were Independents, opposed as much to synodal or Presbyterian forms as to Catholic ones. While they shared with their continental allies the belief in predestination and election, their insistence on independent congregations and an informal way of worship would

---

[15] Stefano Villani, 'Britain and the Papacy: Diplomacy and Conflict in the Sixteenth and Seventeenth Century', in Maria Antonietta Visceglia (ed.), *Papato e politica internazionale nella prima età moderna* (Rome: Viella, 2013), pp. 301–22, at p. 306; see also Chapters 1 and 2 below.

[16] Gigliola Pagano de Divitiis, *English Merchants in Seventeenth-Century Italy*, trans. Stephen Parkin (Cambridge, UK: Cambridge University Press, 1997), on Leghorn or Livorno in particular, pp. 114 ff.; and Stefano Villani, 'Protestanti a Livorno nella prima età moderna', in Uwe Israel and Michael Matheus (eds), *Protestanten zwischen Venedig und Rom in der Frühen Neuzeit* (Berlin: Akademie Verlag, 2013), pp. 129–42, at p. 130.

[17] Marco Barducci, *Anthony Asham ed il pensiero politico inglese (1648–1650)* (Florence: Centro Editoriale Toscano, 2008), p. 47; and Jason Peacey, 'Order and Disorder in Europe: Parliamentary Agents and Royalist Thugs 1649–1650', *Historical Journal*, 40:4 (1997), 953–76.

alienate stricter types of Protestants. Likewise, while the English refugees might find republican allies on the Continent and share civic values with communities in Switzerland and the United Provinces, many moderate republicans as well as royalists had been shocked and alienated by the unprecedented regicide at the hands of the Rump Parliament that tainted not just Charles I's judges themselves but the entire regime associated with this act.[18] Thus the English republican exiles might sometimes misjudge the degree of support they could expect and miscalculate their chances of regaining power in England accordingly.

Some of the locations inhabited by the republican exiles would also become associated with works they produced or published. Ludlow's first exile publication and the only one issued during his lifetime, compiled in Geneva and printed in Yverdon, was a French translation of the trial narratives of some of his fellow regicides intended to rally a wider European Protestant public behind the republican cause.[19] His memoirs, largely written in Vevey, would carry a fake imprint of the town when first published in England, which would make them look more authentic and appeal to a European audience.[20] Almost a century later, Thomas Hollis would donate an annotated presentation copy of the *Memoirs* along with many other English republican works to the authorities of Bern who had once offered protection to the exiles.[21] Sidney probably wrote his *Court Maxims* in Rotterdam, but never followed up on his plans for their publication, while many of the ideas first presented in his *Maxims* would later be incorporated into his more famous *Discourses* (1698). Neville published his playful utopian travel narrative *The Isle of Pines* (1668) shortly after returning from Rome to London, no doubt inspired by his experience of exile. The close relationship he forged to the Medici during his exile meanwhile was reflected most strongly in two of his mature works, the fictitious *Nicholas Machiavel's Letter* (1675) and *Plato redivivus* (1681). The *Letter* first appeared as part of the 1675 translation of Machiavelli's

---

[18] Helmers, *The Royalist Republic*, pp. 101–12.

[19] *Les juges jugez, se justifiants. Ou recit de ce qui s'est passé en la condamnation & execution de quelques uns des juges du dernier defunct Roy d'Angleterre, & autres seigneurs du parti du Parlement* (n.p., 1663); see Chapter 5.

[20] *Memoirs of Edmund Ludlow Esq*, 3 vols (Vivay [sic], 1698–9).

[21] *Memoirs of Edmund Ludlow, Esq* (London: printed for A. Millar; D. Browne, both in the Strand; and J. Ward, in Cornhill, 1751), now kept at the Bern University Library. See Hans Utz, *Die Hollis Sammlung in Bern: Ein Beitrag zu den englisch-schweizerischen Beziehungen in der Zeit der Aufklärung* (Bern: Lang & Cie, 1959); and Urs Leu, 'The Hollis-Collection in Switzerland: An Attempt to Disseminate Political and Religious Freedom through Books in the 18th Century', *Zwingliana*, 38 (2011), 153–73.

Works into English published by the Whig bookseller John Starkey, who also published *Plato redivivus*. Hence, Neville is frequently credited with the translation in standard works on early modern English republican thought.[22] However, I have demonstrated elsewhere why Neville is an unlikely candidate. The Stationers' Register attributes the translation to 'J.B.', and Mark Knights suggests convincingly that this may refer to John Bulteel, who had done several other translations from Italian and French for Starkey. Moreover, Neville never mentions any translation work in his correspondence, nor do Starkey or Cosimo III.[23] His engagement with Machiavelli was of a more theoretical nature. Before we turn to the exiles' literary legacy, however, this book will focus on their more immediate aims and ideas before a wider European background.

The English Republican Exiles in Europe: Transnationalism and Religious Identity

Republicanism in seventeenth-century England was a political philosophy as well as a movement connected to the events surrounding the Civil War. Its proponents engaged with the breakdown of the Stuart monarchy and possible (non-monarchical) alternatives that might be put in its place. While republicanism could be seen as a reaction to short-term political circumstances, contemporary thinkers such as James Harrington suggest that it was rather a response to long-term historical change, challenges to the economic and social structure of the country and the further disintegration of religious unity in the post-Reformation period. While the responses to these issues may have been specific to the particular situation of England at a given moment in time, the challenges themselves were not

---

[22] e.g. Felix Raab, *The English Face of Machiavelli: A Changing Interpretation 1500–1700* (London and Toronto: University of Toronto Press, 1964), Appendix B, p. 272; Caroline Robbins's introduction to Caroline Robbins (ed.), *Two English Republican Tracts* (Cambridge, UK: Cambridge University Press, 1969), pp. 14–15; Blair Worden, 'Republicanism and Restoration, 1660–1683', in David Wootton (ed.), *Republicanism, Liberty and Commercial Society, 1649–1776* (Stanford, CA: Stanford University Press, 1994), pp. 139–93, at p. 144; and Vickie B. Sullivan, *Machiavelli, Hobbes, and the Foundations of a Liberal Republicanism in England* (Cambridge, UK: Cambridge University Press, 2004), pp. 19, 175, 187.

[23] See G. E. B. Eyre and C. R. Rivington (eds), *Transcripts of the Stationers Registers 1640–1708* (repr. Gloucester, MA: Peter Smith, 1967), 3 vols, ii, p. 495, quoted in Mark Knights, 'John Starkey and Ideological Networks in Late Seventeenth-Century England', *Media History*, 11 (2005), 127–45, at pp. 131–2; Gaby Mahlberg, *Henry Neville and English Republican Culture in the Seventeenth Century: Dreaming of Another Game* (Manchester: Manchester University Press, 2009), pp. 210–11; and Gaby Mahlberg, 'Machiavelli, Neville and the Seventeenth-Century Discourse on Priestcraft', *Intellectual History Review*, 28:1 (2018), 79–99.

uniquely English, but part of a broader pattern of social change in Europe
in a period of state formation.[24] Hence we should expect affinities with
similar ideas and movements elsewhere.

Nevertheless, the historiography of seventeenth-century English republicanism to date has been predominantly anglocentric and national as well
as secular in nature.[25] On both counts, this is surprising.[26] Early modern
classical republicanism drew extensively on continental European sources
from ancient Greece and Rome as well as Renaissance Italy; and interest in
these sources was shared by thinkers across Europe, thus providing natural
affinities between men and (less frequently) women of different linguistic
and cultural backgrounds.[27] Confining any study of early modern republicanism to England or the British Isles is consequently arbitrary. It may
reflect the ways in which modern historians work in their own narrow
national contexts, but contributes little to our understanding of the way in
which intellectual life in early modern Europe operated in practice.[28]

Even more at odds with the historical evidence is the secular focus of
much modern scholarship on early modern republicanism, given the
extent to which seventeenth-century thinkers drew on religious sources,
including the Bible and the Talmud as well as other works of the Christian
and Jewish traditions,[29] while the English Civil Wars themselves can be

---

[24] This interpretation was made popular by Hugh Trevor-Roper, 'The General Crisis of the 17th
Century', *Past and Present*, 16:1 (1959), 31–64.

[25] For a similar criticism of the national character of much seventeenth-century historiography, see
Jonathan Scott, '"Good Night Amsterdam": Sir George Downing and Anglo-Dutch Statebuilding',
English Historical Review, 118:476 (2003), 334–56, at p. 334. Scott also bemoans the restraints of
periodisation but, in this instance, does not address the religious question.

[26] Scholarship is changing only slowly. While the religious aspect has been coming into focus more
recently, there are as yet few truly transnational studies.

[27] J. G. A. Pocock's *The Machiavellian Moment: Florentine Political Thought and the Atlantic
Republican Tradition* (Princeton, NJ: Princeton University Press, 1975); Quentin Skinner, *The
Foundations of Modern Political Thought*, 2 vols (Cambridge, UK: Cambridge University
Press, 1978).

[28] However, historians of different fields are slowly coming to adopt a more European perspective.
A recent example is Sarah Mortimer's *Reason and Religion in the English Revolution: The Challenge of
Socinianism* (Cambridge, UK: Cambridge University Press, 2010), p. 4.

[29] Luc Borot, 'Religion in Harrington's Political System: The Central Concepts and Methods of
Harrington's Religious Solutions', in Dirk Wiemann and Gaby Mahlberg (eds), *Perspectives on
English Revolutionary Republicanism* (Farnham: Ashgate, 2014), pp. 149–64; Eric Nelson, *The
Hebrew Republic: Jewish Sources and the Transformation of European Political Thought*
(Cambridge, MA: Harvard University Press, 2010); Lea Campos Boralevi, 'Classical
Foundational Myths of European Republicanism: The Jewish Commonwealth', in Quentin
Skinner and Martin van Gelderen (eds), *Republicanism: A Shared European Heritage*, 2 vols
(Cambridge, UK: Cambridge University Press, 2002), i, pp. 247–61. See also Gordon Schochet,
Fania Oz-Salzberger and Meirav Jones (eds), *Political Hebraism: Judaic Sources in Early Modern
Political Thought* (Jerusalem: Shalem Press, 2008).

seen as a direct result of the European Reformations and have been aptly described as part of the 'European Wars of Religion'.[30] My aim therefore is to write a history of seventeenth-century English republicanism that is both transnational and religious, though I hasten to add that 'religious' does not mean narrowly doctrinal. Republicans were at the same time religious and heterodox, searching for truth, not religious dogma. Therefore they were naturally drawn to various dissenting movements that challenged the boundaries of the established Church. At the same time, while fiercely Protestant, they were not necessarily hostile towards the Catholic faith, but primarily against Catholic structures of church government and prescriptive rules.[31] Hence most republicans would condemn the episcopal structures of the Church of England and the formalism imposed by Presbyterian synods in the same way in which they rejected the 'popery' of the Catholic Church.[32] Yet the republicans' critical and sceptical attitudes towards organised religion were not necessarily indicative of a modernising secularisation process. The nature of religion and popular spirituality changed, but religion had by no means lost its significance. Republicans rather aimed to do away with religious or Church control over secular matters, the involvement of the clergy in worldly government and the tyranny of narrow doctrine over 'spirit and truth'.[33]

---

[30] John Morrill, 'The English Civil War', *Transactions of the Royal Historical Society*, 5th ser., 34 (1984), 155–78; and John Morrill, 'England's Wars of Religion', in his *The Nature of the English Revolution* (London: Longman, 1993), pp. 33–44; Jonathan Scott, *England's Troubles: Seventeenth-Century English Political Instability in European Context* (Cambridge, UK: Cambridge University Press, 2000), p. 29. Responses to the 'wars of religion' thesis can be found in Charles W. A. Prior and Glenn Burgess (eds), *England's Wars of Religion, Revisited* (Farnham and Burlington, VT: Ashgate, 2011). On the curious absence of religion in intellectual history, see John Coffey's 'Quentin Skinner and the Religious Dimension of Early Modern Political Thought', in Alister Chapman, John Coffey and Brad S. Gregory (eds), *Seeing Things Their Way: Intellectual History and the Return of Religion* (Notre Dame, IN: University of Notre Dame Press, 2009), pp. 46–74.

[31] Norah Carlin, 'Toleration for Catholics in the Puritan Revolution', in Ole Peter Grell and Robert W. Scribner (eds), *Tolerance and Intolerance in the European Reformation* (Cambridge, UK: Cambridge University Press, 1996), pp. 216–30; and Gaby Mahlberg, 'Henry Neville and the Toleration of Catholics during the Exclusion Crisis', *Historical Research*, 83 (2010), 617–34.

[32] Peter Lake, 'Anti-popery: The Structure of a Prejudice', in Richard Cust and Ann Hughes (eds), *The English Civil War* (London: Arnold, 1997), pp. 181–210; J. C. Davis, 'Against Formality: One Aspect of the English Revolution', *Transactions of the Royal Historical Society*, 6th ser., 3 (1993), 265–88; and Gaby Mahlberg, 'Le républicanisme anglais et le mythe de l'anticatholicisme', in Nathalie Caron and Guillaume Marche (eds), *La politisation du religieux en modernité* (Rennes: Presses Universitaires de Rennes, 2015), pp. 17–29.

[33] Mahlberg, *Henry Neville and English Republican Culture*, chapter 5; Blair Worden, 'The Question of Secularisation', in Alan Houston and Steve Pincus (eds), *A Nation Transformed: England after the Restoration* (Cambridge, UK: Cambridge University Press, 2001), pp. 20–40.

With a few later exceptions, seventeenth-century English republicans were Reformed Protestants, Independents or freethinkers, not atheists.[34] Given the interest early modern English republicanism of the 1640s and 1650s has received over the past thirty to forty years, the literature on the survival of republican ideas into the Restoration period, or indeed on the English republican exiles who had been forced to leave the country after the return of the Stuarts in 1660, is rather modest.[35] The prevailing narrative on the subject assumes that English republicanism had its heyday in the late 1640s and 1650s during the English Revolution and after the regicide of Charles I, but that the Restoration of the Stuart monarchy was a watershed moment, which the republican cause did not survive – at least not beyond individual radicals inside the British Isles and small and insignificant groups abroad.[36] This view has recently been reinforced by the growing literature on republican exclusivism which sees republicanism proper as strictly non-monarchical.[37] Yet in the late 1670s and 1680s, during the Exclusion Crisis, republicanism raised its head again among

[34] Michael Hunter, 'The Problem of "Atheism" in Early Modern England', *Transactions of the Royal Historical Society*, 35 (1985), 135–57. On freethought, see J. A. I. Champion, *The Pillars of Priestcraft Shaken: The Church of England and Its Enemies, 1660–1730* (Cambridge, UK: Cambridge University Press, 1992).

[35] On Ludlow, the most influential scholarship is C. H. Firth's scholarly edition *The Memoirs of Edmund Ludlow, Lieutenant-General of the Horse in the Army of the Commonwealth of England 1625–1672*, 2 vols (Oxford: Clarendon Press, 1894) and Worden's continuation of his work in Edmund Ludlow, *A Voyce from the Watch Tower: Part Five, 1660–1662*, ed. A. B. Worden, Camden Fourth Series (London: Royal Historical Society, 1987); on Sidney, the most detailed biographical treatment has come from Jonathan Scott's two volumes *Algernon Sidney and the English Republic* and *Algernon Sidney and the Restoration Crisis, 1677–1683* (Cambridge, UK: Cambridge University Press, 1991); on Neville, prior studies include Anna Maria Crinò, 'Lettere inedite italiane e inglesi di Sir (sic) Henry Neville', in Anna Maria Crinò (ed.), *Fatti e figure del Seicento anglo-toscano: documenti inediti sui rapporti letterari, diplomatici e culturali fra Toscana e Inghilterra* (Florence: Olschki, 1957), pp. 173–208; Robbins's introduction to *Two English Republican Tracts*; and the present author's own *Henry Neville and English Republican Culture*. In comparison to the extent of scholarship on English republicanism more widely, these contributions – some of them published a century apart – must seem like a first step only.

[36] e.g. Christopher Hill, *The Experience of Defeat: Milton and Some Contemporaries* (London: Faber, 1984). The persistence of the Restoration as a watershed is reflected in the still common periodisation that lets monographs end or begin in 1660. Historians of the seventeenth century still often specialise in either the Civil Wars and Interregnum or the Restoration, but less commonly in both.

[37] See David Wootton, 'The True Origins of Republicanism: The Disciples of Baron and the Counter-Example of Venturi', in Manuela Albertone (ed.), *Il repubblicanesimo moderno: l'idea di repubblica nella riflessione storica di Franco Venturi* (Naples: Bibliopolis, 2006), pp. 271–304; Eric Nelson, '"Talmudical Commonwealthsmen" and the Rise of Republican Exclusivism', *Historical Journal*, 50:4 (2007), 809–35; and James Hankins, 'Exclusivist Republicanism and the Non-monarchical Republic', *Political Theory*, 38 (2010), 452–82. See also Blair Worden, 'Republicanism, Regicide and Republic: The English Experience', in van Gelderen and Skinner (eds), *Republicanism*, i, pp. 307–27.

debates over the future succession of the Catholic James, Duke of York, which was seen as a threat to the protestant faith and the survival of the Church of England, while Catholicism was also associated with absolutist rule.[38] As Jonathan Scott has demonstrated, during the 1670s and 1680s the country struggled with some of the same issues as it had in the 1640s: the threat of popery and the arbitrary rule of a tyrannical king.[39] Yet, we might ask, if republicanism returned in the Exclusion Crisis, where was it between 1660 and the discovery of the Popish Plot in 1678? As I have aimed to show in my book on Neville, the survival of republican ideas from one government crisis to the next was closely linked to the survival of individuals from the English Civil War period, such as Neville, Sidney or John Wildman, who returned to political activism and political writing in the later part of the century and adapted their demands to the realities of the Restoration regime. Far from toning down their republican or 'commonwealth' principles to accommodate the survival, or rather *re*vival, of the monarchy, however, they were now more interested in constitutional limitations to monarchical rule than in the removal or even murder of a king.[40] The reason why the survival narrative of republican ideas across the Restoration is so thin is that much of the surviving happened not in England or in the British Isles, but in exile in America and Europe.

It is true that the number of English revolutionaries and regicides explicitly excepted from the Act of Indemnity and Oblivion (1660) is small. Only forty-nine of those still alive plus 'the two Persons who appeared disguised upon the Scaffold' were named directly as 'Persons ... concerned in the Murder of King Charles I' and singled out for execution, while the former Lord Protector Oliver Cromwell, his son-in-law Henry Ireton, the president of the High Court John Bradshaw and Thomas Pride, who was responsible for the 1648 purge of Parliament that allowed for the king's trial, were excepted from the Act even after their deaths. Further individuals were subject to 'Penalties not extending to Life'.[41] While the names of the regicides are comparatively easy to establish

---

[38] David Ogg, *England in the Reign of Charles II*, 2nd ed. (Oxford: Oxford University Press, 1984), and John Kenyon, *The Popish Plot* (London: St Martin's Press, 1972).

[39] Jonathan Scott, 'Radicalism and Restoration: The Shape of the Stuart Experience', *Historical Journal*, 31 (1988), 453–67.

[40] Mahlberg, *Henry Neville and English Republican Culture*, pp. 140, 161–3, 172–7, 181–2. This goes against older arguments brought forward by Zera S. Fink, *The Classical Republicans: An Essay in the Recovery of a Pattern of Thought in Seventeenth-Century England* (Evanston, IL: Northwestern University Press, 1945), p. 135, and Pocock, *The Machiavellian Moment*, pp. 406 ff.

[41] 'Charles II, 1660: An Act of Free and Generall Pardon Indempnity and Oblivion', in *Statutes of the Realm*, v.: *1628–80*, ed. John Raithby (n.p., 1819), pp. 226–34.

once the concept of 'regicide' is defined, the definition of what constitutes
a 'republican' is more difficult to determine.[42] Unless an individual left a
considerable trace of written evidence of their political beliefs, we may
need to judge on a case-by-case basis who could be considered as ideological or classical republicans in a clearly identifiable sense rather than simply
opponents of Stuart tyranny or even opportunist collaborators of the
various regimes of the 1640s and 1650s. Besides, not all republicans who
went into exile at the Restoration had been singled out for persecution and
punishment by the Stuart government, making their reasons for leaving
the country less obvious to the distant observer. Nevertheless, the exiles
who went either to the colonies or to the European Continent contributed
through their dispersed existence to the distribution and survival of
English republican ideas abroad and thus to the long-term legacy of the
English Revolution in different countries around the world. Many more
political and religious dissenters also left England for exile abroad despite
not being excepted from the Act of Oblivion. Either they did not trust the
government or they felt more comfortable in their host countries, which
offered them religious liberty besides personal security.

While there is a growing body of literature on the Stuart court and
various royalist communities in exile during the 1640s and 1650s, only the
most spectacular incidents of republican exile movement after 1660 have
been covered.[43] Thus the regicides and major-generals William Goffe and
Edward Whalley, who had escaped to the American colonies, have
attracted the attention of historians and literary scholars mainly because

---

[42] There is some contest over who should be considered a 'regicide', depending on attendance of the
meetings of the High Court of Justice and signature of the final death warrant. See A. W. McIntosh,
'The Numbers of the English Regicides', *History*, 67 (1982), 195–216.

[43] Smith, *The Cavaliers in Exile*; Emma Rees, *Margaret Cavendish: Gender, Genre, Exile* (Manchester:
Manchester University Press, 2003); Anna Battigelli, *Margaret Cavendish and the Exiles of the Mind*
(Lexington: University Press of Kentucky, 1998); Paul H. Hardacre, *The Royalists during the Puritan
Revolution* (The Hague: Nijhoff, 1956). Of the ten chapters in Philip Major's recent edited
collection *Literatures of Exile in the English Revolution and Its Aftermath 1640–1690* (Farnham:
Ashgate, 2010), only two – one by Major himself on William Goffe and one by Jason Peacey on
John Dixwell – deal exclusively with regicides or republican exiles, while Major's recent monograph
Writings of Exile in the English Revolution and Restoration (Farnham: Ashgate, 2013) focuses
primarily on royalist exiles, but also has a chapter on Goffe. Dixwell, Goffe and Edward Whalley
are also the subject of Edward Vallance, '"The Insane Enthusiasm of the Time": Remembering the
Regicides in Eighteenth- and Nineteenth-Century Britain and North America', in Laurent Curelly
and Nigel Smith (eds), *Radical Voices, Radical Ways: Articulating and Disseminating Radicalism in
Seventeenth- and Eighteenth-Century Britain* (Manchester: Manchester University Press, 2016),
pp. 229–50; and most recently Matthew Jenkinson, *Charles I's Killers in America: The Lives and
Afterlives of Edward Whalley and William Goffe* (Oxford: Oxford University Press, 2019).

of their role in Romantic myths and local folklore.[44] Other prominent figures in the literature are John Barkstead, Miles Corbet and John Okey, who had made it to the Continent in 1660 only to find themselves the targets of extraordinary rendition behind the backs of the Dutch authorities less than two years later. They were tried and executed for treason in England in April 1662.[45] Meanwhile, Edmund Ludlow, the most feared of the exiles who had escaped to Europe, is primarily known for his detailed *Memoirs*, which have been exploited mainly for their accounts of the English Civil War and Interregnum period and thus as a 'main source for puritan politics', though less for their detail on Ludlow's life in Geneva, Lausanne and Vevey, despite the obvious links to both Swiss republicanism and the religion of Geneva.[46] This is due in part to the fact that Ludlow's published *Memoirs* were a carefully edited version, produced by the Whig propagandist John Toland in the context of the Standing Army debate of the 1690s, and intended to teach a lesson about the evils of standing armies and the virtues of citizen militias. The edited *Memoirs* were a hagiography of the republicans opposing Cromwell during the 1650s, and were less concerned with the daily lives of the exiles on the shores of Lake Geneva in Switzerland than was Ludlow's original manuscript, 'A Voyce from the Watch Tower', on which the present study draws extensively.[47] For reasons of availability, however, and because of the fact that only part of the original manuscript has survived, Ludlow's original story is still much less frequently used and less well known than the edited version. Richard Greaves, who has done substantial work on the English radicals of the 1640s and 1650s, deals with the English republican exiles in

---

[44] See, for instance, Douglas C. Wilson, 'Web of Secrecy: Goffe, Whalley, and the Legend of Hadley', *New England Quarterly*, 60 (1987), 515–48.

[45] Ralph C. H. Catterall, 'Sir George Downing and the Regicides', *American Historical Review*, 17:2 (1912), pp. 268–89; Greaves, *Deliver Us from Evil*, pp. 92 ff.

[46] Blair Worden, *God's Instruments: Political Conduct in the England of Oliver Cromwell* (Oxford: Oxford University Press, 2012), p. 3; See also Blair Worden, 'Whig History and Puritan Politics: The *Memoirs* of Edmund Ludlow Revisited', *Historical Research*, 75 (2002), 209–37; and Blair Worden, *Roundhead Reputations: The English Civil Wars and the Passions of Posterity* (London: Penguin, 2002), pp. 21–121. The history of eighteenth-century Swiss republicanism has most recently been told in Whatmore, *Against War and Empire*.

[47] For the edited version see Ludlow, *Memoirs*, ed. Firth. The only coherent part of the original manuscript of the 'Voyce' known to have survived, covering the period from February 1660 to the spring of 1677, is held at the Bodleian Library, Oxford, MS Eng. hist. c. 487. The first section of the Bodleian MS, containing what would have been part five of Ludlow's manuscript, was published in an edition by Worden for the Camden Fourth Series in 1987: Ludlow, *A Voyce from the Watch Tower* (hereafter Ludlow, *Voyce*, ed. Worden). For reasons of accessibility, I will subsequently quote from Worden's edition for the edited section and from the original manuscript for the remainder of the text only.

Europe in their entirety in one sub-chapter of his work on the radical underground in Britain, which is far too short to cover the subject, while also relying primarily on English evidence that does not sufficiently capture the situation in the United Provinces, Switzerland or other European countries.[48] Only one incident, the assassination of Ludlow's fellow regicide and exile John Lisle, has received significant attention for its obvious sensationalism.[49] In fact, Lisle's assassination seems to have inspired at least one work of popular history, Hans Peter Treichler's *Die Brigantin: oder Cromwells Königsrichter*, which interweaves the story of Ludlow's exile community in Vevey with that of the abduction of a local noblewoman, while Don Jordan and Michael Walsh's *The King's Revenge: Charles II and the Greatest Manhunt in British History* is as much a piece of hero worship to the adherents of the 'good old cause' as is the recent television series *New Worlds*, which not only adds an array of fictional characters to the mix but also two transatlantic love stories to hold the audience's attention.[50]

The reason why the republican exiles to the American colonies have drawn more attention than those escaping to Europe is twofold. Firstly, the obvious influence of English republican and real Whig ideas on the American movement for independence captured in the wide-ranging literature on the Atlantic republican tradition has dominated the historiography as Americans have attempted to understand the ideological origins of their nation, while British scholars have traced the persistent bond and 'special relationship' between the two countries.[51] Since the beginning of the modern period, Britain has arguably always felt a closer affinity to its

---

[48] Greaves, *Deliver Us from Evil*, pp. 91 ff. Two further volumes of Greaves's work on the radical underground deal with the afterlife of Civil War radicalism. See his *Enemies under His Feet: Radicals and Nonconformists in Britain, 1664–1677* (Stanford, CA: Stanford University Press, 1990) and *Secrets of the Kingdom: British Radicals from the Popish Plot to the Revolution of 1688–1689* (Stanford, CA: Stanford University Press, 1992). See also Richard L. Greaves and Robert Zaller (eds), *Biographical Dictionary of British Radicals in the Seventeenth Century*, 3 vols (Brighton: Harvester Press, 1982–4).

[49] Alan Marshall, *Intelligence and Espionage in the Reign of Charles II, 1660–1685* (Cambridge, UK: Cambridge University Press, 1994); Clive Holmes, 'John Lisle, Lord Commissioner of the Great Seal, and the Last Months of the Cromwellian Protectorate', *English Historical Review*, 122 (2007), 918–36; Brian O Cuiv, 'James Cotter, a Seventeenth-Century Agent of the Crown', *Journal of the Royal Society of Antiquaries of Ireland*, 89:2 (1959), 135–59.

[50] Hans Peter Treichler, *Die Brigantin: Oder Cromwells Königsrichter* (Zurich: Verlag Neue Zürcher Zeitung, 2002); Don Jordan and Michael Walsh, *The King's Revenge: Charles II and the Greatest Manhunt in British History* (London: Abacus, 2013). *New Worlds* was scripted by Peter Flannery and Martine Brant and broadcast on Channel 4 in April 2014. See www.channel4.com/programmes/new-worlds, accessed 18 May 2014.

[51] Caroline Robbins, *The Eighteenth-Century Commonwealthman: Studies in the Transmission, Development and Circumstance of English Liberal Thought from the Restoration of Charles II until the War with the Thirteen Colonies* (Cambridge, UK: Cambridge University Press, 1959); Pocock,

brothers and sisters across the Great Pond than to its European neighbours. However, in the early modern period, at least until emigration to the colonies reached sufficient numbers to merit closer engagement, this was different. Emigration from the British Isles was primarily to Europe, while the seventeenth century with its mass emigration to America might be seen as a turning point. One part of the exiles of the 1660s went to the colonies, and another went to Europe.[52] The second reason for the comparative neglect of the republican exiles in Europe is the wide dispersal of sources across numerous smaller archives in a number of different countries, while a significant part of the secondary literature is also written in languages other than English, often produced by local historians in the exiles' respective host countries.[53] These difficulties relating to access to sources are compounded by the obvious language barriers that pose a major challenge to any researcher.

Sources and Methodology

Research for this book has followed the paths of the English republican exiles into a variety of European countries. Where there was evidence in the State Papers, in private correspondence or other sources of one of the exiles having spent some time in a specific location, I approached the relevant local archives and searched their collections for documents relating to the fugitives or contextual information. Many of these searches proved disappointing, which is perhaps unsurprising in view of the fact that fugitive republicans were concerned to pass undetected and would reveal their true identity only to those with whom they felt safe. Other searches have yielded interesting results. The nature and availability of sources for the exiles differ according to the circumstances.

As Ludlow left a comparatively detailed memoir of his exile and also sought the protection of the local authorities of Geneva and of the council of Bern, the documentation of his stay in Switzerland is relatively good. Among the sources mined for this study are the minutes of the councils of

---

The Machiavellian Moment; Alan C. Houston, *Algernon Sidney and the Republican Heritage in England and America* (Princeton, NJ: Princeton University Press, 1991); Joyce Appleby, *Inheriting the Revolution: The First Generation of Americans* (Cambridge, MA: Belknap Press, 2000); Michael P. Zuckert, *Natural Rights and the New Republicanism* (Princeton, NJ: Princeton University Press, 1994).

[52] Worthington (ed.), *British and Irish Emigrants and Exiles*, p. 1.
[53] On the '[s]carcity of archival evidence', see also Peacey, 'The good old cause for which I suffer', p. 167.

Geneva, Bern and Lausanne held at various state and city archives in Switzerland,[54] the exiles' correspondence, held at the Bern state archive and partly published in the nineteenth century,[55] the manuscript of Ludlow's 'Voyce from the Watch Tower' held at the Bodleian Library in Oxford, in part edited by Blair Worden for the Camden Society,[56] and various printed editions of the work.[57]

For Sidney and Neville the source base is patchier, less coherent and scattered more widely as their refugee status was never made official. Hence it would not make sense to list all the collections that contain brief references to their whereabouts. Nevertheless, for their wider social and political context in Rome the census records in the Archivio Storico Diocesano have been useful, as have been miscellaneous documents in the Vatican Archives and Vatican Library, and in the Biblioteca Nazionale, Rome. The Doria Pamphilj Archives have been consulted for their stay in Frascati and their contact with the Prince Pamphilio. For Sidney's friendship with Cardinal Decio Azzolino and his contacts to the Squadrone Volante I have made use of the Azzolino Archive at the Biblioteca Planettania in Jesi. For Sidney's period in the Netherlands and his contacts with other exiled regicides as well as with the Quaker Benjamin Furly and the English merchant community, I have consulted the Gemeentearchief in Rotterdam as well as the Koningklijke Bibliotheek in The Hague. Correspondence and other documents regarding Sidney's stay in France are also held at the Archives Nationales and the Centre des Archives Diplomatiques in Paris, while the Bibliothèque Nationale in Paris and the Archives Municipales and Archives Départementales de l'Hérault at Montpellier as well as the Archives Départementales de Lot-et-Garonne at Agen have provided contextual information. For Sidney's personal and family papers the Kent History and Library Centre in Maidstone was consulted.

Sources on Neville, including his correspondence, are held primarily in the Berkshire Record Office in Reading and in the Archivio di Stato in Florence, while the Biblioteca Nazionale Centrale in Florence holds a

---

[54] Archives d'État, Geneva, Registres du Conseil, Conseil ordinaire, Petit Conseil, Conseil des XXI; Staatsarchiv, Bern (hereafter StAB), A II, Kanzleiarchiv, Raths-Manuale der Stadt Bern; and Archives de la Ville, Lausanne, Manual du Conseil de Lausanne.

[55] StAB, B III 63, Epistolae virorum clarorum. Copies are also held in the British Library at Add. MS 24850. The letters have been published in slightly shortened form in Alfred Stern (ed.), *Briefe englischer Flüchtlinge in der Schweiz: Aus einer Handschrift des Berner Staats-Archivs.* (Göttingen: Peppmüller, 1874).

[56] 'A Voyce from the Watch Tower', Bodleian Library, MS Eng. hist. c. 487; and Ludlow, *Voyce*, ed. Worden.

[57] *Memoirs of Edmund Ludlow Esq*, 3 vols (Vivay (*sic*), 1698–9); and Ludlow, *Memoirs*, ed. Firth.

range of seventeenth-century printed works relating to Neville. The Tanner Collection and Clarendon Papers in the Bodleian have further material, while the Braybrooke Papers in the Essex County Record Office in Chelmsford include some correspondence between Neville and Clarendon. Needless to say, the State Papers at the National Archives in London and, more recently, the excellent resource that is *State Papers Online* have been invaluable in my quest to track down the republican fugitives. Although not all of my searches have yielded ample results, they have provided me with a better understanding of the wider context of the exiles' lives and the nature of the source material available as well as useful leads to other archives and depositories.

Interest in the European ramifications of English republicanism, meanwhile, has been growing in recent years. Notable contributions to the cross-Channel debate have been made by Rachel Hammersley, who has done more than most to uncover the traces of English republican ideas in the political thought of the French Revolution,[58] while Roland Ludwig has provided a useful context for the reception of the English Revolutions in works of history and political thought of the 1848 Revolutions on the Continent, and Hans-Christof Kraus has looked more broadly at the English constitution after 1689 from a continental perspective.[59] . Naturally, there is a link between the two historiographies of reception and adaptation, as the German-speaking lands in the late eighteenth and early nineteenth centuries absorbed much of the literature of the French Revolution, which in turn had absorbed much of the literature of the English Revolution. Thus much, though not all, of the reception of English revolutionary thought in the German-speaking lands was mediated by French (as well as Dutch) writing. Interesting work on the translation of Sidney into French has been undertaken by Pierre Lurbe, who shows how Sidney's thought was adapted for the French market, while Iwan D'Aprile has recently discovered Harringtonian political thought in the writings of

---

[58] Rachel Hammersley, *French Revolutionaries and English Republicans: The Cordeliers Club, 1790–1794* (Woodbridge: Boydell and Brewer, 2005, paperback ed. 2011), and Rachel Hammersley, *The English Republican Tradition and Eighteenth-Century France: Between the Ancients and the Moderns* (Manchester: Manchester University Press, 2010).
[59] Roland Ludwig, *Die Rezeption der Englischen Revolution im deutschen politischen Denken und in der deutschen Historiographie im 18. und 19. Jahrhundert* (Leipzig: Leipziger Universitätsverlag, 2003); Roland Ludwig, 'Die Englische Revolution als politisches Argument in einer Zeit des gesellschaftlichen Umbruchs in Deutschland', in Heiner Timmermann (ed.), *1848: Revolution in Europa Verlauf, politische Programme, Folgen und Wirkungen* (Berlin: Duncker & Humblot, 1999), pp. 481–504; and Hans-Christof Kraus, *Englische Verfassung und politisches Denken im Ancien Régime 1689 bis 1789* (Munich: Oldenbourg, 2006).

the nineteenth-century Prussian journalist Friedrich Buchholz. Moreover, Jennifer Willenberg's study of the dissemination, translation and reception of English literary works into German during the eighteenth century is an important contribution to the study of cultural transfers.[60] Some of this innovative work has been gathered in a recent collection of essays on *European Contexts for English Republicanism*.[61] However, this volume and the conference from which it emerged were based on the idea that there is a bigger untold story to recover about the interaction of English republicanism with continental thought, and that the collected essays would offer a flavour of this bigger story. More work remains yet to be done on this exciting subject, and this monograph is an attempt to create a more coherent account of the European dimension of English republican thought than has been available to date by establishing connections between different groups of exiles and their intellectual environments. Rediscovering the English republican tradition on the Continent is important for our understanding of cross-Channel connections in early modern Europe as well as a variety of cultural affinities and continuities that may have been overlooked by earlier generations of scholars. Like any book on a large and diverse subject, this one remains work in progress. But the author hopes that her readers will go away and try to fill the gaps in her narrative by following the paths of republicans and regicides cast out by their country for their attempt to create an alternative order.

English Republicanism

Seventeenth-century English republicanism draws on a variety of conceptual 'languages' in John Pocock's definition of the term as 'ways of talking about politics'.[62] The three main languages were those of classical republicanism, Protestant dissent and the common law, which merged with

---

[60] Pierre Lurbe, 'Lost in (French) Translation: Sidney's Elusive Republicanism', in Gaby Mahlberg and Dirk Wiemann (eds), *European Contexts for English Republicanism* (Farnham: Ashgate, 2013), pp. 211–23; Iwan D'Aprile, 'Prussian Republicanism? Friedrich Buchholz's Reception of James Harrington', in Mahlberg and Wiemann (eds), *European Contexts for English Republicanism*, pp. 225–36; Jennifer Willenberg, *Distribution und Übersetzung englischen Schrifttums im Deutschland des 18. Jahrhunderts* (Munich: Saur, 2008).

[61] Mahlberg and Wiemann (eds), *European Contexts for English Republicanism*. A second volume, emerging from the same conference, focuses on different theoretical and methodological approaches to English republican thought: Dirk Wiemann and Gaby Mahlberg (eds), *Perspectives on English Revolutionary Republicanism* (Farnham: Ashgate, 2014).

[62] J. G. A. Pocock, 'The Concept of a Language and the *métier d'historien*: Some Considerations on Practice', in Anthony Pagden (ed.), *The Languages of Political Theory in Early-Modern Europe* (Cambridge, UK: Cambridge University Press, 1987), pp. 20–5, at p. 21.

patriotic feeling and an aristocratic sense of responsibility for the commonwealth.

Classical republicanism goes back to the city-states of ancient Greece and Rome, which nourished the civic humanism embodied by Aristotle's 'political animal'[63] and Cicero's dutiful citizen.[64] Civic humanism elevated the ideal of the virtuous and disinterested citizen over the self-interested and corrupt individual whose politics created only factionalism and strife. In a polity governed by civic humanist ideals, the whole was more than the sum of its parts, and any ruler who furthered his own interest over that of his people was considered a tyrant. To avoid the domination of a factional or individual self-interest over the common good there had to be a balanced mixed form of government composed of the three pure forms of rule: monarchy, aristocracy and democracy.[65] While each of the three in its own way threatened to collapse into its opposite, tyranny, oligarchy or anarchy, a mixture of two or all three forms was able to provide the necessary stability. Moreover, a stable state would rely on the rule of law rather than the leadership of an individual or a group; and the legal framework of the polity ensured the accountability of those in power. In Aristotle's ideal political system, accountability was also provided through a rotation of offices, in which all active citizens had to take their share of the power, at least for a limited period of time, so that they would rule and be ruled in turn.[66] To qualify as active citizens individuals had to be property-holding adult males who could be trusted to defend their polity not just as office-holders but also as soldiers with a stake in their country.[67]

While the secular classical and civic humanist aspect of English republicanism has received wide coverage in the secondary literature, and in particular in the writings of intellectual and conceptual historians, the dissenting Protestant aspect of the English republican tradition has until relatively recently too often been neglected. This Protestant strand of republicanism manifested itself most clearly in the years leading up to

---

[63] Aristotle, *The Politics* and *The Constitution of Athens*, ed. Stephen Everson (Cambridge, UK: Cambridge University Press, 1996), p. 70.

[64] Cicero, *On Obligations*, trans. P. G. Walsh (Oxford: Oxford University Press, 2001).

[65] Polybius, *The Rise of the Roman Empire*, trans. Ian Scott-Kilvert, selected with an introduction by F. W. Walbank (Harmondsworth: Penguin, 1979).

[66] Aristotle, *Politics*, p. 70.

[67] This aspect is also stressed in the work of the Renaissance republican Niccolò Machiavelli, especially in *The Art of War*, ed. Ellis Farnsworth, trans. Neal Wood (Washington, DC: Da Capo Press, 2001); and *Discourses on Livy*, trans. Harvey C. Mansfield and Nathan Tarcov (Chicago: University of Chicago Press, 1996), II.10, II.18, II.20, etc.; but also in his *The Prince*, trans. Russell Price, ed. Quentin Skinner and Russell Price (Cambridge, UK: Cambridge University Press, 1998), chapters 12 and 13.

and of the English Civil War, when opposition to the monarchy of Charles I was often voiced through protest against his religious policies and his usurpation of the role of Christ as God's representative on earth. In its most radical manifestation, Protestant dissent, often referred to by the shorthand 'Puritanism', had an apocalyptic and millenarian dimension, which saw the true Christian believers waiting for the second coming of Christ and the rule of Lord Jesus. This millenarian strand of Protestantism was also often characterised by a strong identification with God's chosen people, the elect, or the Israelite nation, who had to find their way through trials and tribulations to prepare for the return of their Lord.[68]

The classical and the Puritan strands of English republicanism were not as a rule separate, but complemented each other, even though both could be found in individual representatives of English republicanism to varying degrees.[69] The third component of their republican identity was their shared reference to the ancient liberties of free Englishmen embodied in the common law and feeding a native English republicanism imbued with patriotic feeling, which combined with classical and religious values to create a potent mix over the course of the seventeenth century, and which had to prove itself in exile.[70]

As members of a broader political movement, the three English republicans covered in this book shared essential principles: an opposition to patriarchal monarchy by divine right, a strong belief in popular sovereignty and the rule of law and consequently the accountability of rulers and governments, a commitment to religious liberty, and an ethos of public spirit to defend these principles at the risk of their own lives.[71]

---

[68] Avihu Zakai, *Exile and Kingdom: History and Apocalypse in the Puritan Migration to America* (Cambridge, UK: Cambridge University Press, 1992).

[69] Coffey, 'Quentin Skinner and the Religious Dimension of Early Modern Political Thought'.

[70] On the common-law aspect, see in particular J. G. A. Pocock, *The Ancient Constitution and the Feudal Law: A Study of English Historical Thought in the Seventeenth Century* (New York: Cambridge University Press, 1957, repr. 1967). On the combination of different strands of republicanism, see Blair Worden, 'Classical Republicanism and the Puritan Revolution', in Hugh Lloyd-Jones, Valerie Pearl and Blair Worden (eds), *History and Imagination: Essays in Honour of H. R. Trevor-Roper* (Duckworth: Holmes & Meier, 1981), pp. 182–200; Jonathan Scott, *Commonwealth Principles: Republican Writing of the English Revolution* (Cambridge, UK: Cambridge University Press, 2004); Patrick Collinson, *De Republica Anglorum: Or, History with the Politics Put Back* (Cambridge, UK: Cambridge University Press, 1990); Markku Peltonen, *Classical Humanism and Republicanism in English Political Thought, 1570–1640* (Cambridge, UK: Cambridge University Press, 1997); Mark Goldie, 'The Unacknowledged Republic: Officeholding in Early Modern England', in Tim Harris (ed.), *The Politics of the Excluded, c. 1500–1850* (Basingstoke: Palgrave, 2001), pp. 153–94.

[71] I share Jonathan Scott's view that it makes sense to conceptualise English republican thought as a set of principles rather than a narrow doctrine. This enables us to capture a broader movement rather than debating which individuals can be seen as typical representatives of seventeenth-century republicanism. This may make it harder to compile canonical lists, but it acknowledges that it is

Nevertheless, early modern English republicanism was not confined to the commitment to a specific constitutional structure or even kingless government, but was a spectrum of thought that could accommodate radical religious republicans and regicides like Ludlow, classical constitutionalists like Neville, who was willing to accept a single chief executive officer limited by the law, and individuals like Sidney, who shared religious and classical ideas in equal measure and was at best ambiguous on the matter of the regicide. While all three could be seen as condoning the execution of the king as they all served the regicide regime in the 1650s, only Ludlow was a 'regicide' in the narrow sense, because he had signed the king's death warrant. Sidney subsequently praised the deed as 'just' and 'brave', while Neville seemed to care least about the presence or absence of a 'single person' in the constitution as long as this individual was limited by the law, as he made clear both in parliamentary debate and in his later writings.[72] All three could be considered religious Independents or Congregationalists who rejected the formalism of the Church of England as well as Presbyterian synods and denounced the suppression of the 'fanatics'.[73] While Ludlow and Sidney may have been more at home with scriptural arguments and emphasised the importance of worshipping the Lord in Independent congregations as they thought fit, Neville had the clearest vision of the three on what a future church government might look like, envisaging a broadly Erastian structure governed by a parliamentary council within which Independent congregations could thrive.[74] That three figures as disparate as Ludlow, Neville and Sidney can nevertheless all be considered republicans who shared a broadly common vision is documented in the work of their admirer John Toland, who was responsible for the late seventeenth-century editions of both Ludlow and Sidney and may have

---

possible to subscribe to republican principles to a greater or lesser extent and to agree on broader issues while differing on the finer detail. See Scott, *Commonwealth Principles*.

[72] On Sidney's defence of the regicide, see British Library, Add. MS 21506, fol. 55, and Add. MS 32680, fols 9–10, quoted in Scott, *Algernon Sidney and the English Republic*, p. 92; on Neville and the issue of the 'single person', see *Diary of Thomas Burton, Esq. Member in the Parliaments of Oliver and Richard Cromwell, from 1656 to 1659*, ed. John Towill Rutt, 4 vols (London: H. Colburn, 1828), iii, pp. 134–5, 321, and Henry Neville, *Plato redivivus*, in Robbins (ed.), *Two English Republican Tracts*, pp. 61–200, at pp. 185–8. For a full discussion of the issue, see Mahlberg, *Henry Neville and English Republican Culture*, chapter 4.

[73] e.g. Algernon Sidney, *Court Maxims*, ed. Hans W. Blom, Eco Haitsma Mulier and Ronald Janse (Cambridge, UK: Cambridge University Press, 1996), p. 93.

[74] Neville, *Plato redivivus*, ed. Robbins, pp. 75–6, 116–17, 186–7. On his express support for 'private congregations', see *Diary of Thomas Burton*, iv, p. 332.

had a hand in the 1698 Neville edition as well.[75] Likewise, the philanthropist Thomas Hollis, who built on Toland's efforts, aided the revival of
their thought in the eighteenth century by funding ostentatious new
editions of their works and donating them to libraries in the American
colonies in the years before the Revolution as well as to continental
European institutions. He thus contributed to the formation and disper-
sion of a canon of republican works that comprised the writings of
Ludlow, Neville and Sidney alongside those of James Harrington, John
Milton and many others.[76] I will return to this shared republican legacy in
the Epilogue of this book. For now, it should suffice to say that Ludlow,
Neville and Sidney were more than accidental collaborators on the political
stage: they also shared a set of republican principles recognisable both to
their contemporaries and subsequent generations of Whigs and
commonwealthmen. Their varying degrees of flexibility and their ability
to adapt to new environments and create new alliances meanwhile proved
crucial for their experience of exile and the survival of the republican cause.

Definitions of Exile

The *Oxford English Dictionary* defines 'exile' as an '[e]nforced removal
from one's native land according to an edict or sentence; penal expatriation
or banishment; the state or condition of being penally banished; enforced
residence in some foreign land'.[77] This relatively narrow definition goes
back to the city-states of ancient Greece, where warring élites had frequently expelled each other in their struggle for power until the democratic
revolution of the sixth century BC turned the practice of ostracism into an
institutionalised form of banishment through which the people could

---

[75] Worden, *Roundhead Reputations*, p. 100. This is an assumption only, mainly based on the fact that
Neville is part of the canon and was republished around the same time as other republicans.

[76] I would like to thank the late Justin Champion for highlighting this point. Hollis was involved in
the republication of Ludlow's *Memoirs* (1751), Sidney's *Discourses* (1763) and Neville's *Plato
redivivus* (1763). There is a growing literature on his publishing efforts and his numerous
donations to the American colonies as well as to universities and libraries elsewhere in the world,
starting with Caroline Robbins, 'The Strenuous Whig: Thomas Hollis of Lincoln's Inn', *William
and Mary Quarterly*, 7:3 (1950), 406–53; Robbins, *The Eighteenth-Century Commonwealthman*; and
William H. Bond, *'From the Great Desire of Promoting Learning': Thomas Hollis's Gifts to the
Harvard College Library*, introduction by Allen Reddick, preface by William P. Stoneman, special
issue, *Harvard Library Bulletin*, 19:1–2 (2010). Most current work focuses on Hollis's donations
rather than his editorial impact, although the two are necessarily related. See especially the research
conducted by Allen Reddick at Zurich University.

[77] 'Exile, n. 1'. *Oxford English Dictionary*, www.oed.com, accessed 14 June 2014.

assert their influence over the ruling elites and hold them to account.[78] Exile in this sense was a rather specific concept related to established political processes and defined by law. Yet Jan Felix Gaertner claims that the ancient usage of the term could also be much broader, and that 'the English word "exile" is far more precise than the corresponding Greek and Latin terms'. While 'modern derivatives of the Latin word *exilium* imply an involuntary departure, sanctioned by political or judicial authorities, the ancient usage of the corresponding terms φυγή, *fuga*, *exilium*, and their derivatives is less strict', covering 'both the expulsion of groups or individuals and their voluntary departure'.[79] In a broader, more general sense, 'exile' is thus also used to describe '[e]xpatriation, prolonged absence from one's native land, endured by compulsion of circumstances or voluntarily undergone for any purpose'.[80]

The English constitution too allowed for various forms of banishment through either a court or an act of Parliament.[81] Such an act was used, for instance, to exile and permanently banish the former lord chancellor Edward Hyde, the Earl of Clarendon, after he had fled the country following his impeachment for 'Treason and other misdemeanours' in 1667.[82] However, these means were not generally applied to Civil War republicans, although, in some cases, informal arrangements might be made to remove an individual troublemaker from England, as we will see below. Yet, as Jason Peacey has pointed out with reference to the seventeenth-century English regicides and republicans, '[t]o be an exile was to regard one's reason for absence from England as being political in nature and temporary in duration'.[83] The political reasons behind the

---

[78] Sara Forsdyke, *Exile, Ostracism, and Democracy: The Politics of Expulsion in Ancient Greece* (Princeton, NJ, and Woodstock: Princeton University Press, 2005), pp. 1–2.

[79] Jan Felix Gaertner (ed.), *Writing Exile: The Discourse of Displacement in Greco-Roman Antiquity and Beyond* (Leiden: Brill, 2007), p. 2.

[80] 'Exile, n. 1', *Oxford English Dictionary*.

[81] In fact, Magna Carta stated in its thirty-ninth clause that 'No free man shall be seized or imprisoned, or stripped of his rights or possessions, or outlawed or exiled, or deprived of his standing in any other way, nor will we proceed with force against him, or send others to do so, except by the lawful judgement of his equals or by the law of the land.' Magna Carta, www.bl.uk/magna-carta/articles/magna-carta-english-translation, accessed 21 August 2016. See also the reference to this clause in 'Charles I, 1627: The Peticion Exhibited to His Majestie by the Lords Spirituall and Temporall and Co[m]mons in this P[re]sent Parliament Assembled Conc[er]ning Divers Rights and Liberties of the Subjects: With the Kings Majesties Royall Aunswere Thereunto in Full Parliament.', in *Statutes of the Realm*, v, pp. 23–4.

[82] 'Charles II, 1667 & 1668: An Act for Banishing and Disenabling the Earl of Clarendon', in *Statutes of the Realm*, v, p. 628. Only later in the eighteenth century did exile come to be used more regularly as an alternative to capital punishment as outlaws were transported to the colonies as a means of cheap labour.

[83] Peacey, 'The good old cause for which I suffer', p. 167.

republicans' escape to foreign countries is what distinguished them from other types of refugees or emigrants, while the provisional arrangements that characterised their stay abroad suggest that a return to England was at least intended, although for some such as Ludlow and Sidney exile turned into a more permanent arrangement than they might have planned originally. Most refugee republicans left the country out of their own volition – to save their skin – and at least some of them had a reward on their heads. The 1660 Act of Indemnity and Oblivion, passed to determine the fate of the opponents of the monarchy who participated in the Civil Wars and the regicide, had singled out some of them for capital punishment. Others were not named, but still feared for their safety, and yet others left as suspects of the numerous real and imagined plots of the 1660s.[84] I will therefore use the wider, relatively loose definition of 'exile' to capture the multiplicity of reasons that may have moved the individuals discussed here to escape or move abroad.

While their exile may not have been a clearly defined state, English republicans nevertheless attempted to conceptualise their absence from their homeland in meaningful ways. One of these ways was religious and fed the myth of the English as the elect nation through their identification with the ancient Israelites. 'In Israelitish history', the word specifically refers to 'the captivity of the Jews in the 5th century B.C.', which would become an important reference point for at least some seventeenth-century English republican exiles.[85] Ludlow, for instance, saw exile as part of his providential existence, a transitional stage for God's chosen people before the arrival of the millennium with the second coming of Christ. In this way, his ideas were not dissimilar to those of the Puritan migrants to the American colonies.[86] He also believed that the Lord was manifesting 'his favour unto us his poore Exiles' when the plans of the assassins following him and his friends were foiled.[87] In fact, the exiles could resort to rather poetic ways of conceptualising their fate, as did Sidney when in a letter to his father from Italy he described himself in a mixture of maritime metaphors as

[84] 'Charles II, 1660: An Act of Free and Generall Pardon Indempnity and Oblivion', in *Statutes of the Realm*, v, pp. 226–34; Greaves, *Deliver Us from Evil*; Marshall, *Intelligence and Espionage*.
[85] 'Exile, n. 1'. *Oxford English Dictionary*.
[86] On the providential meaning of 'exile' in the Puritan migration to the American colonies, see Zakai, *Exile and Kingdom*.
[87] Ludlow, 'Voyce', fol. 1089.

'a broken Limbe of a Ship-wracked Faction', at times feeling desperate or 'naked, alone, and without Help in the open Sea',[88] while Neville resigned himself to living abroad because he knew he was 'not only hatted but persecuted at home'.[89] These articulations of frustration and helplessness also offer interesting insights into the exiles' sense of belonging, which will be addressed in more detail in Parts II and III.

Exile was then necessary when a society was so focused on political and religious uniformity that there was no space within the system to accommodate dissent, and persecution was rife for those outside the acceptable norms of political conviction and religious belief. Only when new structures and institutions, such as political parties and a legal toleration of various forms of religious dissent, emerged in the later part of the seventeenth century did it become possible to integrate opposition into the system.[90] The individual exile's degree of dissent with the powers that be and his willingness to compromise his own political and religious positions to keep the peace may also have determined the relative possibility of return. There is an entire literature on exile, comprising everything from formal banishment in ancient Greece down to voluntary and inner exile of those escaping Nazi Germany in the twentieth century, which, for reasons of space, cannot be discussed here in any depth.[91] Yet what was common to all those leaving their home was a sense of estrangement and alienation, a love-hate relationship with the country that had rejected them, degrees of resentment mixed with a sense of adventure and the uncertainty over a possible return home. Most importantly, all exiles have always shared the desire to be free.

---

[88] Algernon Sidney, Frascati, to Robert, Earl of Leicester, 23 June/3 July 1661, in Collins (ed.), *Letters*, ii, pp. 720–1, at p. 720. Gaertner notes that 'exile as shipwreck' was a common theme in the ancient world. See Jan Felix Gaertner, 'The Discourse of Displacement in Greco-Roman Antiquity', in Gaertner (ed.), *Writing Exile*, pp. 1–20, at p. 9.

[89] Henry Neville, Florence, to Richard Neville, London, 20 January 1665, Berkshire Record Office, Reading (hereafter BRO), D/EN F8/1/11.

[90] On the emergence of parties and the institutionalisation of opposition politics, see Mark Knights, *Politics and Opinion in Crisis, 1678–81* (Cambridge, UK: Cambridge University Press, 1994).

[91] Examples are Forsdyke, *Exile, Ostracism, and Democracy*; Gaertner (ed.), *Writing Exile*; Said, *Reflections on Exile*; Dirk Wiemann, *Exilliteratur in Großbritannien 1933–1945* (Opladen and Wiesbaden: Springer, 1998); Sharon Ouditt (ed.), *Displaced Persons: Conditions of Exile in European Culture* (Aldershot: Ashgate, 2002); and Lea Campos Boralevi and Paschalis Kitromilides (eds), *Athenian Legacies: European Debates on Citizenship* (Florence: Olschki, 2014). I owe this latter reference to Mark Somos.

Exile and Liberty: The Republican Cause

The key theme of exile, as well as that of republicanism, is liberty. As indicated above, republican liberty is a largely positive concept, based on the active political participation of the citizen in the polis.[92] However, in the context of exile, this ideal liberty was compromised through the regime change in England and the republicans' geographical distance from their home country, which severely limited their political agency. The republican exiles' liberty therefore operated on three different levels: the personal, the political and the religious. Naturally, all three were intertwined and applied to all exiles under examination to a greater or lesser extent.

On a very basic, personal level, the first priority of the exiles was to stay alive and be free to move. This meant they had to ensure they would be out of reach of the sovereign and his government apparatus, which could be achieved only by leaving the country. Thus this personal liberty was largely of a negative kind that depended on the non-interference by others.[93] The real threat of being followed by enemy spies and assassins meanwhile shows how fragile this personal liberty was.

On a political level, the exiles' liberty was also significantly compromised. While choosing exile enabled those on the run to maintain their republican beliefs and to be their own master within the narrow confines of their temporary existence, it meant at the same time that they would be separated from their *patria*. This created an uncomfortable tension between the negative liberty of non-interference by the sovereign and the republicans' desire for positive liberty to shape their own destiny and that of their country. Thus, while political liberty in a republican context is usually associated with the ability to participate actively in the politics of one's home city or country, under certain circumstances, the desire for political liberty can also necessitate voluntary exile, if an individual is unable to be free in their own country, threatened by imprisonment or even death.[94]

---

[92] On different kinds of liberty and their application in a republican context, see Quentin Skinner, *Liberty before Liberalism* (Cambridge, UK: Cambridge University Press, 1998); Quentin Skinner, 'The Republican Ideal of Political Liberty', in Gisela Bock, Quentin Skinner and Maurizio Viroli (eds), *Machiavelli and Republicanism* (Cambridge, UK: Cambridge University Press, 1990), pp. 293–309; and Quentin Skinner, 'A Third Concept of Liberty', *Proceedings of the British Academy*, 117 (2002), 237–68. On the terminology, see also Isaiah Berlin, *Four Essays on Liberty* (Oxford: Oxford University Press, 1969).

[93] Ibid.

[94] Paul Rahe highlights that ancient Greek citizens felt fully human only when they were able to participate in public life. Exclusion or exile was perceived as the worst kind of punishment. See his

This ambiguity becomes most apparent in an undated letter that Sidney wrote around the time the 'fraudulent' indemnity legislation was passed. In it, he considers 'being exiled' from his own country 'a great evil', but while 'the liberty which we [had] hoped to establish' was being 'oppressed' he preferred to be away from it to preserve the liberty of his own thought and actions, claiming, 'better is a life among strangers, than in my own country on such conditions'. Thus he wrote: 'Whilst I live I will endeavour to preserve my liberty, or at least not consent to the destroying of it.' He was even prepared to die for his convictions or forsake his country, saying: 'I have ever had it in my mind, that when God should cast me into such a condition, as that I cannot save my life, but by doing an indecent thing, he shews me that the time is come, wherein I should resign it.' He added, 'And when I cannot live in my own country, but by such means as are worse than dying in it, I think he shews me that I ought to keep out of it.'[95] Ironically, only exile allowed the republicans discussed here to go on supporting their common cause, which combined ideas of political with religious liberty.

The religious was the third and final level of the republicans' liberty ensured by their exile, although the situation was certainly very different for Ludlow, Sidney and Neville. While Ludlow was explicitly categorised as a 'religious refugee' by the local authorities in Bern that granted him their protection and ensured his freedom of worship, Sidney's adherence to networks of Reformed Protestants is counter-balanced by his Catholic contacts in Italy, especially Rome, and elsewhere. Neville was the protégé of the Catholic Ferdinando II of Tuscany and long-standing friend of his son Cosimo, who later succeeded his father as grand duke.[96] Any conclusions about the exiles' religious affiliations and attitudes will therefore need careful differentiation.

What all three of them shared was their commitment to a common cause, and the fulfilment of their Interregnum dream: the establishment of political and religious liberty through popular sovereignty and a rule of law that would allow citizens an active role in political decision-making

---

Republics Ancient and Modern, 3 vols (Chapel Hill: University of North Carolina Press, 1992–4), i, pp. 21–4.

[95] Undated letter by Algernon Sidney to an unidentified addressee, in R. W. Blencowe (ed), *Sydney Papers, Consisting of a Journal of the Earl of Leicester, and Original Letters of Algernon Sydney* (London: John Murray, Albemarle Street, 1825), pp. 199–204.

[96] StAB, A II 454, Raths-Manual der Stadt Bern, vol. 143 (27 January 1662–7 June 1662), entry for 16 April, p. 317. See Chapter 1.

processes for the common good.[97] The extent to which any future government would be able to accommodate a monarchical figure is still contested, but it is probably safe to say that the first priority of English republicans was not the removal of all monarchs.[98] They were first and foremost enemies to tyranny and would probably have agreed to a constitutional monarchy, in which prerogative powers were strictly limited by the law.[99]

Leaving England

Exile usually begins with an individual's realisation that their home country might no longer be a safe place to live, whether because of actual persecution or simply political instability. This realisation is then followed by a decision to leave one's home country to seek freedom and security abroad. For the regicides and republicans who had served the various Interregnum regimes, the need to make this decision came with the Restoration of the Stuart monarchy in 1660. Even though Charles II had promised in his Declaration of Breda in April that he would forgive those who had opposed his father in the Civil War and provide liberty of conscience to all Protestant dissenters, the reality looked very different once he had ascended the throne.[100] Thus 8 May 1660 was a fateful day for many English republicans as the Convention Parliament proclaimed Charles II the lawful monarch of England. With the consent of the elected representatives of the nation, the Stuarts were back on the English throne and the citizens of the English republic once again became the subjects of a monarchy.

---

[97] Mahlberg, *Henry Neville and English Republican Culture*, pp. 4–9; Scott, *Commonwealth Principles*; and Jonathan Scott, 'What Were Commonwealth Principles?', *Historical Journal*, 47 (2004), 591–613.

[98] See the growing literature on the 'monarchical republic' which has been building on Patrick Collinson's seminal article, 'The Monarchical Republic of Queen Elizabeth I', *Bulletin of the John Rylands University Library of Manchester*, 69 (1987), 394–424, and Patrick Collinson, *De Republica Anglorum*. Key contributions include Steve Hindle, 'Hierarchy and Community in the Elizabethan Parish: The Swallowfield Articles of 1596', *Historical Journal*, 42 (1999), 835–51, and Goldie, 'The Unacknowledged Republic'. See also Peltonen, *Classical Humanism and Republicanism*, and Luc Borot, 'Subject and Citizen: The Ambiguity of the Political Self in the Early Modern English Commonwealth', *Revue française de civilisation britannique*, 20:1 (2106), 1–15. A critical engagement with the concept can be found in John F. McDiarmid (ed.), *The Monarchical Republic of Early Modern England: Essays in Response to Patrick Collinson* (Aldershot: Ashgate, 2007).

[99] Mahlberg, *Henry Neville and English Republican Culture*, pp. 4–9.

[100] Declaration of Breda (1660), in 'The Convention Parliament: First Session – Begins 25/4/1660', in *The History and Proceedings of the House of Commons*, i: *1660–1680* (London: Chandler, 1742), pp. 2–25, www.british-history.ac.uk/report.aspx?compid=37614, accessed 24 April 2014.

While Charles himself might have preferred a policy of forgiving and forgetting for his own peace of mind, his new Cavalier Parliament, made up largely of royalists and moderate Presbyterians, soon pushed him towards strict legislation against political and religious dissent.[101] The most significant policies for the republicans were the exceptions made to the Act of Indemnity and Oblivion (1660), for this deceptively named piece of legislation carefully singled out not only surviving regicides but also other key players in Interregnum politics for exemplary punishment.[102] Among the thirty-three individuals 'wholly excepted from the provisions of the Act' were Ludlow as well as a number of other regicides, such as Andrew Broughton, William Cawley, John Dixwell, William Goffe and Nicholas Love, who would at various points make their way to the Continent or the American colonies to escape capture, trial for treason and execution.[103] Even those who were not clearly excepted from the Act did not trust its provisions. Many of those who had been politically active in the Commonwealth either decided to leave the country or remained abroad to save their skin.

By way of comparison with those who decided to leave England after 1660, we might also want to look at republicans who decided to stay behind for a variety of reasons, choosing an alternative response to the Restoration of the Stuarts. They included authors and political actors who retreated into inner exile, such as John Milton, whose oeuvre took a distinctively cryptic turn with *Paradise Lost* (1667). He went into hiding, while two of his Interregnum works were publicly condemned for their treasonous content and publicly burnt.[104] Some former activists had managed to come to an arrangement with the new rulers, with varying degrees of success. Sir Arthur Haselrig is thought to have dropped his

---

[101] For recent summaries and analyses of Restoration politics, see Tim Harris, *Restoration: Charles II and His Kingdoms, 1660–1685* (London: Allen Lane, 2005); N. H. Keeble, *The Restoration: England in the 1660s* (Oxford: Wiley-Blackwell, 2007).

[102] 'Charles II, 1660: An Act of Free and Generall Pardon Indempnity and Oblivion', in *Statutes of the Realm*, v, pp. 226–34.

[103] Keeble, *The Restoration*, pp. 72, 222n.

[104] These were *Eikonoklastes* (1649) and the *Defensio* (1651) in justification of the regicide. See Worden, *God's Instruments*, p. 355, referring to Barbara Kiefer Lewalski, *The Life of John Milton: A Critical Biography* (Oxford: Blackwell, 2000), p. 401. John Goodwin's *Obstructors of Justice* (1649) was destroyed as well. See [Charles II], *By the King: A Proclamation for Calling in and Suppressing of Two Books Written by John Milton: The One Intituled Johannis Miltone Angli pro populo Anglicano defensio contra Claudii Anonymi, alias Salmasii, defensionem regiam, and the Other in Answer to a Book Intituled The Pourtraicture of His Sacred Majesty in His Solitude and Sufferings, and also a Third Book Intituled The Obstructuors of Justice, Written by John Goodwin* (London: printed by John Bill . . . , 1660).

opposition to General George Monck's plans for a restoration of the
Stuarts 'in return for a promise that his own life would be spared', but
was still 'exempted from the Act of Indemnity and imprisoned in the
Tower', where he died in January 1661 'before he could be brought to trial
for treason'.[105] In fact, Ronald Hutton has claimed that '[t]he final
achievement of Monck's efforts on behalf of Hesilrige was that Sir Arthur
died in the Tower instead of upon the scaffold'.[106] The regicide Henry
Marten, who, like Haselrig, was also a close political ally of his Berkshire
neighbour Henry Neville, submitted himself to the authorities on 20 June
1660 and was imprisoned in the Tower to await his trial in October. Even
though he was found guilty he was spared execution, probably 'because
influential royalists were reluctant to create a martyr from someone of his
personal notoriety' or 'because he was active in arguing for the lives of
royalists when supporters of the high court of justice of the Commonwealth wanted retribution for war crimes that extended beyond solely the
figure of Charles Stuart'. Having managed to save his life, Marten was sent
to Holy Island or Berwick Castle, but was transferred in 1665 to Windsor
Castle and in 1668 to Chepstow Castle, where he died in 1680.[107]

Other republicans were associated with plots against the Restoration
government, although it has been argued that many of these plots may
have been fabricated either by eager informers or the authorities themselves
as an excuse for further persecutions and the tightening of laws against
dissenters, such as the so-called Presbyterian Plot of 1661.[108] Following a
series of investigations launched by Lord Chancellor Clarendon and Secretary Edward Nicholas, many of those associated with James Harrington's
Rota Club and the Bow Street circle meeting at John Wildman's Nonsuch
House tavern were rounded up.[109] Harrington himself was arrested on

---

[105] Christopher Durston, 'Hesilrige, Sir Arthur, Second Baronet (1601–1661)', *ODNB*; Keeble, *The Restoration*, p. 73.
[106] Ronald Hutton, *The Restoration: A Political and Religious History of England and Wales 1658–1667* (Oxford: Clarendon Press, 1985).
[107] Sarah Barber, 'Marten, Henry (1601/2–1680)', *ODNB*; and Sarah Barber, *A Revolutionary Rogue: Henry Marten and the English Republic* (Stroud: Sutton Publishing, 2000); on Neville and Marten, see Mahlberg, *Henry Neville and English Republican Culture*, pp. 40, 43–4.
[108] Greaves, *Deliver Us from Evil*, p. 7.
[109] There seems to have been significant overlap between Harrington's Rota Club and the club meeting at Wildman's Nonsuch House tavern in Bow Street. The two are sometimes conflated in the literature, e.g. in *The Political Works of James Harrington*, ed. J. G. A. Pocock (Cambridge, UK: Cambridge University Press, 1977), p. 125. However, Harrington denied having met Wildman at Bow Street. See *The Oceana of James Harrington, and His Other Works; Som Wherof Are Now First Publish'd from His Own Manuscripts. The Whole Collected, Methodiz'd, and Review'd, with an Exact Account of His Life Prefix'd, by John Toland* (London: Printed and are to be sold by the Booksellers of London and Westminster, 1700), pp. xiii–xliv, at pp. xxxii, xxxvi.

28 December 1661 and held in the Tower before being removed to St Nicholas Island off Plymouth.[110] He was then moved to Plymouth itself, where he suffered 'a physical and mental collapse' or 'Melancholy', from which he 'never wholly recovered'. His 'madness' would become famous as it symbolised so powerfully the shock of the Restoration to the republican system, and he ceased to publish altogether.[111] Another member of this circle, the regicide Colonel John Hutchinson, was removed 'from the record of those present at the king's trial' in June 1660, but was captured with some of the other northern rebels after the Yorkshire rising and imprisoned in October 1663. Together with Major Richard Salway and Neville, he was taken to London and put in the Tower. Alas, Hutchinson was less lucky than Salway, who was soon released on good security, and Neville, who, after the intervention of his royalist brother and other influential relatives, was allowed to travel abroad. According to his wife Lucy Hutchinson, both had taken oaths of loyalty to the new regime. John Hutchinson, meanwhile, was moved to Sandown Castle in Kent, where he died in September 1664.[112]

One of the most controversial contemporary figures was Sir Henry Vane the younger, who had made his mark as an active Parliamentarian and famed rhetorician. He was admired by Neville and Ludlow as well as Sidney. Even though Vane was considered 'one of the most hated republican leaders' and a dangerous demagogue, he made no attempt to escape or submit at the Restoration. He was imprisoned in the Tower and later on the Scilly Isles before being tried in King's Bench and condemned to death on 11 June 1662. Vane's sentence was 'commuted to beheading' as 'appropriate to his family's importance', and on 14 June he was executed at Tower Hill. Rumour has it that his final speech was drowned out by musicians under the scaffold.[113] He was buried a day later in the family

---

[110] Toland's 'Life of James Harrington' suggests that he may have been arrested by mistake, as the warrant was issued for 'Sir' James Harrington. See *The Oceana of James Harrington*, ed. Toland, pp. xiii–xliv, at p. xxxi.

[111] *The Political Works of James Harrington*, ed. Pocock, pp. 125–6; *The Oceana of James Harrington*, ed. Toland, p. xxxvii.

[112] P. R. Seddon, 'Hutchinson, John (*bap.* 1615, *d.* 1664)', *ODNB*; Lucy Hutchinson, *Memoirs of the Life of Colonel Hutchinson, with the Fragment of an Autobiography of Mrs. Hutchinson*, ed. James Sutherland (London: Oxford University Press, 1973), pp. 254–5, 272; Keeble, *The Restoration*, pp. 75–6. See also Robbins (eds), *Two English Republican Tracts*, p. 12; Mahlberg, *Henry Neville and English Republican Culture*, p. 60; and Wilbur C. Abbott, 'English Conspiracy and Dissent, 1660–1674', 2 parts, *American Historical Review*, 14 (1909), 503–28, 696–722.

[113] Hutton, *The Restoration*, pp. 162–3.

vault in Kent.[114] Another non-regicide to be tried alongside Vane was the parliamentary general John Lambert, who had been responsible for the first Protectorate's Instrument of Government.[115] After the Restoration, he was put in 'close confinement' in Castle Cornet on Guernsey and in April 1662 'returned to the Tower for trial' with Vane. Both were sentenced to be executed for treason, but Lambert had his sentence commuted to life imprisonment and temporarily returned to Guernsey before being transferred to St Nicholas Island, where he died in 1684. In 1664 some of Sidney's allies, in a plot to depose the Stuart government, attempted to free Lambert from prison so that he could lead an army to invade England from abroad, but they failed and were captured and subsequently executed.[116] Others remained political activists, such as the former Leveller and anti-Cromwellian plotter John Wildman, 'who had been imprisoned at the Restoration, but . . . was released in 1667, entered the service of the Duke of Buckingham, and drifted towards active plotting against Charles II and James II'.[117] The present study is necessarily selective. Its focus will be on three case studies of key republican figures – Algernon Sidney, Edmund Ludlow and Henry Neville – whose publications and archival records make a more detailed examination possible. Yet, as we will see, as their stories intertwine in many complex ways, a broader picture will emerge that allows us to get a better grasp of the changing fortunes of a wider English republican movement after the Restoration.

Algernon Sidney (1623–1683)

Algernon Sidney was the first of the three exiles to keep his distance from England, and his Interregnum career may give us an indication of why. After a brief stint fighting in Ireland to suppress rebellion in 1642 Sidney had joined the Parliamentary forces and was appointed colonel in the Earl of Manchester's regiment of horse in the Eastern Association in April 1644. After honourable conduct at Marston Moor, Sidney became a commander in the New Model Army in April 1645 before returning to

[114] Ruth E. Mayers, 'Vane, Sir Henry, the Younger (1613–1662)', *ODNB;* Keeble, *The Restoration,* pp. 75–6.
[115] Hutton, *The Restoration,* pp. 162–4.
[116] D. N. Farr, 'Lambert, John (*bap.* 1619, *d.* 1684)', *ODNB;* see also Scott, *Algernon Sidney and the English Republic,* pp. 177, 185; and *Calendars of State Papers, Domestic Series (CSPD)* 1665–6, pp. 510–36. Farr wrongly dates the event in 1664, while Scott, following Ludlow's 'Voyce' (p. 1128), has Lambert imprisoned on Jersey. For Vane and Lambert also see Keeble, *The Restoration,* pp. 74–5.
[117] Peacey, 'The good old cause for which I suffer', pp. 174–5.

Ireland in 1647 as governor of Dublin with his brother Philip as Lord Lieutenant of Ireland. In November of the same year, Sidney was also added to the parliamentary Committee for the Affairs of Ireland with his friend Sir John Temple. As Jonathan Scott has pointed out, throughout the Interregnum 'Irish affairs were to remain Sidney's particular speciality'.[118] Sidney also distinguished himself as governor of Dover Castle between 1648 and 1651, although his quartering of soldiers in opposition to army policy brought him dangerously close to a court martial. His main forte, however, remained foreign affairs: meeting ministers of different countries and specialising with Vane in wartime and naval affairs.[119] Like many other classical republicans, Sidney temporarily withdrew from politics after Cromwell's expulsion of the Rump Parliament in 1653, and for much of the 1650s he appears to have focused on family affairs, managing the debt-ridden Strangford estate belonging to his cousin and brother-in-law Thomas Smith, first Viscount Strangford. Only in May 1659, after the restoration of the Rump, did Sidney return to the political stage, primarily as a negotiator in European affairs.[120]

As Scott has convincingly shown, Sidney had sufficiently close involvement in the regicide to fear retribution. Even though his father, the Earl of Leicester, played down his son's role in the proceedings against Charles I, Sidney had both attended several of the court's sessions and publicly proclaimed abroad his support for the regicide as 'the justest and bravest action that ever was done in England, or anywhere'.[121] In Sidney's mind it did not necessarily follow that this would preclude him from all future political office under a monarchy, however. This painful realisation came only later. Abroad to negotiate a peace between Sweden and Denmark on behalf of the Commonwealth regime to secure English trading interests in the Baltic Sound when the Stuart monarchy was restored, he was initially unsure of his next steps.[122] This is evident from the letter he sent to his father Robert, Earl of Leicester, from Stockholm on 27 June 1660 after receiving 'the Newes of the Kings Entry into London'.[123] He even

---

[118] Scott, *Algernon Sidney and the English Republic*, pp. 82, 85, 88.   [119] Ibid., pp. 98–9, 101.
[120] Jonathan Scott, 'Sidney, Algernon (1623–1683)', *ODNB*.
[121] Scott, *Algernon Sidney and the English Republic*, p. 92.
[122] Ibid., p. 125; and Algernon Sidney's letter from Elsinore, November 1659, British Library, Add. MS 32093, fol. 417.
[123] Algernon Sidney, Stockholm. to Robert, Earl of Leicester, 27 June 1660, in Collins (ed.), *Letters*, ii, pp. 690–1.

considered whether or not to stay in his current position, writing, 'I . . . am absolutely uncertaine what Course I shall take, unlesse I find somme other Letters, at my Returne [to Copenhagen], that may instruct me.' He was 'unwilling to stay in a Place, wheare I have bin long under a Character that rendred me not inconsiderable, now that my Powers are extinguished, and I am left in a private Condition'. Yet he also knew it would be an advantage to him 'to have newe Orders from the King'. Therefore he was 'unwilling to put my self out of a Condition of receaving them, unlesse I am theareunto necessitated, or know that none will be sent'.[124] At this stage, Sidney was not entirely averse to holding office under the new king if it was demanded of him, and, as he revealed in the following letter to his father, he did not think he had the right to withdraw from Sweden 'without Order'.[125] As he was waiting for a response from England he also considered it 'a farre greater Respect unto the King, to cease from acting any Thing by Powers not derived from him' and to stay in Copenhagen 'as private Men', instead of 'on a Suddaine to throwe of the Businesse, and to be gone as in a Chase'.[126]

While being aware of the loss of his 'Powers' and his newly acquired 'private' status, Sidney also stayed because he was first and foremost, as he put it, a 'Servant to my Country', for whom public duty was not necessarily bound to a specific government.[127] He also appeared to have sufficient 'Respect' for Charles II, who had been welcomed back into England as king, to wait for his instructions. When no instructions from the new regime were forthcoming, Sidney took his father's advice to move on to Hamburg 'and from thence into *Holland*, or somme Place in Germany, wheare I may lye still a While, and see what is to be expected for me'.[128] For the republicans, it seems, it was all 'wait and see'. Sidney finally decided to go to Rome, explaining: 'I choose this voluntary exile, as the least evil condition that is within my reach. It is bitter, but not soe much soe, as the others that are in my prospect.'[129] While Sidney was travelling via Germany to Italy to secure his own personal safety, the regicide Edmund Ludlow was making his escape to Switzerland.

---

[124] Ibid., p. 690.
[125] Algernon Sidney, Copenhagen, to Robert, Earl of Leicester, 14 July 1660, in Collins (ed.), *Letters*, ii, pp. 691–4, p. 691.
[126] Ibid.   [127] Ibid., p. 694.   [128] Ibid., p. 691.
[129] Algernon Sidney, Copenhagen, to the Earl of Leicester, 29 July 1660, in Blencowe (ed), *Sydney Papers*, pp. 189–94, at pp. 190–1.

Edmund Ludlow (1617–1692)

The republican Edmund Ludlow had fought in the English Civil War on the side of Parliament and had both participated in the trial of Charles I and signed his death warrant in 1649.[130] He was a member of the Commonwealth's Council of State and in 1650 was appointed by Cromwell as second in command to the army leader Henry Ireton in Ireland, carrying the title of lieutenant-general of the horse. While he initially continued in his post after the forcible expulsion of the Long Parliament, Ludlow turned against Cromwell when the latter assumed the title of lord protector at the end of 1653 and became an active member of the republican opposition against the Protectorate. Ludlow's religion might be described as Puritan. More specifically, he was a sectarian Protestant who based his faith firmly on Scripture reading and favoured a near-total separation of state and church, rejected infant baptism and showed some sympathy for the Society of Friends without counting himself one of their number.[131] While agreeing with Cromwell's commitment to liberty of conscience in principle, he nevertheless thought that it was a political move to win over potential opponents.[132] As a radical Puritan and millenarian, Ludlow was a principled opponent of worldly monarchy who considered kings to be impostors and usurpers of God's throne on earth. Like many others, he objected to Cromwell's assumption of quasi-monarchical powers and appears to have agonised over the rights and wrongs of political involvement throughout his life.[133] After several years in relative obscurity during the Protectorate, Ludlow once again assumed several high-profile positions after the restoration of the Long Parliament and was returned to the Convention as MP for Hindon in April 1660. However, his election was declared void in May, when the House of Commons ordered the arrest of the regicides. Fearing further retribution of the Restoration regime at a time when it was still unclear what would happen to the regicides and who would be exempted from the Act of Indemnity and Oblivion, he left the country.[134]

[130] On the contested definition of the term 'regicide', see McIntosh, 'The Numbers of the English Regicides'.

[131] *Voyce*, ed. Worden, pp. 8–9, and C. H. Firth, 'Ludlow [Ludlowe], Edmund (1616/17–1692)', rev. Blair Worden, *ODNB*.

[132] J. C. Davis, 'Cromwell's Religion', in John Morrill (ed.), *Oliver Cromwell and the English Revolution* (London: Longman, 1990), pp. 181–208, at p. 196.

[133] See the chapters below.

[134] In fact, a proclamation for his arrest was issued on 1 September 1660 when he was still in Sussex, waiting for a vessel to carry him abroad. [Charles II], *By the King: A Proclamation for the*

Henry Neville (1619–1694)

Henry Neville was the younger son of a Berkshire country gentry family. While his older brother Richard Neville had been a colonel in the royalist forces during the English Civil War, Henry sided with the Parliamentarians. There is no conclusive evidence of his military engagement for Parliament, but he wrote a number of libertine libels between 1647 and 1650, *The Parliament of Ladies, The Ladies, a second time, assembled in Parliament*, and *Newes from the New Exchange*, lampooning the sexual antics of the House of Lords, the royalists in general and lukewarm Presbyterians in particular, as well as members of the newly established Commonwealth. These pamphlets clearly identify him as a political Independent opposing any compromise with the king, and among others they brought him the reputation of a libertine, while derogatory comments regarding religion would add to his reputation the label of an 'atheist' within the confines of the contemporary usage of that term.[135]

With regard to his political ideas, Neville is best described as a Harringtonian. During the 1650s he was a close collaborator of the political thinker James Harrington, whose ideas he promoted in parliamentary debate. The essence of Harringtonianism was the conviction that England's ancient constitution had collapsed and thrown the country into civil war. This collapse, according to Harrington's theory, was mainly due to economic factors. Changes in land ownership since the Reformation, especially a redistribution of church and Crown lands, had led to a shift of political power away from the monarchy and aristocracy and to the lesser gentry and the commoners represented in Parliament. This popular part of the English government was now seeking to claim its rightful political power, which necessitated various adjustments of the constitution, starting with popular sovereignty and new institutions of self-government which would go hand in hand with a clear limitation of the executive. These Harringtonian ideas had their heyday during Richard Cromwell's Parliament, when a republican faction sought to use Oliver Cromwell's

---

Apprehension of Edmund Ludlow Esquire, Commonly Called, Colonel Ludlow (London: John Bill and Christopher Barker, 1660); and Ludlow, 'Voyce', p. 818. For further details on Ludlow's life and political and military career, see Firth, 'Ludlow [Ludlowe], Edmund', rev. Worden.

[135] On Neville's life and political thought see Mahlberg, *Henry Neville and English Republican Culture*, in particular chapter 3 on his libertinism and chapter 5 on his perceived atheism.

death to establish an alternative government and attempted to limit the protector's powers.[136]

It was not the Act of Indemnity that drove Neville into exile, however, but government suspicion and surveillance in the aftermath of a number of foiled plots against the Stuart monarchy. As he had joined the Rump as a recruiter only in the autumn of 1649, Neville was safe from any accusations of participating in the regicide. However, he had sided with Parliament in the Civil War and sat on the country committee for Berkshire from around 1647 onwards alongside his friend and close political ally Henry Marten, who was a regicide. Neville later became a member of the Commonwealth's Council of State and, like Sidney and Ludlow, turned against Oliver Cromwell after the latter's forcible expulsion of the Rump.[137] He continued to oppose the Protectorate, fighting in vain for a seat in the 1656 election in Berkshire before finally returning to Parliament as MP for Reading under Richard Cromwell after a dispute over a double return.[138] During this time he published several anti-Cromwellian pamphlets, and after the fall of the Protectorate he was once again active as a member of the restored Rump and its Council of State. Neville opposed the Restoration of the monarchy to the very last, declaring against Charles Stuart and his line as late as 3 January 1660.[139] Apparently, this was not his last opposition.

Neville was suspected of conspiracy at least twice after the Restoration, in 1661 and 1663. The State Papers reveal that he was under close surveillance by the secretaries of state, his mail was intercepted, and his movements were monitored.[140] There is evidence that Neville feared for his life, and the Spence Papers suggest that he may have left the country as early as 1661. If this is true, Neville must have temporarily returned to England to be re-arrested in 1663, only to leave the country once again in 1664.[141] In any case, he was the last of our

[136] The most detailed outline of Harrington's economic theory can be found in his *Commonwealth of Oceana* (1656). For Neville's adaptation of Harringtonian ideas to Interregnum politics, see *Diary of Thomas Burton*, iii, pp. 132–5, 229, 321, 331, and iv, pp. 23–5; and to Restoration politics, see Neville's *Plato redivivus*, ed. Robbins, in particular pp. 88–114 on the property-power theory, and pp. 119 ff. on the restructuring of the English monarchy along Harringtonian principles; for an analysis see also Mahlberg, *Henry Neville and English Republican Culture*, chapter 4.
[137] Mahlberg, *Henry Neville and English Republican Culture*, p. 47.
[138] Nicholas von Maltzahn, 'Neville, Henry (1620–1694)', *ODNB*.
[139] Mahlberg, *Henry Neville and English Republican Culture*, p. 162.   [140] Ibid., p. 58.
[141] Beinecke Library, Yale University, New Haven, Joseph Spence Papers MSS 4, Box 4, folder 107. I owe this reference to Mark Knights. Spence was distantly related to Neville as great-grandson of Sir Thomas Lunsford (1610–53). James Sambrook, 'Spence, Joseph (1699–1768)', *ODNB*.

three exiles to leave the country when in the spring of 1664, after a brief spell in the Tower, he made his way to Italy.[142]

Structure of the Book

This book is composed of three parts. The first will outline the 'Networks and Communities' which enabled the three English republicans on the run to survive, settle and build new lives abroad. As will be shown in Chapter 1, these networks and communities often dated back to earlier periods of the exiles' lives and included contacts acquired through personal or family connections, political office or employment, or religious communities. In the case of the latter, these networks and communities might go back over generations and centuries. Chapter 2 will then go into more detail on the local support the exiles received and the dealings they had with their host communities and contacts. As we will see, these were primarily concerned with religious issues.

The second part, on 'Exiles, Assassins and Activism', will address the nature of exile as conceptualised by the republicans themselves as well as their everyday experiences, which included persecution and assassination threats alongside the mundane (Chapter 3), while also looking into plots and conspiracies concocted by the republican exiles themselves, most notably the Sidney plot of 1665 against the backdrop of the Second Anglo-Dutch War, and the way in which exile impacted on the republicans' political ideas (Chapter 4). Part III will discuss the republicans' 'Works of Exile' and to what extent the exiles and their transnational networks contributed to the diffusion and survival of English republican ideas abroad, not only through their personal connections but also through a number of publications, both of their own works and of those of others.

The republicans' works of exile were diverse, but almost all of them (aside from *Les juges*) engaged directly or indirectly with the Second Anglo-Dutch War, which may be regarded as defining the political climate of the mid 1660s. Ludlow's 'Voyce' offers the most detailed account of events from an English republican perspective (Chapter 5), while Sidney's *Court Maxims* directly engages with Anglo-Dutch relations, pleading for closer collaboration of the two Protestant maritime trading countries, and his 'Prophesy' reveals that England's true enemy and the enemy of European Protestantism would always be France (Chapter 6). Neville's *Isle of Pines* meanwhile offers a more critical assessment of the Anglo-Dutch

[142] See below, pp. 66ff.

relationship, highlighting the competition between the two countries as well as their potential for mutual aid and collaboration (Chapter 7). Neither Ludlow nor Neville was, however, able to trust the Protestant republicans across the Channel fully, as personal and national economic self-interest tended to get in the way of any larger common cause. Finally, the Epilogue will reassess our image of the English republican exiles and the significance of their work. Before we look at the fruits of exile, however, we should look at the individuals, networks and communities that enabled them to grow.

PART I

Networks and Communities

CHAPTER I

Cross-Channel Connections

Heavy Fog in Channel. Continent Cut Off.

The Times headline, 22 October 1957[1]

Personal Connections, Local Communities, Transnational Networks

As a study of three exiles and their journeys through a variety of countries, this book employs three analytical categories to describe their interactions along the way: personal connections, local communities and wider transnational networks. Personal connections may exist between a large variety of individuals without necessarily creating a clearly defined group. These form the most basic ties between people through either relationships (family, friendship) or interactions (meetings, correspondence) or both. Communities are more complex. Collectives like parishes, villages or the local gentry tend to be associated with a specific geographical location or area and are usually defined by multiple connections between the different individuals within this community. The connections of a network, meanwhile, are not necessarily confined to a specific location, but may transcend local and national boundaries. They may also change over time. As 'people were connected with many different groups both at any one time and over the course of their lives', there was 'social linkaging across time and space'.[2]

While for the purpose of this book, all communities are considered as forms of networks between a range of individuals with multiple connections between them, not all networks explored here are also communities, as one individual may have ties to other individuals belonging to a variety of different communities. Thus exiles lived within communities, for

[1] *Eigen's Political & Historical Quotations*, http://politicalquotes.org/node/19094, accessed 25 October 2015.
[2] Alex Shepard and Phil Withington, 'Introduction: Communities in Early Modern England', in Alex Shepard and Phil Withington (eds), *Communities in Early Modern England: Networks, Place, Rhetoric* (Manchester: Manchester University Press, 2000), pp. 1–15, at pp. 12, 5.

instance, in the cities and towns of Geneva, Lausanne and Vevey between the 1660s and 1680s; at the Tuscan court or in the international community in Rome in the 1660s; in the cities of Montpellier and Rotterdam in the 1660s, or in the rural Languedoc in the 1670s. They might live there without necessarily being fully integrated into, or part of these communities, while individuals from those communities might be part of their wider networks. The little group of exiles in Vevey might also be seen by itself as a micro-community within a community which at certain times reached out to it or vice versa. The exiles' wider networks, meanwhile, extended from the British Isles across most of Western Europe, involving individuals in Sweden and Denmark, the Holy Roman Empire, the United Provinces, France, Switzerland and Italy. The English Channel was not a barrier, but – as its name says – a channel of communication.[3]

The term 'network' is frequently used, albeit rarely defined in everyday language, since the concept perhaps seems too obvious to need explanation in an age of 'social networking sites' used to share news, contacts and images, or 'networking events' designed for meeting potential employers and clients. The specific concept of the 'social network' employed here is borrowed from the social sciences and is used to refer to 'a structure of connections' in which an 'actor is embedded'. Thus actors are primarily 'described by their relations, not by their attributes'.[4] While I am still interested in the attributes of the actors themselves as individuals and republicans, the network approach is to emphasise that no individual ever acts completely on their own, but is always part of society and embedded in a complex web of relations to others. As Robert Hanneman and Mark Riddle put it, 'the relations themselves are just as fundamental as the actors that they connect'.[5] In comparison to some modern global networks in the worlds of business and communication, the networks dealt with here are comparatively limited and are focused on small groups of people related through a variety of personal, political and religious connections. For the most part, the networks this book deals with are so-called ego networks focused on a central individual (the 'ego') connected to a variety of 'alters' through ties of varying strength.[6] If we take, for instance, Ludlow as the

---

[3] I would like to thank Neil Murphy for this point.
[4] Robert A. Hanneman and Mark Riddle, *Introduction to Social Network Methods* (Riverside: University of California, Riverside, 2005), http://faculty.ucr.edu/~hanneman/nettext/C1_Social_Network_Data.html (unpaginated), accessed 9 August 2015.
[5] Ibid.
[6] Ibid., chapter 9, https://faculty.ucr.edu/~hanneman/nettext/C9_Ego_networks.html (unpaginated), accessed 9 August 2015.

central node of the exile community in Switzerland, his fellow exiles in Geneva, Lausanne and Vevey would be his closest connections, while local friends and supporters, such as Jean de Labadie, Johann Heinrich Hummel or the excellencies of the council of Bern, would be more distant connections, and English contacts moved for the time being to the periphery. In Sidney's case, his ego network would be subject to significant change over time as he changed both location and allegiance, looking for political allies first in the United Provinces and later in France. Historical network analysis has struggled with depictions of change over time, as the static visualisations of networks for the main part capture only specific moments in the lifetime of an ever-changing network. I hope that my narrative will make up for that.

The three exiles studied in this book all knew each other and in turn belonged to other networks without a specific central node (Protestants, republicans). Therefore it is possible to think of them as the centres of their own ego networks on the one hand, while at the same time also being minor or more peripheral figures of larger, sometimes overlapping religious or political networks of English and Dutch, French, Swiss or German Protestants or republicans on the other. While the individuals we are concerned with here could be parts of smaller or micro-communities, such as the group of exiles in Switzerland, their wider networks were necessarily transnational. Because of the nature of early modern politics and society, religion also played an important role in the forming of connections and alliances, even though confessional boundaries were at times crossed in rather unexpected ways.

The Kindness of Strangers? Religious and Political Bonds

Like all fugitives, the English republican exiles had to rely to a great extent on the kindness of strangers. With the political situation subject to change on a daily basis there was a certain unpredictability in the exiles' lives. Yet not all those supporting the fugitive republicans along the way were complete strangers. This chapter will argue that the exiles were able to draw to a considerable extent on pre-existing transnational networks formed during earlier periods of their lives, in particular through their families, their education, their religion and their political activity. Many of these had their origins in England. The republicans' exile networks thus were a mixture of old and new cross-Channel connections.

Research into the circumstances of the republicans' lives abroad helps us to understand the nature of the exile existence in seventeenth-century

Europe more broadly, by revealing the personal contacts that allowed the republican exiles to make their escape from England and find help and support on the other side of the Channel. The documents reveal that all three exiles relied on pre-existing networks that were either based on faith or built during their Grand Tour in their younger years, through aristocratic and family connections or through their political and military activity on behalf of the English Parliament and Commonwealth. These wider networks allowed them to become temporary residents in local communities across Western Europe forging further individual connections necessary for their survival and support. For Ludlow, and to some extent for Sidney, these networks consisted for the major part of Reformed Protestants, in particular ministers, with contacts among local political elites and councils. Ludlow (in Switzerland) and Sidney (in the Netherlands, Germany and France) were in fact tapping into transnational networks of Reformed Protestants going back to the sixteenth century, which established a link between the seventeenth-century exiles and their Marian ancestors.[7] English republicans frequently cited these exiles as role models of resistance to tyrannical rulers who denied their Protestant subjects the right to worship freely in their own country. It is all the more interesting therefore that seventeenth-century republicans not only saw themselves as the spiritual heirs of the Marian exiles, but also made use of European Protestant networks created several generations earlier, which have recently been discussed in the work of Ole Peter Grell, David Trim and Vivienne Larminie among others.[8] This line of enquiry therefore confirms the strong religious influences on seventeenth-century republicanism so often dismissed by a secularising historiography which has primarily focused on the classical sources of English republicanism.[9] Yet most Reformed Protestants in Europe were closer in outlook to English

---

[7] See e.g. Milton, 'Puritanism and the Continental Reformed Churches', pp. 111–12.

[8] Grell, *Brethren in Christ*; David J. B. Trim (ed.), *The Huguenots: History and Memory in Transnational Context. Essays in Honour and Memory of Walter C. Utt* (Leiden and Boston: Brill, 2011), in particular Trim's introductory chapter and his 'The Huguenots and the European Wars of Religion, c. 1560–1697: Soldiering in National and Transnational Context', pp. 154–92; and Vivienne Larminie (ed.), *Huguenot Networks, 1560–1780: The Interactions and Impact of a Protestant Minority in Europe* (New York: Routledge, 2018). Philip Major also highlights the link between different generations of English Protestant exiles in his *Writings of Exile*, p. 36. Ludlow, for instance, writes, 'it's publiquely averred that the Hereticks shall soone know they live in Queene Maryes dayes'. See Ludlow, 'Voyce', p. 937.

[9] This secular historiography has to a large extent been shaped by the Cambridge School of Political Thought, while more recent work on English republicanism is more inclined to embrace religion, notably Michael Winship, 'Algernon Sidney's Calvinist Republicanism', *Journal of British Studies*, 49:4 (2010), 753–73.

Presbyterians than to Independents. Ludlow's hosts in Switzerland in particular came from a Calvinist tradition with a relatively strict synodal structure and formal way of worship – a fact that would create some tensions between the exiles and the local community, as we shall see in Chapter 3, while not proving sufficiently disruptive that it would challenge their brotherly Protestant bond or, worse, lead to an extradition of the fugitives.

Sidney and Neville further benefited from aristocratic and family connections established through either travel or diplomatic service. The Sidney family had connections in the Huguenot south of France dating back to Algernon's youth, when his father Robert, Earl of Leicester, was an ambassador to the country.[10] As Jonathan Scott has shown, Leicester took both his sons on this trip and may have sent them to be educated at the Huguenot Academy of Saumur.[11] Algernon Sidney's correspondence from France in the later 1660s and 1670s reveals that he was drawing on these family connections, including his father's contacts from an earlier period to Henri, Duke of Rohan, and Louis de Bourbon, Prince of Condé, as well as his own to Henri de la Tour d'Auvergne, Viscount of Turenne, Frédéric Maurice, Duke of Bouillon (d. 1652), and his son Godefroy, and François, Duke de La Rochefoucauld.[12] Thus Sidney moved at least temporarily into the local community of Huguenot aristocrats in the south-west of France – the heartland of the Fronde – without necessarily being part of it. Sidney's earlier stay in Rome also benefited from his acquaintance with the exiled former queen Christina of Sweden, whom he had met in Hamburg after his diplomatic mission to Sweden and Denmark, and who would provide useful access to the learned circles and social élites of the Eternal City.[13] Sidney thus became part of the international community in Rome, establishing close connections within the Roman hierarchy of cardinals. The cardinals were part of his wider network, without being part of the same community. Christina was also another link to the Dutch legal scholar Hugo Grotius, who was the former queen's ambassador to Paris when he met the Earl of Leicester, and whose ideas would come to influence Sidney's political thought and writings.[14]

---

[10] Scott, *Algernon Sidney and the English Republic*, p. 75.   [11] Ibid., p. 53.   [12] Ibid., pp. 227–8.
[13] Algernon Sidney, Frankfurt am Main, to Robert, Earl of Leicester, 8 September, 1660, in Collins (ed.), *Letters*, ii, pp. 695–8, at p. 696; and Scott, *Algernon Sidney and the English Republic*, pp. 147–8.
[14] Scott, *Algernon Sidney and the English Republic*, p. 228. On Sidney and Grotius, see Chapter 6 below.

Likewise, Neville was able to draw on old acquaintances at the grand ducal court in Florence, where one of his oldest friends was Ferrante Capponi, a lawyer and by now senior office-holder under Ferdinando II. However, the key figure assisting Neville with many practical issues was Bernardino Guasconi, a former Italian mercenary in the royalist regiment of Neville's older brother Richard. Guasconi was both a travel companion and a key contact at the Tuscan court in the service of the grand duke's brother Leopoldo. As a servant to Leopoldo, who took a keen interest in the sciences, he also acted as an intermediary between the Galilean Accademia del Cimento and the Royal Society in London.[15] Neville became a guest of the community at the Tuscan court and later a temporary resident in the international community in Rome, albeit without any intention to settle. Like Sidney, Neville enjoyed both trust and respect among a range of influential Catholics in the higher echelons of Italian society, contradicting the commonly held assumption that being an English Protestant republican precluded any amicable relations with Catholic contemporaries either at home or abroad.[16] These findings strengthen the argument that cross-confessional contacts might not just have been an opportunist concession to necessity, but also confirmed the republicans' commitment to liberty of conscience beyond dissenting Protestantism. Such cross-confessional contacts furthered the cause of wider toleration, while their existence also suggests that the 'unlikely' alliance between dissenter republicans and Catholics during the 1680s and their collaboration on the 1687 Declaration of Indulgence built on earlier interaction.[17]

While Reformed Protestant networks in Switzerland, Huguenot France and the United Provinces were among the more obvious connections of the English republican exiles, both Sidney and Neville also drew on Catholic networks in Italy, which leads us to the related question of how Catholicism and republicanism might be reconciled. The two key themes the following two chapters will address are thus, first, the transnationalism of the exiles' existence with particular attention to the importance of space and place and, secondly, the religious dimension of the exile experience and the role played by confessional alliances as well as cross-confessional

---

[15] On Ferrante Capponi, see Francesco Martelli, '"Nec spes nec metus": Ferrante Capponi, giurista ed alto funzionario nella Toscana di Cosimo III', in Franco Angiolini, Vieri Becagli and Marcello Verga (eds), *La Toscana nell'età di Cosimo III* (Florence: Edifir, 1993), pp. 137–63; and on Guasconi, see Stefano Villani, 'Guasconi (Gascoigne), Bernardo', *DBI*.

[16] Robbins (ed.), *Two English Republican Tracts*, pp. 13 ff.

[17] Gaby Mahlberg, 'The Republican Discourse on Religious Liberty during the Exclusion Crisis', *History of European Ideas*, 38 (2012), 1–18.

connections. But first we need to look at the departure of the republican exiles and the help they received along the way.

Ludlow's Way to Geneva

Ludlow's manuscript account of his flight to the Continent exaggerates the extent to which his escape was spontaneous and guided by divine providence. His Puritan narrative aimed to fashion him as a servant of God discerning the path the Lord had chosen for him. A closer look at the evidence, however, suggests that his journey must have been more carefully planned and reveals the extent to which he relied on pre-existing contacts, including Calvinist members of the so-called stranger churches in London that connected him to a wider network of Reformed Protestants on the Continent.[18]

Ludlow's decision to leave England took some time to mature, not least because he had a wife whom he was hesitant to leave behind and an estate to look after. Both his wife and several other family members and friends therefore made enquiries about Ludlow's legal status on his behalf before he came to be convinced that exile was the only safe option open to him, after being advised that 'if I stayd I was a dead man'.[19] Ludlow eventually left England by boat, crossing the Channel from Lewes in Sussex to Dieppe in the north of France, where he was received by relations of acquaintances from the French Church in London.[20] In Dieppe, his main contact was the French gentlewoman Mme de Caux (or Caus), who put him up with her family in the country as Ludlow was worried one of the many Irishmen in the town might recognise him on account of his long service in Ireland.[21] However, when he heard of a proclamation for his apprehension, Ludlow feared that he might cause trouble to his contacts in France and decided to move on. He declined an offer to be taken to the United Provinces because he disliked the idea of being in 'a country which depended so much on England' for its trade. Instead, with the Lord's

---

[18] See also Milton, 'Puritanism and the Continental Reformed Churches', pp. 112–14.
[19] Ludlow, *Voyce*, ed. Worden, pp. 102–4 (738–41), 111–12 (747–9); 160–5 ff. (789–94 ff.), 187 (814). The numbers in parentheses refer to the pages of Ludlow's manuscript in the Bodleian Library, Oxford, MS Eng. hist. c. 487.
[20] Ibid., p. 191 (817).
[21] Ibid. The Dieppe-born Huguenot Isaac de Caus was a member of the French Church in London and a friend of the Pembroke family, who were relations of Algernon Sidney. See Vivienne Larminie, 'The Herbert Connection, the French Church and Westminster Politics, 1643–1661', chapter 3 of her edited collection *Huguenot Networks, 1560–1780*, pp. 41–60.

guidance, he decided on Geneva, 'a citty very renowned for liberty and religion'.[22] Ludlow travelled with Mme de Caux's son-in-law Dr Hughes, who had some business to settle in Paris and with whom he was able to converse in basic Latin. In Paris, he got a bill of exchange from Mme de Caux's contact M. Margas, while also making the acquaintance of the English merchant Mr Copley, who showed him his way around Paris before Ludlow departed with the messenger to Lyon. Along his way, Ludlow joined several other travellers bound for Geneva.[23] On his arrival, he was delighted to find himself 'within the teritoryes of Geneve', where he considered himself to be 'in more surety' and in a wholesome environment, because he had 'a great love and inclination to the ayre of a Commonwealth'. He also 'hoped to enjoy the society of mankind, and above all the servants, and ordinances, of Christ'.[24]

Geneva was a remarkable place in the later seventeenth century. Home to Calvin's experiments with Protestant government a century earlier, it had developed into a model city which was attractive to a man like Ludlow, for his political identity was closely bound up with his religious faith. He described himself and his fellow exiles as 'sufferers for the Cause of Christ, & the Libertyes of our Country',[25] while his rejection of the Stuart monarchy was primarily based on the king's perceived usurpation of divine rule, since only God could claim to be a legitimate monarch. Unlike Sidney and Neville, Ludlow remained openly hostile to Charles II, whom he frequently referred to in his memoirs as a 'tyrant' and as the 'present Usurper'.[26] It was both Ludlow's faith and his radical, anti-monarchical republicanism that made Geneva, 'a citty very renowned for liberty and religion', his ideal place of exile.[27]

Military and Civic Connections

Geneva was not part of the Old Swiss Confederacy, but an independent city state only loosely associated with the cantons of Switzerland. This also meant it was reliant to a greater extent than the federated cantons on its big neighbour France, which in the end might have cut short Ludlow's residence in the city as Geneva was reluctant to offer protection against the wishes of the French royal family, which was by marriage related to the Stuarts.[28] Nevertheless, for now, Ludlow lodged with the former soldier

---

[22] Ludlow, *Voyce*, ed. Worden, p. 192 (818).   [23] Ibid., pp. 193–4 (818–20).
[24] Ibid., p. 195 (821–2).   [25] Ludlow, 'Voyce', p. 966.   [26] Ibid., pp. 1072, 1077, 1134, etc.
[27] Ludlow, *Voyce*, ed. Worden, p. 192 (818).   [28] Whatmore, *Against War and Empire*, p. xiii.

Charles Perrot, who had fought as a mercenary for the Parliament during the English Civil War and was married to an Englishwoman.[29] Perrot was descended from a French Huguenot family that had arrived in Geneva as refugees several generations earlier. His grandfather, another Charles Perrot, was a former rector of the protestant Academy of Geneva and a collaborator of the French theologian Theodore Beza, the successor of Calvin and translator of the Greek New Testament.[30] Perrot was also the brother-in-law of Herbert Saladin, another member of the French Church in London and presumably an existing contact of Ludlow's from the 1640s.[31] Like Mme de Caux, he too may have been informed of Ludlow's escape before he arrived in Geneva. As grandson of a rector of the academy and as a member of the city's Council of Sixty, Perrot was well connected among the city's religious and political establishment and thus ideally placed to introduce Ludlow to life in his new temporary home, while also providing him with information and advice on his refugee status.[32] For the best part of eighteen months, this arrangement worked. Ludlow lodged with the Perrot family in the rue des Chanoines, located between the town hall and the Cathédrale Saint-Pierre, adjacent to the house in which Calvin had lived only a century earlier.[33] He enjoyed Swiss hospitality and English beer illegally brewed in the Perrot household.[34] But when news broke in April 1662 that three further regicides, John Barkstead, Miles Corbet and John Okey, had been arrested in the Netherlands by the English envoy George Downing and extradited to England, this idyll was threatened.[35] Together with the regicides William Cawley and John Lisle, who had recently joined him in Geneva, Ludlow enquired via Perrot what the Genevan authorities would do should they be issued with a similar extradition demand.[36] Ludlow feared that the French king might exercise pressure 'upon this little Commonwealth' in the same way he had done on the Grand Pensionary Johan de Witt in the United Provinces,

[29] Ludlow, *Voyce*, ed. Worden, p. 195 (822).
[30] Archives d'État, Geneva (hereafter AEG), Archives du Bureau 1962, Travaux Recherches 65, pp. 291–303; and M. J.-E. Cellérier, 'Charles Perrot, pasteur Genevois au seizième siècle: notice biographique', in *Mémoires et documents publiés par la Société d'Histoire et d'Archéologie de Genève*, xi (Geneva: Jullien Frères, 1859), pp. 1–68; Béatrice Nicollier, 'Beza, Theodor', *HLS*.
[31] Larminie, 'The Herbert Connection'.   [32] AEG, Registres du Conseil (1660), 160, fol. 10.
[33] AEG, Archives du Bureau 1962, Travaux Recherches 65, pp. 291–303.
[34] Ibid.; and Ludlow, *Voyce*, ed. Worden, p. 195 (822).
[35] Catterall, 'Sir George Downing and the Regicides'; Greaves, *Deliver Us from Evil*, pp. 92 ff.
[36] Ludlow, *Voyce*, ed. Worden, pp. 303–4 (922–3).

and that Geneva might be bullied into delivering the regicides. He therefore found it necessary 'to get what assurance we could of our safety whilst we stayed here', while at the same time preparing himself 'to make provission for ourselves elsewhere' if that assurance could not be given.[37]

Geneva's first syndic, Jean Voisine, reassured the exiles that he would inform them of any extradition request before such a thing would be put to the council and, in the worst case, keep their escape routes free. As the holder of the key to the city's water gate, Voisine promised he would unlock it for the refugees, if needed, at night, while also assuring them of a free passage through any of the city gates if they had to escape during the day. He also promised to discuss the matter with his fellow syndic Jacob Dupain.[38] While Ludlow seemed content with the arrangement, Lisle and Cawley considered a verbal promise insufficient to ensure their safety and pressed for a more formal arrangement. Perrot discussed the issue with his cousin Jean Anthoine Dupain, Jacob's nephew, who served as the town's *procureur général* or attorney general.[39] They agreed to petition the council for the exiles' protection. Yet the petition failed and the city was unable to offer the regicides a more formal level of protection – a move Ludlow attributed to internal divisions among the governing élite over their relations to the English government. One of the city's four governing syndics, Odet Lect, was owed a large debt by the English king 'in the right of his wife' and therefore 'obstructed' the exiles' protection and 'threatened those who had a hand therein' in case they intended to surprise the council. So the consideration of the exiles' protection was deferred, and the business withdrawn 'before it was publiquely read'.[40]

---

[37] Ibid., p. 303 (922). Louis XIV's younger brother Philippe I, Duke of Orléans (and Duke of Anjou) was married to Princess Henrietta of England and Scotland, daughter of Charles I and sister of Charles II. The Duchess of Orléans and Anjou played an important role in the persecution of the regicides on the Continent.

[38] Ludlow, *Voyce*, ed. Worden, p. 303 (922–3). For the composition of the city government, see AEG, Registres du Conseil (1662), 162, fol. 4v.

[39] Ludlow, *Voyce*, ed. Worden, p. 304 (923); and AEG, Registres du Conseil (1660), 160, fol. 9v.

[40] Ludlow, *Voyce*, ed. Worden, p. 304 (923). Odet Lect was one of the city's syndics in 1662. Cf. AEG, Registres du Conseil (1662), 162, fol. 4v; and the entry on Odet Lect (1611–85) in Albert Choisy, *Généalogies Genevoises: familles admises à la Bourgeoisie avant la Réformation* (Geneva: Kundig, 1947), p. 211. Lect was married to Renée Burlamachi, the daughter of Philip Burlamachi of Geneva, who settled as a merchant-banker in London in the early seventeenth century and became one of the largest lenders to James I and Charles I. Charles's lax repayments had virtually ruined him. It is likely that the debt Ludlow refers to dated back to this time. See ibid., p. 211, and on Philip Burlamachi: Grell, *Brethren in Christ*, pp. 107–13.

Reformed Ministers

Even more important than Ludlow's military, civic and lay Protestant connections were his links to Protestant ministers. These included the radical preacher Jean de Labadie in Geneva, who was known as the city's 'second Calvin', and Johann Heinrich Hummel, the chief minister of Bern.[41] Both were contacts of the Scottish Calvinist minister John Dury, who had been a close ally of Cromwell's and a key figure in the pan-European irenic movement.[42] The Scots and the English had established many contacts to foreign ministers both through scholarly exchange and through the stranger churches in London, which were gathering places for Calvinist exiles from all over Europe.[43] The continental connections of English Calvinists meanwhile also went back to the Marian exiles who had found refuge in Europe in the 1550s, only to return during the reign of Elizabeth I, when they came to 'play a prominent role in the English Church' and gave it 'a distinctly Reformed flavour'.[44] The Puritans of the English Revolution thus saw themselves as part of a European Calvinist or Reformed network working on a second or further Reformation.[45]

The French-born Labadie had gained notoriety as a former Jesuit and radical convert of the Calvinist Church. He had worked in the Huguenot strongholds of Montauban and the principality of Orange, located like Montauban in the south of present-day France, but then still belonging to the House of Orange-Nassau. It may have been during the early 1650s that he first came into contact with English republicans. Notably, Jean's brother Louis de Labadie had taken part in the Ormée, a local revolution in Bordeaux during the Fronde, whose supporters were inspired by English republican ideas, including the more radical kind promoted

---

[41] On De Labadie, see T[revor] J. Saxby, *The Quest for the New Jerusalem: Jean de Labadie and the Labadists, 1610–1744* (Dordrecht, Boston and Lancaster: Martinus Nijhoff, 1987), p. 103 and n. 60 on p. 358. On Hummel, see Vivienne Larminie, 'Johann Heinrich Hummel, the Peningtons and the London Godly Community: Anglo-Swiss Relations 1634–1674', *Journal for the History of Reformed Pietism*, 2:2 (2016), 1–6; Ludlow, 'Voyce', p. 978 and *passim*.

[42] On Ludlow and Dury, see Worden, 'Introduction' to *Voyce*, p. 14. This Reformed network would later come to include the Dutch scholar Anna Maria von Schurmann (1607–78), who became a leader of the Labadists. See Ludlow, 'Voyce', p. 1378.

[43] Ole Peter Grell, *Calvinist Exiles in Tudor and Stuart England* (Aldershot: Ashgate, 1996); and Grell, *Brethren in Christ*.

[44] Grell, *Brethren in Christ*, p. 178.

[45] See Larminie (ed.), *Huguenot Networks*; Helmers, *The Royalist Republic*, pp. 63–4, 68; and Milton, 'Puritanism and the Continental Reformed churches'.

by the Levellers.[46] At some point, he had even been selected as one of the envoys to go to England to ask Cromwell to support the local republican cause, but it appears that his name was later taken off the list.[47] It was hoped in Bordeaux that the English would send troops to help oust the Prince of Conti and establish a republic in the city.[48] While English support for the Ormiste cause did not translate into military action at the time, both Louis and his brother Jean subsequently appear to have maintained a connection to England via the French Church in London. This connection was strong enough that when Jean De Labadie had to leave Orange in 1659 he contacted Dury in his search for a new home and employment. He was subsequently offered a post in the French Church in London.[49]

In the 1640s, this church had experienced a schism under the French pastor Jean d'Espagne, who was known for his Independent leanings. During the war, he had demanded the foundation of a separate church at Westminster, claiming that the location of the existing church in Threadneedle Street in London's East End was inconvenient for many worshippers. Parliament agreed to the new foundation, and Cromwell first granted d'Espagne and his followers the use of the chapel of Durham House and from 1651 let them use the chapel at Somerset House.[50] Many French and English worshippers moved to the new church, and when d'Espagne became too frail to carry on his ministry, the government sent for Labadie at Orange to take his place. After d'Espagne's death in April 1659, it was Ludlow's fellow republican John Milton, in his role as secretary to the council of state, who wrote to Labadie to offer him the post.[51] Labadie initially accepted, but in June decided to take a position in

---

[46] Saxby, *The Quest for the New Jerusalem*, p. 73. On the impact of Leveller ideas during the Fronde, see Olivier Lutaud, *Cromwell, les Niveleurs et la République* (Paris: Aubier, 1978). I owe this reference to Rachel Hammersley.

[47] Philip A. Knachel, *England and the Fronde: The Impact of the English Civil War and Revolution on France* (Ithaca, NY: Cornell University Press, 1967), pp. 197, 202–3.

[48] Sal Alexander Westrich, *The Ormée of Bordeaux: A Revolution during the Fronde* (Baltimore: Johns Hopkins University Press, 1972), pp. 92, 94.

[49] Saxby, *The Quest for the New Jerusalem*, p. 98.

[50] Durham House was the London residence of the Bishop of Durham. In the 1630s it was the meeting place of the so-called Durham House group, including William Laud and other High Churchmen. Somerset House was a former royal palace, taken by the Parliamentarians during the Civil War. On D'Espagne and the new chapel, see also Larminie, 'The Herbert Connection'.

[51] Saxby remarks that Milton's letter to Labadie is usually dated 21 April 1659 in editions of Milton's *Epistolae familiares*, e.g. *The Works of John Milton: In Verse and Prose*, ed. John Mitford, 8 vols (London: William Pickering, 1851), vii, pp. 406–8; but William R. Parker, *Milton: A Biography*, 2 vols (Oxford: Clarendon Press, 1968), ii, p. 525, says it should be 27 April.

Geneva instead.[52] The English government was not happy about losing him, but bowed to the authority of the Protestant Rome.[53]

After his move to Geneva, Labadie became known for his efforts in the moral reformation of the city, where standards of godliness had markedly dropped since Calvin's times with 'dwindling church attendance' and 'inns open and well frequented at sermon time'.[54] Ludlow himself observed on his arrival that Geneva had 'rather gone backward' since 'the first Reformation' and had not made much progress in either 'doctrine or discipline'.[55] He sympathised with Labadie's clean-up efforts in the city and referred to him approvingly both as a 'true and sincere friend' and as 'a zealous & faithfull minister of the Gospell'.[56] Labadie for his part was still indebted to the English republican regime for its efforts on his behalf. So Ludlow and the other exiles may have felt they could turn to him in April 1662, when the recently reported extradition and trial of the regicides from the Netherlands made them fear for their own lives and they had to leave Geneva.[57] Labadie contacted some of his acquaintances on the council of the Protestant city and canton of Bern, to whom the exiles then applied for their protection and naturalisation.[58] This body granted them permission to settle within the territories of Bern as religious refugees. The council minutes explicitly refer to them as 'Englishmen driven out of their country because of their faith', which shows that the Bern authorities may have perceived the English Civil War primarily as a religious conflict, while it could also be suggested that it was much less contentious for them to grant asylum to religious refugees than to be seen as harbouring a group of regicides in a period when Switzerland aimed to maintain amicable relations with the newly restored Stuart regime in England.[59] The naturalisation of the English exiles was never procured, but they were given refuge in Lausanne on Lake Geneva in the French-speaking Vaud, before they moved – on the advice of the council's treasurer Emmanuel Steiger – to the quieter Vevey the following year. Labadie also put the exiles in touch with another key Protestant ally: the chief minister of Bern Johann

[52] Saxby, *The Quest for the New Jerusalem*, pp. 98–101.   [53] Ibid., p. 105.
[54] Ibid., p. 103. Orange was outside the jurisdiction of France.
[55] Ludlow, 'Voyce', pp. 962, 1237.   [56] Ibid., pp. 951, 923.   [57] Ibid., pp. 916 ff.
[58] Ibid., p. 923. Labadie's contacts may have been Steiger and Weiss, who are frequently mentioned as friends by Ludlow.
[59] StAB, Raths-Manual der Stadt Bern, A II 454, vol. 143 (27 January 1662–7 June 1662), entry for 16 April, p. 317. I owe the latter point to André Holenstein.

Heinrich Hummel, who was to become an important link between the exiles and the local authorities.[60]

Hummel had put in a word for the exiles when they were in need and also thanked the Bern authorities on their behalf because they lacked the necessary language skills to do so themselves. Conveniently, 'this worthy friend of ours Mr Humelius', Ludlow writes, 'having spent some tyme of his Youth in England', had 'attained to the knowledge of our Native Languadge' as well as meeting a variety of Protestants.[61] Indeed, Hummel had spent several years in London, where he came 'within the orbit of' the minister of Rotherhithe, Thomas Gataker, who was to become a moderate Presbyterian member of the Westminster Assembly, and studied with the educational reformer Samuel Hartlib.[62] He visited Oxford and Cambridge and returned to Bern after short stays in France and Geneva. As a leading figure of the canton's Reformed church, which was influenced by the teachings of Luther and Zwingli as well as Calvin but distanced itself from the radical Calvinism of Geneva, he also became an important figure in the irenic movement and a regular correspondent of Dury, who in turn was a close collaborator of Hartlib.[63] Hummel's link to Gataker suggests that he was potentially more inclined towards English Presbyterianism and more moderate in outlook than the Independent Ludlow. In this exceptional situation, however, these differences seemed negligible in comparison to the bigger cause of Reformed religion, even though Ludlow's stay in the Vaud would not remain without its conflicts. Ludlow's Protestant contacts in Switzerland could thus be seen as an outgrowth of his networks in England, extending via Dury and the Hartlib Circle to the pan-European irenic movement for a unity of Protestant churches.[64] The efforts of Dury and Hartlib, together with Johann Amos Comenius, to foster an

---

[60] Ludlow, 'Voyce', p. 965. For Hummel's correspondence with the exiles, see StAB, Epistolae virorum clarorum, B.III.63. Copies are also held in the British Library. The letters have been published in shortened form in Stern (ed.), Briefe englischer Flüchtlinge.

[61] 'Voyce', p. 965.   [62] Larminie, 'Johann Heinrich Hummel', pp. 5–8.

[63] The canton's Reformed church was based on the Berner Synodus of 1532 and the Helvetic Confessions of 1536 and 1562, reflecting these different influences. See Michael W. Bruening, Calvinism's First Battleground: Conflict and Reform in the Pays de Vaud, 1528–1559 (Dordrecht: Springer, 2005), pp. 63 ff. See also Alfred Ehrensperger, Der Gottesdienst in Stadt und Landschaft Bern im 16. und 17. Jahrhundert (Zürich: Theologischer Verlag, 2011); Stern (ed.), Briefe englischer Flüchtlinge, p. xiii, and p. 6, n. 10.

[64] For more detail on the Hartlib Circle and irenicism, see Mark Greengrass et al. (eds), Samuel Hartlib and Universal Reformation: Studies in Intellectual Communication (Cambridge, UK: Cambridge University Press, 1994); and George H. Turnbull, Hartlib, Dury and Comenius: Gleanings from Hartlib's Papers (Liverpool: University Press of Liverpool, 1947).

international network of Reformed Protestants mainly through correspondence would certainly deserve more attention in this context.[65]

Despite the disagreement between London and Geneva over the appointment of Labadie, relations between Interregnum England and Switzerland had been largely amicable, and, as part of Cromwell's ambitious Protestant foreign policy, plans had been under way for a closer alliance. In fact, the mathematician John Pell had been sent to the Protestant cantons of Switzerland in the 1650s as a political agent for the Cromwellian Protectorate to explore possibilities for closer cooperation.[66] Like Dury, Pell was a member of the Hartlib Circle, and both had been engaged by Cromwell in a joint mission to win both the Protestant states and the Protestant churches of Western Europe for an anti-popish, or anti-French, alliance. The status of the exiles in Geneva and Switzerland after 1660 was thus subject to wider diplomatic considerations and depended on the strength of the Protestant cantons to assert themselves against their Catholic neighbours, especially Savoy, but also France and the Habsburg territories. In the event, Bern proved to be stronger and more independent than Geneva, which at the time was only loosely joined to Switzerland, and Ludlow and his fellow exiles depended very much on the goodwill of the local council to provide protection. The exiles' closest friends and allies among the authorities of Bern were the treasurer Emmanuel Steiger and Colonel Weiss, while they also appear to have been on good terms with the president of the council, Avoyer Anton von Graffenried.[67] It was thus due to the exiles' networks in their local community and their good relations with Protestant ministers and local officials that they survived, even though Charles II's sister Henrietta, Duchess of Orléans, had offered money to those who would attempt to 'destroy' Ludlow and his friends. As Ludlow put it, it was assumed that 'we were too much owned by the Magistrates, & too well beloved by the people to have any such thinge offered on us,

---

[65] See also Alfred Stern, *Milton und seine Zeit*, 2 vols (Leipzig: Duncker & Humblot, 1877–9), ii, book 3, p. 27. Of course, Comenius himself was an exile in the United Provinces. See Wilhelmus Rood, *Comenius and the Low Countries: Some Aspects of Life and Work of a Czech Exile in the Seventeenth Century* (Amsterdam: Van Gendt and Co., 1970).

[66] On John Pell (1611–85) and his mission between 1654 and 1658, see Christoph J. Scriba, 'Pell, John (1611–1685)', *ODNB*.

[67] Ludlow, 'Voyce', pp. 944, 978. Ludlow, *Memoirs*, ed. Firth, ii, p. 351n., says that Emmanuel Steiger (1615–70) was a 'member of the Great Council in 1638, Landvogt of Lugano in 1642 and of Grandson in 1645, member of the Little Council in 1652, Landvogt at Trachselwald in 1654, again a member of the Little Council in 1660, and at the same time appointed Treasurer of the "Weltschen-Landen", and in 1664 also chief commander of the forces of the same districts.' Anton von Graffenried (1597–1674) headed the council of Bern as *Schultheiss* from 1651. See his entry in the *HLS*.

and that it was a vaine thinge for any to Imagine the accomplishing thereof.[68] While Ludlow seems to have chosen his exile wisely and carefully, his fellow fugitive Algernon Sidney took some time to find the right place to settle.

Sidney between Copenhagen, Hamburg and Rome

Already while in Copenhagen in September 1659, Sidney had uttered initial doubts about his personal and political future if the royalists in England were to win the upper hand, writing to his father that '[t]his uncertainty of affaires, makes me uncertaine of my owne concernements heare, and my returne home'. Sidney had heard 'reports of the Cavileers's numbers and strenght in England', and they 'weare believed to be very terrible by all heare, except somme of us, that, by knowing theire temper, could guesse at the issue'. At this stage, Sidney still hoped he would be able to bring his diplomatic negotiations to a satisfactory conclusion and lay the foundations for a strong Anglo-Dutch alliance.[69] Yet by November things were still not any clearer because of power struggles in England, where a new Army Committee of Safety had just replaced the Rump's Council of State and communications were disrupted. Sidney remarked in a letter from Elsinore to Bulstrode Whitelocke on the committee that he had not received any reliable information from England since Whitelocke's last letter of 21 September. He complained that the only letters he had received had come 'by chance from persons soe farre from the knowledge of business, that they did not knowe of the liberty granted unto us by the parliament and councell to returne home'. As a consequence, Sidney and his colleagues had 'depended wholly upon the information' received 'from the Holland ministers, for the knowledge of all that hath bin done in England since that time'. So the uncertainty continued, and Sidney did not know where to turn, remarking that 'If the government in England doe continue on the good old principles, I shall be ready to serve them'; however, 'if it returns to monarchy I desire nothing but liberty to retire, finding myself a very unfit stone for such a building'.[70] Yet it would be nearly another year before Sidney was to move on, torn between a sense of

---

[68] Ludlow, 'Voyce', p. 978.
[69] Algernon Sidney, Copenhagen, to Robert, Earl of Leicester, 13 September 1659, in Blencowe (ed.), *Sydney Papers*, pp. 163–8.
[70] Algernon Sidney, Elsinore to [Bulstrode] Whitelocke, 13 November 1689 (*recte* 1659), in Blencowe (ed.), *Sydney Papers*, pp. 169–73.

obligation and love for his country on the one hand and frustration over the success of the royalist faction on the other.

After leaving his ambassadorial position in Sweden and Denmark, Sidney briefly stopped over in Hamburg, where he made use of long-standing English trading connections by staying at the house of Samuel Missenden, a lawyer and secretary to the Merchant Adventurers' Company. The English Company had in recent years experienced turbulent times in Hamburg, both as a result of the Thirty Years War and as a consequence of the regicide and subsequent regime change which had caused disruptions in trade.[71] Since the summer of 1654, there had also been intermittent infighting between competing factions, supporting either the Cromwellian deputy in charge of the company, Richard Bradshaw, or his rival Francis Townley, who had temporarily managed to depose him. As a consequence, Bradshaw's supporters had feared that 'their immunities and privileges' in the city were threatened and called on the Protector for help. By 1659, after Oliver Cromwell's death, matters still had not been settled, as Bradshaw continued his appeals to the government in England.[72] However, Sidney did not comment on any possible effects of this insecurity on his stay there or on his relations with the company at this major turning point in English political fortunes. In fact, as events at a political level were in flux personal connections appear to have mattered more than ever. Even though Sidney and Missenden disagreed on politics (the latter was a royalist at heart), they seem to have been on friendly terms, and Sidney felt obliged to obtain employment for him with the English government in return for his help, reporting to his father that the representative of the English Company was 'desirous to be imployed by the Secretaryes of State, to give Intelligence of what he can learne of the Affaires of Germany, Denmark, or Sweden'. Sidney recommended Missenden as 'a discreet Man, of good Parts, studied well, bread a Lawyer' and as having 'good Credite both with his Countrymen, and others, where he lives'. On a whim, Sidney had 'promised this Employment for him, under thoes that formerly governed, but that he was too Monarchichall for me, and my Brethren'. So Sidney wondered if his father might be able to find him employment under the new rulers as he felt

---

[71] Jürgen Wiegandt, *Die Merchant Adventurers' Company auf dem Kontinent zur Zeit der Tudors und Stuarts* (Kiel: Mühlau, 1972), pp. 101–12.

[72] Ruth Spalding, *Contemporaries of Bulstrode Whitelocke 1605–1675: Biographies, Illustrated by Letters and Other Documents* (Oxford: Oxford University Press, 1990), pp. 19–20. Incidentally, Richard Bradshaw was the nephew of John Bradshaw, the president of the High Court of Justice which had tried Charles I.

'obliged to him, and knowe not how to Recompence him'.[73] This move seems ironic, given that Sidney was trying to get a favour for a friend from the new government that had rejected him, but it is also symptomatic of his ambiguous position. Sidney still thought of himself as a gentleman of quality who should hold sway with the English government even as he was fleeing from its power. Whether through Sidney's intervention or not, Missenden did eventually become an agent for Secretary Joseph Williamson, dispatching intelligence from northern Europe.[74] But once again, Sidney's actions proved that he silently accepted the new government in England without being fully aware of the consequences of the recent regime change for his own position or even the full extent of the danger he might find himself in.

By the end of November, and by then safely settled in Rome, Sidney seemed relieved that he had listened to his father and his friends, who had advised him 'to keepe out of England for a While', judging 'by the Usage my Companions have already received'.[75] This of course alluded to the fate of the ten regicides who had been exempted from the Act of Indemnity and Oblivion and sentenced to death to be publicly hanged, drawn and quartered at Tyburn in October.[76] These included Thomas Scott, with whom Sidney had worked on the Council of State and in the area of foreign affairs, while Sidney's good friend Henry Vane was likewise exempted from the Act, only to be executed two years later.[77] In Sidney's case, it was the monarchy rejecting the republican exile, not the republican exile rejecting the monarchy. The most severe punishment to him mean- while was to remain excluded from public office and from participating in the politics of his home country.

In July 1660 Sidney left Copenhagen for Hamburg, where he met Christina, the former Queen of Sweden and recent Catholic convert, before travelling via the United Provinces and Germany to Italy.[78] Nota- bly, on his way south he passed through Hanau near Frankfurt, which had a small Protestant community from the time of the Marian exiles, and would become the home of several exiles as well as a point of contact

[73] Algernon Sidney, Frankfurt am Main, to Robert, Earl of Leicester, 8 September 1660, in Collins (ed.), *Letters*, ii, pp. 695–9, at p. 699.
[74] National Archives, London (hereafter NA), SP 29/26, fol. 104, undated, 1660?
[75] Algernon Sidney, Rome, to Robert, Earl of Leicester, 19/29 November 1660, in Collins (ed.), *Letters*, ii, pp. 700–1.
[76] See *The Speeches and Prayers of Some of the Late King's Judges* (n.p. 1660).
[77] Scott, *Algernon Sidney and the English Republic*, pp. 50, 101, 94 ff.
[78] Algernon Sidney, Copenhagen, to Robert, Earl of Leicester, 22 July 1660, in Collins (ed.), *Letters*, ii, p. 695.

during the later continental plot of 1665.[79] Yet Sidney did not like Germany much, confiding in his father that he was 'extreamely unwilling to stay in Hamburgh, or any Place in Germany, finding my self too apt to fall too deepe into Melancholly, if I have neither Businesse, nor Company, to divert me'. Besides, he had 'such an Aversion to the Conversation, and Entertainments of that Country' that he 'must have lived as a Hermite, though in a populous Citty'.[80] Passing through Hesse had not improved his view of Germany, although he admitted that part of his unease might have been owed to the fact that the country was still suffering from the long-terms effects of the Thirty Years War, as he observed: 'The People seeme generally fierce, harsh, and rude, much more then the Swedes. Wheather that Temper is natural unto them, or growne by the Coustume of doing and suffering Mischiefs in the Time of the Warre, I am not able to judge.'[81] Rome, in contrast, provided a more congenial environment. Ludlow suggests that Sidney went to Rome because it was less suspicious to the authorities.[82] Maybe it was assumed that an English Puritan might find few allies in a Catholic city. Yet the situation was quite different. Rome was a cosmopolitan place, a political and culture centre, in which English republican exiles hoped to find political safety as well as good company. Despite their Protestantism and rejection of popish superstitions they nevertheless had great respect for the learning and political skill of the cardinals, while they considered the Pope to be as much a political figure as the spiritual head of the Catholic Church. When Sidney arrived in Rome in November 1660 he hoped that 'besides the Liberty and Quiet, which is generally granted all Persons heare', he would be 'admitted into that Company, the Knowledge of which, will very well recompence my Journey'.[83] And recompensed he was.

In Rome, Sidney enjoyed 'the Company of Persons excellent in all Sciences, which is the best Thing Strangers can seeke', and soon made

[79] Algernon Sidney, Frankfurt am Main, to Robert, Earl of Leicester, 8 September 1660, in Collins (ed.), *Letters*, ii, pp. 695–8; George Van Santvoord, *Life of Algernon Sidney: With Sketches of Some of His Contemporaries and Extracts from His Correspondence and Political Writings*, 3rd ed. (New York: Scribner, 1854), pp. 168–9. On the plot, see Ludlow's 'Voyce', pp. 1056 ff.

[80] Algernon Sidney, Rome, to Robert, Earl of Leicester, 19/29 November 1660, in Collins (ed.), *Letters*, ii, pp. 700–1, at p. 700.

[81] Algernon Sidney, Frankfurt am Main, to Robert, Earl of Leicester, 8 September 1660, in Collins (ed.), *Letters*, ii, pp. 695–8, at p. 698.

[82] Ludlow, 'Voyce', pp. 97–8.

[83] Algernon Sidney, Rome, to Robert, Earl of Leicester, 19/29 November 1660, in Collins (ed.), *Letters*, ii, pp. 700–1, at p. 700. On the relationship of English protestants with Rome, see also Edward Chaney, *The Evolution of the Grand Tour: Anglo-Italian Cultural Relations since the Renaissance* (London: Frank Cass, 1998), pp. xi–xii.

the acquaintance of many cardinals and other senior figures in the Catholic Church and the city, presumably through his contact with Christina. Already in November he had 'visited severall Cardinalls' and was planning 'to pay the same Respect to the Cardinal Gizi [*recte* Chigi], Nephew to the Pope', who was traditionally the second most important person in Rome as he controlled access to the head of the Catholic Church. The 'most eminent Persons' he had met were the cardinals Pallavicini and Azzolino as well as an unnamed 'Carmelitano scalzo'.[84] Only few of Sidney's long-standing English contacts in Rome – probably acquaintances from a previous journey – were still alive. He mentions Father Courtney, a former rector of the Jesuit College and now of the Penitentiero di San Pietro, and Thomas Somerset, a canon of San Pietro.[85] His old acquaintance Cardinal Francesco Barberini also seemed 'very little changed since I formerly saw him'.[86] By the time Christmas had passed, Sidney had already 'visited nine or ten' cardinals, 'somme of them the most extraordinary Persons that ever I met with, others equall with the rest of the World'. He was not friendly with all of them to the same degree. 'With somme I pretend only the Performance of a Civility, and desire only a littell Knowledge of them', he confessed, while 'with others I seeke a straighter Conversation, and by frequent Visits endeavour to gaine it'. Among the nine or ten cardinals he had met were Francesco and Antonio Barberini, Chigi, Sacchetti and Spada as well as Pallavicini and Albizzi. His closest contact among them was Cardinal Decio Azzolino, the leader of Rome's Squadrone Volante, a reforming group of cardinals in the electoral college for the papacy, which had secured the protection and patronage of Christina of Sweden. According to Sidney, Azzolino had 'already gained the Reputation of as good a Head as any is in Italy' at the mere age of thirty-six, and the Squadrone Volante was considered 'the principal Instrument in setting the Crowne

[84] The cardinal-nephew Sidney refers to is Flavio Chigi (1631–93). Pietro Sforza Pallavicino (1607–67) was praised by Sidney as the author of the history of the Council of Trent, *Istoria del Concilio di Trento* (Rome, 1656–7), written in response to the work of Paolo Sarpi. Algernon Sidney, Rome, to Robert, Earl of Leicester, 12/22 December 1660, in Collins (ed.), *Letters*, ii, pp. 701–2, at p. 701. The Catholic order of Discalced or Barefoot Carmelites followed the teachings of St Teresa of Avila and St John of the Cross.

[85] Possibly Edward Leedes (alias Courtney) (1599–1677), except that the *ODNB* does not say he was in Rome in 1660/1 (although he may have been). He was rector of the English College in Rome between 1653 and 1656. See Thomas M. McCoog, 'Leedes, Edward (1599–1677)', *ODNB*. On Somerset see also Algernon Sidney, Rome, to Robert, Earl of Leicester, 8/18 April 1661, in Collins (ed.), *Letters*, ii, pp. 708–10.

[86] Algernon Sidney, Rome, to Robert, Earl of Leicester, 19/29 November 1660, in Collins (ed.), *Letters*, ii, pp. 700–1; Van Santvoord, *Life of Algernon Sidney*, p. 172.

upon this Popes Head', while Azzolino's vote was 'one of the best in the College'.[87] The circle around Christina and Azzolino played a key role in the intellectual life of the city, and Sidney was right at the centre of it. The attraction of the Squadrone Volante meanwhile may have been less its religious direction than its intellectual pursuits and political agenda. After all, it was a powerful faction of a powerful political system, and Azzolino, like Sidney, an astute political mind.[88] The Roman political system may even have had a certain attraction for an English republican, for Rome could be considered an 'elective monarchy' that depended on the College of Cardinals as a powerful oligarchy.[89] It may be disputable to what extent preferment to the college was based on either merit or birth and patronage, but there were certainly interesting political observations to be made.

Naturally, Sidney could not resist giving his judgement of the Pope himself, which turned out to be surprisingly mild for an arch-enemy of the papacy. According to Sidney, Fabio Chigi, governing the Catholic Church as Pope Alexander VII, was 'a good Man, of a gentle Nature, free from all Vice, even from his Youth, littell ambitious, or covetuous'. Among his minor flaws was that he was 'sommething too indulgent to his Nephewes'. But overall, Sidney thought, Alexander had a good smattering of education without necessarily being a great thinker. He thought the Pope was 'of a fine Wit, rather then a great Iudgement; a great Delighter in Poetry, History, and that Learning, which is heare called, *Belle Letere*'. Sidney points out that he was 'much better versed in theise, then in deeper Studdyes'. While he was not considered an intellectual heavyweight, Chigi's wit had nevertheless propelled his career, Sidney thought, as 'his first Preferment' had come 'upon Occasion of a Coppy of Verses made by him, in Praise of Urban the 8, given to Padre *Sforza Pallavicini* (then Jesuite, now Cardinal) and by him, shewed to the Pope'. The Pope had been so pleased with the verses that he had asked to meet Chigi, 'then a private Gentleman of Siena; and he being brought to him, by Pallavicini, through a Similitude of Nature and Studdyes, grew kind to him, pers-waded him to turne Prelate, promising Preferrement, and performed it'.

---

[87] Algernon Sidney, Rome, to Robert, Earl of Leicester, 29 December 1660/8 January 1661, in Collins (ed.), *Letters*, ii, pp. 702–4.

[88] Marie-Luise Rodén, *Church Politics in Seventeenth-Century Rome: Cardinal Decio Azzolino, Queen Christina of Sweden, and the Squadrone Volante* (Stockholm: Almquist & Wiksell International, 2000); and Marie-Luise Rodén, 'Cardinal Decio Azzolino and the Problem of Papal Nepotism', *Archivum historiae pontificiae*, 34 (1996), 127–57.

[89] Albeit an 'elective monarchy', in which 'the pope possessed absolute and unrestrained authority during his lifetime'. See Rodén, *Church Politics*, p. 27.

Now that Chigi had reached the very top he was showing his 'Kindnesse to the Family of his Benefactor, made *Pallavicini* a Cardinal, and is thought more his Friend, then to any one of the Colledge'. Moreover, his papal government was 'gentle and easy, neither troubling his Neighbors with great Undertakings, nor his Subiects with too heavy Impositions'.[90]

There is little to suggest that Sidney saw the Pope as anything more than a secular ruler at heart, while he seemed somewhat bemused and alienated by the religious policies of the place, judging from the treatment of heretics. For instance, Sidney reports 'a solemne Abiuration of the Herisy of one whoe sayed he was Christ, and had accordingly chosen his Apostles', but then retired to Germany. 'His Statue was the Day publiquely burnt, *Nel Campo di Fiore*.' In another incident on the same Sunday, the Neapolitan Conte de Mola 'was produced by the Congregation del *Santo Afficio*'[91] for being a Christian who had converted to Judaism and 'induced a Nephewe and tow others of his Kindred to doe the like'. Having repented and abjured that religion, 'he was condemned only to a *Prigione Formale* (as they call it) for his Life; which is a close Place between four Walls of about eight Foot square, with a little Hole open to receauve Meate'. Sidney mockingly remarked that the changing of the man's death sentence to life imprisonment was 'tearmed Mercy', and pointed out that the discovery of his crime had been 'made by his own Daughter' whom he had denied a marriage portion because she had 'chosen a Husband herself'.[92]

Even though Sidney claimed he was too old for the kind of 'Curiosity usual in Strangers', he spent some time exploring Catholic ritual and the alien practices and ceremonies of the holy city. Among the few Christmas ceremonies he attended were the annual 'Funerall Obsequies of Innocent the Tenth', which he considered 'worth seeing'. The previous day he had attended them 'in the Popes Chappell' in the company of thirty-seven cardinals.[93] The most detailed account meanwhile Sidney devoted to the ceremonies of 'Easter Day, being the most solemne Function of the whole Yeare'. Invited by Azzolino, who assisted the Pope in the Easter celebrations as 'Deacon Cardinal', Sidney observed the ceremonies of this special

---

[90] Algernon Sidney, Rome, to Robert, Earl of Leicester, 29 December 1660/ 8 January 1661, in Collins (ed.), *Letters*, ii, p. 704. For Fabio Chigi, Pope Alexander VII from 1655 to 1667, see Rodén, *Church Politics*, p. 58.

[91] Sidney is referring to the Tribunal del Santo Oficio de la Inquisición or Spanish Inquisition.

[92] Algernon Sidney, Rome, to Robert, Earl of Leicester, 29 December 1660/8 January 1661, in Collins (ed.), *Letters*, ii, pp. 702–4.

[93] Ibid.

day from among the cardinals in 'St. Peeters Church', taking his place on one of two benches 'on each Side of the Alter' next to Cardinal Albizzi, who explained to him 'those Parts of the Ceremony that I understood not'. However, out of respect for a religion that was not his own, Sidney withdrew 'behind the Cardinals Bensh' during the consecration and elevation of the host, so that he 'might neither give Scandal, or doe any Thing that I did dislike' or might come to regret later. Sidney also observed the Pope's blessing of the people from a balcony of St Peter's and his giving 'an Absolution of all Sinnes, unto thoes that wear truly penitent', bragging that the Cardinal-nephew Chigi had placed him 'soe neare the Pope' that he could see his book to follow his prayers.[94] Among the most interesting documents of Sidney's stay in Rome therefore were his commentaries on some of the cardinals, complemented by detailed 'characters' he sent to his father.

Both his detailed description of the cardinals and their speculation about the succession of the Pope on account of his illness show his familiarity with concerns of the Squadrone Volante. After Christmas 1660, Sidney wrote to his father that the Pope had not appeared in public at any of the festive ceremonies, which led to much speculation in Rome: 'Somme say he is really sick to such a Degree, that within a short Time, another Successor must be prouided for St. *Peter*. Others think it is only unwillingnesse to be solicited in the Businesses of *Parma* and *Modena*, in which he is resolued to doe nothing.' Sidney himself thought the latter was more likely, while the Pope was also thought to suffer from 'a good Measure of Melancholly, from which Evill the triple Crowne doth not defend him'. Rumours of the Pope's illness may have put Azzolino on the alert, as he was considered 'the principal Instrument in setting the Crowne upon this Popes Head'. Indeed, Sidney reported that there was a rumour in the city that the Pope was sick, 'but at this Time of his first Appearance, he seemed to be soe well in Health, that his former Retirement, is attributed either to his Unwillingnesse to be solicited, or his naturall Melancholy'.[95]

The rumours of the Pope's imminent death seem to have been wildly exaggerated or fuelled by wishful thinking. Noting that the Pope did not seem to have any difficulties in presiding at the four-hour Easter ceremony,

[94] Algernon Sidney, Rome, to Robert, Earl of Leicester, 8/18 April 1661, in Collins (ed.), *Letters*, ii, pp. 710–11, at p. 711.

[95] Algernon Sidney, Rome, to Robert, Earl of Leicester, 29 December 1660/8 January 1661, in Collins (ed.), *Letters*, ii, pp. 702–4, at pp. 703–4.

Sidney wrote to his father, 'they will be much disappointed, whoe hope soone to be choosing him a Successor'. Behind the Pope's 'pale, fallow, and shrivlled' face were 'Eyes, Hands, and Voice' that did 'not shewe him to be fifty Yeares old'.[96] And Sidney's judgement proved right. Fabio Chigi was to live for another six years until May 1667, when he was succeeded by Giulio Rospigliosi as Clement IX. The election of Chigi's successor meanwhile was a major event to test the power and influence of the Squadrone Volante, and Sidney's friend Azzolino continued his defence of nepotism to maintain the power of the papal nephew in court politics.[97] On this matter Azzolino would probably have clashed with Sidney on account of the latter's opposition to any kind of unelected and hereditary power. Luckily, by that time Sidney had safely moved on to the Protestant shores of the French Languedoc.

Nevertheless, Sidney's companions in Rome seem to have taken religious politics with a pinch of salt, judging from the fact that they were able to make fun of both Protestants and Catholics alike. In a little anecdote of an evening's entertainment, Sidney reported that 'a Company of Gentlemen' were passing their time with a game of 'Questions and Commands', and the two proposed were, 'Wheather the Cardinal *Mazzarini*, or Don Luys de Haro, had done most Mischiefe to Spain' and 'wheather *Henry the 8*, of *England*, *Luther* and *Calvine*, or the Popes Nephewes, since their Time, had most preiudiced the Church'.[98]

Neville's Move to Florence

Neville's choice of Italian exile might seem less obvious than that of Ludlow, who headed straight for Geneva and the Protestant cantons of Switzerland, or that of Sidney, who after a long odyssey through Europe (albeit including Rome) was attracted by the Huguenot south of France.[99] In fact, Neville's biographer Caroline Robbins has suggested that it must be seen as highly unusual that a Protestant republican would seek refuge with a Catholic prince like the Tuscan Grand Duke Ferdinando II.[100]

---

[96] Algernon Sidney, Rome, to Robert, Earl of Leicester, 8/18 April 1661, in Collins (ed.), *Letters*, ii, pp. 710–11, at p. 711.

[97] Rodén, 'Cardinal Decio Azzolino and the Problem of Papal Nepotism', pp. 141 ff. In the absence of a direct hereditary successor, the nephews of the Pope had assumed a prominent role in Roman politics.

[98] Algernon Sidney, Rome, to Robert, Earl of Leicester, 13/23 February 1660/1, in Collins (ed.), *Letters*, ii, pp. 705–6.

[99] Ludlow, *Voyce*, ed. Worden, pp. 821 ff.; Scott, *Algernon Sidney and the English Republic*, part 3.

[100] Robbins (ed.), *Two English Republican Tracts*, pp. 13–14.

Yet Neville's 'choice' of exile may not have been entirely his own, and it was less surprising than it might appear at first sight.

Neville had been arrested and was held in the Tower for his alleged involvement in the failed Northern Rising of 1663, which aimed to depose Charles II and restore the Long Parliament.[101] His former ally Ludlow believed that the 'principall cause of Mr Nevils Imprysonement, was upon supposition that he held Correspondence with me'. He also heard that Neville was 'not permitted to stay in England, nor to stirr from the place, he should first choose ... beyond the seas'. However, he was later told that he was 'only forbid correspondence with me', which may explain why there was no direct contact between the two during their exile period. Given the circumstances under which Neville left the country – released from imprisonment as a suspected plotter – the authorities in England may have considered him safely out of the way in Italy. Moreover, as a letter from the Earl of Clarendon indicates, Neville's presence in Italy was considered useful to the government because he would be able to act as an informer on Italian affairs, in particular on the politics of the papacy and 'the little intrigues of the Irish who have always some foolish designe in that Court'.[102] Thus at this stage, Neville benefited from the patronage of one of the most powerful men in England, who protected him from the wrath of the authorities and provided him with a safe retreat. Neville's royalist family connections also played a role.

Henry's older brother Richard, a royalist colonel during the English Civil War and well regarded at the court of Charles II, may have assisted his release from the Tower by vouching for his loyalty to the new regime. A note in the Spence papers suggests that 'Col. Neville entreated [th]e K[in]g to spare him [Henry Neville]; & he granted it, on condi[ti]on [tha]t he s[houl]d leave England.'[103] Richard had been granted access to his brother in the Tower on 10 November 1663 and subsequently may have put in a word for him with the authorities.[104] Likewise, the Fanshawe brothers, Richard and Thomas, distant cousins of Neville on his mother's side, 'were allowed to discourse with Henry Neville in his keepers

---

[101] Mahlberg, *Henry Neville and English Republican Culture*, p. 60. His arrest is related in Ludlow, 'Voyce', p. 997, and Ludlow's worries about his own part in the arrest and Neville's banishment on pp. 1003, 1013.

[102] Essex Record Office, Chelmsford, D/DBy/Z58, copy of a letter from the Earl of Clarendon to Henry Neville, 24 December (1664?).

[103] Beinecke Library, Yale University, Joseph Spence Papers MSS 4, Box 4, folder 107.

[104] A '— Neville' was granted 'accesse to Henry Nevill Esqr & discourse w[i]th him in [th]e p[re]sence of his Keeper' on 10 November 1663. In the context, this is most likely to have been his older brother. See NA, SP 44/15, Entry Book, p. 238, and *CSPD* 1663–4, p. 334.

presence' a week later; and it was probably due to 'the Fanshawe influence that he escaped so easily as he did'.[105] The link between Richard Fanshawe and Clarendon certainly helped. As 'one of the foremost Latinists of his day' Fanshawe was in 1658 appointed as Latin secretary to the exiled king by the future lord chancellor. In October 1663 he had also become a privy councillor.[106] The intervention of Neville's family was timely, as in December Charles II wrote to his sister in France about his plans to execute many of the perpetrators of the Yorkshire plot, and there was uncertainty over who might be singled out.[107] Henry Neville petitioned the king for his release in February and asked for a pass to go abroad.[108] The former was granted in February, the latter in May, enabling Henry to travel via France to Italy in late May or early June 1664.[109] In his letters from Italy, Neville subsequently expressed his gratitude to Clarendon for the 'gracious pardon itt pleased the king to give us' and was keen to reassure the lord chancellor of his submission to the restored Stuart monarchy – so much so, he wrote, that 'in the future course of my life I should count itt a great happinesse if itt should ever fall within my power to expresse my obedience & devotion, by any service, to his Ma[jes]tie'.[110] Italy also seemed an obvious place for Neville to go as he had contacts there dating back to the early 1640s, when he had first visited the country on his Grand Tour.[111] Among those contacts was the Florentine lawyer and family friend Ferrante Capponi, with whom Neville had been in regular contact in the 1640s, and who was to advance to high office at

---

[105] *The Memoirs of Ann, Lady Fanshawe, Wife of Sir Richard Fanshawe, Bart., 1600–72*, ed. Herbert Charles Fanshawe (London: J. Lane: 1907), p. 433n. In a letter to Sir Richard from Florence, Neville, now at 'perfect liberty, & . . . in a place where I want nothing but your leave to serve you', thanks him for 'visiting me in a prison'. See Henry Neville, Florence, to (Sir Richard) Fanshaw, 28 October 1664, Bodleian Library, Oxford, Tanner MS 74, fol. 202.

[106] Roger M. Walker, 'Sir Richard Fanshawe's *Lusiad* and Manuel de Faria e Sousa's *Lusíadas comentadas*: New Documentary Evidence', *Portuguese Studies*, 10 (1994), 44–64, at p. 44; and *The Memoirs of Anne, Lady Halkett and Ann, Lady Fanshawe*, ed. J. Loftis (Oxford: Clarendon Press, 1979), p. 152.

[107] Centre des Archives Diplomatiques du Ministère des Affaires Etrangères, Paris (hereafter AE), Mémoires et Documents, Angleterre, Lettres de Charles II, 1660–1669, 7MD/23, fol. 49: Charles II, Whitehall, to his sister Henrietta, Duchess of Orléans, 10 December 1663.

[108] 'Petition of Henry Neville, prisoner in the Tower, to the King, for liberty and a pass to go abroad', NA, SP 29/92, fol. 21.

[109] Neville's release was granted on 3 February 1664 on the payment of all his fees, and the pass on 20 May 1664. NA, SP 44/16, Entry Book, pp. 23, 127.

[110] Bodleian Library, Oxford, Clarendon MS 84, fols 78–9, Henry Neville, Rome, to the Earl of Clarendon, 3/13 March 1665/6.

[111] Neville was travelling between 1641 and 1645. See Berkshire Record Office, Reading (hereafter BRO), D/EN F8/1/1, Sir John Thorowgood to Richard Neville, 30 January 1641; and Mahlberg, *Henry Neville and English Republican Culture*, p. 40.

the court of Ferdinando II and Cosimo III.[112] The Medici court would come to be an important institution in Neville's life, as both a place of refuge and the source of many new friendships, not least the close bond with Cosimo, manifested in an extensive correspondence exchanged throughout Neville's later years, which would get him into trouble during the Exclusion Crisis, when the fear of Catholics and foreigners in England came to reach new heights.[113] Neville's loyalty to the Medici as both Catholics and princes may come as a surprise from a religious as well as a political point of view. Why should a Puritan politician with a track record of employment in the service of Parliament and the Commonwealth government like Neville serve and be on friendly terms with a Catholic Italian prince like Cosimo, scion of the Italian Medici dynasty?[114]

Seventeenth-century Tuscany was a cosmopolitan centre of learning, culture and commerce. As the birthplace of the Renaissance it held a special status in the artistic and scholarly communities; as a commercial hub it attracted large numbers of international merchants. English diplomats and travelling aristocrats were welcomed at the Tuscan court in Florence, English scholars corresponded with the Accademia del Cimento, and English merchants traded through the port of Livorno.[115] As descendants of an old banking family, the Medici had over time extended their influence as they came to rule the territory as grand dukes and implemented policies that would create a flourishing state. Under Ferdinando I in the late sixteenth century, Livorno, for instance, had become a free port that explicitly offered freedom of religion – a measure that was initially targeted at Jews, but would also make the port attractive to other non-Catholics, including a substantial English merchant community. Initially it was a 'centre for English imports coming into Italy', later it also 'began to attract the goods which were destined for export to England, which arrived by road from all over the country'.[116] And it was crucial for the Levant trade. Under Ferdinando II and Cosimo III, religious toleration came to be limited, but Protestant ministers continued to live in the town, and the

---

[112] Richard Neville sends his regards to him via Bernardino Guasconi. See Richard Neville, London, to Bernardino Guasconi, Florence, 18/28 November 1660, in Crinò, 'Lettere inedite', pp. 176–7, and Martelli, 'Ferrante Capponi'. For Neville's friendship with Capponi, see Capponi's letters from Rome at BRO, D/EN F8/2/1–2.

[113] Mahlberg, *Henry Neville and English Republican Culture*, chapter 5.

[114] See Robbins (ed.), *Two English Republican Tracts*, p. 14.

[115] Crinò (ed.), *Fatti e figure del Seicento anglo-toscano*.

[116] Pagano de Divitis, *English Merchants in Seventeenth-Century Italy*, p. 87.

exercise of non-Catholic religious worship was silently tolerated as long as the faithful did not flaunt their creed publicly.[117] It may have been here in Tuscany, then, that Neville learnt to appreciate the religious toleration he would later come to promote in his political writings.[118] There were many practical reasons for maintaining good relations across the confessional divide, diplomatic, intellectual and commercial.

Yet if Neville needed any further justification for his friendship with the Medici family, and in particular Prince Cosimo, the later Grand Duke Cosimo III, he could easily find one in the writings of his erstwhile collaborator James Harrington, who considered the Medici to be a family risen to rank and political power through their own merit.[119] While the Medici were princes, therefore, from a classical republican point of view, their position was not that clear-cut. Although they had acquired the hereditary title of grand dukes of Tuscany, they could be seen as an exception among the princes of Europe because they had arguably acquired their princely power not by inheritance, but on the basis of their wealth and merit and had over time come to strengthen it through the further acquisition of land. Thus they could be seen as self-made princes, whose power rested on their own labour. According to Harringtonian theory, in which political power naturally follows the ownership of property, they could thus be seen as legitimate rulers.[120]

It is true that other republicans may have seen this differently. Sidney considered the 'duchy of Tuscany' to be a tyranny comparable to Greece or the Kingdom of Naples, and the government of the 'duke of Florence' to be no better than that of 'the Great Turk' or 'the king of Spain', as their inhabitants had not chosen to live under their rule.[121] But Sidney himself did not appear to be too picky in the choice of his associates, given that he would more than once attempt to involve the King of France in his schemes, first in a plot to overthrow the Stuart government in the 1660s and again in the 1670s, when he was in negotiation with the French

---

[117] Ibid., pp. 114 ff.; Villani, 'Protestanti a Livorno nella prima età moderna'; and Stefano Villani, 'Unintentional Dissent: Eating Meat and Religious Identity among British Residents in Early Modern Livorno', in Katherine Aron-Beller and Christopher Black (eds), *The Roman Inquisition: Centre versus Peripheries* (Leiden: Brill, 2018), pp. 373–94.

[118] e.g. Neville, *Plato redivivus*, ed. Robbins, pp. 156–7.

[119] James Harrington, *The Prerogative of Popular Government* (London: T. Brewster, 1658), p. 17. The passage reads: 'It is true, the Family of the Medice's were both Merchants, and made a Bank into a Throne: but it was in a Commonwealth of Merchants, in a small Territory, by great purchases in Land, and rather in a mere confusion then under any settled government . . . .'

[120] See Harrington, *The Prerogative of Popular Government*, p. 17.

[121] Sidney, *Discourses*, ed. West, chapter 2, section 6 (p. 108).

ambassador Paul Barillon.[122] On the other hand, the Medici's self-image may have differed from that of other hereditary families. In any case, they remained remarkably unaffected by criticism of princely rule. When the English Whig bookseller John Starkey sent Cosimo III a copy of his recently printed Machiavelli edition with a manuscript page inserted on the legitimacy of rebellion to unjust rulers in 1675, the potentially treasonous words of the inserted manuscript did not elicit any known outrage,[123] while Cosimo reacted with similar equanimity to Neville's attack on the Catholic Church in his Exclusion Crisis pamphlet *Plato redivivus*.[124] A cynic might see this benevolent oversight as the result of Cosimo's limited understanding of the English language, which he had been attempting to learn. But there is nothing to suggest that the Duke's respect for Neville was anything but genuine.[125] Likewise, both Ferdinando II and his son had been patrons of the German scholar Johann Michael Wansleben, who spent several months in Tuscany at the house of the English merchant Charles Longland, where he produced a digest of

---

[122] Scott, *Algernon Sidney and the English Republic*, chapter 11, and Scott, *Algernon Sidney and the Restoration Crisis*, pp. 108 ff.

[123] *The WORKS of the Famous Nicolas Machiavel, Citizen and Secretary of FLORENCE: Written Originally in ITALIAN, and from Thence Newly and Faithfully Translated into ENGLISH* (London: printed for John Starkey at the Miter in Fleetstreet, near Temple-Bar, 1675). The gold-leaved folio edition presented to Cosimo III is part of the Magliabechiana Library (shelfmark MAGL. 19.5.67), now part of the Biblioteca Nazionale Centrale in Florence. The most interesting feature of the book is a handwritten page inserted into 'Nicholas Machiavel's LETTER to ZANOBIUS BUONDELMONTIUS IN VINDICATION Of Himself and His WRITINGS' authored by Neville, which follows 'The Preface to the Reader' and is not – as could be assumed from the table of contents – the last piece in the volume. The offending passage on rebellion states: 'whosoever then takes up armes to maintaine the politick constitution or Goverment of his Country in the condition it then is, I meane to defend it from being chainged or invaded, by the craft or force of any man (although itt be the Prince or cheife magistrate himselfe) provided that such taking up of armes be commanded or authorised, by those who are by the orders of that government, legally intrusted with the custody of the liberty of the people & foundation of the Goverm:t. this I hold to be so farr from rebellion that I beleeve it Laudable, nay, the duty of every member of such commonwealth, for that, who fights to support & defend the Goverment he was borne & lives under cannot deserve the odious name of rebel, but he who endeavors to destroy itt.' Themes of this passage are echoed in Sidney, *Discourses*, ed. West, chapter 3, section 36 (pp. 522–3). For Starkey's gift to Cosimo, see Francesco Terriesi to Cosimo III, 19 February/1 March 1674/5, Archivio di Stato, Florence (hereafter ASFi), Mediceo del Principato 4241, c. 308, published in Crinò, 'Lettere inedite', p. 199; and Mahlberg, 'Machiavelli, Neville and the Seventeenth-Century Discourse on Priestcraft'.

[124] Cosimo III to Francesco Terriesi, 26 July 1681, ASFi, Mediceo del Principato 4243, c. 167, published in Crinò, 'Lettere inedite', p. 205.

[125] Anna Maria Crinò, *Il Popish Plot nelle relazioni inedite dei residenti granducali alla corte di Londra (1678–1681)* (Rome: Edizioni di Storia e Letteratura, 1954), p. 214.

Harrington's major works.[126] This suggests that contemporaries were more able than modern historians to distinguish between intellectual debate on the one hand and political allegiance on the other. Moreover, cross-confessional and cross-party alliances were not out of the question if they served a common political goal, as we will see in Chapter 2.

Conclusion

Far from being spontaneous creations arising from an immediate need, the exiles' networks reveal long-standing links between transnational confessional groups as well as personal, aristocratic and political connections forged over lengthy periods of time. While connections between English radicals and communities in the United Provinces at this time are commonly acknowledged in the secondary literature, this chapter has extended our view to other communities in the Huguenot areas of France and Reformed Protestants in Geneva, Switzerland and the Holy Roman Empire. The most surprising insight may be that we need to add the Italian states to our list of friendly host countries for English republican exiles. The city of Rome in particular plays an important role in our story, not just as the centre of Catholicism, frequently vilified by contemporary Protestants, but also as a cosmopolitan city of learning and culture, which hosted a broad array of people from a variety of confessional backgrounds. Besides, the Medici grand dukes of Florence were known for their anglophilia, which reflected their economic and scholarly connections with England. Dividing Europe simply along confessional lines would therefore be misguided.

The movements of the exiles thus give us a more personalised insight into the political and confessional make-up of seventeenth-century Europe as well as uncovering unexpected connections that appear to contradict established assumptions about confessional and political allegiance. The next chapter will turn to the exiles' interaction and engagement with the local communities that protected them and the tensions and synergies arising from their cross-confessional connections.

---

[126] Gaby Mahlberg, 'Wansleben's Harrington, or "The Fundations & Modell of a Perfect Commonwealth"', in Mahlberg and Wiemann (eds), *European Contexts for English Republicanism*, pp. 145–61.

CHAPTER 2

Local Support, Confessional and Cross-Confessional Connections

[B]etter is a life among strangers, than in my own country on such conditions.

Algernon Sidney, undated letter to an unidentified addressee[1]

I find a sensible difference between being civilly treated, . . . valew'd and esteem'd by princes abroad, and not only hatted but persecuted at home.

Henry Neville to Richard Neville, 20 January 1665[2]

[T]hough we had some Enemyes, we had many more friends.

Edmund Ludlow, 'A Voyce from the Watch Tower'.[3]

Introduction

Over time, as temporary arrangements turned into more permanent situations, the new networks built by the English republican fugitives came to supplement and replace some of their pre-existing connections. Having outlined these different networks in the first chapter, this book will now focus on the activities within these networks and the extent to which they could aid or stifle the exiles' republican agenda as they were confined to unfamiliar places and had their agency limited by local political conditions. It will be argued that the situation of the exiles changed as they became more closely integrated into their host communities. On the one hand, they became more able to rely on local support. On the other, their presence could also lead to friction between their hosts and their hosts' own political allies. While remaining confined to their exile and reliant on the protection of their hosts, however, the republicans could obtain

---

[1] Algernon Sidney, undated letter to an unidentified addressee, in Blencowe (ed.), *Sydney Papers*, pp. 199–204.
[2] BRO, D/EN F8/1/11, Henry Neville, Florence, to Richard Neville, London, 20 January 1665.
[3] Ludlow, 'Voyce', p. 1186.

information about England through their various channels and find opportunities for political agency that would allow them to influence the situation in their home country.

Ludlow's Swiss Protestant Networks

An example of the operation and extent of local support was Ludlow's move from Geneva, first to Lausanne and then to Vevey on the shores of Lake Geneva – a move necessitated by religious and political considerations. While Geneva remained a major Protestant centre throughout the seventeenth century, a significant part of its territory had returned to Catholicism under Bishop Francis de Sales in the early seventeenth century, and the Catholic Duke of Savoy, Charles Emmanuel I, had in 1602 attempted to recapture it. Both Savoy and France were neighbours to be reckoned with and best not provoked. Moreover, as we have seen in Chapter 1, members of the Council of Twenty-Five wanted to maintain good relations with Restoration England as well as with neighbouring France, so it was not politic for them to harbour English regicides. The regicide had sent shock waves throughout Europe and alienated a good many people who might otherwise have supported the republican cause. It had been a contentious issue also among the Reformed Protestants of Europe, many of whom may have felt closer to the English Presbyterians than to their more radical Independent brethren, even as they were offering their help to the republican refugees.[4] Thus, diplomatically, the exiles' hosts had to walk a fine line. When Ludlow and his friends no longer felt safe in Geneva they received help from Hummel and the local authorities in Bern, who promised to give them protection. So the little group of exiles, at this time only consisting of Ludlow, Cawley and Lisle, moved to the French-speaking Lausanne in the Pays de Vaud, where on 16 April 1662 all three were issued official letters of protection. Only the text of Lisle's letter has survived, stating that this 'English gentleman', who had come to Lausanne as a 'member of the Reformed Church' and 'making profession of his evangelical religion', had been granted permission to 'retreat to our lands to live there as a gentleman of honour and of good and singular reputation under our protection as long as he may wish'.

---

[4] Dirk Wiemann, 'Spectacles of Astonishment: Tragedy and the Regicide in England and Germany, 1649–1663', in Mahlberg and Wiemann (eds), *European Contexts for English Republicanism*, pp. 33–48; Helmers, *The Royalist Republic*, pp. 101–8.

The letter asked the bailiff and inhabitants of the Vaud to respect the council's decision and to enable Lisle to live in safety. Identical patents were issued to both Ludlow and Cawley.[5] Soon afterwards, the 'Mess[ieurs] les Anglois' were given their own seats in the Reformed church of St François by order of the town council.[6]

From late September, more refugees joined the little community. The first to arrive were the regicide William Say, Colonel John Biscoe and Sergeant Edward Dendy, followed in October by the regicide Nicholas Love, Andrew Broughton, one of the clerks to the high court of justice which tried the king, and the former MP and recent councillor of state Slingsby Bethel. The regicide Cornelius Holland was the last to arrive, in November.[7] In the spring of 1663, the exiles' friend Emmanuel Steiger then suggested a move to the quieter and safer Vevey, and Ludlow as well as Lisle, Cawley, Say, Love, Bethel and Holland decided to leave, while Dendy and Broughton stayed behind in Lausanne, although Broughton was to move to Vevey at a later stage. Biscoe and John Phelps, who alongside Broughton had acted as clerk to the court that tried Charles I, meanwhile, decided to leave the exile community in Switzerland to go and trade in the United Provinces and Germany.[8] Phelps re-appears on record in 1666 in the Netherlands, where he was involved in the earlier stages of Sidney's plot to invade England, but did not follow through when Sidney allied with the French.[9] His name was on 'a list of exiles in enemy service summoned on 21 July to surrender themselves within a given time to the English government.' He later died in Vevey.[10] It has been suggested that the mayor of Lausanne was hostile to the exiles, despite the council's official welcome, which may have prompted Steiger's suggestion to move to a smaller and less conspicuous place like Vevey.[11] After several assassination attempts on the exiles in Vevey, however, Lisle decided to return to Lausanne. His decision to go back on his own was to prove fatal. The next

---

[5] Archives Cantonales et Vaudoises, Lausanne (hereafter ACV), BA 33-4, Weltsch Spruch-Buch der Statt Bern, Décrets Romands Nr. 4, p. 66. This letter is reproduced in Stern (ed.), *Briefe englischer Flüchtlinge*, pp. 23–4.

[6] ACV, D 56, Manual du Conseil de Lausanne – registre des décisions concernant les affaires particulières du public (8 October 1661–20 September 1666), fol. 55r, Mardis 3.e Juin 1662 (Tuesday, 3 June 1662).

[7] Ludlow, 'Voyce', p. 964.

[8] Stern (ed.), *Briefe englischer Flüchtlinge*, p. vii; Ludlow, *Memoirs*, ed. Firth, ii, p. 344; Ludlow, 'Voyce', p. 965; C. H. Firth, 'Phelps, John (*b.* 1618/19)', rev. Timothy Venning, *ODNB*. It is unclear when exactly Phelps had arrived in Lausanne.

[9] See Chapter 4.   [10] Firth, 'Phelps, John'.   [11] Ludlow, 'Voyce', p. 985.

entry relating to him in the council minutes of Lausanne dated Thursday, 11 August 1664 is the order to lay his body to rest after he had been shot dead by a stranger that morning. He was to be buried in the same Church of St François where he had only recently been given a pew.[12]

Given their precarious situation, Ludlow and the other exiles could count themselves lucky to have found a friendly welcome in Vevey. They were staying in the private home of one of the town's local councillors Samson Dubois and were received into the community with presents and many warm words which confirmed to them the support of Bern.[13] Yet there is some dispute in the secondary literature about the exact location of Ludlow's abode in Vevey. While this seems a trivial matter, Ludlow's circumstances are important because they tell us about his friends and contacts in the town, about concerns over his security, and finally about measures taken by the local community to protect him.

In the 'Voyce', Ludlow reports that he lived in the house of the councillor Dubois, which suggests that the local authorities backed his stay in Vevey so wholeheartedly that they were even prepared to act as hosts. At the same time, this move signalled to the town's inhabitants that the exiles were welcome and should be treated with respect. In fact, the friendly welcome Ludlow and the others received proves as much, and Dubois's house was not chosen by accident. Its location provided access to the bell on the tower of one of the town's gates which Ludlow could ring in an emergency. Having researched the ownership of properties in the town, G. R. De Beer found that the only house fitting this description and owned by Dubois was the Hôtel de la Balance, located close to one of the town's western gates, the Porte Saint-Saveur. The current address of this house is 49 rue du Lac, and it now carries a plaque commemorating Ludlow's stay there between 1662 and 1689.[14] Yet locally, for a long time a different house was known as Ludlow's home – a house located on the spot of the present (Grand) Hôtel du Lac, on the east side of the early modern town. This house used to have a sign carrying Ludlow's motto, *Omne solum forti patria quia patris*,[15] and the year 1684. De Beer

---

[12] ACV, D 56, Manual du Conseil de Lausanne – registre des décisions concernant les affaires particulières du public (8 October 1661–20 September 1666), fol. 200v, Jeudi xi Aoust 1664 (Thursday, 11 August 1664). On the assassination itself, see Chapter 3.

[13] Ludlow, *Memoirs*, ed. Firth, ii, p. 344; and Ludlow, 'Voyce', p. 1075.

[14] G. R. De Beer, 'Anglais au Pays de Vaud', *Revue historique Vaudoise*, 59 (1951), pp. 56–78, at pp. 57–8.

[15] 'To the brave every land is a fatherland because it is of the father.' The first part is taken from Ovid's *Fasti*. The addition 'quia patris' gives it a religious twist and is presumably by Ludlow himself.

concluded that this discrepancy could only be explained by the fact that Ludlow must have moved during the more than thirty years he spent in Vevey, and he suggests as a possible date the year 1689, in which Ludlow briefly went back to England. De Beer thought Ludlow would probably have moved to a new place on his return to Vevey.[16]

A report in the State Papers produced by the government agent James Cotter in February 1677, however, has Ludlow living in the house of 'one Jean Heunt or Heurt Binet', a merchant of Vevey. Presumably, this was Ludlow's new abode, to which he attached his motto and which became locally known as his home.[17] The reference to Binet is also interesting because Ludlow mentions him in the 'Voyce' as an acquaintance of Dubois. Maybe this acquaintance facilitated Ludlow's move from one house to the other. However, in the light of the report from the State Papers, Ludlow must have moved before February 1677, not in 1689 as De Beer assumed. This would also mean that Ludlow did not take the sign with his motto with him from one house to the next, as De Beer suggests, but that he only acquired it in 1684 *after* his move from the Porte Saint-Sauveur to the location of the current Hôtel du Lac.[18] The exact location of Ludlow's lodgings thus matters because it helped the townsfolk to protect the exiles against assassins – an issue we will return to in Part II. His move during the 1670s also shows that the close-knit community in which the English exiles had found refuge remained concerned for their safety and that individual members of that community would help each other out to provide appropriate lodgings, whether motivated by individual kindness or their shared Protestant faith. Personal connections, meanwhile, were also important for Sidney and Neville, both of whom found refuge in Catholic Italy.

Catholics and Dissenters

Sidney's primary connection in Rome had been the recent Catholic convert and former Swedish queen Christina, who in turn introduced him to her friend Decio Azzolino and the other cardinals of the Squadrone Volante. Through this network of senior Catholic clerics and cultural movers and shakers, Sidney gained access to the highest echelons of

See De Beer, 'Anglais au Pays de Vaud', p. 59, and *Publii Ovidii Nasonis Fasti*, rev. from the text of J. B. Krebs (London: John W. Parker and Son, 1854), 'Liber primus', verse 493.

[16] De Beer, 'Anglais au Pays de Vaud', p. 60.   [17] Ó Cuív, 'James Cotter', p. 150.

[18] De Beer, 'Anglais au Pays de Vaud', pp. 57, 60.

Roman politics and society, which allowed him to continue his diplomatic mission by other means. After all, the newly established Restoration regime in England was still working out the finer detail of the political and religious settlement, and senior figures at the Roman Curia had an interest in knowing what path Charles would take with regard to religious toleration and the future of his Catholic subjects. Catholics in the three kingdoms on their part also sought the support of the Curia on behalf of their cause. It was therefore no accident that Sidney should have sought the contact and friendship of a senior civil servant in the papal Secretariat of State who was exchanging secret correspondence with leading political figures in England over the religious terms of the Restoration settlement.[19] Among the correspondents lobbying Azzolino for their cause was Sir Richard Bellings, an Irish Catholic courtier of Charles II who served as knight secretary to the Catholic Queen Catherine of Braganza.[20] The king's Catholic subjects did not just yearn for religious liberty, they also wanted a cardinal to represent the Catholic hierarchy in their country. In England this hierarchy had died out in 1585 with Thomas Goldwell, Bishop of St Asaph, who had spent his final years as an exile in Rome. Subsequently, Cardinal William Allen had represented English Catholicism until his death in 1594, and in 1598 Pope Clement VIII had conferred the authority over the Catholic clergy in England to the archpriest George Blackwell, before Pope Gregory XV appointed first William Bishop and then in 1625 Richard Smith as Bishop of Chalcedon, an office holding the status of an apostolic vicar. Smith was threatened with arrest in 1628 and took refuge in the French embassy, before leaving England in 1631 and settling in France. After Smith's escape across the Channel, 'English Catholics were governed by the chapter of the secular clergy that had been set up by Smith.'[21]

The favoured candidate for the English cardinalate was Ludovic Stuart d'Aubigny (1619–65), a relative of the king and almoner to Queen Catherine.[22] The Stuarts of Aubigny were established in France, but also temporarily resided in England and Scotland and thus provided another continental link of the Stuart family. Aubigny was also known as a close friend and ally of the Cardinal of Retz, a former Frondeur who was now

[19] See Biblioteca Planettiana, Jesi, L'Archivio Azzolino, Lettere a Decio Azzolino, 1661–3, 102.
[20] See Tadhg Ó hAnnracháin, 'Bellings, Richard (c. 1603–1677)', ODNB.
[21] Villani, 'Britain and the Papacy', pp. 308–10.
[22] Aubigny had conducted an informal Catholic wedding ceremony between Charles and Catherine before their official wedding presided over by Gilbert Sheldon, Bishop of London. See Cyril Hughes Hartmann (ed.), Charles II and Madame (London: William Heinemann, 1934), p. 43.

rehabilitated and back in favour with the French king. According to Ruth Clark, Aubigny had previously played a part in the rapprochement between Cromwell and the Catholics as a potential bishop.[23] He could thus be seen as a consensus candidate that both dissenters and Catholics might have been willing to accept and that could bring advantages for both. There are several letters from 1661 addressed to Azzolino on this matter among his papers in Jesi. Most of them are not signed, so they are difficult to attribute. But they are well informed on the affairs of England and deal with the plans for an English cardinalate as a serious option. One of them, however, written in French, is signed by Bellings and suggests that both the king and his chancellor had previously written in favour of Aubigny. Bellings writes that 'our destiny', that is the destiny of English Catholics, depends on the outcome of the matter, and underlines the urgency of his cause, saying that he is speaking out 'in the interest of religion'.[24] To what extent loyalty to the monarch could be reconciled with his subjects' Catholic faith, however, would determine much of the debate about toleration, as we will see below.

Meanwhile, Charles II's Roman Catholic subjects were petitioning the House of Lords for liberty of conscience, and Bellings's ally George Digby, Earl of Bristol, supported their cause in the chamber.[25] Bristol is an interesting figure here, as he was both the cousin of the Blackloist Sir Kenelm Digby, who had promoted a reconciliation of Catholics with the Cromwellian regime, as well as a former ally of Clarendon's, but had forfeited the latter's friendship through his conversion to Rome in the 1650s.[26] Much to the annoyance of Clarendon, he now devoted his energy to a parliamentary campaign for 'the removal of the penal laws from the English Catholics'. With his support for the Catholic cause Bristol was slowly becoming one of Clarendon's foremost opponents in the Lords as well as an unlikely ally of the dissenters.[27] The correspondence between

[23] Ruth Clark, *Strangers and Sojourners at Port Royal: Being an Account of the Connections between the British Isles and the Jansenists of France and Holland* (Cambridge, UK: Cambridge University Press, 1932), pp. 76, 80.

[24] Biblioteca Planettiana, Jesi, L'Archivio Azzolino, Lettere a Decio Azzolino, 1661–3, 102, B. [or R.] Bellings, London, to Cardinal Azzolino, 8 October 1661.

[25] See 'Petition of Roman Catholics, about Them', *Journal of the House of Lords*, xi: *1660–1666* (London: His Majesty's Stationery Office, 1767–1830), pp. 275–7, 10 June 1661; and Biblioteca Planettiana, Jesi, L'Archivio Azzolino, Lettere a Decio Azzolino, 1661–3, 102 [anon.], 24 June 1661.

[26] Paul Seaward, *The Cavalier Parliament and the Reconstruction of the Old Regime, 1661–1667* (Cambridge, UK: Cambridge University Press, 1989), p. 218.

[27] Ibid., pp. 219, 229–30. According to Seaward, Bristol was also the only MP later arrested on suspicion of involvement in the 1663 Yorkshire Plot.

English Catholics and Rome meanwhile seems to suggest that the papacy had genuine hopes of gaining a secure foothold in England, if not of re-converting it to Catholicism, which would also have had implications for the toleration of non-conforming Protestants. In order to understand the negotiations around the issue of liberty of conscience in the Restoration religious settlement and the republicans' interest in it we need to understand some of the connections and common ground between Catholics and Protestants on the Continent which show the tenuousness of confessional labels and categories.

Intriguingly, the figure of Aubigny connects English Catholics to the Jansenists at Port-Royal, where the would-be cardinal was educated.[28] Jansenism, named after the Dutch theologian Cornelis Jansen (1585–1638), was a theological movement inside the Catholic Church which followed the teachings of St Augustine of Hippo. The Five Propositions derived from Augustinian teachings focused on original sin and the corruption of man, the need for divine grace, and the rejection of free will.[29] In France, the Jansenists were considered as republicans by Louis XIV, who associated them with opposition to absolutist rule, while their emphasis on conscience also led them to advocate independence from Rome and made them fierce opponents of papal infallibility.[30] In England, it was in particular the Jansenists' belief in predestination that linked them to Calvinism and led their opponents to see them as the Puritans among the Catholics. In fact, the English royalist divine Richard Watson considered the Jansenists 'a pack of villains, worse ten times, if possible, than the Puritans'.[31] Beliefs shared between Jansenists and English non-conformist Protestants meanwhile suggest that there might be some points of contact between them, and that they might have provided the key to a rapprochement between Catholics and Protestants.

An important feature of Jansenist thought is the separation of religious from political allegiance. That is, Jansenists did not believe that Catholics owed their loyalty first to the Pope and only then to the secular ruler, which usually made Catholics potential traitors in Protestant countries.

---

[28] On Aubigny, the Jansenists and the cardinalate, see Clark, *Strangers and Sojourners*, pp. 75–115.
[29] Ibid., p. xix. See also Dale Van Kley, 'The Jansenist Constitutional Legacy in the French Prerevolution 1750–1789', *Historical Reflections/Réflexions historiques*, 13:2–3 (1986), 393–453, at pp. 397–8.
[30] Thérèse-Marie Jallais, 'English Harringtonian Republicanism in France and Italy: Changing Perspectives', in Mahlberg and Wiemann (eds), *European Contexts for English Republicanism*, pp. 179–93, at pp. 181–3.
[31] Clark, *Strangers and Sojourners*, p. 45.

Writers associated with Jansenism, such as the Irish clergyman John Callaghan, also 'upheld the principle of obedience to kings and their magistrates of whatever religion', which meant that the Stuarts' Catholic subjects would be able to find accommodation within a Protestant regime, and in return could safely be tolerated.[32] While Callaghan was accused of heresy, his argument provided an important bridge between the two Christian confessions.[33] If Catholics were to be tolerated, any argument for a suppression of Protestant dissent would be significantly weakened.

Through the Jansenist connection, Sidney's Catholic circles in Rome were more closely related to his contacts in France than might first appear. It is particularly intriguing that individuals in Sidney's close environment shifted between the Protestant and Catholic faiths themselves, which again shows the instability of religious labels as well as the impossibility of linking those labels unfailingly to a set of secular policies. Notably, the French general Henri, Viscount of Turenne, who had been born into the Huguenot house of La Tour d'Auvergne and initially fought with the opposition during the Fronde of 1648 to 1653, was to reconcile with the monarchy later and converted to Catholicism in 1668. As a former Frondeur he had also been linked to the Cardinal of Retz, who had been arrested in 1652 and was temporarily imprisoned for his part in the French civil wars. By 1662 Retz was likewise rehabilitated at court and resumed an official role as envoy to Rome, but had to resign his claims to the Archbishopric of Paris.[34]

Jansenism also encouraged the doctrine of Gallicanism, which had originated in France but found followers in a number of European countries.[35] Like Jansenists, Gallicans did not acknowledge the superior authority of the Pope, but considered him a *primus inter pares* among the bishops. Gallicanism would thus have appealed to both Anglicans and constitutionalist republicans, such as Harrington and Neville, who favoured an Erastian church government.[36] During Oliver Cromwell's Protectorate the doctrine had played a part in the thought of the Blackloists, whose leader Thomas White had been the 'official agent of

---

[32] Ibid., p. 34.   [33] Ibid., p. 37.
[34] Jean François Paul de Gondi, Cardinal of Retz (1613–79), was a French churchman, writer and agitator in the Fronde. As the descendant of a Florentine banking family introduced into France by Catherine de' Medici he provided a further connection between Paris, Rome and Florence. On his role in the Fronde, see Colin Jones, 'The Organization of Conspiracy and Revolt in the *Mémoires* of the Cardinal de Retz', *European Studies Review*, 11 (1981), 125–50.
[35] On the relationship between Jansenism and Gallicanis, see Van Kley, 'The Jansenist Constitutional Legacy', esp. pp. 399–401, 404.
[36] Jallais, 'English Harringtonian Republicanism', pp. 184–7.

English Catholics in Rome between 1625 and 1629'. His *Grounds of Obedience*, published in 1655, emphasised the centrality of freedom of conscience – a good they hoped to obtain from Cromwell in return for their loyalty.[37] Their efforts had thus not been unlike the Catholics' attempts to secure freedom of conscience under Charles II. While Sir Kenelm Digby had been involved in the former project, his cousin Bristol was now associated with the latter, in a move that provided continuity between Interregnum and Restoration activism as well as revealing some interesting personal connections. The project at stake was not insignificant: if political allegiance could be separated from religious affiliations, or religion be subjected to civil authority, liberty of conscience could be granted without any greater risk to the sovereign power. This story needs to be explored in more depth elsewhere, but there are clear indications that the links between English non-conformist Protestants and (different types of) Catholics have been underrated.[38] In the event, however, Aubigny was refused the cardinal's cap – primarily, as Ludlow thought, because he had 'without Lycence from the Pope' conducted the secret Catholic wedding service between the Catholic Infanta of Portugal, Catherine of Braganza, and Charles II, 'who went under the Notion of a Protestant'.[39]

Sidney's and Neville's Catholic Connections

Sidney the republican diplomat was an excellent networker used to socialising in the highest circles. Soon after his arrival in Rome, he moved to Frascati on the invitation of the Prince Pamphilio, nephew of the previous pope, who had offered him a place to live in his Villa de Belvedere.[40] While Sidney's last preserved letter from Italy to his father is dated 24 July 1661 from Frascati, he stayed in the country for another two years, planning to visit Naples, Sicily and Malta.[41] He finally left Italy in 1663 when after several years of relative inertia and time for contemplation he thought he could return home to make a difference there.[42] Sidney may well have made his first plans for an invasion of England with foreign

---

[37] Ibid., pp. 190–1. On White and the Blackloists, see also Stefania Tutino, *Thomas White and the Blackloists: Between Politics and Theology during the English Civil War* (Aldershot: Ashgate, 2008); and Stefania Tutino, 'The Catholic Church and the English Civil War: The Case of Thomas White', *Journal of Ecclesiastical History*, 58:2 (2007), 232–55.

[38] See also Mahlberg, 'Le républicanisme anglais et le mythe de l'anticatholicisme'.

[39] Ludlow, 'Voyce', p. 937.

[40] Algernon Sidney, Frascati, to Robert, Earl of Leicester, 3 June/13 June 1661, in Collins (ed.), *Letters*, ii, pp. 718–19; Van Santvoord, *Life of Algernon Sidney*, p. 175.

[41] Van Santvoord, *Life of Algernon Sidney*, p. 179.   [42] Ludlow, 'Voyce', pp. 977–8.

support at this time. In a letter to his father, he expresses his desire to raise troops to fight under the emperor in Hungary; but these plans may just have been a thinly veiled attempt to obtain the command of an army that might be employed for a variety of causes,[43] for his next moves look like the beginning of a campaign to drum up support for future military action from the Continent, although Ludlow thought that Sidney now considered it 'seasonable to draw towards his Native Country, in Expectation of an Opportunity wherein he might be more Active for their Service'.[44] Both may be true. In any case, Sidney was ready for action on behalf of the republican cause. On his way north from Italy, he visited the exiles in Vevey and entered his name in the book of the Academy of Geneva before moving on to Basel in August.[45] From there, he must have moved on to Flanders, Germany and the United Provinces before settling in the south of France. Shortly after Sidney had left the eternal city, his relative Henry Neville arrived from Florence.[46]

Like Sidney, Neville was on an unofficial diplomatic mission, but one of a different kind. As Clarendon's reluctant spy he too became closely entangled in Catholic politics and society, tasked no doubt with finding out more about the dealings of Catholics from the three kingdoms with the Papal Curia. In fact, Clarendon's throwaway remark about 'the little intrigues of the Irish who have always some foolish designe in that Court' must be read in that context.[47] Clarendon was referring to the likes of Bellings, who had promoted Aubigny's cause in 1661 and travelled to Rome in 1663 to resolve the issue of 'dual loyalty' – to the Pope and to the king – that faced the Irish and other Catholic subjects of Charles II.[48] In the meantime, Clarendon had managed to rid himself of another Catholic enemy, George Digby, the Earl of Bristol, whose failed attempt at getting the Chancellor impeached in the Lords for high treason had awkwardly led to his own removal from the court.

In July 1663 Bristol had accused Clarendon 'of making the king suspicious of parliament; and of enriching himself and his friends by

---

[43] Algernon Sidney, Brussels, to Robert, Earl of Leicester, 1/11 December 1663, in Collins (ed.), *Letters*, ii, p. 725; and Ludlow, 'Voyce', p. 1004.

[44] Ludlow, 'Voyce', p. 977.

[45] Suzanne Stelling-Michaud (ed.), *Le livre du recteur de l'Académie de Genève (1559–1878)*, 6 vols (Geneva: Librairie Droz, 1959–80), v: *Notices biographiques des étudiants, N–S*, p. 568.

[46] They are described as second cousins by Maltzahn, 'Neville, Henry', *ODNB*. However, Rachel Hammersley has pointed out to me that they are more likely to have shared a first cousin.

[47] Essex Record Office, Chelmsford, D/DBy/Z58, copy of a letter from the Earl of Clarendon to Henry Neville, 24 December [1664?].

[48] See Ó hAnnracháin, 'Bellings, Richard'.

selling offices'. Most interestingly, he had also charged Clarendon with 'trying to alienate the affections of the people from the king by favouring Catholics (and particularly by organising Bellings's mission to Rome on Aubigny's behalf) and then seeking popularity by setting himself up as the chief bulwark of the protestant religion'. Thus Bristol accused Clarendon of backing a policy – the establishment of Aubigny as cardinal – that his own faction in other circumstances would have supported. In letters to various cardinals, Bellings is said to have pressed them 'to induce the Pope to confer a Cardinal's cap on the said Lord D'Aubigny, promising, in case it should be attained, exemption to the Roman Catholics of England from the penal laws in force against them'. And with this address to the Pope 'for that Ecclesiastical Dignity for One of His Majesty's Subjects and Domestics', Bellings had, 'as far as from One Action can be inferred, traiterously acknowledged the Pope's Ecclesiastical Sovereignty, contrary to the known Laws of this Kingdom'. As Paul Seaward has noted, even many contemporaries 'found Bristol's charges incomprehensible', and several 'wondered why a papist should make allegations of popery'. But his strategic move makes perfect sense in his quest to obtain religious toleration, as Bristol's aim was to remove Clarendon as its prime opponent.[49]

It also appears that Clarendon himself may have been playing a double game, and that he had initially backed the scheme to obtain a cardinalate for Aubigny, as suggested by Bellings's letter of 1661, only to weary of the idea later when he came to grasp the full implications of a Catholic restoration and its unpopularity among the king's subjects. For one, Ludlow too believed that Clarendon had instigated the scheme.[50] He reports on Bristol's charges in his memoirs.[51] And he even shows a certain sympathy for his cause, saying that Bristol 'was much applauded & prayed for by the people ... after he had delivered the said Articles', though later Ludlow expresses hope that both Clarendon (whom he prefers to call by his birth name Hyde) and Bristol 'may goe out at the same doore they entred the Stage'.[52] In the struggle with Bristol, Clarendon would retain the upper hand for now and manifest his reputation as a defender of the

---

[49] 'Articles of High-Treason, and Other Heinous Misdemeanors, Exhibited against Edward, Earl of Clarendon, Lord High-Chancellor of England, in the House of Lords; on the 10th of July, 1663. By the Earl of Bristol', in *A Collection of the Most Remarkable and Interesting Trials.*, 2 vols (London: R. Snagg, 1775), i, pp. 261–3, at p. 262. See also Seaward, *The Cavalier Parliament*, pp. 228–9; and Alan Marshall, *The Age of Faction: Court Politics, 1660–1702* (Manchester: Manchester University Press, 1999), pp. 93–105.

[50] Ludlow, 'Voyce', p. 937.   [51] Ibid., pp. 969–72.   [52] Ibid., pp. 972, 976.

Church of England in its episcopalian form. However, Bristol would be re-admitted to the court in 1664 after renouncing his Catholicism and become instrumental in Clarendon's fall in 1667. These religious struggles, and indeed attempts to remove him from the chancellorship, are key to understanding Clarendon's interest in Rome and his desire to have an informer there, even though he may have misjudged the reliability of his client, for Neville was in fact sympathetic to the Catholics' and dissenters' shared cause of liberty of conscience. He was also an italophile as well as a pragmatic opportunist in his dealings with Catholics.[53]

As a friend of the Medici, Neville lived the life of a courtier while in Tuscany. We can glean from his letters from the 1660s that he engaged in courtly pastimes at Florence and Pisa, such as balls, the game of *coconetto*, hunting and playing cards, and that he missed these familiar entertainments when he moved to Rome.[54] While Florence was useful for gaining a foothold in Italian society, Rome was the main focus of Neville's mission. He took up lodgings on Via del Corso in the vicinity of the Piazza del Popolo and the Piazza di Spagna in the parish of San Lorenzo in Lucina, which was popular with foreigners from all over Europe and an ideal place for anyone interested in gossip and gathering intelligence. According to the 1666 census, Neville lived in Rome with both English and Italian servants, which would have eased his integration into Roman society.[55] His most important contacts in Italy aside from Ferdinando II meanwhile were Ferrante Capponi, who by now had come to be one of the first ministers at the Tuscan court, and Bernardino Guasconi, who had fought as a mercenary captain on the royalist side during the English Civil War and was a close friend of his brother Richard.[56] In the company of an English royalist captain of Italian extraction, Neville was well equipped for the task in hand. Guasconi had returned to Florence after having been saved from death under the Cromwellians.[57] In fact, it is more than likely that he accompanied Neville to Florence in late May or early June 1664, as

---

[53] See Mahlberg, *Henry Neville and English Republican Culture*, chapter 5; and Gaby Mahlberg, '"All the conscientious and honest papists": Exile and Belief Formation of an English Republican: Henry Neville (1619–94)', in Barbara Schaff (ed.), *Exiles, Emigrés and Intermediaries: Anglo-Italian Cultural Transactions* (Amsterdam and New York: Rodopi, 2010), pp. 61–76.

[54] Henry Neville, Rome, to Bernadino Guasconi, 9 January 1666, in Crinò, 'Lettere inedite', pp. 183–4; and Henry Neville, Rome, to Bernadino Guasconi, 1 August 1665, ibid., p. 181.

[55] Archivio Storico Diocesano, Rome, Parrochia S. Lorenzo in Lucina, Stati D'Animi 1666.

[56] Martelli, 'Ferrante Capponi'; and Henry Neville, Babylon [i.e. Rome], to Bernadino Guasconi, 19 September 1665, in Crinò, 'Lettere inedite', pp. 182–3.

[57] Thus, ironically, an Italian royalist mercenary spared by the republicans was the close friend and likely travel companion of a republican spared by the royalists.

indicated by several draft letters addressed by Ferdinando to Charles II and the Duke of York, in which he anticipates Guasconi's arrival at the Tuscan court.[58] Through his service for the royalist cause, Guasconi had become an honorary Englishman, and in 1661 he eventually became naturalised, changing his name to 'Bernard Gascoigne' in October. He returned to England in the spring of 1667 to enter Charles II's service after three years in Italy, and on 20 June was made a fellow of the Royal Society.[59] In the meantime, he was Henry Neville's friend and confidant.

Guasconi was well connected at the Tuscan court, a regular correspondent of the grand duke's brother, Prince Leopoldo, and a member of the acclaimed Galilean Accademia del Cimento under the prince's patronage.[60] This connection also involved Lorenzo Magalotti, who had entered Leopoldo's service in 1659 and took part in the meetings of the Accademia, of which he became secretary in May 1660. Magalotti became a well-paid courtier in Florence, where he resided permanently from 1667. In the summer of 1667, Magalotti and Paolo Falconieri – another of Neville's acquaintances – undertook the first of three journeys that would take him to the major cities of Europe.[61] Magalotti among others was later to accompany Ferdinando's son Cosimo to England, where the party would stay with the Neville family.[62] Neville's contacts at the Tuscan court also included Cammillo del Palagio, Giovanni Salviati and Lorenzo del Rosso, all of whom would remain his correspondents once he had returned to England.[63] While in Italy, however, Neville's closest friend and guide

---

[58] ASFi, Mediceo del Principato 165, Minute di Lettere e Registri, Ferdinando II, 1664–6, fols 77–8, Ferdinando II to Charles II, 24 May 1664, and Ferdinando II to the Duke of York, 24 May 1664. Stefano Villani, however, suggests that Guasconi had already returned to Italy in January 1664. See 'Guasconi (Gascoigne), Bernardo', *DBI*.

[59] Villani, 'Guasconi (Gascoigne), Bernardo'. He received a pass to return to England on 11 March 1666/7. See *CSPD* 1666–7, p. 556, quoted by W. J. Cameron, *New Light on Aphra Behn: An Investigation into the Facts and Fictions Surrounding Her Journey to Surinam in 1663 and Her Activities as a Spy in Flanders in 1666* (Auckland: University of Auckland Press, 1961), p. 98n.

[60] See Crinò, 'Lettere inedite', pp. 176–7; and Villani, 'Guasconi (Gascoigne), Bernardo'. On the Accademia del Cimento see Paolo Galluzzi, 'Nel "teatro" dell'Accademia', in Paolo Galluzzi (ed.), *Scienziati a corte: l'arte della sperimentazione nell'Accademia Galileiana del Cimento (1657–1667)* (Livorno: Sillabe, 2001), pp. 12–25. There are a number of letters from Guasconi to Leopoldo from the late 1660s in ASFi, Mediceo del Principato 5538.

[61] BRO, D/EN F8/2/5, Paolo Falconieri, Amsterdam, to Henry Neville, 2 July 1669, and D/EN F8/2/6, Paolo Falconieri, Rome, to Henry Neville, 6 August 1679. See also Luigi Matt, 'Magalotti, Lorenzo', *DBI*.

[62] [Lorenzo Magalotti], *Travels of Cosmo the Third, Grand Duke of Tuscany, through England, during the Reign of King Charles the Second, 1669* (London: J. Mawman, 1821), p. 279.

[63] BRO, D/EN F8/2/4, Cammillo del Palagio, Rome, to Henry Neville, 12 July 1671; D/EN F8/2/3, Giovanni Salviati, Florence, to Henry Neville, 5 August 1673; D/EN F8/2/7, Lorenzo del Rosso, London, to Henry Neville, 25 January 1674.

remained Guasconi. It is through Guasconi's correspondence that we learn about Neville's stay in Rome. Alas, only a small part of Neville's whereabouts and activities in Rome can be reconstructed from the limited evidence.

An important circumstance of Neville's stay in Rome was his acquaintance with a range of high-ranking Catholic clergymen. Like Sidney, Neville moved in Roman circles that allowed him access to princes as well as cardinals.[64] Thus he counted among his acquaintances the Prince Giovanbattista Pamphili, the nephew of Pope Innocent X who had previously hosted Sidney at his villa in Frascati.[65] Although it is not clear whether Neville stayed with him as well, he was sufficiently close to the prince to ask him for a favour on behalf of Guasconi, to take his trusted servant when the latter left for England.[66] Neville further reported seeing the Cardinal of Retz, who was used to putting on a show in Rome and also mentions contacts with cardinals, though there is no evidence that he had the same access as Sidney to the circles of Queen Christina and the Squadrone Volante, nor would he have felt comfortable in their company.[67] Neville's letters make it clear that his circles in Rome proved a challenge. He wrote to Guasconi that he had been trying to be 'a good courtier of Rome', but that he found it hard as someone who had 'always been the satyr' to learn the art of flattery he was now obliged to perform.[68] Aware of the irony of his current state, he even claimed to have prepared a little piece in writing that he could use in different situations to address the worthies in Rome: 'we suffer these heats gladly (because they don't talk about anything else) as long as your Eminence can stand it with his health and grace and so continue to help exalt the Church of God with his honourable labours, as long as he can maintain through his merit the path to reign it some time with glory and happiness'.[69] This little piece had the advantage that it could be 'equally said to all', and he would 'sometimes

---

[64] On Sidney and the cardinals, see Scott, *Algernon Sidney and the English Republic*, pp. 151–9.

[65] 'Henry Neville, Frascati, to Bernardino Guasconi, 30 October 1666', and Henry Neville, Rome, to Bernardino Guasconi, 23 November 1666, in Crinò, 'Lettere inedite', pp. 184–5; and Algernon Sidney, Frascati, to Robert, Earl of Leicester, 3 June/13 June 1661, in Collins (ed.), *Letters*, ii, pp. 718–19, at p. 718.

[66] Henry Neville, Frascati, to Bernardino Guasconi, 30 October 1666, and Henry Neville, Rome, to Bernardino Guasconi, 23 November 1666, in Crinò, 'Lettere inedite', pp. 184–5.

[67] Henry Neville, Babylon [i.e. Rome] to Bernardino Guasconi, 19 September 1665, in Crinò, 'Lettere inedite', pp. 182–3.

[68] Henry Neville, Rome, to Bernardino Guasconi, 1 August 1665, in Crinò, 'Lettere inedite', p. 181.

[69] Ibid.

give it to his Excellence, sometimes to his Highness [Ferdinando II]', who would 'not take it badly'. Neville then told Guasconi,

> When I have gained special service with one of these lords and when I come to have great obligation with him, I will write to his most illustrious Lordship to talk to the Grand Duke to make him pope at the first vacant seat, I know that he will do it for you, and all believe here for certain that the papacy is a benefice of which his most Serene Highness has the patronage for now.[70]

Neville also felt that he was not able to enjoy Rome properly because his stay in Florence had ruined him, so that he could 'no longer see either a prince or a court with admiration and devotion or join in with similar pleasure'.[71] Rome certainly did not strike him as a particularly pious place. Therefore he asked Guasconi if he had contacts in France to have prayers said for his love life in the oratory of S. Futino near Orleans, 'which is so famous for the issue of women' because 'we do not have such devotion in Rome'.[72] This disrespect for the Catholic Church and its clergy between the lines of Neville's correspondence would later become more evident in 'Nicholas Machiavel's letter' and in his political treatise *Plato redivivus*.[73]

There were also tensions between Neville's company in Rome and his libertine lifestyle. He explained to Guasconi that he had found 'penitence' in Rome rather than the 'delights and prudence' he had been looking for, and that he feared that 'instead of becoming a sage' he would 'leave Rome as a saint'. He already saw himself as 'a martyr' for 'not going to women', which made him 'feel all burnt inside and full of ulcers on the outside', while Guasconi was still able to enjoy 'the beautiful cities and ladies of Florence'.[74] Later, though, Neville found distraction in an affair with a married woman and complained to his friend about the strict rules of Roman society that did not allow him to divert himself openly with her.[75] While finding his amusement elsewhere, Neville kept a low profile and steered clear of his own countrymen. He assured Clarendon in a letter from Rome: 'I doe very rarely frequent the company of any of our nation,

---

[70] Ibid.   [71] Ibid.

[72] Henry Neville, Babylon [i.e. Rome], to Bernardino Guasconi, 19 September 1665, in Crinò, 'Lettere inedite', pp. 182–3.

[73] On Neville's anti-clericalism, see Mahlberg, *Henry Neville and English Republican Culture*, chapter 5, and Mahlberg, 'Machiavelli, Neville and the Seventeenth-Century Discourse on Priestcraft'.

[74] Henry Neville, Rome, to Bernardino Guasconi, 1 August 1665, in Crinò, 'Lettere inedite', p. 181.

[75] Henry Neville, Babylon [i.e. Rome], to Bernardino Guasconi, 19 September 1665', in Crinò, 'Lettere inedite', pp. 182–3; and Henry Neville, Rome, to Bernardino Guasconi, 9 January 1666, ibid., pp. 183–4.

& never but extreamly upon my guard.'[76] Neville was clearly afraid of spies and assassins as well as of compatriots who showed their displeasure more openly. In Tuscany, where he spent considerable time at the grand ducal court, the English resident Sir John Finch was his 'greatest enemy'; for Neville was likely to cause diplomatic complications as a republican on the run on the one hand, but also as the brother of a royalist and the protégé of Clarendon on the other. In any case, Finch snubbed him, although it is not clear whether this was simply due to personal animosity or to an order of the English secretary of state.[77]

We cannot be sure if Neville ever received official permission to return to England from the Stuart regime, for his letters indicate that he would return at his own risk and potential peril. By late October 1666 Neville had decided that it was time for him to go back, however unwilling he was to leave the comfort and security of Italy. He wrote to Guasconi from Frascati in the hope that the two men would be able to travel to England together the following spring.[78] Apparently, Neville had been entrusted by various 'gentlemen of quality' with important papers which were burnt in the Great Fire of London and felt obliged to return to see what he could salvage.[79] Yet he was putting off the journey until the summer, while Guasconi was preparing for his trip back to England. The circumstances under which the latter was leaving suggest a rather secretive endeavour: Guasconi decided to travel 'incognito' on his own without any servants that might give him away, planning instead to recruit new servants along the way should he need any. Meanwhile, he was keen to leave his trusted servant Mr Guglielmo with the Prince Pamphili in Rome with the possible intention of taking him back on his return.[80]

Neville was still in Rome in June 1667, as evidenced by an intercepted letter in the State Papers from Richard Neville addressed to his brother, but he must have returned to England some time after the fall of his patron Clarendon.[81] Within a year he was back in England, where he was to

---

[76] Bodleian Library, Oxford, Clarendon MS 84, fols 78–9, Henry Neville, Rome, to the Earl of Clarendon, 3/13 March 1665/6.

[77] Henry Neville, Rome, to Bernardino Guasconi, 8 January 1667, in Crinò, 'Lettere inedite', pp. 186–7.

[78] They may have wanted to avoid the discomfort of travelling in winter.

[79] Henry Neville, Frascati, to Bernardino Guasconi, 30 October 1666, in Crinò, 'Lettere inedite', p. 184.

[80] Henry Neville, Rome, to Bernardino Guasconi, 23 November 1666, in Crinò, 'Lettere inedite', p. 185.

[81] NA, SP, 29/206, 21 June 1667, fol. 134, Richard Neville, Billingbear, to Henry Neville, Rome, 20 June 1667, sent by James Hicks to Secretary Williamson.

publish his satirical utopian travel narrative *The Isle of Pines* in late June 1668.[82] As suggested by Joseph Spence, Neville may have returned for a brief spell in England to sort out his affairs and then gone back to Italy. According to Spence, Neville briefly travelled to England to see Belle Haydon, the sister of Richard Neville's wife Katherine, although Spence does not say exactly when. The republican may also have been back and forth between 1660 and 1664, so that 1664 was the second time he left the country after the Restoration.[83]

Neville's movements during the Restoration show him clearly as an opportunist. He benefited from his brother's royalist connections to escape imprisonment and persecution in England. During his Italian exile he acted, albeit rather half-heartedly, as an informer for Clarendon until the latter's fall from grace in 1667 and kept an eye on affairs in Rome. Neville was ideally placed through his knowledge of Italian and existing friendships at the Tuscan court and in Rome and even suggested to Clarendon that he could imagine taking up office for Charles II. By the time Neville returned to England meanwhile Clarendon himself had lost his position and was an exile in Montpellier, where his paths may have crossed those of Sidney, who had recently arrived there via Flanders, Germany and the United Provinces.[84] On the second leg of his exile journey, after his Roman interlude, Sidney rediscovered his Protestant connections in the Netherlands, Germany and France.

Sidney's Protestant Connections

Jonathan Scott suspects that Sidney's 'initial approach to Flanders and Holland in 1663 may indeed have had its background in the subsequently failed Yorkshire plot of that year', for this plot had 'its own Dutch connection' and its 'defeated remnants ... subsequently made their way to Holland in early 1664'.[85] According to Ludlow, Sidney spent the following winter in Flanders.[86] In early December Sidney was in Brussels, writing to his father that he was considering serving the Emperor in

---

[82] The first part of his narrative was licensed on 27 June 1668. See Henry Neville, *The Isle of Pines; or, A Late Discovery of a Fourth Island near Terra Australis, Incognita ... Licensed June 27. 1668* (London: Allen Banks and Charles Harper, 1668).

[83] Beinecke Library, Yale University, Joseph Spence Papers, MSS 4, Box 4, folder 107. Spence suggests that Neville 'must have been chiefly out of England from 61 to 68'.

[84] Indeed, it is likely that Neville returned to England because he had lost his patron and protector in England. He may therefore no longer have been safer in Italy than he was at home.

[85] Scott, *Algernon Sidney and the English Republic*, p. 172.   [86] Ludlow, 'Voyce', p. 977.

Hungary as a military leader.[87] However, the government was not happy to put him in charge of troops for fear of what he might do with them. Possibly in pursuit of this aim, Sidney withdrew to Germany and in late 1664 found himself temporarily living in the southern city of Augsburg, where the former lord chief justice Oliver St John had sought refuge after the Restoration.[88] Sidney had been followed by a group of royalist assassins headed by a man known as Andrew White. By the time White and his men reached Augsburg, however, Sidney had moved on yet again. As Scott suggests, the republican must have returned to the Netherlands before the outbreak of hostilities between the English and the Dutch on 22 March 1665.[89]

Later in 1665, the group of exiles involved in Sidney's plot to invade England from abroad was based in Rotterdam. It included John Phelps, Nicholas Lockyer, John Biscoe, William Say, Slingsby Bethel and William Scott. The latter was the son of the regicide Thomas Scott, who had been executed in October 1660. Unfortunately for the plotters, he soon started supplying the English government with information via the royalist agent Aphra Behn, who was based in the United Provinces from late July 1666.[90] His descent gave him credence with the other plotters, while his desire to survive the Restoration may have instigated his working relationship with Behn. To what extent his intelligence contributed to the failure of the Sidney plot is not certain. But it is through him that we know that the Quaker merchant Benjamin Furly was the 'most trusted person' among the exiled 'fanaticks' and no doubt useful on account of his occupation and his local knowledge.[91] Furly was also Sidney's chief 'local' contact, and the republican may have lodged at his house in Scheepsmakershaven when writing his *Court Maxims*.[92] As Sarah Hutton points out, Furly's abode in Rotterdam was located on a major trade route from England to Europe,

---

[87] Algernon Sidney, Brussels, to Robert, Earl of Leicester, 1/11 December 1663, in Collins (ed.), *Letters*, ii, p. 725.

[88] William Palmer, 'St John, Oliver (c. 1598–1673)', *ODNB*.

[89] Ludlow, 'Voyce', p. 1063; Algernon Sidney, 'The Apology of Algernone Sydney, in the Day of his Death', in *Discourses Concerning Government. By Algernon Sidney, Esq; to Which Are Added, Memoirs of His Life, and an Apology for Himself* (London: printed for A. Millar, 1751), pp. xxx–lii, at p. xxxi; and Scott, *Algernon Sidney and the English Republic*, pp. 172–4.

[90] Cameron, *New Light on Aphra Behn*, pp. 11–13.

[91] NA, SP 29/120, Aphra Behn to Major James Halsall, 4 September 1666 (O.S.), quoted in Cameron, *Aphra Behn*, pp. 60–1, at p. 61.

[92] Scott, *Algernon Sidney and the English Republic*, p. 180; Sarah Hutton, 'Introduction' to Sarah Hutton (ed.), *Benjamin Furly 1646–1714: A Quaker Merchant and His Milieu* (Florence: Olschki, 2007), pp. 1–10, at pp. 4–5; and Luisa Simonutti, 'English Guests at "De Lantaarn": Sidney, Penn, Locke, Toland and Shaftesbury', in Hutton (ed.), *Benjamin Furly*, pp. 31–66, at p. 39.

'well-placed to receive travellers in transit to and from England' or stuck somewhere in between. There were so many Englishmen in this part of town that it became locally known as 'Little London' in the eighteenth century. Through his political and religious inclinations, Furly attracted in particular 'political and religious dissidents', and among those calling at his house over the years were Anthony Ashley Cooper, his secretary John Locke, John Toland, Anthony Collins and Algernon Sidney – a list that reads like the canon of commonwealth authors.[93] Already by the end of 1666, 'Furly's house had ... become a landmark and a meeting-place for the Rotterdam Quakers', and as part of the Quaker meeting culture, Furly's Lantern Club or 'De Lantaarn' emerged, and Sidney may have participated in its gatherings.[94]

As Douglas Catterall has shown, men, women and children from the British Isles formed the largest group of migrants in seventeenth-century Rotterdam. The British contingent was even larger than the German and Flemish ones. A major attraction was the religious liberty provided by the Dutch authorities, allowing for the establishment of both an English and a Scots church in the city. Many of their leaders were 'strongly Calvinist' religious refugees fleeing the policies of Charles II and James II. They saw Rotterdam both as a safe haven and 'a base for resistance to the Stuarts'.[95] After the Restoration, there had been a new influx of English people into Rotterdam as significant 'numbers of disaffected persons' were coming 'dayly out of England into this country', as Downing observed. They had set up at Rotterdam 'an Independent, Anabaptist, and Quakers Church, and doe hire the best houses, and have great bills of exchange come over from England to them'.[96] The large numbers of English-speaking foreigners also meant that someone like Sidney might easily find like-minded people, while at the same time not attracting too much attention, as the sight of an Englishman was common enough in these parts. However, I have not been able to find any references to Sidney in the records of either of the English or Scottish churches.[97] It is more likely that he worshipped as part of an Independent congregation or attended Furly's

[93] Hutton, 'Introduction' to Hutton (ed.), *Benjamin Furly*, p. 2.
[94] Simonutti, 'English Guests at "De Lantaarn"', pp. 38–9.
[95] Catterall, *Community without Borders*, pp. 25, 44, 248.
[96] Sir George Downing, The Hague, to Lord Chancellor Clarendon, 14/24 June, 1661, in T. H. Lister, *Life and Administration of Edward, First Earl of Clarendon; With Original Correspondence, and Authentic Papers Never Before Published*, 3 vols (London: Longman et al., 1837–8), iii, pp. 139–44, at p. 144.
[97] Gemeentearchief, Rotterdam, 225 Engels-Episcopale St Mary's Church ('Klein Londen', English Church) and 962.01 Schotse Kerk (Scottish Church).

Quaker meetings.[98] From the Netherlands and Germany, Sidney finally moved to France and temporarily settled in Montpellier.

As Jonathan Scott has shown, Sidney's time in France was divided between the Languedoc in the south-east from around 1666 to 1672–3 and Guyenne and Bordeaux in the south-west from around 1672–3 to 1677, with several longer visits to Paris that are recorded in the memoirs of Turenne and by the author and politician Jean-Baptiste Lantin. Both Sidney's location and company were important: Montpellier and the Languedoc as well as the area around Bordeaux between La Rochelle on the Atlantic coast and Nérac further south-east inland were traditionally Huguenot regions.[99] The town of Montpellier was considered a key Protestant stronghold in the south of France. It was slightly larger than Geneva, but less densely populated, numbering some 25,000 inhabitants at the time of Sidney's arrival, according to the contemporary account of the natural philosopher John Ray, who travelled the area for research. About two-thirds of the town's population were Catholic and one-third Protestant, with the Protestants occupying two churches in the town, which they called 'temples' to distinguish them from the Catholic 'églises'. Ray further reported that the city's streets were 'very narrow, short and crooked, without any uniformity or beauty at all'. They were 'so intricate' that it took six months 'to understand them all, and learn the way from place to place'. Many of the city's houses were 'well built of free stone, which were they set well together in order would make 3 or 4 handsome streets'. The town did not have any 'large Piazza or market-place'. However, he noted, the 'number of Apothecaries in this little City is scarce credible, there being 130 shops, and yet all find something to do'.[100]

Montpellier attracted numerous foreign visitors like Ray because of its outstanding reputation for scholarship, mainly owing to the university's medical faculty, which dates back to the twelfth century. Given the popularity of the town with English scholars, it may not come as a surprise

---

[98] John Dury also was in Rotterdam in the 1660s. See Catterall, *Community without Borders*, pp. 133n., 263.

[99] Scott, *Algernon Sidney and the English Republic*, pp. 223–4.

[100] John Ray, *Observations Topographical, Moral, & Physiological; Made in a Journey through Part of the Low-Countries, Germany, Italy, and France: With a Catalogue of Plants Not Native of England, Found Spontaneously Growing in Those Parts, and Their Virtues* (London: Printed for John Martyn, Printer to the Royal Society, at the Bell in St. Paul's Church-yard, 1673), p. 454. Montpellier's local historian Henri Michel puts the number of the city's inhabitants in the late seventeenth century at c. 22,500, some 7,000 of which were Huguenots. See 'Montpellier du milieu du XVIIe siècle à la fin du XVIIIe siècle', thèse d'état, Université de Paris I, Panthéon-Sorbonne (1993), p. 229. See also Borys Herszenhorn, 'John Ray, botaniste anglais, à Montpellier en 1665–1666', *Bulletin historique de la ville de Montpellier*, 13:1 (1990), 21–5.

that Montpellier was home to several Anglophiles, among them the Protestant apothecary – one of the 130 mentioned above – Jaques Puech, who was host to several Englishmen on their passage through the town. Puech's most famous visitor was John Locke, who stayed at his house between 1675 and 1677.[101] It is possible that he also gave a home to Sidney during his stay between 1666 and 1670. At least Sidney was well acquainted with the medical community thriving in the town. His doctor for a time was Charles Barbeyrac, another friend of Locke's, with whom Barbeyrac shared an interest in the circulation of the blood, while Barbeyrac's nephew Jean carried on the tradition of Protestant political thought as the foremost translator of Samuel Pufendorff.[102] Sidney's acquaintances in the scientific and scholarly community were complemented by Protestant contacts. In fact, there was considerable overlap between the scholarly and the Protestant community in the Languedoc. Among Sidney's other acquaintances in Montpellier was, for instance, the Protestant minister David Abernathy, a descendant of the Scottish academic Adam Abernathy, who became the head of the university's arts faculty in 1608 before taking up medicine and serving at the local Hôtel-Dieu Saint-Éloi.[103] Apparently, during his stay in the town Sidney assisted the younger Abernathy by providing proof of his Scottish origins, although the purpose of this remains elusive.[104]

Sidney's most illustrious or rather infamous countryman in Montpellier meanwhile was Edward Hyde, Earl of Clarendon, who had retreated to France after his fall from grace as lord chancellor and first minister following the English defeat in the Second Anglo-Dutch War. Clarendon lived in Montpellier from around 1667 to 1671, working on his *History of the Great Rebellion*, and the two men's paths are likely to have crossed as exiles, expatriates and émigrés have always had the habit of flocking together.[105] There were also numerous contacts between Reformed Protestants in Switzerland and Huguenot communities in the south of France as well

---

[101] *Dictionnaire de biographie héraultaise, des origines à nos jours: anciens diocèses de Maguelone-Montpellier, Béziers, Agde, Lodève et Saint-Pons*, ed. Pierre Clerc et al. (Montpellier: Librairie/ Édition Pierre Clerc, Les Nouvelles Presses du Languedoc Éditeur, 2006), ii, p. 1564. Puech had taken over his father's shop in the Pas-Etroit, the present-day rue du Bras-de-Fer. We know he was Protestant from his marriage certificate. Archives Municipales Montpellier, Église Réformée, Mariages 1658–63, GG 369, fol. 47. *Dictionnaire de biographie héraultaise*, i, pp. 153–4.

[102] *Dictionnaire de biographie héraultaise*, i, pp. 153–4.

[103] Ibid., i, pp. 20–1; Archives Municipales, Montpellier, Table des Mariages de Montpellier.

[104] Archives de Lot-et-Garonne, Serie J, Fonds Lagrange-Ferregues, p. 185, quoted in Scott, *Algernon Sidney and the English Republic*, p. 232n.

[105] *Dictionnaire de biographie héraultaise*, i, p. 548. Many other Englishmen retired in Montpellier, such as Robert Montague, third Earl of Manchester (1634–83), who moved to France in 1681.

as links to England. This would become particularly obvious after the revocation of the Edict of Nantes in 1685, when many French Huguenots left either for Switzerland or England, in particular London. Puech was among those who settled in London.[106] In short, our republicans were right at the heart of a transnational European Protestant network, while also benefiting from friendly relations with Catholics, some of whom were highly critical of papal powers.

Sidney and the Frondeurs

While settled in the south of France, Sidney made several extended trips to Paris. During a visit in 1670, he met Henri de La Tour d'Auvergne, Viscount of Turenne, at Versailles, while his stay in the capital also 'coincided with that of the Northumberland family who occupied the Hotel Bationere for the first half of the year'. Interestingly, the Duke of Buckingham was in Paris at the same time, and the Duke of York suspected that the two were plotting together. While there is no evidence for that, Sidney did use his knowledge of the Secret Treaty of Dover for an attempt at 'political rehabilitation', contacting the English king via Turenne and Louis XIV.[107] The record we have of their conversation, held presumably some time in July 1670, is brief, but instructive. Once again, as he had suggested in 1660, Sidney was ready to 'render his services to the King of Great Britain', although Turenne reported that his feelings were 'entirely Parliamentarian'. The policies of his fellow Parliamentarians followed 'three great principles', he claimed: 'the ruin of the Dutch', the 'cutting down of the Spanish' and 'a close union with France' for the 'augmentation of their commerce'. Sidney's most interesting remarks, however, relate to religion, in particular his allies' support for liberty of conscience. Presbyterians and Independents would never be quiet unless they obtained liberty of conscience, Sidney said, and they felt 'less hatred for the Catholic religion than for the government of bishops'. Sidney also expressed himself convinced that if liberty of conscience were provided, the country would be quiet, and that nobody wanted war at this moment. If Charles II were to come to an agreement with the heads of the various sects over liberty of conscience he would have nothing to fear from them, and,

---

Puech assisted in the embalming of his body. See Louis Dulieu, *La pharmacie à Montpellier, de ses origines à nos jours* (Avignon: Les Presses Universelles, 1973), p. 276.
[106] Dulieu, *La pharmacie à Montpellier*, p. 276.
[107] Bibliothèque Nationale de France, Paris (hereafter BNF), MS Français 23254, Lantiniana, fols 97–101; Scott, *Algernon Sidney and the English Republic*, pp. 232–3.

'to the contrary', would be able to rely on their fidelity and loyalty.[108] As Scott points out, 'One of the hearers at the other end of this advice was the Duke of York who, as James II, was to institute just such a policy in 1687–8.'[109]

While Scott is keen to stress Sidney's Huguenot connections throughout, he is also aware that Sidney was a political opportunist and at this stage willing to give an alliance with the Catholic French monarchy a chance.[110] Yet he skims over the small matter of Turenne's conversion to Catholicism in 1668, which was certainly key to his activities in the diplomatic service of Louis XIV, but also helps us understand his relativism with regard to religious denominations. Religion was something that could be changed if politics required it, while politics might also bend to religion if necessary.[111] Thus Turenne was having talks with Sidney as a former Frondeur who had turned employee of the French king and was negotiating on behalf of his master, trying to reach an accommodation between Charles II and the dissenters and republicans. Likewise, Sidney seemed open towards a toleration of Catholics, or at least feared them less than he did High Anglicans. In fact, as Scott has shown, 'this whig martyr ... "feared the Prince of Orange more than the Duke of York"', as he would tell the French ambassador Paul Barillon during the Exclusion Crisis.[112] This may have been due to his Catholic connections in Rome and elsewhere, and may even have been related to his friendship with Turenne, who had crossed the religious divide. While Scott discusses these comments only in relation to Sidney himself, it can be shown that Sidney's proposals for liberty of conscience in England and collaboration between the king and the leaders of the various sects may have been backed by a wider circle of republicans, dissenters and (former) exiles. In fact, these demands and suggestions are very close to the ideas put forward both by Neville in *Plato redivivus* and by William Penn in his proposals for toleration in England, which influenced the policies of the later James II.[113]

---

[108] The text follows a letter of Louis XIV to Colbert from St Germain, 29 July 1670, AE, Correspondance Politique, Angleterre, 8CP/99, 1670, Supplément, pp. 270–1: 'Relation de ce que le S.r Philipe Sidné a dit a M.r de Turenne dans une visite qu'il luy a rendue, envoyé a M.r Colbert le 30.e Juillet 1670'.

[109] Scott, *Algernon Sidney and the English Republic*, pp. 232–3.   [110] Ibid., p. 234.

[111] After all, Turenne had a good model for that policy in Henry IV, who allegedly told a friend that 'Pairs vaut une messe' ('Paris is worth a mass') after his strategic conversion to Catholicism in 1593.

[112] Scott, *Algernon Sidney and the English Republic*, pp. 2, 153.

[113] See Mahlberg, *Henry Neville and English Republican Culture*, chapter 5.

Scott rightly points out that Sidney's conversation with Turenne contradicts his earlier support for the United Provinces (and the predictions of the 'Prophecy' he had sent to Furly), but it may also reflect a certain disappointment of Sidney with De Witt in 1665–6 and indicate that he had set his hopes on France now. Of course, it may have been a case of sheer opportunism, not alien to Sidney. That Charles II was not keen to see Sidney back in England too soon becomes apparent from the fact that it took the Earl of Leicester another three years to get permission for Algernon to visit England. On this occasion, however, Sidney did not take up the opportunity. Instead, he initially returned from Paris to the Languedoc, before moving around 1672–3 to Nérac, where he stayed for the remainder of his exile.[114] During the final stage of his long exile journey Sidney thus swapped the busy urban life of Montpelllier and Paris for that of the country.

Nérac and Gascony

Nérac is a small town in Gascony in the south-west of France. It is located in the southern part of the present-day department of Lot-et-Garonne about halfway between Bordeaux and Toulouse, and was then the capital of the Pays d'Albret. The lands had been acquired by Frédéric-Maurice de La Tour d'Auvergne, Duke of Bouillon, who had fought against the Crown in the Fronde, a series of aristocratic revolts between 1648 and 1653, which initially opposed the government of Cardinal Mazarin during the regency of Anne of Austria and ultimately aimed to limit the powers of her son, the French king Louis XIV. Frédéric-Maurice had fought with his brother Henri, Viscount of Turenne, and de La Rochefoucauld alongside the governor of the Guyenne, the Prince of Condé, before Turenne turned against Condé at Gien in 1652 to bring hostilities to an end. As Scott points out, it was at this time, when Cardinal Mazarin's men laid siege to Bordeaux and 'sacked de la Rochefoucauld's estate at Verteuil' that the area became 'a centre for radical political ideas (including regicide) imported from the English Republic'.[115] Scott here alludes to the time of the Ormée, during which closer connections between English republicans and French radicals were forged, as we have seen in the previous chapter. However, these connections were complex, and they reveal divisions among the opponents of the French government as well as among various strands of English republicanism.

---

[114] Scott, *Algernon Sidney and the English Republic*, pp. 233–5, 239.   [115] Ibid., p. 227.

The Ormée was a radical revolt within the Fronde in the city of Bordeaux. The so-called Ormistes, mainly consisting of the city's 'middle and lower sectors', including 'smaller merchants, modest tradesmen, minor functionaries, artisans' and such like, 'felt excluded from civic power' and aimed to overturn the local social order. Condé and his aristocratic allies in contrast opposed the extensive powers of the monarchy, but had no interest in touching the social order as such. While they may have welcomed the Ormistes as fellow opponents of the Crown, they did not want them to go too far.[116] However, the French rebels had attracted the attention of the English Commonwealth. In the autumn of 1651 – when Henry Neville was serving as a councillor – the English republican government represented by the Council of State sent several envoys to Guyenne 'to investigate the possibility of an alliance with the Fronde'. The Frondeurs on their part too sent an agent to England to obtain military aid. The idea was for the Commonwealth to send troops, and in return to secure religious freedom for the Huguenots and Condé's help in transforming France into a republic. One of the English envoys in France was the former army colonel Edward Sexby, who was to promote rather radical ideas based on the political thought of the English Levellers in Bordeaux.[117] Indeed, Sexby even translated the third edition of the Leveller *Agreement of the People* (1649) into French to encourage the Ormistes to establish a popular assembly elected by a universal franchise (only excepting women, servants and beggars) and a council of state to exercise executive power when the assembly itself was not in session.[118] Most importantly, Sexby translated the Leveller call for freedom of conscience for English Protestant dissenters into a general call for the toleration of different faiths, which in this case meant French Protestants.[119]

Until the summer of 1653, both Condé and the Ormistes variously called on Cromwell and the English government for more substantial help against the French monarchy – at a time when Sidney was serving on the

---

[116] Perez Zagorin, *Rebels and Rulers 1500–1660*, 2 vols (Cambridge, UK: Cambridge University Press, 1982), ii, p. 218; and Laurent Curelly, '"Do look on the other side of the water": de la politique étrangère de Cromwell à l'égard de la France', *E-rea*, 11:2 (2014), section 3, http://journals .openedition.org/erea/3751, accessed 1 January 2019.

[117] Zagorin, *Rebels and Rulers*, ii, p. 218; Knachel, *England and the Fronde*, pp. 162–4; and Alan Marshall, 'Sexby, Edward (c. 1616–1658)', *ODNB*.

[118] The call for a Council of State differed from the original Leveller idea to have the country ruled by a committee of Parliament in the periods between sessions. Cully, '"Do look on the other side of the water"' (sections 9–14), suggests that this was a compromise that avoided a clash with the current government of England.

[119] Ibid., section 11.

Council of State and was involved in foreign policy negotiations. But the response the Frondeurs received was at best half-hearted. Laurent Cully suggests that any 'support' for the French rebels was little more than an attempt to 'fan the flames' rather than a commitment to engage on the side of any part of the Fronde in a war against the French government. Instead, Cromwell did not want to jeopardise commercial ties between England and France and secretly maintained relations with Mazarin.[120] As late as July 1653, the English were 'preparing 10 ships for the Reliefe of Bourdeaux' loaded 'with Corne and other Provisions', but there had not been any military aid.[121] Radical English critics would later bemoan Cromwell's lack of support for the French Protestants, and like Sexby himself turn against him after he dissolved the Rump and assumed the powers of Lord Protector.[122] Sidney, Neville and Ludlow did so too, although it is at this stage not possible to reconstruct how deeply, if at all, they may have been involved in any concrete negotiations.

While Ludlow, whose sympathy for the English Levellers was known and who mentions Sexby's mission to France positively in his memoirs, would have been most likely to support the Ormistes, Neville consistently argued in his speeches during the 1650s and his later writings for a constitutional limitation of monarchical powers. He agreed with the Levellers on the outdated nature of the House of Lords, while his Harringtonian theory of political change also included a widening of the political nation below the ranks of the gentry, which makes it likely that he sympathised with the Ormiste cause.[123] Sidney meanwhile was not known as a social radical, but rather aligned with Condé's party. He was welcomed by his aristocratic friends when he came to stay in this part of the world long after the dust of the Fronde had settled. Frédéric-Maurice, Duke of Bouillon, had obtained the Duchy of Albret through a treaty with Louis XIV in 1651. When he died the following year, it passed to his son Godefroi-Maurice, who briefly stayed in Nérac in 1667 and again between

---

[120] Ibid., sections 4–8, 16–17.
[121] NA, SP 46/189, fol. 162v, Thurloe Papers, vol. 4, p. 269; and SP 18/38, f. 194, Theodorus to Viscount Conway, 25 July 1653.
[122] Cully, 'Do look on the other side of the water', section 15.
[123] Firth, 'Ludlow, Edmund', rev. Worden; and Ludlow, *Memoirs*, ed. Firth, i, pp. 414–15; Neville favoured a senate-like structure to replace Cromwell's 'other house' of army grandees. Failing that he was also willing to accept a reformed House of Lords that was stripped of its hereditary status and assigned a clear role in the law-making process. See *Diary of Thomas Burton*, iii, p. 321, 331, iv, pp. 23–5; and Neville, *Plato redivivus*, pp. 193–4; Mahlberg, *Henry Neville and English Republican Culture*, pp. 105, 152–6, 173–5.

1684 and 1686.[124] In the interim, the castle appears to have been little used, allowing Sidney to make himself at home there.[125] Scott stresses that his period in the south of France not only allied Sidney to 'the principal remnants of the last great noble rebellion – the noble Fronde', but also gave him access to 'a particular French aristocratic circle', which allowed him to assume a social position far above that of a younger son in England. As 'the south of France did not share England's rigid primogeniture and . . . aristocratic titles were inherited by all a noble's sons' he was able to live the life of 'Le Comte de Sidney'. This was an environment in which he felt very much at home without being burdened with the stigma of the poor younger son.[126] Indeed, Sidney appears to have pursued his aristocratic ambitions at the same time as cultivating his rebel connections. Yet the links between the Sidney family and the French Frondeurs went even further.

The children and grandchildren of Henri de La Tour (Prince of Sedan and Duke of Bouillon), for instance, had close relations with Christina of Sweden, whom Sidney had befriended in Hamburg. Hugo Grotius, whose political theory strongly influenced Sidney, had become friendly with Leicester while serving as her ambassador. In this way, culture, religion and political cause 'transcended national boundaries', and Scott rightly stresses the 'internationality' of both the republican cause and the cause of religious liberty. He also observes that Sidney was not so much an Englishman in exile as 'a citizen of the European cities' as well as a country gentleman, although it should be added that this kind of cosmopolitanism was by no means unusual among the contemporary aristocracy or even among ordinary merchants and traders, whose livelihoods forced them to spend significant periods of their lives abroad or travelling.[127] Yet it may be easy to overlook this part of the early modern way of life when looking at it from the perspective of the modern, albeit declining nation state.

While Sidney was a citizen of Europe, he also maintained connections to and temporarily housed visitors from England or the British Isles. The Archives Départementales de Lot-et-Garonne reveal that on 13 May 1674 Sidney's home served as a wedding venue for Suzanne Groundon, daughter of Pierre de Groundon of Devonshire, and Oliver Cheyney, son of François de Cheney of Essex, who were married by a Huguenot pastor.

[124] G. de Lagrange-Ferregues, 'Présence des ducs de Bouillon à Nérac', Revue de l'Agenais, 90:1 (1964), 29–35.
[125] G. de Lagrange-Ferregues, 'Un régicide anglais à Nérac', Revue de l'Agenais, 91:3 (1965), 173–8.
[126] Scott, Algernon Sidney and the English Republic, pp. 224–5.   [127] Ibid., pp. 228–9.

Alas, it remains unclear why the couple had chosen to marry there, how long they stayed, or what their connection to Sidney may have been.[128] There is an outside chance that the spelling (or the transcription) of the wife's family name 'Groundon' was not correct, and that the couple were in fact relations of the Goudour or Goudoun family of Nérac, whose ancestors hailed from the British Isles and whose name had been adapted into French.[129] At least this would explain why the couple would have decided to get married at Sidney's home.

The main source for Sidney's time in Nérac, meanwhile, is his letter to the Duke of Bouillon, addressed to his steward or agent in Paris, M. Bafoyl, and dated 14 January 1677.[130] With the help of previous fieldwork done by one of Nérac's local historians, G. de Lagrange-Ferregues, and Jonathan Scott, we can learn several things from this one letter. Firstly, we learn that Sidney must have arrived in Nérac around 1672–3, as he mentions that he has been there some four years.[131] The amount of detail with which Sidney reports not only on local politics but also local gossip reveals that he must have been well integrated in his local community and have known the relevant authorities and local officeholders, such as Paul de Mazelières, *gouverneur* and *intendant* of Albret, the assessor 'Poale' or Poul and the lawyer 'Mesparote' or Masparault, whom the Duke of Bouillon had recently added to his council.[132] Alas, Sidney thought very little of the men in the duke's service. Poul was 'nothing but an idiot', who did everything Mazelières told him, while the other was so incompetent that 'few people ... would trust him with a case of one ecu'.[133] He also warned that Mazelières was trying to introduce more people into the duke's service who should not be trusted, such as the two 'Cas[i]mont' brothers, the younger of whom had 'absented himself for having lately assassinated an officer in his bed'.[134]

---

[128] Archives Départementales (hereafter AD), Lot-et-Garonne, Fonds Lagrange-Ferregues, Serie J, referring to Registre des mariages benie en l'eglise reformee de Nérac 4E 199/17.

[129] See AD, Lot-et-Garonne, Fonds Lagrange-Ferregues, 11 J 13, Notes sur Nérac (Familles), i, pp. 147–9. In fact, Lagrange-Ferregues suspects that the Goudours may have been Scottish, as there were many people of Scottish extraction in the area, and that their name originally might have been 'Goodour'. It could also have been Gordon. L[ucile] Bourrachot, 'Des Écossais en Agenais au XVe siècle', *Revue de l'Agenais*, 106:4 (1979), 283–91.

[130] AN, R/2/82, Algernon Sidney, Nérac, to M. Bafoyl, Paris, 14 January [1677]; Lagrange-Ferregues, 'Un régicide anglais à Nérac'; and Scott, *Algernon Sidney and the English Republic*, p. 239 ff.

[131] AN, R/2/82, Algernon Sidney, Nérac, to M. Bafoyl, Paris, 14 January [1677].

[132] On Mazelières and the Masparault family, see AD, Lot-et-Garonne, Fonds Lagrange-Ferregues, 11 J 13, Notes sur Nérac (Familles), i, pp. 39 and 287–9.

[133] AN, R/2/82, Algernon Sidney, Nérac to M. Bafoyl, Paris, 14 January [1677].

[134] Ibid. The brothers in question were Jean-Paul and Pierre de Casmont. Pierre, the younger one, had been in trouble with the law, although the sources do not specify why. See also AD, Lot-et-Garonne, Fonds Lagrange-Ferregues, 11 J 13, Notes sur Nérac (Familles), i, pp. 91–2.

While these seem trivial matters, it is important that locally the employ-ment policies of the Duke of Bouillon were considered at least in part a religious matter in this Huguenot heartland, and that the duke was keen to show that he treated Catholics and Protestants with equal fairness. As Sidney reported, the Comte de la Sere believed that 'M. de Bouillion would not want people of his religion since he did not accept those that had been commanded to be of his council'. [135] He was keen 'to show himself fair in matters of religion to show that a Huguenot might be false, a thief, a prisoner or an assassin in the same way as a Catholic.'[136] This indicates that if Sidney associated himself with a tolerant local nobleman like the Duke of Bouillon he was likely to approve of his open ways, which reinforces the point made above about Turenne and Sidney's potential openness towards Catholics.

The majority of his letter meanwhile is concerned with hunting and the conservation of game in the Pays d'Albret. It shows that Sidney had sufficient leisure to engage in one of his favourite pastimes, which the English aristocracy and gentry shared with their French counterparts. At a closer look, it also reveals some local problems and Sidney's role in sorting them out. At least he felt sufficiently responsible to report to Bafoyl what he thought the issues were and how they might be resolved. After all, Sidney's letter makes it clear that he had given a promise to Bafoyl 'to inform you on the affairs of this country', possibly as a favour for being allowed to reside on the estates of the Duke of Bouillon.[137] For a while now poaching had been a major problem on the duke's land, and Sidney makes suggestions as to how the rapid decline of game in the area might be stopped.

Part of the reason why Sidney became so upset about the poaching may have been his underlying anger at the Duke of Bouillon for having to account for his own hunting practices. Thus he wrote to Bafoyl he could hardly 'believe that M. de Bouillion asks me to give a count of the game I have killed'. For his own peace of mind, and to prove that he was beyond reproach, he assured Bafoyl that his people had told him 'that in the four years all has not amounted to sixty pairs of partridges, two thirds of which were from last year.' The real problem, according to Sidney, was that there

---

[135] 'Comte de la Sere' refers to Louis, Comte de la Serre (d. 1693), Seigneur de Francescas et de Ligardes, Lieutenant-Général des Armées du Roi et de la Haute-Guyenne, Sénéchal d'Agenois et de Condomois. See *Dictionnaire de la noblesse: contenant les généalogies, l'histoire et la chronologie des familles nobles de France*, ed. Aubert de la Chesnaye Des Bois and Jacques Badier, 19 vols in 4 (Paris: Schlesinger, 1863–76), vii, p. 177. The Comte de la Serre was a Catholic.

[136] AN, R/2/82, Algernon Sidney, Nérac, to M. Bafoyl, Paris, 14 January [1677].   [137] Ibid.

was no keeper on the land to watch and report the local poachers. 'On arriving from Paris', which must have been several weeks previously, Sidney reported, he had seen 'two men shooting in the plain, close to the town', and was never able to 'go for a walk without hearing gunshots'. Sidney therefore suggested that the Duke of Bouillon should follow the method of the Duke de La Rochefoucauld, 'on whose lands one never hears talk about poison or violence: a gentleman in charge of the hunt and a man in charge of the revenue: both are good for the area and serve without offending anyone'. The same principle was successfully followed by Mme d'Hauterive at Ruffec near Vertueil.[138] This shows both that Sidney was keen to defend his good name and that he expected his word to count enough with the duke that he would be heard and the poaching problem would be resolved. It also shows that Sidney knew de La Rochefoucauld at Verteuil and Mme d'Hauterive at Ruffec well enough to know about the ways in which they were managing their estates. He had essentially become part of the local French nobility. Scott highlights in particular Sidney's connection to de La Rochefoucauld, who 'was not only a retired *frondeur*' but later was to become 'one of the period's most celebrated writers as well'. His *Maximes morales* were 'first published (illegally) in the Netherlands' in 1664 and subsequently in France in 1665, 'around the time Sidney's own *Court Maxims* were being written'.[139]

Aside from local politics, gossip and poaching, Sidney was primarily interested in news from England, in particular in the letters he had received the previous week.[140] The visit to Paris that Sidney mentions in his letter from Nérac probably was that of autumn 1676, when he first got the opportunity to return to England. In Paris, Sidney had met his uncle Henry Savile and his grand-nephew George Savile, the eldest son of Lord Halifax, who had visited via Saumur. After his return to England, Henry Savile made enquiries through Henry Coventry about the possibility of a pass for Sidney to visit England, and soon afterwards the disgraced republican received a letter from Coventry confirming that he could come to England and would be unmolested by the king.[141]

---

[138] Ibid.   [139] Scott, *Algernon Sidney and the English Republic*, p. 243.
[140] See AN, R/2/82, Algernon Sidney, Nérac, to M. Bafoyl, Paris, 14 January [1677].
[141] Scott, *Algernon Sidney and the English Republic*, pp. 245–7.

Conclusion

This chapter has illustrated the kind of local support the exiles benefited from during their period of refuge, while also outlining some of the aims they pursued in their host countries. While at first sight the different confessional environments might appear confusing and we might question what business Protestant English republican exiles might have in a Catholic country like Italy, on closer examination it becomes clear that all of the exiles were on a Protestant mission, albeit not always in the most direct and obvious way.

While Ludlow saw Protestant Switzerland as his providential exile, where he was protected by like-minded co-religionists, Sidney's and Neville's activities in Italy suggest a political concern with the religious settlement of Restoration England which was in part negotiated with the Roman Curia since Charles II's Catholic subjects and indeed the king himself were concerned to accommodate their faith within the requirements of a Protestant monarchy. For a brief period during the early 1660s, therefore, both Sidney and Neville were intent on gathering intelligence on the religious future of their country, which depended to a considerable extent on the position of Rome and England's relations with the papacy.

Sidney's move to a more permanent exile in the Huguenot south of France meanwhile suggests that the religious struggles in England had been laid to rest for the time being or that hope for an accommodation of nonconformist Protestants had drifted out of sight, while Sidney retreated to the background of politics. During the mid-1660s, meanwhile, when religious battles were very much alive and the Second Anglo-Dutch War gave republicans hope for change, the situation of the exiles was particularly uncomfortable. Conflicting interests, distrust and fear affected the daily lives and experiences of the exiles during their time in Europe, as the next part of this book will show.

PART II

Exiles, Assassins and Activism

CHAPTER 3

The Nature of Exile and Its Dangers

Don't bother with a nail in the wall
Hang your coat over the chair!
Why provide for four days?
You'll return tomorrow!
. . .

When people pass, pull your cap into your face!
Why consult a foreign grammar book?
The message that calls you home
Will be written in familiar language.
Bertolt Brecht, 'Gedanken über die Dauer des Exils'
('Thoughts on the duration of exile') (1937)[1]

Introduction: Everyday Life in Exile

The English republican exiles conceptualised their situation in many different ways as they were forced to adapt to their new lives abroad. Besides practicalities, such as language skills, money supply and living under false identities, safety was a key everyday concern, as was maintaining contact to their home country. In fact, as indicated in the previous chapter, one of the main activities of the exiles was gathering intelligence and information about the political situation in England and in Europe more broadly, which would help their political cause. This happened both through the personal networks addressed in Part I and through the close study of newsletters, papers and pamphlets from a variety of sources. Looking at the everyday lives of the exiles, this chapter will engage with the nature of exile and loyalty to the republican cause in a precarious situation.

---

[1] The original reads: 'Schlag keinen Nagel in die Wand / Wirf den Rock auf den Stuhl! / Warum für vier Tage vorsorgen? / Du kehrst morgen zurück!/ . . . / Ziehe die Mütze ins Gesicht, wenn die Leute vorbeikommen! / Wozu in einer fremden Grammatik blättern? / Die Nachricht, die dich heimruft / Ist in bekannter Sprache geschrieben.' See Bertolt Brecht, 'Gedanken über die Dauer des Exils' (1937), in *Svendborger Gedichte* (London: Malik, 1939), pp. 80–1.

It will also address the various attempts on the republicans' lives that were a continuation of the royalists' earlier revenge mission to hunt down and kill the perpetrators and supporters of the regicide as well as officials and backers of the Commonwealth. This chapter will explore how the exiles managed their day-to-day existence abroad while being faced with a permanent threat to their lives.

Languages

As we have seen in the previous chapters, the republicans' privileged education and upbringing helped them along the way, as did their previous travel experience. This included the command of foreign languages, in particular French and Latin. While complaining to his father that 'the Want of Language, hinders me from conversing with thoes ordinary People I travaile with' as he was making his way across the German lands, Sidney also reported that he was able to get by on French and Latin among more educated society, 'wheareby I have recovered something of what I had forgotten of the one, and learnt a littell more then I knew of the other'. In fact, Sidney was sufficiently fluent in French to pass 'as a French man' in the Low Countries.[2] Each language served a different purpose, facilitating conversation with one of the two different groups of people Sidney encountered on his journey. Thus 'the first serves me amongst Persons of Quality; the other helps me to the Conversation of Priests, whoe, in all the Countryes that I have passed through, are the most ignorant People that ever I met with of that Profession, excepting that most of them speake a littell Latine'.[3] While hitting out at the ignorance of priests was a matter of course for most English republicans, Sidney apparently changed his mind about the profession once he arrived in Rome and must have made a lot more use of his Latin in the company of Azzolino and the cardinals of the Squadrone Volante.

Neville, in addition, had a solid knowledge of Italian, as we can gather from his letters to Italian friends and acquaintances. He always wrote to them in their mother tongue, while they in turn responded in Italian.[4]

---

[2] 'Sir George Downing, The Hague, to Lord Chancellor Clarendon, 9/19 June 1665, in T. H. Lister (ed.), *Life and Administration of Edward, First Earl of Clarendon; with Original Correspondence, and Authentic Papers Never Before Published*, 3 vols (London: Longman et al., 1837–8), iii, pp. 379–85, at p. 384.
[3] Algernon Sidney, Frankfurt am Main, to Robert, Earl of Leicester, 8 September 1660, in Collins (ed.), *Letters*, ii, pp. 695–8, at p. 696.
[4] See, for instance, Neville's Italian correspondence at BRO, D/EN/F8/2.

He probably acquired this skill on his Grand Tour during the 1640s, when he first stayed in Florence and in Rome, while French and Latin would have been part of his schooling and university education. In his various writings, Neville made frequent use of Latin quotations from Roman poets such as Martial and Ovid, while also referring to ancient Roman authorities such as Cicero on politics.[5] When his stepfather Sir John Thorowgood died, he left Henry all his 'printed bookes and all such books as are written in Italian or French' in his will, which documents the two men's shared love of foreign languages, literature and learning.[6] Neville's knowledge of Italian in particular was now useful for conversing with his hosts and getting by in a foreign country.

Likewise, Ludlow was able to converse in Latin on his journey to Switzerland and had at least some French, even though he modestly claims that it was not very good; but his comments on the French translation of the dying speeches and prayers of the regicides suggest otherwise, as we will see in Part III below.[7] The exiles also composed their own addresses to the authorities of Bern in French, and Ludlow himself recalls addressing his Swiss hosts in French when telling them about 'that strange revolution in England', while also quoting lengthy French passages in his 'Voyce'.[8] Nevertheless, Ludlow and his fellow exiles frequently made use of Hummel as a translator and go-between when negotiating with the Bern authorities and other officials, either for political reasons or because Ludlow did not want to risk being misunderstood or embarrassing himself in important dealings.[9]

Finances

Financial support was an issue for those having to leave England without much notice or, in Sidney's case, without having had the chance to make any advance provision. As was common for other exiles elsewhere, however, Sidney, Neville and Ludlow would receive some money and supplies from home, while also benefiting from the hospitality and patronage of

---

[5] Henry Neville's *Newes from the New Exchange, or the Commonwealth of Ladies, Drawn to the Life, in Their Severall Characters and Concernments* (London, 1650), has quotations from both Martial and Ovid on its title page. He referred to Cicero, for instance, in *Plato redivivus*, p. 83.
[6] See NA, PROB.11/265/209, and Mahlberg, *Henry Neville and English Republican Culture*, p. 32.
[7] See Ludlow, *Voyce*, ed. Worden, pp. 193–4 (818–20).
[8] Ludlow, 'Voyce', p. 986, and for the French letters sent to him by M. de la Flechère, pp. 1047–48; see also *Memoirs*, ed. Firth, ii, pp. 348–9.
[9] See, for instance, StAB, B III 98, Epistolae ad decanos bernenses, 1661–1743, item 41, Edm[und] Philipp[s] al[ias] Ludlow to Johann Heinrich Hummel, 10 June 1670.

wealthy individuals abroad or even supplementing their income with
pensions from their host countries.

The situation was tough for Ludlow, who, like many other regicides,
had his estate sequestered by the government on the Restoration. Even
though he had advised his bailiff in time to sell his stock in Ireland and
gather his rents from his tenants in anticipation of the need for a possible
sudden escape, the bailiff had not acted quickly enough, and Ludlow
appears to have lost most of his property. Some time around May 1660,
his possessions in Ireland were taken; and after his escape to Switzerland
his estates in England were confiscated too.[10] But he was lucky enough to
have relatives who looked after him and made sure he always had enough
to live on. Having the money readily accessible on his journey without
carrying too much cash was a major logistical issue. Money was problematic when one crossed borders in early modern Europe. Like the grand
tourists of the period, the exiles would therefore make use of bankers and
their foreign agents, some of them merchants, who would provide them
with cash for their bills of exchange.[11] Of course, this only worked if prior
arrangements had been made in England. Thus Ludlow received money
from home 'by direction of my dearest relation' that was transferred
through bills of exchange via international bankers, such as Monsieur
Margas of Paris, who sent Ludlow a 'bill of exchandge . . . for six hundred
crownes' to Switzerland, 'chargeable upon a merchant of Geneve' on his
arrival.[12] Yet, aware of his precarious situation, Ludlow was frugal and
careful not to spend his money all at once. As he wrote, 'having betweene
fifty and threescore pounds of the stock I brought out of England with me
yet left, and not having any letters of advice touching this mony' he asked
Margas in Paris 'to deteyne the money in his hand till I shoud heare from
my wife concerning it'.[13] Before Elizabeth joined her husband in
Switzerland she had also 'procured a subsistence' for the couple 'to be
settled', while her mother too made a considerable contribution to their
income, 'making a comfortable provission for her [daughter], for the
present & future, turning parte of her yearely Revenue into ready mony'.[14]
Later in his life, when funds from England were drying up, Ludlow was
receiving pensions from both Geneva and Bern, as the Irish informer

[10] Ludlow, *Voyce*, ed. Worden, pp. 124–5 (760); Ludlow, *Memoirs*, ed. Firth, ii, p. 267 and n. (on the
sequestrations in Ireland) and p. 327 (on the confiscation of Ludlow's English property).
[11] See Jeremy Black, *The British Abroad: The Grand Tour in the Eighteenth Century* (New York: Alan
Sutton, 1992), p. 87. The similarities between (royalist) exiles, grand tourists and other expatriates
has also been observed by Smith, *The Cavaliers in Exile*, chapter 5.
[12] Ludlow, *Voyce*, ed. Worden, pp. 196, 193.   [13] Ibid., p. 196.   [14] Ludlow, 'Voyce', p. 1176.

James Cotter reported to the secretary of state in February 1677.[15] These pensions may have been part of what Ole Grell has called the wider 'charitable relief operation' set up by the Calvinist networks the exiles moved in.[16]

Neville presumably received funds from his brother Richard and his family, who were the only people in England he remained in regular contact with throughout his exile. As he reveals in a letter, he wrote to his brother Richard twice a week, usually Tuesdays and Fridays, and did not 'intend to faile you except I am sick or in Viaggio'. Alas, only a small fraction of their correspondence has survived.[17] We do not know whether he had any additional sources of income in Florence or Rome or whether Clarendon subsidised his stay abroad in exchange for information.

Of the three exiles discussed here, Sidney seems to have struggled the most financially, not least because relations with his family were strained. The Earl of Leicester wanted his son to return to England as soon as it was safe to do so and had ordered him to come back in the spring of 1661. In the meantime, Algernon was lost for a place to 'live for the present' and was wondering 'how he may be maintained', as he told his father via his friend Sir John Temple, who also called on Leicester to 'take care of his subsistence'. Temple was concerned that Algernon was 'in very great danger' and, out of desperation, might decide to go 'to serve against the Turk' as a way to make a living.[18] Leicester for his part did not seem to feel responsible for his son's maintenance and complained in a letter that Algernon rarely wrote to him and, when he did so, seemed interested only in money.[19] While in Rome, Algernon frequently complained about not having sufficient funds to support an adequate lifestyle. In particular, he found it shameful to live on a shoestring budget 'in a Place farre from

---

[15] *CSPD* 1676–7, p. 577, and NA, SP 29/391, fol. 102, cited in Ó Cuív, 'James Cotter', p. 150. It is possible that Cotter was charged with checking up on Ludlow as Sidney had been exploring opportunities to return to England around this time (see Chapter 2). The authorities were apparently still suspicious of the exiles and their motives. Exiles elsewhere where also struggling to get by financially. For example, the regicide John Dixwell in New England probably 'lived in straightened financial circumstances. He pursued no employment or trade, relying instead upon a small estate inherited from his first wife, which was supplemented in December 1680 by a small gift of land by the local authorities.' As described in Peacey, 'The good old cause for which I suffer', pp. 167–80, at p. 170.

[16] Grell, *Brethren in Christ*, p. 2.

[17] BRO, D/EN F8/1/12, Henry Neville, Florence, to Richard Neville, London, 20 January 1665. In this letter, Henry notes that he received only five of the ten letters his brother had spoken of.

[18] Sir John Temple, from Durham Yard, to the Earl of Leicester, 21 November 1660, in Blencowe (ed.), *Sydney Papers*, pp. 245–6.

[19] The Earl of Leicester, London, to his son Algernon Sidney, 30 August 1660, in Blencowe (ed.), *Sydney Papers*, pp. 205–13, at p. 205.

Home, wheare noe Assistance can possibly be expected, and wheare
I am knowne to be of a Quality, which makes all lowed and meane
Wayes of Living shamefull and detestable'.[20] Yet he was too proud to
ask his father directly for support, hoping that this would be forthcoming without any further prompting. Thus Sidney sent his father the
rather ambiguous, passive-aggressive message from Rome that 'If theare
be noe Reason for allowing me any Assistance out of the Family, as long
as theare is a Possibility for me to live without it, I have discharged
you. ... I shall with Silence suffer what Fortune soever doth remaine unto
me', adding, however, that 'I confesse I thought another Concluson might
reasonably have been made upon what I had sayd, but I leave that to your
Lordships Judgement and Conscience'.[21] With father and son appearing
similarly proud and stubborn, this conversation was clearly going
nowhere.

As we have seen in Chapter 2, however, Sidney found other means of
supporting himself and maintaining his aristocratic lifestyle in Rome by
relying on the hospitality of the Prince Pamphili, who offered him lodgings
at his Villa de Belvedere in nearby Frascati.[22] Yet even there he complained
that the hospitality did not include much more than free lodging and good
company, and that the 'Civilityes' he received from 'thoes, whoe are in the
Height of Fortune and Reputation' were 'too aery, to feed and cloath a
Man'.[23] But more practical help may have been at hand elsewhere.
According to Sidney's biographer John Carswell, the republican's friendship with the merchant Benjamin Furly, with whom he later stayed in
Rotterdam, may help 'to explain how he kept going for so long financially
without any apparent support from his family'. While Carswell does not
suggest that Furly would have given Sidney an income, he nevertheless
thinks that he may have lent Sidney enough money to survive on the basis
of the latter's 'expectations on his father's death'.[24] It also appears that
Sidney may have lived free of charge on the estate of the Duke de Bouillon

[20] Algernon Sidney, Rome, to Robert, Earl of Leicester, 22 April/2 May 1661, in Collins (ed.), *Letters*,
ii, pp. 716–17, at p. 717.
[21] Algernon Sidney, from Rome, to Robert, Earl of Leicester, 29 January/8 February 1660/1, in
Collins (ed.), *Letters*, ii, p. 704.
[22] Algernon Sidney, Frascati, to Robert, Earl of Leicester, 3/13 June 1661, in Collins (ed.), *Letters*, ii,
pp. 718–19; Van Santvoord, *Life of Sidney*, p. 175.
[23] Algernon Sidney, Frascati, to Robert, Earl of Leicester, 23 June/3 July 1661, in Collins (ed.), *Letters*,
ii, pp. 720–1, at p. 720.
[24] John Carswell, *The Porcupine: The Life of Algernon Sidney* (London: John Murray, 1989), p. 152.

in Nérac in return for guarding the castle and providing regular reports on local affairs, as we have seen in Chapter 2.[25]

Assumed Names

Among the practical safety precautions taken by the exiles was also the assumption of false names and identities. Thus Edmund Ludlow took the prudent decision to call himself Edmund Philips, while William Cawley went under the name of 'W[illiam] Johnson', and John Lisle was known by the surname 'Fi[e]ld'.[26] The letter-writer who signed himself John Ralfeson in his correspondence with Hummel is later identified in the 'Voyce' as Cornelius Holland, who had joined the exiles in Lausanne in November 1662.[27] Yet the exiles' cover was far from perfect, as their original names too easily shone through. Ludlow alias Philips had kept his own Christian name while assuming the surname of his maternal grandfather, Richard, which was Phelips or Philips.[28] Cawley too continued to use his first name, William. Besides, the exiles soon dropped their cover in their correspondence with Hummel, so that anyone intercepting the letters would immediately have been able to identify them. Philip Major, who sees the assumption of a new name as part of a 'rhetoric of exile', has suggested that the exiles' retention of parts of their original names, such as their own Christian name or at least their initials, may have represented an attempt to retain part of their identity and a sense of self amid a situation that required them to break with the past and start afresh.[29] But there were also other naming policies.

[25] In his letter to Bafoyl of 14 January [1677], Sidney speaks of 'the promise I have made you to inform you on the affairs of this country'. AN, R/2/82.

[26] StAB, B III 63, Epistolae virorum clarorum; Archives de la Ville, Lausanne, D56, Manual du Conseil de Lausanne – registre des décisions concernant les affaires particulières du public (8 October 1661–20 September 1666). The name was also sometimes spelt 'Philt'; see StAB, A II 460, Raths-Manual der Stadt Bern, vol. 149 (1664), p. 102.

[27] Ludlow, 'Voyce', pp. 1068, 964. He was the eldest son of Ralph Holland (1581–1625). See Jason Peacey, 'Holland, Cornelius (1600–1671?)', *ODNB*. Heinrich Thiersch originally thought 'Ralfeson' must have been Nicholas Love, who was among the exiles still alive in the 1670s when some of the letters were written. See Albert Maag, 'Die Republik Bern als Beschützerin englischer Flüchtlinge während und nach der englischen Revolution', *Berner Zeitschrift für Geschichte und Heimatkunde*, 2:3 (1957), 93–118, at p. 97; and Heinrich W. J. Thiersch, *Edmund Ludlow und seine Unglücksgefährten als Flüchtlinge an dem gastlichen Herde der Schweiz* (Basel: Felix Schneider, 1881), p. 15.

[28] Firth, 'Ludlow, Edmund', rev. Worden.

[29] Philip Major, '"A poor exile stranger": William Goffe in New England', in Major (ed.), *Literatures of Exile*, pp. 153–66, at p. 164.

Algernon Sidney, for instance, occasionally called himself Philip Sidney in honour of his famous great-great-uncle Sir Philip, author of the *Arcadia*. While this led to confusion with his brother, another Philip Sidney, however, it did little to conceal his origins or indeed his true identity.[30] Too famous was the original holder of that name. Only Neville appears to have felt little inclination to change his name, nor was he required to. The authorities in England knew of his whereabouts, and his Italian hosts seem to have adopted him as one of their own countrymen, frequently referring to him as signor 'Arrigo' – a name he adopted to sign off his correspondence.[31]

Informers, Spies and the Assassination of John Lisle

Even though the exiles had managed to escape from England or abandoned their Commonwealth posts, they were by no means safe. With all the schemes and secret dealings republicans were involved in, they knew very well that they were likely to be followed by government spies and random adventurers who hoped for personal gain through a betrayal or assassination. The royalist hunt for regicides, republicans and Commonwealth officials abroad had begun almost immediately after the execution of Charles I, with the Commonwealth ambassadors Isaac Dorislaus and Anthony Ascham among the first victims.[32] The native Dutchman and scholar Dorislaus had been 'the judge advocate of the army under the earl of Essex' and had helped to draft the charge against Charles Stuart. He was killed by royalist thugs on his mission to The Hague. Ascham, who had defended the regicide and supported the Engagement to the new regime in his published writings and was 'alleged to have assisted with the charge against the king', was murdered by royalist exiles soon after his arrival in Madrid.[33] Jason Peacey and Marco Barducci have argued that it was unlikely that the king's son, who was soon proclaimed Charles II in Scotland, explicitly commissioned the killings, but his express resolve 'to be severe avengers of the innocent blood of our dear father', 'to pursue and

---

[30] AE, Correspondance Politique, Angleterre, 8CP/99, 1670, Supplément, pp. 269–70, 'Du Roy a M.r Colbert, S.t Germain, Le 29. Juillet 1670'; and Camille-Georges Picavet, *Les dernières années de Turenne (1660–1675)* (Paris: Calmann-Lévy, 1919), p. 266.

[31] See Neville's Italian correspondence in Anna Maria Crinò, 'Un amico inglese del Granduca Cosimo III di Toscana: Sir Henry Neville', *English Miscellany*, 3 (1952), 235–47, and ASFi, Mediceo del Principato 4241.

[32] Peacey, 'Order and Disorder'; on Ascham see also Barducci, *Anthony Ascham*.

[33] Peacey, 'Order and Disorder', p. 954.

bring to their due punishment those bloody rebells who were either actors or contrivers of that barbarous and inhumane murder' and to 'chace, pursue, kill, and destroy' them as 'traytors and rebells' was most certainly understood as a call to arms by his loyal followers.[34] Peacey and Barducci also argue that senior royalists in the administration of Charles I, such as Hyde, James Graham, Marquis of Montrose, and Francis, Lord Cottington – then exiled on the Continent themselves – were most certainly involved in the plots to kill the republican agents, if not their masterminds. The motives for the killings extended beyond mere revenge, however, as Charles II was looking for both political allies and financial backers of his claims.[35] The hunt for the regicides and their allies then was also supported by members of the extended royal family scattered around Europe through marriage, such as the Duchess of Orléans, sister of Charles II, or the Queen of Bohemia, sister of the executed king.[36] To an extent, the attacks on the republican exiles after the Restoration were thus the continuation of an ongoing revenge spree and battle for authority, except that power relations had now changed and the republicans were no longer government officials of an unpopular regime, but refugees belonging to an underground opposition movement.[37] If anything, they were now even more vulnerable and reliant on personal contacts, their own wits and their ability to disappear in a crowd.

Sidney fully expected to be followed by English spies and responded to his precarious situation with relative equanimity. He wrote to his father from Rome that he was 'heare well enough at Ease, and believe I may continue soe, unlesse somme Boddy from the Court of England doth think it worth theire Paines to disturb me'.[38] In any case, Sidney kept a distance from his countrymen in exile and was alert to any rumours about him. He wrote to his father from Rome that 'the Court heare' had ordered the Internuntio in Flanders to make enquiries about his 'Birth, Person, and Quality', and that information had been given that 'I was ever found to be violent against Monarchy, a Friend unto Roman Catholiques, one that in

[34] British Library, London, Add, MS 15856, fols 22–22v, 26, 26v, 30, 31, quoted by Peacey in 'Order and Disorder', p. 953.

[35] Peacey, 'Order and Disorder', pp. 953–4, 966–7, 970–2, and Barducci, *Anthony Ascham*, pp. 46 ff.

[36] See Chapter 1 and Peacey, 'Order and Disorder', p. 958.

[37] E.g. after the Restoration, in October 1662, the former army officer Joseph Bampfield was recruited as an agent for the government of Charles II to spy on republicans and dissenters in the United Provinces. He later worked for Johan de Witt. See Alan Marshall, 'Bampfield, Joseph (1622–1685)', *ODNB*.

[38] Algernon Sidney, Rome, to Robert, Earl of Leicester, 19/29 November 1660, in Collins (ed.), *Letters*, ii, pp. 700–1, at p. 700.

our last Troubles, meddled little with private Businesse, and that had made my Fortune, by the Warre, with some other Things like unto theis'. These observations about his background were 'Part true, and Part false; but none that I can learne which doth me any Prejudice'. Naturally, the Roman authorities had been 'put upon this Enquiry, by the foolish prating of some Priests, who spoke of me, as the only Enimy the King had left, and that I being taken away, his Majesty might reagne in Quiet'.[39] While Sidney lightly dismissed these rumours, he nevertheless seemed relieved to see many strangers leave town after Holy Week, as he 'never found any Inconvenience heare, but by theire Company, and Neighbourhood'.[40]

With a permanent threat of persecution and assassination emanating from the English government and its allies, the exiles were at times helpless and understandably bitter towards their own country. While Sidney claimed he was not shaken by the 'Misfortunes' into which he had fallen 'by the Destruction of our Party'[41] in England, he nevertheless reported at times feeling desperate or 'naked, alone, and without Help in the open Sea'.[42] According to his 'Apology', government spies and assassins followed him around Europe, stalking him not only in Rome, but also in 'Flanders and Holland', and even when he had withdrawn 'into the most remote parts of Germany', one 'Andrew White, with some others' were sent to murder him.[43] On the outbreak of the Second Anglo-Dutch War, when Sidney was in Augsburg, 'ten ruffians were despatched by authority of the king's government to assassinate him' and 'might have accomplished their infamous purpose, if he had not before their arrival retired from that city into Holland, being called thither on some matters of business'.[44]

Unwelcome attention from adventurers and assassins was even worse for the regicides in Switzerland, who had a price on their heads. Proclamations for the apprehension of Ludlow as well as Edward Whalley and William Goffe had been issued as early as September 1660, just after Ludlow had

[39] Algernon Sidney (from Rome?), to Robert, Earl of Leicester, 8/18 April 1661, in Collins (ed.), Letters, ii, pp. 708–10, at p. 709.
[40] Ibid., p. 710.
[41] Algernon Sidney, Rome, to Robert, Earl of Leicester, 22 April/2 May 1661, in Collins (ed.), Letters, ii, pp. 716–17, at p. 717.
[42] Algernon Sidney, Frascati, to Robert, Earl of Leicester, 23 June/3 July 1661, in Collins (ed.), Letters, ii, pp. 720–1, at p. 720.
[43] 'The Apology of Algernon Sydney, in the Day of his Death', in Discourses (1751), pp. xxx–lii, at p. xxxi. The incident is not reported in the State Papers.
[44] Van Santvoord, Life of Sidney, p. 178; Ludlow, 'Voyce', p. 1063; and Ludlow, Memoirs, ed. Firth, ii, p. 382.

left the country.[45] The exiles also soon heard rumours that the king wanted them extradited, though the information could not be substantiated.[46] In the following years, Ludlow frequently reported on suspicious people spotted in the vicinity of Vevey and Lausanne, and informers' reports in the State Papers illustrate the terror in which the fugitives must have lived.[47] One report notes that the exiles left their houses only on a Sunday, presumably to attend divine service, while another shows that Ludlow was preoccupied by both false and true alarms announcing danger and that he had put up his bed in the loft of a granary, where he could pull up the ladder at night.[48]

Such precautions were wise in the political climate, as regicides and republicans had been hunted down and killed by royalists before. Only in 1661 had John Barkstead, Miles Corbet and John Okey become the subjects of an extraordinary rendition from the United Provinces despite the steadfast refusal of the Grand Pensionary Johan de Witt to deliver his protégés. The story of the extradition of the three regicides was both a diplomatic incident and a serious bone of contention that marred the relationship between the United Provinces and the English exile community. It was also often cited as proof that De Witt could not be trusted. Barkstead, Corbet and Okey had managed to escape to the Continent after the Restoration. While Corbet settled in the United Provinces, Barkstead and Okey had been living in Hanau near Frankfurt in the west of Germany, while also occasionally visiting their friends and allies across the border.[49] One of their trusted contacts in the Netherlands was Abraham Kick in Delft.[50] Alas, this Kick was a turncoat who had become an informer for the English envoy in the Netherlands, Sir George Downing, who, as a former Cromwellian, had accommodated with the new government and, to prove his loyalty, persecuted the regicides in the Netherlands with particular zeal.[51]

Downing had on several occasions attempted to get an arrest warrant for the regicides from De Witt, who refused to grant his wish as it was against the principles of his country to deliver political offenders on the run, and

[45] [Charles II], *By the King: A Proclamation for the Apprehension of Edmund Ludlow*; and [Charles II], *By the King: A Proclamation for Apprehension of Edward Whalley and William Goffe* (London: Christopher Barker and John Bill, 1660). The situation was similar for John Dixwell in New England. See Peacey, 'The good old cause for which I suffer', p. 171.
[46] Ludlow, *Memoirs*, ed. Firth, ii, p. 359.   [47] Ibid., p. 382.
[48] SP 29/86, fols 17–18, at fol. 17r (19 December 1663); SP 29/101, fols 29–30, at fol. 30v; and *CSPD* 1663–4, p. 662 (8 August 1664).
[49] Catterall, 'Sir George Downing and the Regicides', pp. 275, 283.   [50] Ibid., p. 274.
[51] Ibid., p. 269; Scott, 'Good Night Amsterdam', pp. 340–1.

there was no extradition treaty between the two countries on the basis of which England could have demanded the arrest and delivery of the regicides.[52] However, Downing put pressure on De Witt, who was concerned 'to secure good terms in the [trade] treaty then being negotiated between the provinces and England', and a warrant was finally issued. With the help of Abraham Kick, Downing then managed to trap the regicides at Kick's house, kidnapped and arrested them, and later obtained permission to extradite the regicides to England, where they were tried for treason and executed shortly afterwards.[53]

De Witt may have been conned by the English government and its zealous agent Downing, but the case certainly diminished the exiles' trust in the ability of foreign governments to ensure their protection. And assassination attempts did happen, in particular after the failed Yorkshire Plot of October 1663, when political and religious dissenters came to be persecuted with renewed zeal both at home and abroad and the hunt for opponents of the government once again became an opportunity for adventurers looking for a reward from the Crown. Such an adventurer had set his eyes on the exiles in Switzerland in the form of an Irishman named John Riordan, who kept Secretary Bennet informed of his plans, although it is not possible to say to what extent he acted on directions from England. But his presence in the area around Lake Geneva had the exiles on the alert. As Ludlow reports in his 'Voyce', in the autumn of 1663, some time after their move to Vevey, the exiles were informed of 'an Irish man going under the name of Riardo, and belonging, as he said, to the Dutchess of Orleans' who had arrived at Turin and 'formed a design against our lives'.[54] He passed himself off as a 'Burgundian officer' and was later spotted in various parts of Savoy and the Vaud.[55] The fear of his intentions was so real that, as a precaution against an attempted assassination, the exiles even changed their lodgings for a night during a fair in the town, in case any intruders should hide among the crowd, and 'had the favour of the Towne to have their Usuall Guard for the keeping of all

---

[52] Catterall, 'Sir George Downing', p. 270.
[53] Ibid., p. 278; Greaves, *Deliver Us from Evil*, p. 93. For Ludlow's version of events, see his *Memoirs*, ed. Firth, ii, pp. 330–4.
[54] Ludlow, 'Voyce', p. 993; quotations from Ludlow, *Memoirs*, ed. Firth, ii, pp. 359–61. There are a number of variations of his name in the contemporary sources, but it is clear from the context that 'Riardo' is to be identified with 'Riordan', 'Riordens' or 'Rierdan' and that Lisle's death was his first success, which he presumably hoped would provide him with future employment from the English king.
[55] *CSPD* 1663–4, 8 August 1664, pp. 661–2.

thinges quiet & peaceable during the tyme of the faire, much enlarged'.[56] Nothing happened then, but the fear remained.

Soon afterwards, in November 1663, a possible assassination attempt on the exiles under Riordan's direction was foiled. A number of 'ruffians' had been spotted loitering around town on the evening of 14 November, and it was assumed that they would strike the next day when the exiles went to hear the sermon. On 15 November, early in the morning, a suspicious boat hailing from Savoy was then discovered on the lake with arms covered by straw hidden in its bottom. The boat looked ready to set off, while the suspected villains had apparently 'cut the Withes (that held the oars) of all the Towne Boates, that they might not be persued in case they accomplished their designe'. Some of the suspects had been seen in the town later in the day. But when the suspects realised that the town authorities were onto them, they did not dare to strike and returned across the water to Savoy.[57] The events left such an impression on the exiles that one of them soon afterwards wrote to a friend in England describing 'an attempt made by four Frenchmen, two Savoyards, two English and Irish, and two others, with their servants, to waylay himself and Mr. Phillips [*recte* Ludlow] on their way to church at Geneva, and murder them', but that the thing 'was prevented by the care of their landlord, and the zeal of the people on their behalf', which 'made the villains glad to escape as fast as possible'.[58]

It is notable that attempts on the exiles' lives may have been masterminded by men acting on behalf of the English royal family, but that locals were also involved in their designs. One of the suspects acting with Riordan, for instance, was Louis Deprez of Thonon, a Savoyard, who had his own issues with the Bern authorities and may have acted for personal profit as well as revenge: as Ludlow reports, following a long lawsuit Deprez had recently taken possession 'of some Lands which he held in the right of his wife, & lay in their Teritoryes' which had been 'sequestered from him by their Excellencies, for that he had violently taken her who afterward became his wife out of their Country'.[59] This abduction of a local noblewoman, Demoiselle de Pierrefleur of Orbe, and the subsequent property dispute had caused a great stir in the area, but may

---

[56] Ludlow, 'Voyce', p. 995; and Ludlow, *Memoirs*, ed. Firth, ii, pp. 359–61.

[57] Ludlow, 'Voyce', p. 999; and Ludlow, *Memoirs*, ed. Firth, ii, pp. 361–2. See also Ó Cuív, 'James Cotter', p. 140.

[58] *CSPD* 1663–4, c. December 1663, p. 398. The calendars falsely identify the letter-writer as Ludlow himself. But since he writes about 'Mr Phillips' alias Ludlow in the third person, it must have been another exile from the group.

[59] Ludlow, 'Voyce', p. 1001; and Ludlow, *Memoirs*, ed. Firth, ii, pp. 362–3.

also have contributed to a deterioration of relations between Bern and Savoy, making the 'wronged' outsider into a willing ally of the English monarchy.[60]

Despite his failed attempt on the exiles' lives, Riordan kept a close watch on them, writing to the secretary of state that he believed they 'might be reclaimed by a letter from the king demanding them as parricides, to whom all Europe has refused an asylum'. He also recommended that if such a demand was to be made in Bern, 'the roads from Vevay should be guarded, lest they try to escape'. If Bern refused their extradition 'they might be taken by force', since the place was 'but half a league from Savoy'. Riordan was also sure that 'all save the puritan cantons would seize them, on the least letter from the King'.[61] While his advice was not followed, he continued his guard in Vevey. Months later he observed with some satisfaction that his presence in the area had unnerved the otherwise calm Ludlow, who had 'grown frenzied with terror' at the sight of any strangers in town. As the agent reported to Secretary Bennet on 8 August 1664, 'on seeing him and two others enter the church on Sunday', Ludlow 'would not leave it without an escort of magistrates, though there were seven others with him, all armed'. In fact, the regicide was hiding 'with such precaution that no stranger can accost him'. He had 'his hounds and horses' and was sleeping 'in the attic of a barn, drawing in the ladder after him'.[62] By the time Riordan was writing to Secretary Bennet, Lisle had already moved back to Lausanne in the hope of leaving the dangerous company of Ludlow, only to become the prime target himself.[63] Riordan falsely believed that the whole group had 'retired to Lausanne', which may have been what led him and his accomplices to strike there next.[64]

The murder of John Lisle was among the most spectacular cases of its kind as it happened in bright daylight in Lausanne on the morning of Thursday, 11 August 1664. There are different accounts of the event. But all agree that Lisle was shot in the back on his way to hear the morning sermon at the church of St François and that the assassins were Irish and had probably been sent across the border from France. One of the assassins had been waiting for Lisle at a barber's shop by the churchyard, and then, 'following him into the church-yard, . . . drew a carabine from under his

---

[60] On Deprez, see in particular Stern (ed.), *Briefe englischer Flüchtlinge*, pp. xvii, 24–32.
[61] *CSPD 1663*, 19 December 1663, p. 380; and NA, SP 29/86, fols 17–18.
[62] *CSPD 1663–4*, 8 August 1664, pp. 661–2.
[63] Ludlow, 'Voyce', p. 1020; Ludlow, *Memoirs*, ed. Firth, ii, p. 367.
[64] *CSPD 1663–4*, 8 August 1664, pp. 661–2.

cloak, and shot him into the back'. His accomplice had been waiting with a horse, which he then used to escape. The assassins allegedly shouted 'vive le roi' ('long live the king') before riding off towards the town of Morges, some seven or eight miles west along the shore of Lake Geneva.[65] Further details are contested. Thus it remains unclear whether there were two or three assassins, what their correct names were, and which of them fired the deadly shot.

In his 'Voyce' Ludlow reports that he had been informed by a fellow Englishman who passed through Vevey on his way north from Rome that 'the Irish man who shot Mr Lisle was named Ocroli, and he who assisted him was named [James] Cotter, having a Brother who serves Hides son, [and] that Ocroli & Cotter had both served in the Duke of Yorkes Regiment on this side of the sea'.[66] In another account of September 1664, the French ambassador to London, the Comte de Comenge, told his fellow diplomat Hugues de Lionne that an Irishman named 'Riordens' had killed one of the exiles in broad daylight in Lausanne.[67] While all three Irishmen had been staying in the area, first in Vevey and subsequently in Lausanne, at the time, probably only two of them had carried out the actual attack.[68] A later account, entitled *A New Journey to France* (1715), named the assassins as Miles Crowly, James Cotter and John Rierdan, with Crowly (or Ocroli) responsible for the killing and the others as his accomplices.[69] It seems most likely, however, that Riordan was the mastermind, while his accomplices did the work, as Riordan was the main informer communicating with Secretary Bennet, while the other men involved appear only as minor actors. In any case, following Lisle's assassination, security was stepped up in Vevey and other towns and villages in the region for the protection of the exiles, so that any suspects would be more easily caught. The only town not participating appears to have been Lausanne, which seems to confirm Ludlow's suspicion that the local authorities – the 'subordinate majestrates' rather than 'their Excell[en]cies

---

[65] Ludlow, 'Voyce', pp. 1028–30. See also the council minutes from Lausanne and Bern: Archives de la Ville, Lausanne, D 56, Manual du Conseil de Lausanne – registre des décisions concernant les affaires particulières du public (8 October 1661–20 September 166), fol. 200v, 11 August 1664; and StAB, A II 460, Raths-Manual der Stadt Bern, vol. 149 (1664), p. 89, entry for 18 August 1664.

[66] Ludlow, 'Voyce', pp. 1261–2; and Ó Cuív, 'James Cotter'.

[67] AE, Correspondance Politique, Angleterre, 8CP/82, January–October 1664, fols 195–6.

[68] Ó Cuív, 'James Cotter', p. 140.

[69] Ibid., pp. 141–3. The State Papers also mention a Thomas Macdonnell, who had some employment promised 'for service done in relation to the regicide Lisle' some time in 1663 or later. This may have been in connection with the assassination. See *CSPD* 1663–4, p. 419.

themselves' – were sympathisers of France and may have failed to prevent Lisle's assassination for political reasons.[70]

Not long after the assassination of Lisle, Ludlow also received a warning of a poison plot against his life via a friend in Vevey and was able to take precautions by having the suspect 'searched and Examined', although he did not have sufficient proof to have him arrested. But the suspect was at least asked to move on to Moutre, which Ludlow considered 'a great meanes to discourage & prevent him in his designe'.[71] While Ludlow remained relatively calm after Lisle's murder and decided to stay put, 'thinking it much better to be in a Condition to make opposition against my Enemyes, then to live in a continuall feare of being discovered', William Say was certainly warned by Lisle's death that he could be next, as both of them had served as Justice John Bradshaw's assistants at Charles Stuart's trial. So Say decided to leave for Germany in the company of Colonel Biscoe, urging Ludlow to follow suit.[72] But the latter remained stubborn and determined to face his enemies rather than run from them, despite repeated warnings by Monsieur de la Fléchère that his kinsman Deprez was likely to persist in his attempt to harm the exiles.[73] De la Fléchère then was himself murdered by Deprez, who went on the run before being seized and sent to Yverdon Castle.[74] Some time in August, Deprez was eventually tried by the Bern authorities, sentenced to death and executed.[75] Deprez's removal certainly must have come as a great relief to the exiles, as he was known as a brutal man and had the local knowledge that his Irish allies would have lacked. But he was far from the only threat to their lives. According to Ludlow's nineteenth-century editor, Charles Firth, 'Similar attempts either to assassinate the exiles, or by diplomatic means to procure their expulsion, continued till 1669, and possibly even later.'[76] Yet the phase of most intense danger was over by the 1670s.

The only one of the three exiles who was not followed was Henry Neville, as the government was already informed of his whereabouts

---

[70] Ludlow, 'Voyce', pp. 1035–6, 1039.
[71] Ibid., pp. 1051–2. One suspect in the poison plot was the local apothecary M. Enno.
[72] Ibid., p. 1038; and Ludlow, *Memoirs*, ed. Firth, ii, pp. 373–4 and 373n.
[73] Ludlow 'Voyce', p. 1044; and Ludlow, *Memoirs*, ed. Firth, ii, pp. 374–5.
[74] Ludlow 'Voyce', pp. 1045–6, 1075; and Ludlow, *Memoirs*, ed. Firth, ii, pp. 376, 385. He later escaped from Yverdon and was taken into protection by the magistrates of Fribourg (Ludlow, 'Voyce', pp. 1061, 1069). He was later re-arrested and put back in Yverdon Castle (ibid., p. 1074).
[75] Ludlow, *Memoirs*, ed. Firth, ii, pp. 386–7; Ludlow, 'Voyce', pp. 1089–91.
[76] Ludlow, *Memoirs*, ed. Firth, i, 'Introduction', pp. xliv–xlv. Another suspicious person, a Frenchman, arrived in Vevey around June 1665, but was quickly removed by the authorities (Ludlow, 'Voyce', p. 1067).

through his arrangement with the lord chancellor. Nevertheless, Clarendon kept tabs on Neville, whose reports on the intrigues in Rome were not as forthcoming as his patron might have wished: at least so the lord chancellor complained to Neville's brother Richard in 1666, when Henry did not send any news; and, for good measure, some of the correspondence between the Neville brothers was intercepted by the agents of the secretary of state in case anything should be missed.[77]

Friends and Foes

Fear of assassins was not the only problem the exiles had to deal with. As we have seen above, both Sidney and Neville struggled with the unwanted attention of foreign envoys and countrymen, while relations between Ludlow's exile community and his hosts were not always as good as they could have been, not least because of competing Catholic and Protestant factions in the area and the powerful neighbour France exercising additional pressure. The fragile relationship between Bern and the French was further challenged by the intervention of English royal agents, who in August 1668 approached the excellencies of Bern over a possible extradition of the regicides. Ludlow's worst fears about a possible repetition of the Dutch extradition drama around Barkstead, Corbet and Okey had come true. He suspected a plot between the queen mother, the Duchess of Orléans, and the disgraced former lord chancellor Hyde, who was by now himself an exile in the southern French city of Montpellier. Despite his removal from public office Hyde remained a loyal servant of the Stuarts, not least because he had become part of the wider royal family through the marriage of his daughter Anne to the Duke of York.[78] Ludlow had learnt from one of his allies and informers, 'Mr Arduus', a merchant of Fribourg, that the key agent in the plot was 'one Monsieur Roux, a quick witted nimble tongued & confident Frenchman'.[79] Roux had taken lodgings in the Vaud with Monsieur Balthasar, who had made his money 'by Plunder & Rapine in the King of France his service', married a French lady and was suspected of being a secret Catholic, even though he outwardly presented

[77] Bodleian Library, Oxford, Clarendon MS 84, fols 78–9, Henry Neville, Rome, to Clarendon, 3/13 March 1666; and NA, SP 29/206, 21 June 1667, fol. 134, Richard Neville, Billingbear, to Henry Neville, Rome, 20 June 1667, sent by James Hicks to Secretary Williamson.

[78] Ludlow, 'Voyce', pp. 1178–9.

[79] Ibid., p. 1179. He may be the same Roux who in England in 1668 would pass himself off as 'M. de Marsilly, who had been employed in Switzerland by his colonel, the Maréchal de Schomberg'. See Hughes Hartmann (ed.), *Charles II and Madame*, p. 250.

himself as a Reformed Christian.[80] On a visit to Balthasar, the local councillor Colonel Weiss had learnt about the plans for an extradition and informed Steiger, the treasurer in Bern, who was then able to give warning to the exiles. While the community around Ludlow had been repeatedly reassured of their hosts' loyalty to them and that they would not be delivered to the English authorities, the threat remained real.[81]

Roux approached Weiss again after his return from Geneva to negotiate a deal. The Frenchman informed Weiss that 'the King of England had a desire to enter into a more strict League with the Canton of Berne, then with the other Cantons, provided that they would deliver those into his hands with in their Territoryes who had judged his father to death'. As an additional incentive for the betrayal, he also offered a substantial reward or bribe, promising 'that he who should bring the first notice therof, should have fifty thousand Crownes presented to him'. According to Ludlow, Weiss rejected the offer 'as being unworthy of their Excellencies, and unsuitable to the Custome of the Switz to betray those who put themselves under their Protection'. He also let it be known to the King of England that he would have to contact the authorities in Bern directly if he had any issues with them.[82] In response, the Bern authorities received a note via two syndics of Geneva from a friend close to the King of England to repeat the request, while also insinuating to the local authorities that Ludlow and his friends were not of the same religion as the Reformed Christians of the Vaud – presumably in an attempt to sour relations between the exiles and their hosts in Vevey.[83] The letter had the desired effect in so far as the excellencies of Bern contacted Hummel to enquire about the religious practices of their protégés, and Hummel in turn wrote to the exiles for a justification, 'though as he was pleased to write, he well understood the Customes and conscientious Reasons of the Independents in England'. He was therefore 'convinced that this was nothing but an artifice of our Enemyes to render us odious to their Excellencies & the Inhabitants of this Country, by charging against us, what concerned the Law of our God, for want of other occasion'.[84]

Ludlow made it clear in his 'Voyce' that he did not think the exiles differed from their host community in terms of religious doctrine. However, he conceded that they did keep themselves to themselves at times for the purpose of worship because they did not consider their fellow Protestants in Switzerland to be of the same purity of religion as themselves. Yet

[80] Ludlow, 'Voyce', p. 1180.   [81] Ibid., p. 1181.   [82] Ibid., pp. 1182–3.
[83] Ibid., pp. 1184 ff.   [84] Ibid., p. 1184.

for Ludlow this was not a matter of choice. The exiles were just following divine orders. He conveyed to Hummel that 'we had not a freedome to communicate with any in that holy Ordinance of the Lords Supper, of whom we had not particular satisfaction of a worke of grace in their hearts, and that their conversation was suitable thereto'. For the true followers of Christ were 'a vissible Church consisting of Living stones, to wit of Beleevers, who by mutuall consent walke together and watch over one another in the use of all Christs Ordinances'.[85] For good measure, Ludlow threw in a number of biblical passages to show that the Lord disapproved of the godly associating with their flawed brothers and sisters,

> that two could not walke together except they were agreed, Amos. 3.3. that we are not to be unequally yoaked. 2 Cor. 6. 14. That an Oxe & an Ass were not to be plowed with, That a Garment of lynnen & woolen was not be worne, Deut. 22. 10. 11. That the Priest was commanded to put a difference betweene the holy, & unholy Levit. 10. 10. Ezek. 44. 23. That they who separate the pretious from the vile, shall be as the Lords mouth. Jer. 15. 19.[86]

With such biblical backing and the desire to follow the 'Liberty of our owne Consciences', the exiles hoped they 'should still under their Excellencyes protection be permitted to leade quiet and peaceable lives in all Godlyness & honesty'.[87] So Ludlow and his friends referred all these concerns to their ever-obliging friend Hummel.

In a letter to the chief minister of Bern, John Ralfeson (alias Cornelius Holland) justified their absence from the communion table, stressing that 'wee hold and Professe, the same doctrinall points of Christian faith, w[i]th you, and other the best reformed Churches or places in the world doe', but the exiles also did not receive the Lord's Supper 'amongst ou[r]selves, for divers reasons, wherei[n] . . . in due tyme, wee hope [to] give you satisfaction'. He then continued to reassure Hummel that the exiles did 'severall tymes in the weeke, pray w[i]th one another, and speake to one another out of the Scriptures', and that they had no intention to offend their hosts. Holland then asked Hummel to make their case to the authorities, knowing that the latter was 'better able to produce argum[en]ts out of Scripture, and otherways, to this purpose'.[88] As we do not hear any more of the issue, we can assume that the dispute was smoothed over by Hummel, who understood the exiles' needs and was keen to preserve

---

[85] Ibid., pp. 1184–5.   [86] Ibid.   [87] Ibid.

[88] StAB, B III 98, Epistolae ad decanos bernenses, item 35, John Ralfeson (alias Cornelius Holland), Vevey, to Johann Heinrich Hummel, 23 August 1668.

harmony between his foreign protégés and his own flock. So peace between the exiles and their hosts was restored and they were assured 'that though we had some Enemyes, we had many more friends'.[89] Bern also declined to have an agent of the English king residing locally.[90]

News and Intelligence from England and Elsewhere

While the exiles were staying abroad, England was never far from their minds, or, as Philip Major has put it, many exiles saw themselves 'as being caught between worlds, with England always a very present absence'.[91] They attempted to stay abreast of news from home through private correspondence, public newsletters and a range of printed news and pamphlet publications. Gathering news and intelligence was not just a sentimental pursuit: it was key to the exiles' security and essential for any underground political activity and future planning. Lack of news therefore remained a constant worry.

Sidney, for instance, complained that his friends in England did not supply enough news, fearing that 'the Knowledge of that [which relates unto *England*], would disturbe my Solitude' and thus were making him 'as much a Stranger unto all that is done theire, as to the Affaires of China'. The fear of becoming a 'stranger' meant that Sidney now wrote to his father 'constantly . . . , at the least, once a Fortnight', but complained that he did not receive much in response, though we do not know if this was due to his father's indifference or the watchful eye of the English secretaries of state, who may have intercepted letters from the earl to his errant son.[92] Correspondence was opened so frequently that Sidney specifically remarked on the fact when a letter arrived with its seal still intact.[93] A certain amount of distrust was clearly in order, as we know from a number of letters to and from the fugitives that were intercepted along the way and now survive in the State Papers, such as a letter from Ludlow's circle about a foiled assassination attempt in late 1663, and another of

---

[89] Ludlow, 'Voyce', p. 1185; StAB, B III 98, Epistolae ad decanos bernenses, item 35, John Ralfeson (alias Cornelius Holland), Vevey, to Johann Heinrich Hummel, 23 August 1668,.

[90] Ludlow, 'Voyce', p. 1187.

[91] Major, 'A poor exile stranger', in Major (ed.), *Literatures of Exile*, p. 166.

[92] Algernon Sidney (from Frascati?) to Robert, Earl of Leicester, 14/24 July 1661, in Collins (ed.), *Letters*, ii, pp. 721–2, at p. 721.

[93] Even before Sidney became a proper exile, he remarked on Bulstrode Whitelocke's letter: 'I observed the seal was untouched, which was a better fortune than doth befall many letters that come this way.' See Algernon Sidney, Copenhagen, to Bulstrode Whitelock, 1 March 1660, in Blencowe (ed.), *Sydney Papers*, pp. 176–80, at pp. 176–7.

1667 from Colonel Richard Neville to his rebellious younger brother Henry in Rome.[94] Letters were an important way to strengthen and complement the personal networks addressed in Chapter 1. In particular, as the exiles moved around in Europe, letters could ensure regular contact with those left behind. As the exiles set out on their journey, their personal networks at home often turned into epistolary networks, while previously more distant European networks temporarily turned into personal ones.[95] The sources of news were manifold, including among others printed materials of various kinds to supplement more personal channels of information.

Letters and news publications sent from home were key to staying in touch with the affairs of England. Ludlow frequently mentions 'letters from my relations',[96] and he reports that members of his exile community used to hear from their contacts in London every two or three weeks, except when a suspicious visitor arrived in the spring of 1665 and this regular correspondence was 'wholly Interrupted' for four or five months.[97] In the aftermath of the Yorkshire Plot there had clearly been plans by the English secretary of state, Henry Bennet, Earl of Arlington, to monitor 'the correspondence between the fugitives in Lausanne and their party in England, by inducing some persons of those now in the island, by promise of reward, to feign an escape and fly to them'.[98] This may have been a later instance of such an attempt as negotiations for the Sidney plot were underway. The suspicious visitor who had arrived in Switzerland the previous winter was an Englishman using the name of Thomas Schugar to look for employment in teaching mathematics in Bern. He had sought the help of Hummel, claiming that he had previously been 'a papist, a Priest, and a servant to the Queen mother of England' who had converted first to Lutheranism and subsequently to Calvinism. However, Hummel had become suspicious when Schugar took too much of an interest in the affairs of the exiles and decided to inform Ludlow and his friends of this potential danger. Thus when Schugar approached the exiles themselves they were forewarned, and the agent, 'finding himselfe discovered & suspected ... tooke a Resolution to retorne to Geneve the

---

[94] Ibid. On the interception of Ludlow's letter, see *CSPD* 1663–4, p. 398, and on Neville's correspondence, NA, SP 29/206, 21 June 1667, fol. 134, Richard Neville, Billingbear, to Henry Neville, Rome, 20 June 1667, sent by James Hicks to Secretary Williamson.
[95] I owe this observation to Mark Somos.   [96] Ludlow, 'Voyce', p. 817.
[97] Ibid., p. 1222. He also mentions 'my correspondent' in London in a letter to Hummel of 25 January 1671/2, StAB, B III 98, Epistolae ad decanos bernenses, p. 534.
[98] *CSPD* 1663–4, p. 380.

next morning'.[99] Ludlow suspected that the interruption of his correspondence with England was related to Schugar's presence, as the flow of news had stopped around the same time as the latter arrived in Geneva. Something very similar had previously happened to Oliver St John when Schugar came to stay with him near Augsburg.[100] It seems that the exiles and their trusted contacts were astute at identifying potential threats and agents of the Crown, even though this did not stop the Stuarts from trying to disrupt the exiles' peace and lines of communication again and again. So the exiles had to rely on their trusted networks.

Among Ludlow's most important contacts and correspondents in England was Slingsby Bethel, a republican merchant, later sheriff of London, and a distant relative of Algernon Sidney.[101] He and his wife provided support for Elizabeth Ludlow, who had initially stayed behind in England and came to visit Switzerland with the Bethels in October 1662. Ludlow reports that 'our very good freind' Bethel stayed with the exiles for a month.[102] By all appearances he was a trusted family friend, who later also came into possession of Ludlow's manuscript memoirs and may have set in motion their publication process.[103] He also tried in vain to persuade Ludlow to participate in the Sidney plot.[104] Yet according to Worden, 'Ludlow's most regular contact in London' was his 'good friend, & correspondent' Walter Thimblelton,[105] a dissenter and an 'ally of Morgan Lloyd and Hugh Courteney', the latter of whom had been imprisoned in Newgate for refusing to take the Oath of Allegiance to Charles II.[106] Moreover, government agents also knew of Ludlow's regular correspondence with Thomas Gardiner a fringe maker at the White Horse in the Poultry, and his 'very good freind'.[107]

Ludlow's most constant source of information about England and advisor in personal and political matters, however, remained his wife, who had stayed behind in England for several years before joining her husband in Vevey. He describes his 'deare wife' as someone 'whose heart was as much got for the ... promoting of this worke [i.e. the godly and

---

[99] Ludlow, 'Voyce', pp. 1221–2.
[100] Ibid., p. 1222; and Ludlow, *Memoirs*, ed. Firth, ii, pp. 419–20.
[101] Gary S. De Krey, 'Bethel, Slingsby (*bap.* 1617, *d.* 1697)', *ODNB*.
[102] Ludlow, 'Voyce', p. 964. Bethel's name was inserted into the manuscript later.
[103] Ludlow, *Voyce*, ed. Worden, pp. 13, 18–20.   [104] Ludlow, 'Voyce', p. 1080.
[105] Ibid., p. 1443; and Ludlow, *Voyce*, ed. Worden, pp. 10, 13. This could be the Captain Thimbleton who was to be apprehended 'to answer to what is objected against him on the King's behalf'. See *CSPD 1661–2*, 10 November 1662, p. 552.
[106] *CSPD 1661–2*, 19 June 1661, p. 12.
[107] Ludlow, *Voyce*, ed. Worden, p. 13; and Ludlow, 'Voyce', pp. 1096, 1348.

republican cause] as any other'; and she observed the political situation in England and advised her husband on the best course of action.[108] Ludlow also employed his wife, 'who had a heart full freight with love & zeale for the publique Cause' as a go-between to communicate his advice on the plot to his allies in London.[109] She eventually came to join Ludlow in exile some time in late September or early October 1663 to make his banishment 'as easy & as comfortable' as she could.[110] Worden suspects that some of Elizabeth's knowledge of English politics was 'probably derived from connections which she succeeded in establishing at Charles II's court', while the letters of John Lisle's wife Alice (née Beconshaw), who had contacts at Whitehall, and Bulstrode Whitelocke's son James, who temporarily came to stay in Geneva, were other possible sources of information about the political goings-on in England.[111]

Besides personal correspondence and newsletters, gazettes and newspapers as well as other miscellaneous pamphlet publications played an important role in the lives of the exiles even though they would have arrived with several weeks' delay. Blair Worden has found ample references to printed material from England in the manuscript of Ludlow's 'Voyce'; and while there is not the same amount of evidence for the other two exiles, we can assume that they had similar channels of information.[112] Among the pamphlets Ludlow referred to in the 'Voyce' were 'The Discovery of Mr. Baxter's Enmity to Monarchy';[113] a declaration by Charles II 'for the composing of the differences betweene the episcopall and presbyterian party' with a French response, which also shows that Ludlow followed both the English-language and the French-language press;[114] Dr. Heylin's *'booke which he lately published, chardgeing Mr. Calvin with laying the foundation of the warr in England, and with owneing principles destructive to monarchy'*; and 'a booke intitled Philanax Anglicanus, first written in Latin and then in English, asserting that rebel and Presbyterian

---

[108] Ludlow, 'Voyce', p. 941.   [109] Ibid., pp. 1059, 1143–4.
[110] Ibid., p. 1176. John Phelps accompanied Elizabeth Ludlow from Holland to Switzerland. See Ludlow, 'Voyce', p. 1181; *CSPD* 1663–4, p. 291. Bethel's wife had also joined her husband around this time. According to Firth, *Memoirs*, ii, p. 330n., Cawley's wife stayed in England.
[111] Ludlow, *Voyce*, ed. Worden, pp. 13–14, and Ludlow, 'Voyce', p. 1040 on Alice Lisle and pp. 1181, 1332–3, 1348 on James Whitelocke.
[112] For the following references to publications, I have drawn on the editor's footnotes in Ludlow, *Voyce*, ed. Worden, pp. 13–14, and expanded on them.
[113] Ibid., p. 172 (800). This may relate to Richard Baxter's refusal of preferment after the Restoration. I have not been able to find a pamphlet of that title, however.
[114] Ibid., p. 269 (891).

are inseparable'.[115] Ludlow's reading also included newspapers, while he also kept track of royal declarations and parliamentary proceedings to follow political developments back home in England.[116] Thus he learnt from the 'first Gazet [he] saw' after his arrival in Geneva that the authorities believed Colonel Whalley and Colonel Gough (or Goffe) had returned to England and were offering a hundred pounds to anyone 'who should seize upon either of them'. Ludlow also thus learnt that there was a price of three hundred pounds on his own head, and that the authorities believed he might still be in England.[117] He also received news about the Presbyterian Plot of 1661, in which many of his allies were implicated and later imprisoned in the Tower, including James Harrington, John Wildman, Henry Ireton, Samuel Moyer and Praisegod Barebones; and 'the newes bookes for severall weekes after took occasion to speake of the horridness of this plot, without meantioning any particculars'.[118] It was not least this lack of detail that led Ludlow to suspect that the plot was based on the 'lyes and fictions' of the government 'carrying on their mischieveous designes' and using bare rumours to justify arbitrary arrests and imprisonments of opposition members.[119]

According to Worden, '[t]he principal route of intelligence from England to Switzerland seems to have been through Paris and Lyons', where Ludlow had contacts 'with merchants and messengers' along the postal route.[120] In Paris, Ludlow did his banking with 'Mr. *Margas*' and made the acquaintance of 'Mr. Copley, an English merchant', from whom he 'received much civillity and freindship'.[121] One of Ludlow's more distant contacts on that route was 'one Mr Arduus a merchant of freeburgh [Fribourg] (& consequently a Papist) residing at Lyons, a Correspondent

---

[115] Ibid., p. 282 (903). Dr Heylin's book may have been P[eter] H[eylin], *The Stumbling-Block of Disobedience and Rebellion Cunningly Laid by Calvin in the Subjects Way, Discovered, Censured and Removed* (London: Printed by E. Cotes for Henry Seile over against St. Dunstans Church in Fleet street, 1658). The latter book is *Philanax Anglicus: Or a Christian Caveat for All Kings, Princes & Prelates, . . . Faithfully Published by T.B. Gent.* (London: for Theo: Sadler, 1663).

[116] Ludlow, *Voyce*, ed. Worden, p. 13n.

[117] Ibid., p. 196 (822). According to Worden, ibid., p. 13n., Ludlow's source could have been *Mercurius politicus*, 39 (20–7 September 1660). In any case, the gazettes probably referred to the king's proclamations for the apprehension of Ludlow, Whalley and Goffe cited above.

[118] Ludlow, *Voyce*, ed. Worden, p. 291 (911). According to Worden, ibid., p. 13n., Ludlow's source could have been *Mercurius publicus*, 48–9, 52–3 (21 November 1661–2 January 1662).

[119] Ludlow, *Voyce*, ed. Worden, p. 291 (910).

[120] Ibid., p. 14. For some of the main postal routes from England to Europe, see Peter Fraser, *The Intelligence of the Secretaries of State and Their Monopoly of Licensed News 1660–1688* (Cambridge, UK: Cambridge University Press, 1956), map between pp. 64 and 65.

[121] Ludlow, *Voyce*, ed. Worden, p. 193 (819).

of Monsieur Du Four [or Du Foux] ... of Vevey'[122] – the same Arduus who had warned the exiles of Roux's attempt to effect their extradition on behalf of the English and French courts. A 'Mr Parre a Gentleman & freind of myne living at Vevey' also received information from Paris via Lyon about a possible assassination plot against Ludlow, which he communicated to him.[123]

Ludlow also had access to French and Dutch newspapers, pamphlets and 'letters of intelligence'.[124] Among the publications he mentions are the 'French Gazet', or *Gazette de France*,[125] and the 'french Intelligencer',[126] as well as French 'Publique Gazzets'[127] and unnamed 'Libels being published at Paris'.[128] He also refers several times to 'french & dutch manuscripts',[129] 'the manuscripts which came from Paris',[130] 'the French manuscript [from Paris]'[131] or just 'the manuscript',[132] as well as to other accounts from Paris,[133] or to 'letters out of France'[134] and 'Letters from Paris'.[135] He also mentions a letter 'from a friend in Holland' – no doubt another republican exile with contacts to rebels in England and Scotland – and other 'Letters from Holland'.[136] Ludlow had apparently more personal contacts in the United Provinces than in France. Yet among the newsletters and published material, French sources are mentioned slightly more frequently than Dutch, as they may have been more easily obtainable in Switzerland through sheer geographical proximity. However, his preference for publications from France was not necessarily a linguistic issue, as many Dutch publications at the time were written in French as well. Yet, as Worden notes, Holland became 'a major source of intelligence, especially during the Anglo-Dutch war of 1665–7', while Ludlow also 'received regular supplies of information from Savoy and Germany'.[137] Information on possible threats, for instance, had come from Turin, which at the time was the capital of the Duchy of Savoy, which bordered on the territories of Bern and gave access to both France and Italy.[138] One of Ludlow's contacts in the duchy is identified as 'Mr Torneri our freind in Savoy',

---

[122] Ludlow, 'Voyce', p. 1179. Firth has 'Du Fort' or 'Du Four', 'merchant of Vevey': *Memoirs*, ed. Firth, ii, p. 382. Another time, however, he calls him a 'merchant of Geneva' (ibid., p. 425).
[123] Ludlow, 'Voyce', pp. 1051–5.   [124] Ludlow, *Voyce*, ed. Worden, p. 14.
[125] Ludlow, 'Voyce', pp. 893, 950.   [126] Ibid., p. 1316.   [127] Ibid., p. 1383.
[128] Ibid., p. 1106.   [129] Ibid., p. 1263.   [130] Ibid., p. 945.
[131] Ibid., pp. 1050, 1133, 1137, 1189, 1260, 1314.   [132] Ibid., p. 1246.   [133] Ibid., p. 1063.
[134] Ibid., p. 1089.   [135] Ibid., p. 1179.
[136] StAB, B III 63, Epistolae virorum clarorum, item 20, Edmund Phillipps [Ludlow] to Johann Heinrich Hummel, 7 October 1667, reproduced in Stern (ed.), *Briefe englischer Flüchtlinge*, and in *Memoirs*, ed. Firth, ii, pp. 492–6, pp. 491, 495.
[137] Ludlow, *Voyce*, ed. Worden, p. 14.   [138] Ludlow, *Memoirs*, ed. Firth, ii, pp. 359–60.

who appears to have been a double agent, also working for Charles II.[139] Part of Ludlow's intelligence also stemmed from his Protestant circles, not least Hummel in Switzerland and Dury, who travelled Europe on behalf of the irenic movement.[140]

Conclusion

As this chapter has shown, the republican fugitives had to overcome many practical obstacles on their journey to the Continent and during their life abroad. While the communities that had taken them in were largely welcoming and supportive, they also occasionally slipped into indifference or even hostility when the exiles threatened to become a political liability. The murder of Lisle is significant because it shows that however many efforts the host communities made to protect the fugitives, nobody was able to shelter them completely from secret assassins and intrigues. The international manhunt also shows how much the surviving regicides and republicans were still feared as a destabilising force to the English monarchy even after the failure of the Yorkshire Plot, and how much their whereabouts and activities remained a transnational European matter of concern. It was therefore important for the republicans to be always on their guard and to stay up to date with current affairs both in England and in Europe more widely. Being one step ahead of the enemy mattered not just as a means of self-defence, however; it was just as important for taking action against the government in England. For the situation of political and religious dissenters back home was worsening day by day, with dissenters filling the prisons and a new set of penal laws issued in the so-called Clarendon Code.[141] With dissatisfaction growing among opponents of the Stuarts at home and abroad, Sidney had found the patriotic task he had been waiting for. Over the next couple of years, we find him criss-crossing Europe in an attempt to raise an army to invade England from abroad to restore the Long Parliament and republican rule.[142] It is with this underground plotting activity and the development of the English republican cause in Europe that the next chapter is concerned.

---

[139] Ludlow, 'Voyce', p. 1060.
[140] Ludlow, *Voyce*, ed. Worden, p. 14, and Ludlow, 'Voyce', pp. 903, 900, 1037 (on Dury), and 978 ff., 993, 1001, 1060, 1062, 1181, 1184 ff., 1216, 1221, 1233, 1363, 1378 (on Hummel).
[141] This included the Act of Uniformity (1662), the Conventicle Act (1664) and the Five Mile Act (1665).
[142] Being a good citizen and patriot can in some cases mean acting against one's own country: see David Held, 'Cosmopolitanism, Democracy and the Global Order', in Maria Roviso and Magdalena Nowicka (eds), *The Ashgate Research Companion to Cosmopolitanism* (Farnham: Ashgate, 2011), pp. 163–77, at p. 170.

CHAPTER 4

Plots, Conspiracies and Ideas

[W]e meete with too many of that sullen proude trybe abroad, who
have still a smack of their antient ranchor against his Ma[jes]tie . . .
Charles II's agent in Tuscany, Joseph Kent, to Joseph Williamson,
26 October 1663[1]

Introduction: The Republican Underground
at Home and Abroad

The English republican exiles on the Continent were being watched by the
authorities in England and followed around Europe by spies and assassins.
Yet they were not just their persecutors' passive victims. They also had an
agenda of their own that involved a major intelligence-gathering operation,
targeted publications to promote their cause and active plotting against the
Stuart government. As we have seen above, the fugitive regicides and other
prominent Commonwealth republicans were not the only ones who had
made their way to the Continent. Their wider networks included dissenters from the British Isles who had left their native country over the
years in search of liberty of conscience, so that there was a substantial exile
and expatriate community in Europe who remained in close contact
with their friends and relatives at home, as well as Reformed European
Protestants. The majority of these exiles and émigrés were based in the
United Provinces, where liberty of conscience and economic opportunities
provided a welcoming environment, while others were scattered across
the Huguenot regions of France and the Protestant states and cities of the
Holy Roman Empire. These networks also became fertile ground for
plotting.

News and rumours of republican plots had been unsettling the English
monarchy ever since its restoration. The aim of such plots was either to

---

[1] NA, SP 98/4, fol. 265r, Joseph Kent, Livorno, to Joseph Williamson, 26 October 1663.

restore the Long Parliament of the 1640s, to create a republican order and establish liberty of conscience or, failing that, to destabilise the Stuart regime in protest at its repressive policies. Some of the rumours circulating about republican plots were true, others false. Some may even have been planted by government agents themselves to justify a backlash against members of the opposition. Bungling informers, opportunists and a tendency to mass hysteria among the people meanwhile have made it as hard for modern historians as it must have been for contemporary observers to establish what was really going on.[2] Two of the alleged plots are particularly relevant in the present context, as the round-ups that followed included a number of prominent republicans from the exiles' immediate environment: the so-called Presbyterian Plot of 1661 and the Yorkshire Rising or Northern Plot of 1663.

The first of these was probably a government fabrication intent on weakening the opposition through a number of arbitrary arrests. In the aftermath of this Presbyterian Plot, a number of republicans and dissenters, including James Harrington and John Wildman, were arrested, while others, such as Henry Neville, were put under surveillance.[3] The fact that Edmund Ludlow too had been a chief suspect, even though he had left the country many months before, illustrates the absurdity of some of the accusations being made.[4] Yet there is a danger that the numerous fabrications might lead us to dismiss too easily the actual existence of a fairly coherent republican underground. This underground did not form under the Restoration. It had never ceased to exist. For it was simply composed of the monarchy's old enemies: former Civil War Parliamentarians, members of the Commonwealth and Protectorate governments, Levellers, religious dissenters and sectarians. Some of the different opposition groups now came to form alliances of necessity to fight the restored government together – among them many republicans.

An underground community of republicans opposed to Oliver Cromwell's increasingly centralising and autocratic tendencies had begun to emerge following his expulsion of the Rump Parliament in 1653, and it forged stronger links during the Protectorate. For instance, before the 1656 general elections Henry Neville, Sir Arthur Haselrig and Sir Henry Vane the younger had been plotting together to have themselves elected to

---

[2] For a detailed discussion of Restoration plots, see Greaves, *Deliver Us from Evil*; and Marshall, *Intelligence and Espionage*.
[3] Mahlberg, *Henry Neville and English Republican Culture*, p. 58.
[4] Greaves, *Deliver Us from Evil*, p. 71.

the new Protectorate Parliament in an attempt to prevent the election of Cromwell's select candidates who were backed by the major-generals.[5] Likewise, during the 1659 Parliament of Richard Cromwell, a group of commonwealthmen had allied against the Cromwellians and Presbyterians or crypto-royalists to promote a restructuring of the constitution along Harringtonian principles to provide checks on the new Protector and prevent him from assuming arbitrary powers.[6] Neville in particular was an important link between Harrington's Rota Club meeting at Miles Coffee House between 1659 and 1660 and the commonwealthmen in Parliament,[7] while Harringtonians were also associated with a pamphlet entitled *The Armies Dutie* (1659), authored by Neville, Henry Marten, John Lawson, John Wildman, John Jones and Samuel Moyer, and the *Humble Petition of Divers Well-Affected Persons* (1659), which repeated some of the earlier publication's demands for constitutional reform along Harringtonian lines. Neville had presented the petition to Parliament to promote popular sovereignty and a Harringtonian division of powers, including the institution of an executive magistracy, for the reshaping of the English constitution.[8] Notably, a number of republicans tried to the very last to prevent a restoration of the Stuarts through their attempts at exerting influence on General George Monck after his arrival in London, but were disappointed by his actions.[9] Contacts between a wider group of commonwealthmen continued into the Restoration period, while new alliances with disaffected elements from the dissenting community more widely were also formed on the spur of the moment. Historians studying this disaffected underground have disagreed in their assessment of its relative coherence and the question to what extent it could be considered 'radical'.

---

[5] Mahlberg, *Henry Neville and English Republican Culture*, pp. 48 ff.; Christopher Durston, *Cromwell's Major-Generals: Godly Government during the English Revolution* (Manchester: Manchester University Press, 2001); Christopher Durston, "'Settling the Hearts and Quieting the Minds of All Good People": The Major-Generals and the Puritan Minorities of Interregnum England', *History*, 85 (2000), 247–67; and Christopher Durston, 'The Fall of Cromwell's Major-Generals', *English Historical Review*, 113 (1999), 18–37.

[6] Mahlberg, *Henry Neville and English Republican Culture*, pp. 54 ff.; J. G. A. Pocock, 'Machiavelli, Harrington, and English Political Ideologies in the Eighteenth Century', *William and Mary Quarterly*, 22 (1965), 549–83.

[7] Pocock, 'Machiavelli, Harrington, and English Political Ideologies'; Mahlberg, *Henry Neville and English Republican Culture*, pp. 56, 143, 160.

[8] *The Armies Dutie* (London, 1659); *Humble Petition of Divers Well-Affected Persons . . . to the Supreme Authority, the Parliament of the Common-Wealth of England* (London, 1659). See Mahlberg, *Henry Neville and English Republican Culture*, p. 55.

[9] Mahlberg, *Henry Neville and English Republican Culture*, p. 56.

While Richard Greaves assumes that there was an organised political underground in post-Restoration Britain, he nevertheless tends to downplay the real danger emanating from this discontented body of 'radicals' as he focuses to a great extent on government hysteria, concluding that it is in many cases impossible to judge whether a plot was real or imagined.[10] Conversely, Alan Marshall argues that the continuities in opposition activism have been underestimated, yet hesitates to apply the term 'radicals' to 'the men who lived in the dark underbelly of Restoration politics' for fear of sounding 'anachronistic' because the term was not used at the time.[11] Instead, the individuals concerned were known among their contemporaries as 'fanaticks' or 'commonwealthsmen', or they were often described as 'Levellers', even though any sort of coordinated Leveller movement had disappeared from view in the 1650s. While Marshall acknowledges the existence among the plotters of a relatively 'articulate' group of 'commonwealthsmen and Levellers', as he calls them, he considers their ideological background to have been primarily religious, but 'not necessarily republican in nature'.[12] In making this assumption, Marshall seems to suggest that religious and political ideas could easily be separated from one another, while also downplaying the republican motives behind much of the plotting. The description of the opposition as 'radical', however, can be justified in so far as that the men and women engaged against the Crown wanted to see a fundamentally different form of government in England: one based on popular sovereignty and liberty of conscience for a broad range of dissenters.[13] And there were concrete attempts to topple the Stuart government.

The most substantial attempt within England to achieve that goal was the Northern Rising or Yorkshire Plot of 1663, in the aftermath of which Neville was arrested and imprisoned in the Tower.[14] According to informers' reports surviving in the State Papers and various correspondences, the rising had been planned for 6 October, when troops were due to gather in Gildersome in the West Riding of Yorkshire with the aim of taking several other towns and advancing on the capital to topple the monarchy, restore the Long Parliament and establish liberty

[10] See in particular his 'Introduction' to *Deliver Us from Evil*. Admittedly, many of the plots were a bit of both. There was evidence of opposition activity, seditious speech, etc., but the authorities could never prove that there was an actual plot.
[11] Marshall, *Intelligence and Espionage*, pp. 10, 12. [12] Ibid., p. 15.
[13] On the problems with 'radicalism', see Glenn Burgess and Matthew Festenstein (eds), *English Radicalism 1550–1850* (Cambridge, UK: Cambridge University Press, 2007).
[14] See Chapter 1.

of conscience.[15] While the rising itself failed, it is nevertheless notable, not just for the fears it raised and the flurry of arrests that followed in its wake, but also for its transnational dimension. The plotters in England stood in contact with the exile community on the Continent, in particular the dissenters and republicans who had withdrawn to the United Provinces and were thought to have supplied their brothers and sisters at home with money and arms.[16] This same exile community would also later become instrumental to Algernon Sidney when he attempted to gather men and resources for his very own plot to invade England from abroad with the help of foreign troops, as we will see below.

The first part of this chapter will therefore trace Sidney's attempts to win the support both of the exile community as well as foreign governments for his project to return England to republican rule. The second part will assess how the nature of the English republican cause was transformed over the course of the 1660s as its main agents changed from being free and elected representatives of a Commonwealth government to becoming persecuted underground activists and exiles acting in secrecy and often considerable danger. It will be argued that republican ideas and principles remained relatively constant across the perceived Restoration watershed and over the course of the 1660s and 1670s, even though the republicans' means to achieve their goals were severely constrained. This chapter will also address the extent to which the exiles relied on and collaborated with foreign governments, notably those of the United Provinces and France, in an attempt to achieve their aims. The Second Anglo-Dutch War played a key role in the process as the last major opportunity for concerted republican action before the Exclusion Crisis and the Rye House Plot of the 1670s and 1680s. However, the mutual distrust between the various opponents of Charles II and the Stuart monarchy also meant that the success of the republican cause would remain hopelessly out of reach.

The Aborted Sidney Plot of 1665

As we have seen above, Sidney left Rome in the summer of 1663. He no longer felt safe in this melting pot of foreigners where he had been followed by royalist assassins and was seeking new ways and means to

---

[15] Bodleian Library, Oxford, Clarendon MS 80, fol. 77; *CSPD* 1663–4, 12 October 1663, p. 298; Mahlberg, *Henry Neville and English Republican Culture*, p. 59.

[16] Mahlberg, *Henry Neville and English Republican Culture*, p. 59; Pincus, *Protestantism and Patriotism*, p. 229.

reclaim power for the republican faction in England. He may even have
been aware of the Northern Rising planned for the coming October and
felt it was the right moment to act. In the first instance, his aim was to
make contact with the wider exile community in Europe in order to gather
support for his plans. On his way north towards the United Provinces,
where the largest numbers of English and Scottish exiles were based,
Sidney stopped in Switzerland in the autumn to visit Ludlow in Vevey
and consult with him about the possibility of future action against the
Stuart government. As a gift, he brought him a pair of pistols from
Lombardy that would come in useful for the task in hand.[17]

As a distinguished former military leader, Ludlow was still considered
one of the most feared republicans alive. He was frequently implicated in
plots and suspected of leading uprisings in England throughout the early
1660s, even though we have no record of him leaving Switzerland during
that time. But it was widely assumed that he would be the most likely
candidate to lead a successful rebellion against the Stuarts. This idea was
apparently shared by Sidney, who approached him for help and advice in
the first instance.[18] The Northern Plot was backed by exiled dissenters in
the United Provinces, who supplied the rebels in England with money and
weapons. Maybe Sidney had already been toying with the idea of following
such a rising with a foreign invasion. But nothing concrete appears to have
materialised from his meeting with Ludlow before Sidney continued his
journey north. On his way, he stopped over at Geneva to pay his respects
at the famous Academy, enter his name in the visitors' book and leave the
rather loaded inscription: 'sit sanguinis ultor justorum' – 'let there be
revenge for the blood of the just'.[19]

While Ludlow seemed quite comfortable in his lodgings on the Swiss
Riviera and gave no sign of wanting to take action against the English
government, Sidney moved on to Brussels, from where he announced in a
letter to his father in early December that he was hoping to spend the
following summer as a 'Volunteere in Hungary' in 'the Service of the
Emperor' heading 'a good strong Boddy of the best Officers and Soldiers of
our old [Parliamentary] Army; both Horse and Foot' to defend the
Habsburg monarchy against the Ottoman Empire in the Austro-Turkish

---

[17] Ludlow, *Memoirs*, ed. Firth, ii, p. 346; and Ludlow, 'Voyce', p. 977.
[18] Firth, 'Ludlow, Edmund', rev. Worden.
[19] The inscription and its translation are reported by Scott, *Algernon Sidney and the English Republic*,
   p. 171, referring to Charles Borgeaud, *Histoire de l'Université de Genève: l'Académie de Calvin
   1559–1798*, i, pp. 442–3. For his stay in Geneva, see also Stelling-Michaud (ed.), *Le livre du recteur
   de l'Académie de Genève*, v, p. 568.

War (1663–4).[20] This could be seen either as a desperate attempt to secure an income through his mercenary services or as a first step towards securing military support for a possible operation in England. Probably it was both. Yet Sidney soon appears to have changed his mind. Instead of going to Hungary, he withdrew for some time to the German city of Augsburg, where his former parliamentary ally Oliver St John had settled during the early 1660s. There he only just escaped an assassination attempt in the spring of 1665 before moving on to the United Provinces to explore further opportunities for action and drum up support.[21] It was here, in the company of many other dissenters, including Furly, that Sidney further developed his plan to set an end to Charles II's government by invading England from abroad with the help of foreign troops and also started writing the *Court Maxims* as his political manifesto and call to arms, as we will see in Chapter 6.[22]

Sidney's nineteenth-century biographer George Van Santvoord claimed – and many historians have repeated his claim since – that the outbreak of the Second Anglo-Dutch War over access to trading routes at sea in March 1665 gave the English republicans new hope. They saw the Protestant and republican Dutch as natural allies, as they too were enemies of Charles II, while also sharing a similar religious and political outlook. In particular the 'liberal sentiments' of the Grand Pensionary Johan de Witt, 'known to be thoroughly in accordance with those of the English republicans, were such as to give encouragement to the exiles, many of whom looked forward to the success of Holland as the prelude to the restoration of the Commonwealth'.[23] Van Santvoord's positive view of the Dutch was clearly shaped by his own Whiggish sentiments, which looked ahead to William of Orange's successful invasion of England more than twenty years later.[24] But Sidney's contemporary allies treated the whole situation with more caution, not least because the two republics had not always seen eye to eye in the previous decades and there was a certain amount of

---

[20] Algernon Sidney, Brussels, to Robert, Earl of Leicester, 1/11 December 1663, in Collins (ed.), *Letters*, ii, p. 725.

[21] Oliver St John had initially, in 1662, exiled himself to Basel in Switzerland, where Sidney may have met him during his visit in August 1663, but later moved on to Augsburg. See Palmer, 'St John, Oliver'; and the entry on Sidney in Stelling-Michaud (ed.), *Le livre du recteur de L'Académie de Genève*, referring to the 'Fremdenbuch' of Basle.

[22] Scott, *Algernon Sidney and the English Republic*, p. 180; Hutton, 'Introduction' to Hutton (ed.), *Benjamin Furly*, pp. 4–5; and Simonutti, 'English Guests at "De Lantaarn"', p. 39.

[23] Van Santvoord, *Life of Algernon Sidney*, p. 181.

[24] Even Scott cannot completely escape them despite his otherwise most successful attempt to demolish Whig myth.

ideological disagreement. As Steven Pincus has pointed out, many English republicans in the early 1650s came to see the Dutch as bad republicans and bad Protestants, because they had been unwilling to write off the House of Orange completely and enter into a deal with the English for an aggressive Protestant foreign policy, which prevented any closer union at the time.[25] Arthur Weststeijn meanwhile has drawn attention to the fact that the Dutch also rejected English advances in the 1650s because they, in turn, did not see the English as proper republicans. To them, the English Commonwealth was nothing but an illegitimate regicide regime that was no better than the monarchy of Charles I. They also regarded the high degree of centralisation in the English polity as contradicting their own republican principles, in particular after the rise of Oliver Cromwell as its leader and quasi-monarchical figure. The Dutch federal system as a league of provinces, meanwhile, demonstrated a very different understanding of a republic.[26] The fact that the Dutch were now dealing with republicans many of whom had themselves been critical of Cromwell may have eased the situation. But any new alliance between Dutch and English republicans would have had to overcome a number of obstacles, and trust would have to be rebuilt on both sides. What seems most remarkable in this context is that the English republican faction, now operating from their continental exile, acted almost as if they were still the legitimate rulers of England, deprived of their rightful position by the incoming king and intent on reclaiming their power at the next opportunity. In keeping with this attitude, the exiles tried to revive and recreate their old alliances from the Commonwealth period with the choice of William Nieuwpoort, the former Dutch ambassador to the Rump, as their chief contact. In fact, the exiles attempted to pick up where they had left off before the Restoration.

According to Ludlow's manuscript account, the start of the Second Anglo-Dutch War was considered an opportunity to act, both because English and Dutch republicans shared a common enemy in Charles II and because the English government would be too preoccupied with foreign affairs to have much capacity left to police the political underground at home. In early 1665 a contact of the exiles in the United Provinces was therefore employed to 'feele the pulse of the Dutch, touching their uniting with the honest party in England against Charles Steward'.

---

[25] Pincus, *Protestantism and Patriotism*, pp. 27–8.
[26] Arthur Weststeijn, 'Why the Dutch Didn't Read Harrington: Anglo-Dutch Republican Exchanges, c. 1650–1670', in Mahlberg and Wiemann (eds), *European Contexts for English Republicanism*, pp. 105–20.

The go-between made 'hopefull progress', as Ludlow reported – so much so that one of his fellow regicides and exiles in Vevey, William Say, made his way to the United Provinces 'for the certifying of himself & others in the truth of the particulars', while Sidney turned to Ludlow for help, asking him for a meeting in Basel.[27] There is no evidence that Ludlow ever attended such a meeting, and he also seems to have been immune to the pleas of Say, who urged him in various letters to come to the United Provinces and offer his help and support to the cause by joining the plotters' councils. Say tried to assure Ludlow that the Dutch would make safe allies and provide security for the exiles during their undertaking, while their joint action against the English monarchy would also help the Protestant party in France, who feared for their own safety. In the meantime, Say had also met with Nieuwpoort, who promised the exiles that 'they had in their fleete thirty thousand men, of which a third parte were Land souldiers, which should be disposed of as a councell heere of our own should advise & direct, . . . and that their whole fleet should be at our Comand in Order to promote our designe'.[28]

The Dutch for their part seemed perfectly serious about backing the exiles. Among others, Nieuwpoort urged them to set up a council of English republicans and Dutch representatives to discuss further moves in their common design. The plan hatched by Sidney, Say and others was to free another military man, Major General John Lambert, from prison in Guernsey and to put him and Ludlow in charge of the troops.[29] While they were still pressing Ludlow to join the plot, Sidney and Say continued their talks with Nieuwpoort at his country house. According to the information Ludlow received in a letter from Say in late May, rebels in England and Scotland were 'ready to rise at 5 days warning' and 'a very considerable Body' of them was 'ready to draw together in the North, and also in the West of England, and that all thinges [were] as well as they [could] wish'. The exiles were asking for 4,000 foot soldiers to land at Newcastle, 'which is promised to be delivered to them, & which they hope to posess as soone as the fight is over'. In another letter, Sidney confirmed: 'thinges are ready, parties will appear in the North, the west, & London, Newcastle will be delivered, to any who with a small force will come to take it' – a role that had been earmarked for Ludlow, so that he should 'make all Imaginable hast' to come and join the plotters. As their plans developed, Sidney increasingly put pressure on Ludlow to come to

---

[27] Ludlow, 'Voyce', p. 1056.   [28] Ibid., p. 1058.
[29] Ibid., p. 1059. Ludlow wrongly has Jersey instead of Guernsey.

the exiles' aid. When he hesitated, they even accused him of 'not only disliking the meanes, but the thinge itselfe, to wit, the publique Cause' and jeopardising their plans by his absence. Slingsby Bethel too urged Ludlow to make up his mind and tell the plotters clearly whether he was to join or not, so that they could proceed accordingly. But Sidney was the one most insistent – to no avail.[30]

Ludlow's refusal to participate in the plot eventually led to a temporary fall-out between the two men. Ludlow had long had serious reservations about Sidney's plan and about dealing with the Dutch, who, as he objected, were not trustworthy because they 'prefer[red] their Trade before the honour of God & Christ'. His particular bugbear meanwhile was the extraordinary rendition of Barkstead, Corbet and Okey, with the knowledge, though not necessarily consent, of De Witt three years previously, while he was also unwilling to risk his position in Switzerland, as the authorities of Bern had advised Ludlow to stay away from any plotting that might upset relations between the Swiss and Restoration England. Besides, Ludlow recently had word from an acquaintance that Lisle's assassin was now after him, and so had decided to withdraw for a while.[31]

In the meantime, the Dutch had suffered a significant setback at the Battle of Lowestoft on 13 June. They had lost sixteen ships, and the rest had withdrawn across the North Sea. The fleet's commander Jacob van Wassenaar, Lord of Obdam, had died, and it would take a significant restructuring of the fleet, with Michiel De Ruyter at its head, Cornelius Tromp as second in command and De Witt himself acting as a deputy, to turn Dutch fortunes around.[32] The Dutch losses meanwhile had also dealt a blow to the exiles' expectations. Ludlow had received information from his contacts in London that there were 'Divissions . . . amongst our party' which also did not give 'ground for so great hopes'.[33] Yet this did not deter Sidney for now. Despite Ludlow's concerns over the extraordinary rendition of the three regicides, and convinced that De Witt had been tricked by Downing in delivering them, he personally travelled to The Hague to negotiate with the Grand Pensionary.[34] But the talks soon came to a halt.

---

[30] Ibid., pp. 1065–6, 1079–80.
[31] Ibid., pp. 1056–7, 1059. This withdrawal was, among other things, intended to confuse the enemy, who was thus led to believe that Ludlow might have left Switzerland to join the plotters (ibid., 1059–60).
[32] Herbert H. Rowen, *John de Witt: Statesman of the 'True Freedom'* (Cambridge, UK: Cambridge University Press, 1986), pp. 115–17.
[33] Ludlow, 'Voyce', pp. 1069–71, 1079.
[34] Catterall, 'Sir George Downing and the Regicides', p. 278.

Whether because of Ludlow's unwillingness to lead the military operation or a lack of trust in Sidney's ability, De Witt seemed convinced neither by the feasibility nor even by the desirability of such a plot.[35] After all, during the Commonwealth England had risen to become a genuine competitor at sea, while the Restoration monarchy seemed relatively negligible in comparison. Why change that balance of power by assisting the English opposition? According to Downing, De Witt had advised the plotters after the Battle of Lowestoft that 'matters were not yet ripe for [th]em, by reason of [th]e late defeate'. But if William Scott was to be believed, the exiled republicans had not yet given up: '*one Captaine Philips*' was 'to *goe for England* to sound and prepare humours there, [tha]t so they may have something of grounded to propose to *De Witt*', and '*one Collonell Woogan*', whom Downing believed to be another regicide, was to follow shortly. The plotters were also expecting 'several more of their *fellows here*'.[36] By the end of 1665 the plotters had removed their headquarters to Rotterdam, but, amid divisions between the exiles themselves, not much else had happened.

However, the plotters were not willing to give up so soon. Some 'friends to the Commonwealth' also had high expectations that 1666 was 'a tyme to be doing something for the honest Interest'. It was 'the Year of the Beast' from the Book of Revelation, the year 'in which many of the Lords people hoped to see the accomplishment of great thinges in order to the pulling downe of AntiChrist; and the setting up of Christs Kingdome', and Ludlow was once again called upon to help.[37] According to the news he received from the United Provinces, the Dutch were prepared to help the English dissenters, but the 'mixt Counsels' were now to take place at Paris, where the French king was reportedly willing to offer 'all security Imaginable'.[38] Thus the French were drawn into the plot as allies of the Dutch after declaring war on England in January 1666. While this move strengthened the opposition to the English monarchy, it also involved another party in the plot that may not have shared the same aims and objectives with English and Dutch republicans and may eventually have contributed

[35] Van Santvoord, *Life of Algernon Sidney*, p. 182.
[36] Sir George Downing, The Hague, to Lord Chancellor Clarendon, 23 June 1665, in Lister, *Life and Administration of Edward, First Earl of Clarendon*, iii, pp. 385–9, at p. 388. Note that Ludlow used the alias Philips (see Chapter 3 above). Maybe the exiles were still hoping to use him as a go-between.
[37] Ludlow, 'Voyce', p. 1107. See David Brady, '1666: The Year of the Beast', *Bulletin of the John Rylands University Library of Manchester*, 61 (1979), 314–36; Warren Johnston, *Revelation Restored: The Apocalypse in Later Seventeenth-Century England* (Woodbridge: Boydell, 2011), pp. 56–8.
[38] Ludlow, 'Voyce', p. 1111.

to its failure. Louis XIV was first of all interested in weakening the English government rather than helping to re-establish a republic, and many of the exiles were highly suspicious of the popish power.[39] However, the involvement of the French was not necessarily the sole choice of Sidney, who had turned to Louis XIV for help after having failed to convince De Witt of his project, as is sometimes suggested.[40] The referral to the French king was also a result of the close collaboration at this point between the Dutch and the French against Charles II. De Witt recommended Sidney to the French ambassador in the United Provinces, the Comte d'Estrades, and asked him to provide passports for Sidney and Ludlow, who were allegedly waiting in Frankfurt at the time, to go to France. D'Estrades reassured Louis that Sidney and Ludlow were 'deux personnes de grand mérite' – two individuals of great merit – who desired to see the French king to discuss important issues.[41]

We do not know exactly what Sidney promised the king of France, but it may have been a bit rash to suggest that Ludlow was ready to join the scheme, or even waiting for a passport in Frankfurt. To all intents and purposes Ludlow was still in Switzerland and remained stubborn in his refusal to join a conspiracy he considered doomed from the start. According to the manuscript of Ludlow's memoirs, he had received various letters from allies in the United Provinces informing him of the scheme and urging him to participate. And the terms seemed fair enough. According to John Phelps, 'de Wit, Newport & others of the honest party in Holland are hearkening after what may be done by the discontented party in England, expressing themselves most willing to assist them'. For the suggested meeting in Paris, Ludlow was offered 'all security Imaginable from the King of france', and he was to 'be lodged at the Embassadors of Hollands howse'. There, 'a Treaty' was to be concluded 'Joyntly by the King of france & Holland' with Sidney and Ludlow 'with all faithfulness & secrecy'. Phelps had further added that it was 'not a motion at Randome, but of great intentness, the King of France having already offered lardgely in it' and therefore asked for Ludlow's thoughts on the matter. Ludlow was further assured that 'the whole body of friends in that Citty [of Rotterdam]' involved in the affair 'had fixed their Eyes, and heart

---

[39] *Mémoires de Louis XIV, écrits par lui-même, composés pour le grand dauphin, son fils, et addressés à ce prince*, ed. J. L. M. de Gain-Montagnac, 2 vols (Paris: Garnery, 1806), ii, p. 242.

[40] Scott, *Algernon Sidney and the English Republic*, p. 181.

[41] AD, Lot-et-Garonne, Fonds Lagrange-Ferregues, 11 J 18, 'Un régicide anglais à Nérac', pp. 180–9, at p. 184. This is confirmed by K. H. D. Haley, *An English Diplomat in the Low Countries: Sir William Temple and John de Witt, 1665–1672* (Oxford: Clarendon Press, 1986), p. 90.

upon me & Col Sidney', promising him 'safe conduct' and 'full assurance for my abode there, to the utmost of what I could expect'. They urged Ludlow to follow 'the Lords Call to a glorious worke, wherein the Interest of the Lords people throughout the world was concerned'. Once again, both Say and Sidney wrote to Ludlow in Switzerland urging him to change his mind and join the plotters. Sidney's letter asked Ludlow for a meeting at Basle, where he hoped he would be able to 'easily remove any scruples of Conscience' Ludlow might still have, if only he could speak with him. And Sidney even apologised for his earlier angry outbursts at Ludlow to win him for the project. Likewise, Say urged in another letter to Ludlow that all depended on him, as Ludlow reported: 'all there [in Rotterdam], will goe with me If I goe, but if I refused, he believed not a man would stir'.[42]

Sidney had already met his French contact, Louis XIV's resident at Metz, who gave him the letters of safe-conduct for both himself and Ludlow ordered by d'Estrades. But Ludlow rejected his advances yet again.[43] He had made some concessions, saying that he might be able to collaborate with the Dutch if they acknowledged fault in the extradition of Barkstead, Corbet and Okey, but it was out of the question that he would ever trust the French. There may have been a degree of paranoia in Ludlow's attitude, but he suspected that some of the hired assassins that had followed the exiles to Switzerland, and had already claimed the life of Lisle, had been sent by the French court.[44] Moreover, France was the ultimate home of absolutism, Catholicism and everything the exiles hated and despised. Collaboration with the French made the plot entirely unacceptable both to Ludlow and eventually also to some of the other exiles around Phelps, who preferred to rely on Dutch support only.[45] By this time Ludlow had come to the conclusion that the exiles' negotiations at Paris had become 'not only fruitless but dangerous' because it was unlikely that the French would assist them, unless they could show they had 'a party so considerable, as to make it effectuall', but also not least because the French king was at the same time corresponding with Charles II, and Ludlow feared that Louis might betray the plotters to his cousin.

---

[42] Ludlow, 'Voyce', pp. 1111–13.
[43] Scott, *Algernon Sidney and the English Republic*, p. 183; Ludlow, 'Voyce', p. 1114; and Van Santvoord, *Life of Algernon Sidney*, pp. 182–3.
[44] Ludlow, 'Voyce', p. 922. The French clearly knew of the assassination of Lisle in Switzerland, although there is no proof that they instigated the plot. AE, Mémoires et Documents, Angleterre, 7MD/29, Négotiations, 1662–4, fols 169v–170r. On the assassination of Lisle, see Chapter 3.
[45] Phelps may have changed his mind after consulting with Ludlow. He would return to Switzerland soon afterwards.

Ludlow thus agreed with the faction around Phelps, who had decided to withdraw to the United Provinces, while Sidney travelled to Paris accompanied by the former Cromwellian chaplain Nicholas Lockyer and Colonel John White.[46] According to the *Mémoires* of Louis XIV, Sidney asked for 100,000 écus to produce a great uprising in England.[47] But the king was reluctant to risk such an amount of money 'on the word of a fugitive'. He committed 20,000 instead and promised more later if he could see results.[48] Alas, at this stage, Sidney had already lost the backing of the majority of the exiles, while Ludlow declined a new invitation to join Phelps and his faction in the United Provinces. With support waning on all sides, Sidney finally decided to act without Ludlow. He 'volunteered to command the invasion [of England] directly from Paris leading the French troops' himself. However, his scheme failed when he tried to free Lambert from prison in Guernsey with the help of two Frenchmen, who were discovered and executed.[49] Sidney had failed.

The remaining hopes of the exiles in the United Provinces now rested on Ludlow almost until the very end of the Second Anglo-Dutch War and its conclusion with the Treaty of Breda. When the Dutch fleet was setting sail for England in the summer of 1667, Ludlow was once again approached by his countrymen in the United Provinces to come over and engage on the side of the Dutch against the English. His specific task would have been to command land forces on the Dutch fleet – a task that was for the time being assigned to Colonel Doleman, 'an Englishman' as well as 'an Experienced Officer and wellwissher to the publique Interest', who had refused to surrender to the English government. But Ludlow could not be persuaded, as he did not get sufficient assurance from the Dutch government that it regretted its part in the seizing of the three

---

[46] Ludlow, 'Voyce', p. 1122; and Scott, *Algernon Sidney and the English Republic*, p. 184. Although Ludlow does not give first names here, this must have been Nicholas Lockyer, who was a chaplain under Oliver Cromwell in Scotland in 1651, not 'John' Lockyer as Scott assumes. Nicholas Lockyer had fled to Rotterdam in September 1666 to 'escape prosecution under the Act of Uniformity.' See E. C. Vernon, 'Lockyer, Nicholas (1611–1685)', *ODNB*, and Anne Laurence, *Parliamentary Army Chaplains, 1642–1651* (Woodbridge: Boydell, 1990), p. 75. 'Colonel White' is John White, identified in Ludlow's *Memoirs* as one of the men recalled to England 'to surrender themselves into the hands of some justice of the peace in the county where they should land'. *Memoirs of Edmund Ludlow: With a Collection of Original Papers, and the Case of King Charles the First* (London: printed for T. Becket and P. A. de Hondt, and T. Cadell, in the Strand; and T. Evans, in King Street, Covent Garden, 1771), p. 453.

[47] 1 écu was worth 3 livres tournois. In today's money this may have been (very) roughly a million pounds.

[48] *Mémoires de Louis XIV*, pp. 242–3. Scott quotes this passage from a later edition of the *Mémoires* in *Algernon Sidney and the English Republic*, p. 184. I have made use of his translation.

[49] Ludlow, 'Voyce', pp. 1124, 1127–8.

regicides at Delft and would ensure the safety of the English republicans fighting on its side. He had his suspicions confirmed after the Raid on the Medway, when it became clear to him 'that the Dutch had never any reall Intention to doe the honnest party of England any good', but instead looked after their own self-interest, unwilling 'to doe any thinge that might render their Accord with Charles Steward difficult'. For in the Treaty of Breda they still promised 'to deliver up such whom they call Regicides, bound into the Hands of their Enemyes'.[50]

The Failure of the Plot

Thus the plot did finally fail. But it would be wrong to assume that it failed because there was no republican cause to speak of.[51] It failed over the mutual distrust of the different parties who were joined in an unlikely and rather unhappy alliance. Ludlow did not trust the Dutch after the extra-dition of Corbet, Barkstead and Okey; and he did not trust the French either, who had been sending assassins across the border to target the regicides. Louis XIV (and possibly De Witt too) did not trust Sidney to succeed with his plans, not least because Ludlow refused to back the scheme and participate as its military leader. And finally, the exile com-munity split over the best plan of action. We might also question whether or not the Dutch and French in fact trusted each other, given that the Dutch negotiated a peace with the English to end the Second Anglo-Dutch War in 1667, but the French three years later separately agreed in the Secret Treaty of Dover to supply money and troops to the English king, which saved him from having to call a Parliament and would enable him to return the country to Catholicism, while the English promised their support of France against the Dutch. Thus the French king remained undecided over whose side he was on. The only sure thing was that he wanted to dominate England in both cases: either through destabilising it by helping the opposition, or by keeping Charles II in permanent depen-dency on his financial support.

However, while the French king was playing a double game, so was Sidney. In 1670 he travelled from Montpellier, where he had temporarily withdrawn from politics and plotting, to Paris to meet his old friend Turenne, who had formerly been a man of the Fronde but had eventually taken the side of the king and become leader of his troops as well as a

---

[50] Ibid., pp. 1144–5, 1148, 1151, 1152–4.
[51] See Van Santvoord, *Life of Algernon Sidney*, pp. 182–3.

diplomatic agent. In their talks at Versailles, Sidney approached France once again in the hope of coming to an arrangement with Charles II. In their conversation, held around July 1670, which has been discussed in Chapter 2 above, Sidney offered his 'services to the King of Great Britain', saying that he was motivated by the three key principles of his fellow Parliamentarians, which were aimed at 'the ruin of the Dutch', the 'cutting down of the Spanish' and 'a close union with France' for the 'augmentation of their commerce'. However, he was also hoping for liberty of conscience, which he saw as the only thing that could end the conflict between the Crown and the dissenters. As we saw earlier, Sidney also appeared favourable towards extending liberty of conscience to Catholics, who were less hated by republicans than were the Anglican hierarchy.[52]

However, it is fair to assume that Sidney's appealing offer was nothing more than another attempt to curry favour and pursue his own interests. In the longer term, he certainly had no intention of supporting a closer Anglo-French alliance. On the contrary, he had predicted less than four years previously, just after the failure of his European plot when he had withdrawn to Montpellier, that the French domination of the Continent was about to come to an end. From his exile in the Languedoc, he had sent his friend Furly in Rotterdam a mysterious 'Prophesy of St Thomas the Martyr', which refers to an apocalyptic struggle between Catholics and Protestants in Europe, in which the '*Lilly*' (France) would lose its crown to the 'Son of Man' with backing from the 'Land of the *Lion*' (the United Provinces), the 'Land of Wool' (England) and the '*Eagle*' (the empire).[53] Whether this curious pamphlet is a document of Sidney's intense religiosity or rather a thinly veiled political message in the wake of his failed plot, or both, it clearly shows that France was no more than a temporary pawn in his game.

While the actual Sidney plot failed or failed to materialise for lack of money, organisation and, most importantly, mutual trust between the parties involved, we should nevertheless caution against seeing this failure as the end of the republican cause. While republicans did not achieve a

---

[52] See AE, Correspondence Politique, Angleterre, 8CP/99, 1670, Supplément, pp. 270–1, Louis XIV, St Germain, to Colbert, 29 July 1670.

[53] *Copy of a Prophecy Sent to B:F: in the Year 1666 from Montpelliers by the Late Honourable Alguernon Sidney Esqr. & by Him Accidentally Found among Old Papers This 18/28 February 1689.* Copies can be found in the Koninklijke Bibliotheek in The Hague at KB Pflt 11838 and in the British Library at 1103.f.27(15) and 1103.f.27(16). Endorsed by Furly, the original survives in the Bodleian Library, Oxford, MS Engl. Letters C200, fols 24–5. See Scott, *Algernon Sidney and the English Republic*, p. 231 and n., as well as Carswell, *The Porcupine*, pp. 151–2. I shall discuss this mysterious prophecy in more detail in Chapter 6.

restoration of the Commonwealth, liberty of conscience for religious dissenters or popular sovereignty with a fully accountable government, the negotiations among republicans and with their allies at home and abroad kept their aims alive. They also produced a document trail as well as a number of republican works that were published by later generations detailing the hopes and fears of contemporary activists and political thinkers. Without them we would know little about the evolution of republican ideas over time and the survival of policies into mainstream political culture over the course of the seventeenth and eighteenth centuries. With their political writings and transterritorial activism, the republican exiles in Europe thus contributed to an ongoing political discourse about good government that is too important to be dismissed. And as the republican cause evolved, so did the exiles' ideas and identities as political agents.

The Evolution of English Republican Ideas in Exile

When the Stuart monarchy was restored in May 1660, the situation for English republicans had changed almost overnight. Many of those who had previously been respected military leaders and government representatives lost their social position and were reduced to the status of persecuted fugitives. Their personal, political and religious liberty was severely curtailed as they withdrew into the political underground or into foreign exile, and their survival came to depend to a considerable extent on the help they received from old and new allies. Nevertheless, the republican cause survived, not least because those who defended it still clung to their hope of once again restoring the Commonwealth government in England and, in the case of the exiles, of returning home. None of the three exiles discussed here permanently turned their back on their home country. On the contrary, they continued to see themselves as patriots and defenders of their cause and their country, no matter what government it was currently under. However, with their experience of flight, persecution and underground political activism, the exiles underwent significant changes of their political roles and identities. The remaining part of this chapter aims to capture some of these longer-term developments through the language the republicans used to describe their exile experience. In what follows, we will see that the refugees' initial feelings of rejection, hatred, displacement and fear soon gave way to more pragmatic approaches to their enforced life abroad and helped to create new alternative roles and identities.

Seventeenth-century English republicans had several different yet related political and religious identities. On the one hand, republican thinkers modelled themselves on the Western European classical humanist ideal of the citizen going back to Aristotle and Cicero, stressing the centrality of political participation, which they linked with their more immediate demands for popular sovereignty, the rule of law and full accountability of political rulers in their own country, as we have seen above. On the other hand, most English republicans were at the same time Reformed Protestants or Puritans who saw themselves as members of God's invisible Church around the world.[54] Their self-image was therefore at once political and religious, national and transnational. This independent sense of public duty also meant that the pursuit of their aims did not prevent them from temporarily serving or submitting to different governments, or indeed considering military action against the government of their own country.

English republicans defined the role of the citizen with Aristotle as that of an individual who participated 'in the administration of justice, and in offices',[55] i.e. as that of an active member of the political nation, endowed with political agency by the authorities of the state. While they used the term 'citizen' itself primarily with reference to the Greek and Roman city-states, they nevertheless shared its notion of public duty, virtue and merit in their own political context for the members of the English polity.[56] All citizens were equal in principle, but special merit and virtue could advance an individual to leadership.[57] Citizens could therefore act either in a private or in a public capacity, if they acted in a leading role that elevated them over their fellow citizens. While the change of regime in the spring of 1660 changed their employment and personal situation, it did not change the republicans' sense of public duty. In fact, their sense of themselves as political actors was to an extent independent of the government they served, which agrees with the observations made by Patrick Collinson, Steve Hindle, Mark Goldie and others on the compatibility of an ethos of

---

[54] John Coffey, 'Puritanism and Liberty Revisited: The Case for Toleration in the English Revolution', *Historical Journal*, 41:4 (1998), 961–85; J. C. Davis, 'Religion and the Struggle for Freedom in the English Revolution', *Historical Journal*, 35:3 (1992), 507–30; Worden, 'Classical Republicanism and the Puritan Revolution'; Blair Worden, 'Providence and Politics in Cromwellian England', *Past and Present*, 109 (1985), 55–99.

[55] Aristotle, *Politics*, p. 62.

[56] e.g. Sidney in the *Court Maxims* stresses 'virtue' and 'piety' (p. 2) as key characteristics of good subject-citizens and courtiers. The 'seeds of virtue' (p. 3) in a courtier show the quality of his standing, while 'virtue' should be 'cherished' (p. 7).

[57] See Sidney, *Discourses*, ed. West, chapter 2, section 1, pp. 79–80, referring to Aristotle's *Politics*.

citizenship with monarchical structures.[58] Republicans saw themselves as servants of their country first and foremost, while their country's form of government might be subject to change.

As we have seen above, Sidney had originally stated that he would not be able to serve a monarchy. He had still claimed until shortly before the Restoration that he would retreat if the Stuarts returned to power. Yet he changed his mind as soon as it was clear that a return to some form of monarchical rule was inevitable.[59] However, he emphasised throughout that his service was to England rather than to the Stuart regime, and stubbornly refused to apologise for his service to the Commonwealth even as he was seeking employment under the monarchy. Thus he wrote to his father in late May 1660 that he had 'served England' as an ambassador when negotiating a peace between Sweden and Denmark to secure trading interests in the Baltic Sound, 'and consequently him that is at the head of it'. If he was to serve the Stuarts in future it would be only because the people had consented to a restoration and things had been conducted according to the rule of law: 'Since the Parliament hath acknowledged a king, I knowe, and acknowledge, I owe him the duty and the service that belongs unto a subject, and will pay it. If things are carried in a legall and moderate way, I had rather be in employement, than without any.' Sidney was well aware, however, that the new regime might not trust him enough to see him in office, in which case he claimed to be 'almost as well contented with a private life, or liberty to goe beyond sea'. He even wrote a letter to the new king, to be delivered via his uncle Northumberland, although we do not know whether this letter ever reached its addressee. If it did, it cannot have been very effective since Sidney's pride led him to 'omitte the points that I judge to be most useful, which are congratulation and acknowledgement of our faults, in having bin against this king, or his father'. He was simply not able to act against his own principles. 'The truth is', he wrote, 'I could hope for noe gooed in a business that I should beginne with a lye, and chose rather to say, only such things as concerne our negociation, or relating to the future, are such as I will make good.'[60]

That Sidney had found it hard to take his leave from active politics is most obvious in his letter written to his father from Stockholm on 27 June

---

[58] For a compatibility of civic duty with a monarchical framework, see Collinson, 'The Monarchical Republic', and Collinson, *De Republica Anglorum*; Hindle, 'Hierarchy and Community'; Goldie, 'The Unacknowledged Republic'. See also Borot, 'Subject and Citizen'.

[59] See Chapter 1.

[60] Algernon Sidney, Copenhagen, to Robert, Earl of Leicester, 28 May 1660, in Blencowe (ed.), *Sydney Papers*, pp. 181–8, at pp. 187–8.

1660 after receiving 'the Newes of the Kings Entry into London'.[61] As we have seen above, for a while he had been seriously considering whether or not to continue in his current position. On the one hand, he was 'unwilling to stay in a Place, wheare I have bin long under a Character that rendred me not inconsiderable, now that my Powers are extinguished, and I am left in a private Condition'. On the other hand, he was unwilling to leave, in case the King might decide to send him 'newe Orders'.[62] Sidney made a clear distinction between his office and public function, and his 'private' condition, apparently preferring the former. And he was ready to receive the king's order. He also stayed because he was first and foremost, as he put it, a 'Servant to my Country', for whom public duty was not necessarily bound to a specific government. He also appeared to have sufficient 'Respect' for Charles II, who had been welcomed back into England as king, to wait for his instructions. Only when no instructions from the new regime were forthcoming did Sidney take his father's advice to stay abroad for the time being.[63]

By the end of July 1660, he was still 'doubtfull' of his 'condition in England'. Letters from his friends in England had made it clear to him that although he would have been able to retire 'into as private a life as any man in England is in', his own experience from the Cromwellian days had shown him that a life of dependence on his political enemies would not be particularly comfortable. Sidney acknowledged that he owed 'all duty and service unto the king' as his 'lawfull soveraigne', but he also knew that he would never feel completely safe unless the king showed him through an official act of favour that he had forgiven him for his opposition during the Civil War and Interregnum period. So he decided to stay across the Channel. He would have liked to share his diplomatic experience with Charles II, but he felt that both he and his efforts had been 'disowned and slighted' to such an extent that he stood little chance of being heard. He chose 'voluntary exile' as 'the least evill condition' in his reach. He had not yet decided where to settle, but he knew for certain that he disliked 'all the drunken countries of Germany, and the north' and was also at this stage 'not much inclined to France' yet. So he decided on Italy for the time being.[64]

---

[61] Algernon Sidney, Stockholm, to Robert, Earl of Leicester, 27 June 1660, in Collins (ed.), *Letters*, ii, pp. 690–1.
[62] Ibid., p. 690.
[63] Algernon Sidney, Copenhagen, to Robert, Earl of Leicester, 14 July 1660, in Collins (ed.), *Letters*, ii, pp. 691–4, at pp. 691, 694, 691.
[64] Algernon Sidney, Copenhagen, to the Earl of Leicester, 28 July 1660, in Blencowe (ed.), *Sydney Papers*, pp. 189–94, at pp. 189–91.

All the while, however, Sidney was aware that he might 'never ... returne' to see his father or his 'owne countrey again'. He knew that this was in part his own fault as he did not show any remorse for his actions during the Civil War and Interregnum period, none of which he considered 'as a breach of the rules of justice or honour', and he was too proud to change his mind, saying that 'I had rather be a vagabond all my life, than buy my being in my own country at soe deare a rate'. Like Ludlow, he was guided by God and his conscience, claiming that 'I walk in the light God hath given me; if it be dimme or uncertaine, I must beare the penalty of my errors.'[65]

While Ludlow was an outspoken enemy of monarchy in principle, in Sidney's case it was initially the monarchy rejecting the republican exile, not the republican exile rejecting the monarchy – at least not yet. The most severe punishment for Sidney was to remain excluded from public office and from participation in the politics of his home country.[66] As we have seen above, he considered exile to be a 'great evil' and felt rejected by a country that would not accept him on his own terms.[67] Sidney seemed also more preoccupied by his loss of social position than by any unwanted attention. He was painfully aware of the mismatch between his 'Quality' and station in life and his poor circumstances, which forced him not only to remain abroad, but to live a life well below his aristocratic upbringing. While he was forced by his situation to rely on the kindness of strangers, he nevertheless felt proud to announce to his father that one of these strangers was the Prince Pamphilio, 'Nephewe to the last Pope', who had given him 'very convenient Lodgings in his Villa de Belvedere [near Rome], which is one of the finest of Italy', and that he was enjoying the fresh air of Frascati, while 'every boddy at rome' was 'panting and gasping for Life in the Heat' of June.[68] Sidney rejoiced that even as a 'Vagabond' in this world, 'forsaken of my Friends' and poor, he was yet finding 'Humanity and Civility from thoes, whoe are in the Height of Fortune and Reputation'.[69]

---

[65] Algernon Sidney, Hamburg, to the Earl of Leicester, 30 August 1660, in Blencowe (ed.), *Sydney Papers*, pp. 194–8.
[66] Cf. Rahe, 'Introduction' to *Republics Ancient and Modern*, i, pp. 22–3 on the Greek practice of ostracism.
[67] Undated letter from Algernon Sidney to an unidentified addressee, in Blencowe (ed.), *Sydney Papers*, pp. 199–204, at p. 199. Cf. 'Exile and Liberty' in the Introduction, above.
[68] Algernon Sidney, Frascati, to Robert, Earl of Leicester, 3/13 June 1661, in Collins (ed.), *Letters*, ii, pp. 718–19, at p. 718.
[69] Algernon Sidney, Frascati, to Robert, Earl of Leicester, 23 June/3 July 1661, in Collins (ed.), *Letters*, ii, pp. 720–1, at p. 720.

Sidney was defiant, but his sense of rejection was apparent. While foreign aristocrats were able to see his value and status, his own country apparently did not. This realisation may have hardened him towards the government of Charles II and contributed to his plans for a foreign invasion of England with exile support. As time went on, and once the planned invasion of England had failed, however, Sidney began to make renewed attempts at regaining favour with the monarchy and receiving permission to return home, first through his friendship with Turenne and later through his family's own government connections. His attempts to return to England should not be seen as a reconciliation with the Stuart monarchy, though. They were more likely to have been motivated by the realisation that he would have better opportunities to effect political change from inside the country than from abroad. He still considered himself entitled to some kind of public role, as can be seen from his later attempts to win a parliamentary seat in the 1670s and his struggles against corruption in the electoral system.[70] Sidney finally obtained permission to return to England in April 1677, just months before his father's death – doubtless not least because he was the son of an influential aristocratic family of long standing which had rendered many services to the Crown.[71]

Neville too made a great show of loyalty to the king after his release from the Tower in 1664. In his letters from Italy, he expressed his gratitude to his patron and protector Clarendon for the 'gracious pardon itt pleased the king to give us' and was keen to reassure the lord chancellor of his submission to the restored Stuart monarchy – so much so, he wrote, that 'in the future course of my life I should count itt a great happinesse if itt should ever fall within my power to expresse my obedience & devotion, by any service, to his Ma[jes]tie'. Like Sidney he showed a degree of acceptance of the Restoration government for now, even though this acceptance was the result of necessity rather than choice. However, we should not be fooled by the apparent trust that Neville put in Charles II. In Italy, Neville kept a low profile and steered clear of his own countrymen as far as he could. He assured Clarendon in a letter from Rome: 'I doe very rarely frequent the company of any of our nation, & never but extreamly upon my guard' – a statement that suggests that he was similarly afraid of the wrong sort of attention, if not necessarily of assassination.[72] Like Sidney, Neville had experienced a similar sense of rejection by his own

---

[70] Scott, 'Sidney, Algernon'.   [71] Scott, *Algernon Sidney and the English Republic*, p. 248.
[72] Bodleian Library, Oxford, Clarendon MS 84, fols 78–9, Henry Neville, Rome, to the Earl of Clarendon, 3/13 March 1665/6.

country, to which he responded with defiance. While staying at the court of Ferdinando II in Florence, he wrote to his brother: 'I find a sensible difference between being civilly treated, ... valew'd and esteem'd by princes abroad, and not only hatted but persecuted at home.'[73] Both Sidney and Neville felt rather snubbed by the restored monarchy, which deprived them both of their political role and social status. However, Neville was intent on compensating that rejection by getting as much pleasure as possible out of his stay abroad. As we have seen above, Neville enjoyed both the court life in Tuscany and an affair with a married woman, while also socialising among the rich and powerful in Rome and reluctantly learning the art of flattery. In fact, he seems to have enjoyed Italy so much that he would have shown little inclination to return to England any time soon. Neville frequently expressed his esteem for the 'paradise' of Italy,[74] while his letters to his friend Guasconi from Rome in 1666 show that Neville would have been reluctant to leave Italy, had it not been for his duty towards his friends at home, for which he was even willing to risk imprisonment. Again, it was duty and responsibility for the affairs of others that eventually motivated Neville to return home. The specific circumstances he cited as the reason for his return were important papers entrusted to his care that had been damaged in the Great Fire of London.[75] Nevertheless, he still waited another year before eventually travelling back.

Like Sidney, Neville had benefited from his family connections, which helped his rehabilitation in English society after his period of plotting and exile was over. Both he and Sidney had shown a certain degree of pragmatism and opportunism in their dealings with the Restoration government in order to be able to return to their home country. For both, this had involved giving themselves over to the hands of more powerful royalist relatives and acquaintances and refraining from any open oppositional activity the government might frown upon. This did not mean they had abandoned the republican cause, but it meant that they were willing to let it rest while the time was not right. Both, however, returned to political activism and writing during the government crises of the 1670s and 1680s and contributed to the revival of the republican cause as soon as they saw a chance to promote constitutional change.

---

[73] BRO, D/EN F8/1/11, Henry Neville, Florence, to Richard Neville, London, 20 January 1665
[74] Henry Neville, Rome, to Bernardino Guasconi, 1 and 8 January 1667, in Crinò, 'Lettere inedite', pp. 185–7.
[75] Henry Neville, Frascati, to Bernadino Guasconi, 30 October 1666, in Crinò, 'Lettere inedite', p. 184.

Ludlow meanwhile showed little zest for any form of direct political action. Even though he was an experienced military man, he was the most hesitant of the three exiles to return to the political scene. Naturally, this was in part due to his status as a regicide and a wanted man, even many years after the Restoration. But religious doubts also held him back. Ludlow's political identity was closely bound up with his religious faith and his belief in divine providence, which had carried him to Geneva. In the 'Voyce', he ruminated on 'the great mercy and overruling hand of God' in bringing him safely through France, where he could easily have become prey to 'corrupt interests' had his identity been discovered. 'But the Lord hid me in the hollow of his hand.' And Ludlow prayed, 'O that I might be so affected therewith as to sacrifice the remainder of my life entirely to his praise and service.' He conceptualised his exile primarily in religious, rather than classical republican, terms. Thus he described himself and his fellow exiles as 'sufferers for the Cause of Christ, & the Libertyes of our Country', while his rejection of the Stuart monarchy was primarily based on the king's usurpation of divine rule, as only God could claim to be a legitimate monarch.[76] Unlike Sidney, Ludlow was from the start openly hostile to Charles II, whom he frequently referred to in his draft memoirs as a 'tyrant' and as the 'present Usurper'. Conversely, the friendly welcome received by the exiles in Switzerland 'layd a great Obligation on us to bless the Lord, who had raysed up so many to favour us & our righteous Cause in a forreigne & strandge Land'.[77]

Ludlow also took foiled assassination attempts against the exiles as a sign of the Lord's favour, while he considered the increasing numbers of plague victims in London during the 1660s to be divine punishment for the sinful government of Charles II. Thus Ludlow remarks, 'as the Lord pursues our Enemyes, so doth he Emynently manifest his favour unto us his poore Exiles', and 'the wisedome & goodness of the Lord in providing & presenting us an Asylum is the witness he hath enabled us to beare for Christs Prerogative of ruling in the Consciences of his people, when the powers of the Earth are so generally against him, and his annoynted'.[78] There is little here of the sense of rejection by his country that we have seen with Sidney and Neville. Ludlow saw himself as one of the righteous for whom his exile had a deeper spiritual meaning. He readily submitted to his fate as an outcast and waited for signs from God to lead him. There

---

[76] Ludlow, 'Voyce', p. 822. Some very similar language can also be found in the eighth dialogue of Sidney's *Court Maxims*.

[77] Ludlow, 'Voyce', pp. 1072, 1077, 1134, 966.   [78] Ibid., pp. 1089, 1192.

were occasional hints that he would consider political or military action if he was called upon, but he did not feel safe to return to England until after the Glorious Revolution of 1688–9 had brought in a new government and the hope for an amnesty. Even then, he was not able to stay.

Republican Nostalgia and Visions

Even as the republican exiles where lying low and temporarily condemned to inaction, they still remained nostalgic about the past and continued to dream of an alternative republican order in their home country. Conversations with foreigners in their host countries revealed their idealised view of England in the 1640s and 1650s, giving a hint of what the exiles may have envisaged for their fatherland. One example of such a conversation is that of Sidney with Jean Baptiste Lantin, recorded in a memoir of the councillor to the Parlement of Dijon.

After hearing the news of his pass to visit England, Sidney must have visited Paris at least one more time. During this visit in 1677, he often dined with Lantin, who at the time was lodging in the rue de Tournon. As Lantin recorded, the two would take their dinner at the 'l'hostel d'Antragues' (or 'l'hôtel d'Entragues'), where he experienced Sidney as an 'homme d'esprit' or 'man of wit', but of a somewhat exaggerated republicanism. Apparently, Sidney felt some nostalgia for the time of Oliver Cromwell, but even more for the time preceding that of the 'usurper'.[79] At these dinners, Sidney elaborated on his vision of the republic, and Lantin gives us a remarkable summary of his interpretation of events and republican aims during the 1640s and 1650s. Thus Lantin explains that the English had aimed to model their government on the ancient republics of the Jews before the time of the kings, of Sparta and Rome, and on the more recent example of Venice, taking the best from each of them to create a 'perfect composition'. Three magistrates would have held a key role: the general of the army, the admiral of the navy and the chancellor in charge of the administration of justice, each of whom would have exercised their power for no more than a year, while a permanent council was to supervise their work. There were also financial officers who had to report to their superiors from time to time, while their tenure of office was also limited. There also had been an army consisting of an infantry of 60,000 and a cavalry of 20,000 men as well as 60 well-equipped war ships. When the parliamentary army was on the march, none of the soldiers would have

[79] BNF, MS Français 23254, Lantiniana, fol. 99.

been heard swearing, while games of cards or dice were prohibited, as were prostitutes, and each soldier would have carried an English copy of the Bible in his pocket, while also being well trained through physical exercise.

It is obvious that this vision Sidney outlined bore only a distant resemblance to the realities of the 1640s and 1650s and that he may have idealised the potential of the republican government from a distance, but the compartmentalisation of duties under a number of executive officers who served on a rotational system is also reminiscent of earlier Harringtonian proposals, while the idea of a 'Cons[eil] perpétuel' or 'permanent council' is close to the proposals of Vane and Milton for a standing senate, although Lantin does not report whether this council, according to Sidney, would be made up of either citizens or saints.[80] Sidney was also sure that if Cromwell's son-in-law Henry Ireton had not died in 1651, the republic could have been fully established and Ireton could have prevented the rise of Cromwell by seizing power for himself. Instead, ambition had driven Cromwell like an insolent servant who had been waiting a long time for his turn, even though he knew he could not keep royal power in his family.[81] Sidney also told Lantin about the verse he wrote into the visitors' book at Copenhagen: 'manus haec inimica tyrannis / ense petit placidam cum libertate quidem' ('This hand, an enemy to tyrants, seeks peace and liberty by the sword').[82] Yet, Sidney remarked, all tyrants and usurpers pretended to be enemies of usurpers and tyrants and aimed to re-establish liberty only to oppress the people with even more violence afterwards, and this is what Cromwell had done in Sidney's view.[83] The conversations between Sidney and Lantin also reveal that the republican valued religion above all, but that after the study of theology or the knowledge of God and religion there was no more worthy employment for an honest man than politics.[84] Among the books Sidney rated most highly were Hugo Grotius's *De jure belli ac pacis* (1625) and Juan Márquez's *El gobernador christiano* (1612). His admiration for Grotius is well known. He cited the scholar, for instance, on the Dutch Revolt in his *Court Maxims*, or on the limited power of magistrates as well

---

[80] Ibid., fol. 100. Cf. Henry Vane, *A Healing Question* (London: printed for T. Brewster, 1656); John Milton, *The Ready and Easy Way to Establish a Free Commonwealth*, 2nd ed. (London: Printed for the Author, 1660); Martin Dzelzainis, 'Harrington and the Oligarchs: Milton, Vane, and Stubbe', in Wiemann and Mahlberg (eds), *Perspectives on English Revolutionary Republicanism*, pp. 15–33.

[81] BNF, MS Français 23254, Lantiniana, fol. 100.

[82] This translation is based on Scott, *Algernon Sidney and the English Republic*, pp. 46, 133.

[83] BNF, MS Français 23254, Lantiniana, fol. 101.

[84] On Sidney's religion, see Winship, 'Algernon Sidney's Calvinist Republicanism'.

as on regular parliaments and other matters in the *Discourses*.[85] His respect for the Spanish Augustinian and natural-law theorist Márquez at first sight might be less obvious.[86] However, Sidney shared with him the conviction that the ruler was always subject to positive law. This positive law, according to Márquez, must conform to natural law, which ultimately conformed to the divine will. This was a position that Sidney had just confirmed to Lantin by giving primacy to religion as well as by his frequent recourse to biblical authority in his *Court Maxims*. He clearly shared Márquez's view that Scripture should be taken as a source of advice on statecraft and practical politics. He may also have appreciated Márquez's criticism of Jean Bodin.[87] Moreover, Sidney expressed his admiration for the great legal knowledge of John Selden, who had been consulted by the great and the good and also shared his interest in the Hebrew commonwealth.[88] While Sidney and Lantin exchanged views on a range of topics, meanwhile, this record of their conversations shows most of all how present the world of the English republic still was for Sidney and how much he was still clinging on to his old dreams and ideals. Republican rule in England was by no means a thing of the past. And a return to England for Sidney also meant a return to politics in some form.

Conclusion

As I hope to have shown, the republican exiles who either failed to return to England after the Restoration or had to leave England for fear of their lives never broke with their home country or their public role. Despite the return of the monarchy, Sidney, Neville and Ludlow were aware of their position in society and the political realm, even though their focus may have shifted from the role of representatives of their nation to that of underground activists. In this new position, the republicans' liberty and agency was severely curtailed and they had many hard choices to make between opportunism and inaction. While Sidney tried and failed to stage

[85] Sidney, *Court Maxims*, p. 99; and Sidney, *Discourses*, ed. West, pp. 115, 529.
[86] Sidney may have read the work in the French translation of 1621. For Márquez's translation and reception, see Harald E. Braun, 'The Bible, Reason of State, and the Royal Conscience: Juan Márquez's *El governador christiano*', in Harald E. Braun and Edward Vallance (eds), *The Renaissance Conscience* (Oxford: Wiley-Blackwell, 2011), pp. 118–33, at p. 132.
[87] Braun, 'The Bible, Reason of State, and the Royal Conscience', pp. 119–20, 130; Luis Carlos Amezúa Amezúa, 'La soberanía en "El gobernador cristiano" (1612), de Juan Márquez', *Anuario de filosofía del derecho*, 21 (2004), 75–106; Werner Stark, *The Sociology of Religion: A Study of Christendom*, 5 vols (New York: Fordham University Press, 1966–72), iii, p. 145.
[88] BNF, MS Français 23254, Lantiniana, fol. 101.

a republican plot to restore the Commonwealth in England with the help of foreign troops, Neville's plotting career had come to an abrupt end with his detention in the Tower and subsequent release as the lord chancellor's protégé. Ludlow meanwhile refrained from any underground political action, waiting and hoping to receive a sign from heaven that would guide him on the right path. All three exiles, however, had their views on where they saw England on the political stage and their hopes for the future, and the safest and freest way to express them was through writing. The third and final part of this book will therefore be dedicated to the exiles' political observations, ideas and visions.

PART III

Works of Exile

The works of seventeenth-century English republicans tend to be studied either individually or as part of a more or less coherent republican canon that would come to influence later generations of thinkers in the British Isles and in the American colonies. They are less often situated in the immediate creative context of their authors' lives, not least because intellectual biographies were out of fashion for quite some time.[1] The collective approach to the study of canonical works is due to attempts to find common themes or shared principles across time and space, albeit at the expense of the particular.[2] In the third part of this monograph I will attempt a reading, or re-reading, of several republican works associated with the exiles in their specific contemporary context. My aim is not only to highlight the ways in which the extraordinary circumstances of their production may have impacted on the texts themselves, but also to show how the writing and, in some cases, publication of these works was a continuation of the republican cause by other means – a form of political activism with sometimes serious consequences. In this way, the works of the exiles on the Continent resembled those of other contemporary republicans who decided to stay in England but withdrew into inner exile, such as John Milton.

Literary scholars have come to question the assertion that Milton's *Paradise Lost* (1667) represents 'a guilty retreat from politics and withdrawal into a quiescent concern with individual spirituality'. Instead, they have read the epic as a 'defiant' republican text that continued to criticise

---

[1] This trend seems now to be reversing, with major studies of James Harrington, John Lilburne and John Locke either recently released or currently in preparation by Rachel Hammersley, Mike Braddick and Mark Goldie.

[2] See Quentin Skinner's critique of 'timeless ideas' in 'Meaning and Understanding in the History of Ideas', *History and Theory*, 8 (1969), 3–53.

monarchical power.[3] Likewise, Katherine Gillespie has seen Lucy Hutchinson's *Memoirs* of her husband Colonel John Hutchinson – a close ally of Ludlow, Neville and Sidney – and her biblical epic *Order and Disorder* (1679) as a recovery of 'her husband and republicans in general from oblivion' as she supplants 'their images as demonic rebels condemned to hell' and replaces it 'with that of virtuous republican men whose dedication to the cause earned them a saint's rest in heaven and the satisfaction of seeing their dream realized on earth'.[4] The works by Sidney, Neville and Ludlow were similarly defiant in their criticism of the now restored monarchy and their refusal to give up on the republican cause. While the works discussed are not at all times self-conscious reflections on the experience of exile, I nevertheless aim to show to what extent the exiles' shared experiences described in their correspondence, such as memories of war, persecution, flight, displacement and instability, as well as faith, are also present in their published works and works intended for later publication.

These works of exile were not necessarily great works of literature or political thought, but most of all were works arising from a very specific situation in their authors' lives, often written in haste, limited by censorship and more often than not left unpublished during their authors' lifetimes. While works like Neville's *Isle of Pines* and Ludlow's *Memoirs* became integrated into the republican canon constructed over several generations by editors and philanthropists such as John Toland and Thomas Hollis, Sidney's long-lost *Court Maxims* acquired its canonical status only relatively recently.[5] The enigmatic 'Prophecy' that he sent to

---

[3] Katherine Gillespie, *Women Writing the English Republic, 1625–1681* (Cambridge, UK: Cambridge University Press, 2017), p. 285, referring to Armand Himy, '*Paradise Lost* as a Republican "tractatus theologico-politicus"', in David Armitage, Armand Himy and Quentin Skinner (eds), *Milton and Republicanism* (Cambridge, UK: Cambridge University Press, 1995), pp. 118–34, at p. 119; David Norbrook, *Writing the English Republic: Poetry, Rhetoric, and Politics, 1627–1660* (Oxford: Blackwell, 2001); Barbara Kiefer Lewalski, 'Paradise Lost and Milton's Politics', *Milton Studies*, 38 (2000), 141–68; Reid Barbour, 'Recent Studies in Seventeenth-Century Literary Republicanism', *English Literary Renaissance*, 1:3 (2004), 387–417. Similarly, Laura Lunger Knoppers sees Milton's *Paradise Regain'd* and *Samson Agonistes* (both 1671) 'as part of oppositional discourse, fostering hope and fortifying resistance in dissenters and political radicals'. See her '"Englands Case": Contexts of the 1671 Poems', in Nicholas McDowell and Nigel Smith (eds), *The Oxford Handbook of Milton* (Oxford: Oxford University Press, 2009), pp. 571–88, at p. 587.

[4] Gillespie, *Women Writing the English Republic*, p. 286.

[5] The status of Neville's *Isle of Pines* is ambiguous. While it was among the English republican works republished by Hollis in the eighteenth century, it later seems to have dropped out of the canon – either because scholars did not fully comprehend its political dimension, or because its genre was not considered appropriate for serious discussion. Notably, it was republished together with the first of Neville's *Parliament of Ladies* pamphlets. See The Parliament of Ladies . . . *and* The Isle of Pines, ed. Thomas Hollis (London, 1768).

Furly from Montpellier meanwhile is still rarely discussed in the secondary literature at all, not least because its religious and millenarian style is alien to the secularised historiography of classical republicanism that had also turned Ludlow from a radical Puritan into a defender of citizen militias. And the *Court Maxims* have only recently been rediscovered by Michael Winship as an intensely Calvinist text, leading among others Sidney's foremost biographer Jonathan Scott to reassess the significance of the author as a religious as well as a civic republican.[6] The *Court Maxims* foreshadow many of the themes addressed in Sidney's more famous posthumously published *Discourses*, while also sharing features with Ludlow's 'Voyce from the Watch Tower' and Neville's *Isle of Pines*, not least their engagement with the legitimacy of monarchy, the state of religious dissent and the events, circumstances and consequences of the Second Anglo-Dutch War (1665–7).

All three authors discussed here were opposed to hereditary patriarchal monarchy by divine right. Ludlow's arguments for a republic and against monarchy are primarily based on recent events. Thus he stresses the significance of the Long Parliament as the only true, legitimate power elected by the people, stating that it should never have been dissolved, while the Stuart monarchy for him is lacking in legitimacy because it is an unaccountable secular power usurping God's role on earth. His arguments for a republic and against monarchy are mainly drawn from Scripture, such as the famous passage on tyranny from I Samuel 8. Some of the same scriptural arguments are also employed by Sidney, who in addition expands on some of the more practical absurdities of the hereditary system; this links him to Neville, who ridicules patriarchal monarchy and its alleged scriptural foundations in *The Isle of Pines*.

Similarly, the republican exiles discussed here were all concerned with the issue of religious liberty and dissent. Its strongest advocate was Ludlow, who continuously complained about the oppression suffered by 'the people of God' in England and who sought protection among his Reformed Protestant networks on the Continent. In contrast, Sidney looked at the suppression of dissent more as a systemic problem because he considered it to be the natural consequence of a monarchy backed by an episcopal church. Religious liberty to him could flourish only under a

---

[6] Winship, 'Algernon Sidney's Calvinist Republicanism'; and Jonathan Scott, 'Patriarchy, Primogeniture and Prescription: Algernon Sidney's *Discourses Concerning Government* (1698)', in Cesare Cuttica and Gaby Mahlberg (eds), *Patriarchal Moments* (London: Bloomsbury Academic, 2016), pp. 73–9, at p. 74.

republican form of government. This interpretation of religious liberty as essentially a constitutional issue was also shared by the Harringtonian thinker Neville, who in his major late Restoration work *Plato redivivus* saw political and religious liberty as a natural consequence of economic developments that had come to favour the lesser gentry and the commoners represented in Parliament since the Reformation. However, in his *Isle of Pines* Neville also describes a religion based on the study of the Scriptures and communally practised in informal meetings as 'natural' to the English.

A reformed Protestant faith and a desire for political liberty were also what seventeenth-century English republicans shared with the Dutch, which is why the English exiles after the Restoration attempted to revive their relations with the government of the Grand Pensionary of Holland, Johan de Witt. Many English dissenters had found a new home across the Channel over time, and when preparations for a Second Anglo-Dutch War were getting underway in late 1664, some within the English exile community perceived an opportunity for a joint Protestant republican undertaking as well as a revival of the English Commonwealth. Those in favour of political and military action against the Stuart monarchy supported a plot to invade England with help from the Dutch as well as the French. Those against immediate action meanwhile were guided by caution and an intense distrust of either Dutch or French motives for assisting the exiles. Both sides had a point.

It could be argued that English dissenters and republicans shared a common cause with Protestant republicans in the United Provinces. There had been past attempts at a closer union between the Dutch and the English nations dating back to the time of the English Commonwealth and the First Anglo-Dutch War (1652–4). The aim was a joint Protestant foreign policy to fight attempts at universal monarchy by the French. After Cromwell's dissolution of the Rump in 1653, the English Council of State even presented a proposal to the Dutch to merge the two states in 'a federal union in which each country would maintain intact its own domestic laws', while 'its decisions and appointments would require the approval of the other'. Cromwell's intention was 'to block restoration of the Prince of Orange', and, in return, 'he even offered to abandon the Navigation Act' of 1651 that was so damaging to Dutch trade.[7] In the end, however, this did not happen, as the two countries were also competitors for trade and

---

[7] Rowen, *John de Witt*, p. 41; and Pincus, *Protestantism and Patriotism*.

colonial empire, and self-interest on each side was stronger than any commitment to a common cause.

Moreover, the parallels between the two republican countries were 'more apparent than real'.[8] Dutch republicanism was based on the 'rejection of the tyranny of the kings of Spain' and thus a national movement against rule by a foreign power, while English republicanism developed from a Civil War in which the forces of Parliament had won victory over those of the king. Originally, Dutch republicanism 'had not been directed against the Princes of Orange' at all, even though republicans would later come to reject the stadtholderate.[9] Also, the Dutch Republic was a confederation of provinces, which made it more difficult to take decisions and speak with a common voice, while the English Commonwealth had a strong centralised government – a point that English republicans frequently commented on.[10] Both Milton and Sidney thought that the confederate structure of the United Provinces made the country more vulnerable overall. Milton felt that the sovereignty of each Dutch province was 'oft times to the great disadvantage of that union', while Sidney agreed that the constitutions of the United Provinces 'seem to have a more particular regard to the preservation of the liberties and privileges of each town and province than to the welfare of the whole'. To him the Dutch commonwealth seemed to be 'a vast building of loose stones, which not well cemented, threatens ruin'. However, he also contended that the Dutch people's 'delight in liberty and prosperity, their desire to maintain it, has kept them unanimous in defence against all enemies, though some did think a little accident might disorder and dissolve it'.[11] Dutch Calvinists and English Puritans may also have shared the same faith and were able to agree on dogma, but they held very different views on church government. Like most other continental Reformed churches, 'the Dutch Reformed church was presbyterian in structure, while in Britain the Presbyterians were losing out to the congregationalist Independents', and many Dutch republicans balked at the English regicide. The situation

[8] The quote is from Rowen, *John de Witt*, p. 21. More recently, see also Weststeijn, 'Why the Dutch Didn't Read Harrington'.
[9] Rowen, *John de Witt*, pp. 20, 21.
[10] Arthur Weststeijn, *Commercial Republicanism in the Dutch Golden Age: The Political Thought of Johan & Pieter de la Court* (Leiden: Brill, 2012), pp. 223–4.
[11] John Milton, *The Readie and Easie Way to Establish a Free Commonwealth; and the Excellence Thereof Compar'd with the Inconveniences and Dangers of Readmitting Kingship in This Nation*, 2nd ed. (London: printed for the Author, 1660), p. 96; and Sidney, *Court Maxims*, pp. 172–3.

became even more complex as 'the Stuart cause became entangled with the Orangists' hopes and plans'.[12]

Charles I's eldest daughter, Mary, had been married to William II, and during the Second Civil War in 1648 the future Charles II had moved to The Hague, where he would spend part of his exile at the Dutch court. The premature death of William II in late 1650 meant that Charles's nephew would become the next Prince of Orange as William III – the man who would much later invade England and succeed to the Stuart throne. However, the fortunes of the Prince of Orange were declining as Holland took over leadership of the United Provinces. Much of Charles II's exile thus coincided with the early years of the First Stadtholderless Period in the United Provinces (1650–72), or 'True Freedom', during which the stadtholder was absent in five of the seven provinces, and the rise of the republic under De Witt. The republican government thus coexisted with the Orange dynasty, and an alliance of De Witt's republican party with the English dissenters could easily have upset this delicate balance, while the failure of a common undertaking would have benefited the Orangist interest. It may therefore be understandable that Dutch republican support for the English exiles was not as easily forthcoming as they would have hoped. Nevertheless, the desire was always there to bring the two nations closer together. The possibilities of such an alliance, as well as the future of the political and religious government of their home country, were considered by all three of our authors.

---

[12] Rowen, *John de Witt*, p. 21.

CHAPTER 5

Ludlow's Protestant Vision

'My lord, I stand continually upon the watch-tower in the daytime, and I am set in my ward whole nights ...'

Isaiah 21:8[1]

I had acted according to my light, for the glory of God and the good of mankind.

Edmund Ludlow, 'A Voyce from the Watch Tower'[2]

Introduction: Ludlow as Author and Editor

In the early 1660s, Ludlow was working on two literary projects at the same time. One was his autobiographical 'A Voyce from the Watch Tower', on the Civil War and its aftermath, published in heavily edited form as his *Memoirs* towards the end of the seventeenth century; the other was a less well-known, yet equally significant, translation and editorial project narrating the final days of some of his fellow regicides, largely based on the infamous *Speeches and Prayers of Some of the Late King's Judges* (1660) with some additional content. The two projects are closely related, as the French pamphlet and the process of its publication are documented in the 'Voyce' and may indeed have inspired the writing of the latter. Work on the French edition of the *Speeches and Prayers*, which appeared in 1663 under the title *Les juges jugez, se justifiants*, must have started before the writing of the 'Voyce' as one contains a description of the other. Yet the two projects went hand in hand.

Les juges jugez is the work of a religious and political activist attempting to make the fate of Ludlow's executed brothers known across Protestant Europe. The 'Voyce' is the manuscript of an autobiography or memoir, which was published after its author's death in a carefully edited version

---

[1] Bible quotations are from the King James Version unless otherwise stated.
[2] Ludlow, *Voyce*, ed. Worden, p. 801.

167

that was to serve a political purpose of its own, yet the manuscript shares the former work's desire to render a particular version of recent political events. At the same time, it is a much more personal document of the period. It combines a memoir of the Civil War and Interregnum years in the British Isles with a running commentary of contemporary events as they unfolded during Ludlow's exile – sometimes with extensive quotes from newsletters, printed news publications and official documents – and his personal experiences as an exile in a foreign country. Underlying his writing is a strong spiritual perspective that casts all events into a divine plan and order, whether they are developments on a national or international scale, such as the restoration of the Stuart monarchy,[3] the Plague,[4] the Great Fire of London[5] and the Second Anglo-Dutch War,[6] or very personal circumstances of his exile, such as the fact that he had found a welcoming community in Vevey,[7] or that he was followed and targeted but never caught by assassins.[8] Regarding Ludlow's style and perspective on events, two things are noteworthy. First, he writes as a former statesman and military leader in his confident assessment of politics and warfare: indeed, much of his memoirs consist of detailed descriptions of political events, military operations and the minutiae of battles. Secondly, he also writes as a believer and true follower of the Lord, humbly commending himself into the hands of God and seeing where his providence will take him. In many ways, Ludlow's style and rhetoric reminds us of that of Oliver Cromwell himself in the absolute priority he gives to God's will in his life and his actions, while the individual often retreats behind his purpose and mission.[9]

As Blair Worden has told the story of Ludlow's 'Voyce' and its transformation by John Toland into the carefully edited *Memoirs* most clearly and eloquently, there is no need here to cover the same ground.[10] However, it may be worth pointing out that Toland's edition not only stripped Ludlow's narrative of its religious flourishes, but in doing so also diminished the significance of the exile context in which it was written. While

---

[3] Ludlow, 'Voyce', p. 1132.   [4] Ibid., pp. 1072, 1089.
[5] Ludlow describes the fire as the Lord's manifestation of 'his displeasure to this sinfull & Apostate Citty'. See ibid., pp. 1132, 1130.
[6] Ibid., pp. 1069–71, 1161, etc.   [7] Ibid., pp. 1074, 1090.
[8] Ibid., pp. 998, 1021, 1089, 1160, etc.
[9] J. C. Davis, *Oliver Cromwell* (London: Arnold, 2001), chapter 6, 'Man of God', pp. 112–37.
[10] See Worden's introduction to Ludlow, *Voyce*, 'Whig History and Puritan Politics' and *Roundhead Reputations*. Mark Goldie has recently contributed further details on Toland in *Roger Morrice and the Puritan Whigs: The Entering Book of Roger Morrice 1677–1691* (Woodbridge: Boydell, 2007), i, chapter 5, esp. pp. 212 ff.

Switzerland remained the setting for Ludlow's story, it no longer appeared to have the same significance for Ludlow's religious identity that it had in the 'Voyce'. Naturally, when Toland brought out his first edition of the *Memoirs* in 1698–9 (see Figure 1), he was more interested in drawing attention to problems in England and less in a larger European Protestant cause. In fact, the language of religious enthusiasm had become distinctly suspicious by the later seventeenth century.[11] The Standing Army debate of the late seventeenth and early eighteenth centuries that formed the backdrop to Toland's editorial project was about England's military strength; it was a patriotic cause that highlighted England's special situation rather than its role as one among many European nations. The issue at stake then was the English constitution and the liberties of free Englishmen.[12] To recover some of the work's religious context, however, the second part of this chapter will focus on the 'Voyce' as the story of a spiritual journey of exile which attempted to make sense of the lives of the English regicides in Switzerland in relation to their place in Protestant Europe and the wider world. In this sense, the 'Voyce' and the martyrology of *Les juges* can be seen as complementing each other. Both works share the aim to set the record straight and keep the memory of the republican cause and the regicides alive for posterity, while the latter also served a more immediate political purpose.

Les juges jugez, se justifiants (1663)

Les juges jugez, se justifiants, published in 1663, is a pamphlet based on a number of different English- and French-language sources narrating the stories of thirteen regicides as well as the MP Sir Henry Vane and the Parliamentary general John Lambert, who were excepted from the 1660 Indemnity Act and tried for treason.[13] All but one of them were

---

[11] Worden, 'The Question of Secularisation'; Blair Worden, 'The Commonwealth Kidney of Algernon Sidney', *Journal of British Studies*, 24 (1985), 1–40, at pp. 25–6; and J. P. Carswell, 'Algernon Sidney's "Court Maxims": The Biographical Importance of a Transcript', *Historical Research*, 62:147 (1989), 98–103, at pp. 100–1.

[12] On the standing army debate of the eighteenth century, see among others Lois Schwoerer, *No Standing Armies* (Baltimore: Johns Hopkins University Press, 1974); Pocock, *The Machiavellian Moment*, chapter 12.

[13] With some changes and additions, the following section is based on my article '*Les juges jugez, se justifiants* (1663) and Edmund Ludlow's Protestant Network in Seventeenth-Century Switzerland', *Historical Journal*, 57 (2014), 369–96. The article contains full transcripts of the relevant passages from the French text.

Edmund Ludlow Esq.
Liev.! Gen.!!

Figure 1   *Memoirs of Edmund Ludlow Esq.* (Vivay [*sic*], 1698), vol. i, frontispiece.
© The British Library Board. RB.23.a.11981

executed between October 1660 and June 1662.[14] The first part of the pamphlet was commissioned by Ludlow following the first ten executions of regicides in an act to honour his fellow travellers on the path of righteousness. He had seen to the translation of the regicides' stories during his stay in Geneva, which dates the origins of the work back to the period between late October or November 1660, when Ludlow first heard of the executions of his former allies, and his move to Lausanne in April 1662.[15] The second part of the pamphlet consisted of additions made by the printer as events were unfolding.

Ludlow had been deeply affected by the deaths of those who had fought alongside him for their common cause, and he agreed with the point made by 'one of our first ten Martyrs', John Carew, 'that the faithfull witness' that the executed regicides 'bore to the Kingly Office of Christ' would be 'of great use & advantadge to the Churches of Christ beyond the Seaes'. He therefore saw it as his 'duty' to see to the publication of their 'occasionall speeches' made to friends shortly before their execution, together with the speeches held 'at the place of their Execution, and the breathing of the Spirit in their prayers'. The speeches, as he put it, were to be published 'for the conviction, conversion, edification & strengthening of others'. Ludlow had commissioned the texts to be translated into French when he was in Geneva and now saw to their printing.[16] The text on which Ludlow's commissioned translation was based was a copy of *The Speeches and Prayers of Some of the Late King's Judges* (1660; see Figure 2).[17] The pamphlet itself was contentious, having been published clandestinely in London in at least four editions under slightly varying titles. It was among the works seized in a number of printing shops around London

---

[14] The full title of the pamphlet is *Les juges jugez, se justifiants. Ou recit de ce qui s'est passé en la condamnation & execution de quelques uns des juges du dernier defunct Roy d'Angleterre, & autres seigneurs du parti du Parlement* (n.p., 1663). For the 'Act of Indemnity', see 'Charles II, 1660: An Act of Free and Generall Pardon Indempnity and Oblivion', in *Statutes of the Realm*, v, pp. 226–34. Both Vane and Lambert were also excepted from the Act, despite not being regicides. Vane was executed in June 1662, while Lambert was reprieved.

[15] Ludlow, 'Voyce', p. 948.

[16] Ibid., p. 948. John Carew was the second of the regicides to be executed, on 15 October 1660.

[17] The full title is *The Speeches and Prayers of Some of the Late King's Judges, viz. Major General Harison, Octob. 13. . . . Together with Severall Occasionall Speeches and Passages in Their Imprisonment till They Came to the Place of Execution. Faithfully and Impartially Collected for Further Satisfaction. Heb. 11.4 And by it he being dead, yet speaketh* (n.p., 1660). Ludlow, who was kept informed of events in England through a stream of letters and news publications sent to him by friends and family, must have been in possession of a copy of the first imprint of *Speeches and Prayers*, some passages of which he also included almost verbatim in his 'Voyce'. See J. B. Williams [J. G. Muddiman], 'The Forged "Speeches and Prayers" of the Regicides', *Notes and Queries*, 11th ser., 7 (1913), 301–2, and 8 (1913), 341–2, 383, 442, 502–3.

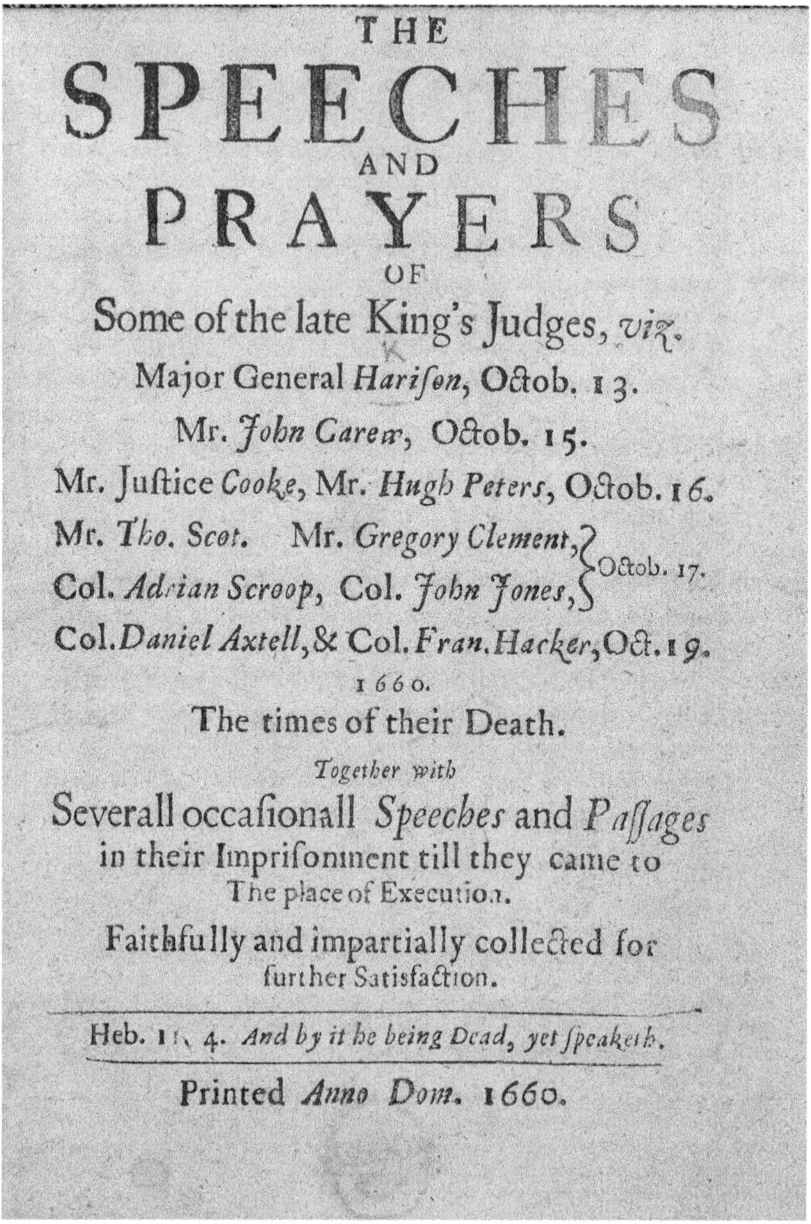

THE
SPEECHES
AND
PRAYERS

OF

Some of the late King's Judges, *viz*.

Major General *Harison*, Octob. 13.

Mr. *John Carew*, Octob. 15.

Mr. Justice *Cooke*, Mr. *Hugh Peters*, Octob. 16.

Mr. *Tho. Scot.* Mr. *Gregory Clement*,⎱
Col. *Adrian Scroop*, Col. *John Jones*,⎰ Octob. 17.

Col. *Daniel Axtell*, & Col. *Fran. Hacker*, Oct. 19.

1660.

The times of their Death.

Together with

Severall occasionall *Speeches* and *Passages*
in their Imprisonment till they came to
The place of Execution.

Faithfully and impartially collected for
further Satisfaction.

Heb. 11, 4. *And by it he being Dead, yet speaketh.*

Printed *Anno Dom.* 1660.

Figure 2   *The Speeches and Prayers of Some of the Late King's Judges* (n.p., 1660), title page.
© The British Library Board. G.3888

during Sir Roger L'Estrange's clampdown on the opposition press after the passage of the 1662 Licensing Act and singled out as 'Treasonous and Seditious' in the new surveyor's *Considerations and Proposals* (1663) for the regulation of the press.[18] The *Speeches and Prayers* would also play a role as incriminating evidence in the arrests made in the context of the 1663 Northern Rising against the Stuart regime.[19] The pamphlet contains narratives of the final days of several of the men responsible for the trial and execution of Charles I in 1649 and now condemned to death for treason by the Restoration regime of Charles II, together with several speeches and prayers and some miscellaneous material, such as letters to friends and family or, in one case, a sermon. The regicides are named on the pamphlet's title page as Major General Thomas Harrison, John Carew, Justice John Cook, Hugh Peters, Thomas Scott, Gregory Clement, Colonel Adrian Scroop, Colonel John Jones, Colonel Daniel Axtell and Colonel Francis Hacker. The text's emphasis is on the suffering of the regicides, dying as 'martyrs' for the 'cause' of religious and political liberty, and their readiness to die in the knowledge that they might be considered guilty by human law, but justified in their actions by God.[20] Numerous passages said to have been spoken by the convicted traitors refer to the justice of their cause and their willingness to die in the knowledge that they would soon be reunited with their creator.[21]

Modern historians have primarily focused on the authenticity of the *Speeches and Prayers*, with the majority taking them at face value and others considering them as forgeries.[22] However, the debate is futile, as contemporaries had been well aware of the fictitious, or at least partially fictitious, nature of the speeches and prayers committed to print. In the pamphlet itself we find phrases such as he 'uttered words to this Effect', indicating that the text transmitted the sense rather than the exact wording of what

---

[18] Roger L'Estrange, *Considerations and Proposals in Order to the Regulation of the Press: Together with Diverse Instances of Treasonous, and Seditious Pamphlets, Proving the Neceßity Thereof* (London: printed by A.C., 1663), p. 11. The 'treasonous' passages are from 'The Publisher to the Reader' of the *Speeches and Prayers*: 'That men may see what it is to have an Interest in Christ in a Dying hour, and to be Faithful to his Cause', and from p. 41: 'I look upon it [the Murther of the King] as the most Noble and high Act of Justice that our Story can Parallel.'
[19] See Williams [Muddiman], 'The Forged "Speeches and Prayers"'; and Greaves, *Deliver Us from Evil*, chapter 7. The government had tried to suppress this publication in 1661. See Elizabeth Clarke, 'Re-reading the Exclusion Crisis', *Seventeenth Century*, 21 (2006), 141–59, at p. 153.
[20] e.g. *Speeches and Prayers*, pp. 14, 6, 13, 16.   [21] Ibid., pp. 4–5, 6.
[22] Compare Matthew Jenkinson, *Culture and Politics at the Court of Charles II: 1660–1685* (Woodbridge: Boydell, 2010), p. 38, with Williams [Muddiman], 'The Forged "Speeches and Prayers"'.

had been said.[23] What mattered to contemporaries was that the *Speeches and Prayers* represented what the regicides and the other convicts *would have* said.[24] Thus Ludlow points out that his printer at Yverdon had added to the official news account of Vane's dying hour 'the substance of what he would have spoake at the tyme of his Execution had he not bin hindred', and that in adding what must be purely fictional material he had 'in some measure done him right'.[25] Of course, it is impossible for us to ascertain what the men sentenced to death for treason actually said before they died. The significance of the *Speeches and Prayers* lies in their propaganda value.[26] It is to be expected that they were carefully edited for effect by supporters of the cause, as had been the case with the sixteenth-century narratives of suffering of the Marian exiles related in John Foxe's *Book of Martyrs*, to which they are often compared and on which the *Speeches and Prayers* may in fact have been modelled.[27] This propaganda value was also clear to Ludlow, who was determined to make the texts more widely available to a greater audience beyond England and the English-speaking world.[28] Ludlow reports in the 'Voyce' that his plan to publish the *Speeches and Prayers* in French met with considerable opposition from an unnamed fellow exile. Nevertheless, he saw it as his 'duty' to go ahead with his project 'in relation to God, the deceased Martyrs & witnesses, to the faithfull that remained, & to our selves', even though he conceded to the omission of a few things 'for peace sake'.[29] That is, Ludlow exercised a certain degree of self-censorship in his defence of the regicides to produce a pamphlet that would be suitable for a foreign audience, while the work's printer would make further editorial interventions which Ludlow perceived as a potential dilution of the speeches' message. To understand

---

[23] *Speeches and Prayers*, p. 15.

[24] It is also possible that some of the speeches had been written down before they were delivered and therefore existed in manuscript form.

[25] Ludlow, 'Voyce', p. 950.   [26] Jenkinson, *Culture and Politics*, pp. 38 ff.

[27] Thomas S. Freeman and Sarah Elizabeth Wall, 'Racking the Body, Shaping the Text: The Account of Anne Askew in Foxe's "Book of Martyrs"', *Renaissance Quarterly*, 54 (2001), 1165–96; and Ludlow, *Voyce*, ed. Worden, p. 9. However, the Marian martyrs had been denied their dying speeches 'on pain of having their tongues cut out', which was perceived as the act of an 'unjust and tyrannical regime'. The authorities were presumably aware of the propaganda effect. See Andrea McKenzie, 'God's Tribunal: Guilt, Innocence, and Execution in England, 1675–1775', *Cultural and Social History*, 3 (2006), 121–44, at p. 126. Ludlow's fellow exile John Lisle had two speeches drafted for his possible trial and execution, in case he should be captured and repatriated by Charles II's agents. After Lisle was shot in Lausanne in 1664, Ludlow included transcripts from Lisle's papers in his 'Voyce' (pp. 1083–7). See Holmes, 'John Lisle', p. 930.

[28] It was to be expected that copies of the pamphlet would travel to the American colonies, where many Puritans lived.

[29] Ludlow, 'Voyce', pp. 948–9.

the rationale of these omissions and changes, and the nature and purpose of the work that eventually emerged, we need to have a closer look at the French translation (see Figure 3).

The first part of *Les juges* was a close literal translation of the English *Speeches and Prayers*, even though various minor adjustments added a considerable number of pages to the French version of the text. To begin with, French grammar and sentence structure added a bit of length, while the pamphlet's size was also increased by the choice of a larger font and additional paragraph breaks, which roughly doubled in length the part of the text based on the *Speeches and Prayers* alone despite some of the cuts and omissions outlined below.[30] In addition, more care was taken with the typesetting, as passages of direct and indirect speech were rendered in italics throughout, more consistently than in the English original.[31] The printer also consolidated the pamphlet's structure, for instance by moving Justice Cook's 'Letter to his Daughter' forward from page 82 in the English to pages 83 to 85 in the French version to follow his scaffold speech, while Cook's letters to various friends and to his wife were moved to the back of the French version.[32] Unlike the original English pamphlet, the French version also has a table of contents in the back.

The textual omissions conceded by Ludlow included a sermon preached by Hugh Peters on Psalm 42, which is briefly referred to in the narrative but not reproduced in full length, and the last part of Scott's narrative, consisting of one prayer as well as six lines from another.[33] Both parts of the Scott section were presumably removed because they digressed from the immediate description of events or may have gone too far into detailed religious exegesis for a wider audience. In addition, several passages from pages 80 to 81, containing miscellaneous material relating to various regicides, were either re-arranged, moved elsewhere or omitted.[34] Further

---

[30] The original English text had 96 pages, while the French translation – despite several omissions – had 202 pages. The full French pamphlet including the additional material had 235 pages plus an additional table of contents.

[31] However, the English text has the scaffold speeches all in italics, which the French text has not.

[32] The letters to his friends appear in the English version between pp. 36 and 50 and on p. 57, and in the French translation between pp. 177 and 206 and between pp. 218 and 220. The letters to his wife appear in the English text between pp. 50 and 56, and in the French pamphlet between pp. 206 and 218.

[33] In the *Speeches and Prayers*, the sermon can be found on pp. 58–60; the French text refers to the sermon on p. 87. The last part of Scott's narrative can be found on pp. 67–8 and 72 in the *Speeches and Prayers*.

[34] e.g. additional passages on Jones were moved forward to join up with the other text relating to him, while conversely the short paragraph on Clement was moved back. Two passages on Scroop and Cook were omitted.

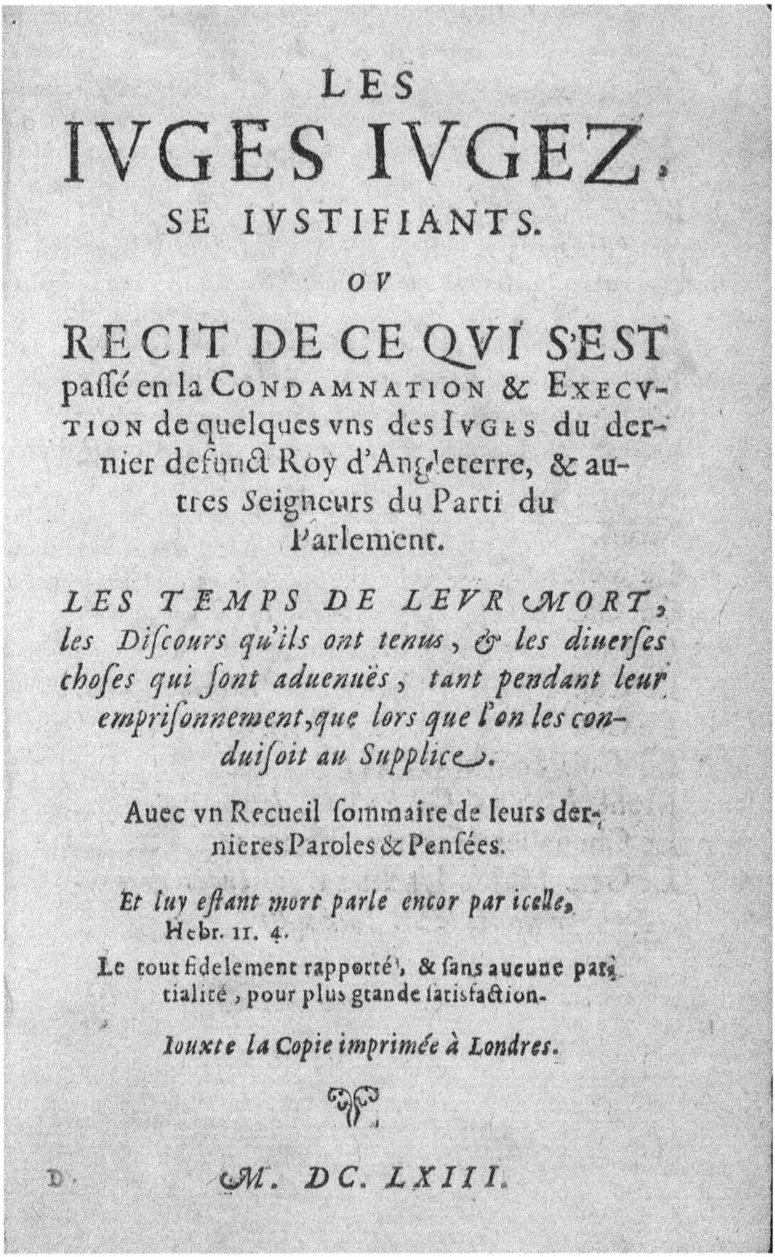

LES
IVGES IVGEZ,
SE IVSTIFIANTS.
OV
RECIT DE CE QVI S'EST
paſſé en la CONDAMNATION & EXECV-
TION de quelques vns des IVGES du dernier defunct Roy d'Angleterre, & autres Seigneurs du Parti du
Parlement.

LES TEMPS DE LEVR MORT,
les Diſcours qu'ils ont tenus, & les diuerſes
choſes qui ſont aduenuës, tant pendant leur
empriſonnement, que lors que l'on les con-
duiſoit au Supplice.

Auec vn Recueil ſommaire de leurs der-
nieres Paroles & Penſées.

Et luy eſtant mort parle encor par icelle,
Hebr. 11. 4.
Le tout fidelement rapporté, & ſans aucune par-
tialité, pour plus grande ſatisfaction.

Iouxte la Copie imprimée à Londres.

D. *M. DC. LXIII.*

Figure 3 *Les juges jugez, se justifiants* (n.p., 1663), title page.
© The Bodleian Library, University of Oxford

omissions were of a comparatively minor nature, sometimes comprising only a few lines of text at a time.[35] It remains unclear whether these passages were taken out because the printer took offence at them or because they did not fit the layout, as they do not appear significantly different in tone or content from the remaining text.[36]

However, Ludlow did have several very specific complaints about a number of unauthorised changes the printer had made to the text, which he considered to be 'gross mistakes' tending 'to the disadvantadge of the worke'.[37] He points out that 'the Epistle to the Booke' omitted 'the first reason' for publishing the work, namely 'to prevent the wrong which might be done to the deceased, by false & Imperfect Coppyes (& more especially to the Name of God)'.[38] The printer had also dropped 'the fourth reason', which had equally offended L'Estrange, 'that men may see what it is to have Interest in [Christ] in a dying hower, ... and to be faithfull to his cause'.[39] These named errors and omissions, Ludlow claims, are only 'a taste of the rest'.[40] He complains that the printer had rather toned down the anger Cook had expressed in a letter to a friend at several traitors or turncoats 'who had once owned the Cause, & now betrayed it'. The original English letter says that 'they will wish at the last day, they had bin Jewes, Turkes & Indians, for that the more of light, the greater their Apostacy & Ingratitude', but in the French translation the following words are omitted: 'and sure they will have a peculiar Judgement by themselves, for they doe openly prefer the Cause of Barrabas, before the Cause of Jesus'.[41] Ludlow further notes that in the report about Axtell and Hacker being drawn to Tyburn 'after the relating of the Ropes being tyed about their Necke, & a burning fire kindled before their faces', the following words were omitted: 'and being there ready to receive that sentence which Nature would have sunke under, if grace had not supported'.[42] The missing part would have emphasised the extraordinary courage the regicides had displayed in the face of death, which was considered a sign of

---

[35] e.g. *Speeches and Prayers*, pp. 18–19, 22, 93.

[36] It is most likely that they were removed to 'streamline' the text into a more coherent narrative.

[37] Ludlow, 'Voyce', p. 949.

[38] 'To the Reader', in *Speeches and Prayers* as compared with 'Au lecteur' in *Les juges*. However, 'le tort qu'on avroit pû faire aux defuncts, par des Copies fausses & imparfaites' is mentioned, while the reference to God is indeed missing.

[39] 'To the Reader', in *Speeches and Prayers*. Again, the French has 'En quatriesme lieu, afin que l'on puisse voir que c'est que d'avoir interest en Christ à l'heure de la mort', but not the further reference to 'his cause'. See also L'Estrange, *Considerations and Proposals*, p. 11.

[40] Ludlow, 'Voyce', p. 949.   [41] Ibid. Compare *Speeches and Prayers*, p. 42, with *Les juges*, p. 186.

[42] Ludlow, 'Voyce', p. 949. Compare *Speeches and Prayers*, p. 88, with *Les juges*, pp. 138–9.

God's grace in them. Ludlow's final criticism of the French text relates to the closing passage of the English pamphlet, which reports on the hanging of Axtell and Hacker. The *Speeches and Prayers* remark on the extraordinarily civil and respectful behaviour of the onlookers. According to the pamphlet, only two people in the crowd had shouted at the hangman to pull away the cart more quickly to speed the death of the two 'Rogues, Traytors, [and] Murtherers'. But the hecklers were silenced by a man in the crowd who asked them to respect the situation.

After listening to Axtell's 'speech and prayer' the hecklers were so moved that they withdrew to cry. Ludlow complained that the final part of the sentence, which described how 'that man who before desired them to be Civill, went after them, and beheld them to his great admiration, as himselfe reported', was missing.[43] Again, Ludlow thought the omission removed some of the scene's emotive force and thus the full impact of the regicides' words on the people. He thought that the mistakes and missing (half) sentences weakened the pamphlet's message and the symbolism of the martyrs' actions. The work printed in Yverdon clearly differed from what Ludlow had intended.

Besides complaining about unauthorised omissions from the translation, Ludlow was also furious about several of the printer's unsolicited additions that had become necessary as the production process was overtaken by events. Ludlow had commissioned the original French translation well before April 1662, when only the first group of regicides had been executed. By the time the printer was preparing the pamphlet for the press, the three regicides arrested in the Netherlands, Barkstead, Corbet and Okey, had also been tried and executed in late May. So he may have wanted to include their speeches and prayers for a comprehensive and up-to-date work.[44] Moreover, Vane and Lambert, both ardent defenders of the 'good old cause' though no regicides, had also been condemned to death in June. Notably, Lambert was still included in the pamphlet, although his sentence had been commuted to life imprisonment, which the printer may not have been aware of. Lambert was kept a close prisoner on Guernsey before being transferred in 1670 to St Nicholas Island, where he died a natural death in 1684.[45] Vane was executed shortly after his trial. As Ludlow had not given the printer any material on the new cases, the latter used some information on the trial of Corbet, Barkstead and Okey

[43] Ludlow, 'Voyce', p. 949. Compare *Speeches and Prayers*, p. 96, with *Les juges*, p. 159.
[44] Catterall, 'Sir George Downing and the Regicides'; Greaves, *Deliver Us from Evil*, pp. 92 ff.
[45] Farr, 'Lambert, John'.

'taken out of the French Gazet'.[46] This was easy to do as the material was available in French and did not need to be translated. However, Ludlow disapproved of the version of events reported in the French-language press, for the *Gazette de France* was more or less a government organ that probably favoured the perspective of the English authorities.[47] Ludlow thought that the paper had distorted the account of events and complained that according to the narrative included by the printer, Corbet, Barkstead and Okey had been watched by the king's and the sheriff's guards so that 'they might hinder the people from offering up themselves those sacrifices'. Yet 'the trueth', according to Ludlow, was that 'they were so strongly guarded least the people should succour them' because they had come to be convinced that the regicides were 'butchered for having asserted their Libertyes'.[48] Once again, he felt that the account was not doing justice to the regicides' popularity and the validity of their cause.

Finally, the printer took details of 'the Tryall & Condemnation of Sir Henry Vane that renowned Patriot' from 'another Gazet', which, in Ludlow's opinion, had also treated him somewhat unfairly: 'his Christian Resolution, his faithfull asserting of the Cause of God, & his Country, his Learned & prudent management of the defense of what he had done for the promoting thereof' were 'termed prolix repeating of the same thinges, Insolent & Injurious carriadge towards his Judges, & ground of a new accusation against him'. Vane had also been charged with 'falling into disgressions very extravagant'.[49] Given that Vane was widely known as a man who could talk for hours, these accusations may not have been entirely unfounded, if rather hard to stomach for an ardent admirer. Ludlow defended his friend, saying that Vane had not wanted 'couradge to owne a good Cause', so that even 'his greatest Enemyes' had to acknowledge 'he was qualified with partes to manage it to the best advantadge'.[50] To redeem himself, meanwhile, the printer 'in his Preamble to a more Exact relation of that affaire which [had] come from London in a Publique manuscript, & was printed by him in the End of the said Booke', along with Vane's scaffold speech, had done the right thing by the great republican hero and saint. Thus Ludlow was content that he should 'make

---

[46] Ludlow, 'Voyce', p. 950.
[47] If 'French Gazet' indeed refers to the *Gazette de France*, published in Paris between 1631 and 1915. Alas, as yet I have not been able to locate the account of Barkstead, Corbet and Okey that Ludlow refers to here.
[48] Ludlow, 'Voyce', p. 950.   [49] Ibid. See *Les juges*, p. 172.   [50] Ludlow, 'Voyce', p. 950.

no further mention thereof, but leave it to the Lord to cleare up the
Innocency of his witnesses'.[51]

Aside from the additional content, the printer had also increased the
volume of the publication through the use of a larger font size and a new
layout. From a merely economic point of view, this seems counter-
intuitive as paper was the most expensive part in the book production
process, and money had to be found for the printing,[52] but the increased
size of the volume would have raised not only its material value but also the
pamphlet's physical weight and thus added to its perceived significance as a
work about the new English martyrs. The pamphlet's physical volume thus
complemented the weight of its contents, which would have made perfect
commercial sense. For the marketing of the pamphlet, meanwhile, the title
page and the title itself were crucial. Unlike the English title page, the
French version displays neither the regicides' names nor their execution
dates. The English names would have meant little to a francophone
audience, while the dates may have been removed because the events were
no longer 'news' by the time the translation was ready for distribution.
The work had become more of a compendium of all the people recently
executed in the name of the good old cause and thus was transformed
from a hastily assembled underground news publication into a more
timeless piece. In the process, the most important change was made to
the title itself.

The neutrally descriptive *The Speeches and Prayers of Some of the Late
King's Judges* was rendered in French as *Les juges jugez, se justifiants* – or
'The judges judged, justifying themselves'. The new French title put the
emphasis on both justice and the concept of 'justification' in all its
semantic breadth and ambiguity in a legal as well as religious context, for
'justification' could be understood both as a defence of the regicides'
actions and as the Protestant doctrine of justification by faith. Ludlow
himself elaborates at length on the rationale for the chosen title. Again, the
printer may have taken the initiative with his own business in mind. As
Ludlow notes: 'under pretence that it was necessary to annex a Title for the
better sale of the Booke, & because none was sent him, we thinking it not

[51] Ibid. I have not been able to identify the original of the 'Publique manuscript' referred to here, but
its contents are likewise reproduced in Ludlow's 'Voyce', p. 930. The French pamphlet (p. 225)
concedes that the fictitious speech was added: 'Les Amis du Chevalier Henry Vane estans restés mal
satisfaits de ce qui a esté produit ci devant.'
[52] Robert Darnton, *The Business of Enlightenment: A Publishing History of the* Encyclopédie *1775–1800*
(Cambridge, MA: Harvard University Press, 1979), p. 185.

necessary, he intitles it Les Juges Jugez'.[53] This title, according to Ludlow, was 'thought a high Reflection upon those faithfull witnesses who had made their Appeale to the great Tribunall'. Yet, the regicides 'being satisfied in their owne Conscience, as to the Justice of what they had done and for which now they suffered, and being also cleared in the Judgements of all unbyassed & disinterested persons', it was initially thought 'that it ought rather to be intituled Les Juges Jugez & Justifiez'.[54] But as 'more was to be said in their Justification, it was thought fit rather that to Les Juges Jugez should be added se Justifians'.[55] This seemed to Ludlow an appropriate title, and the printer too seemed 'well satisfied with the amendment'. However, Ludlow had expected the extended title to be 'inserted in the Topp of every leafe', while 'instead thereof it was only added to ... the frontispeece of the Booke, which might be added, or not, at pleasure'.[56] Ludlow considered the extension to the title crucial for the proper understanding of the pamphlet and to ensure that the reader would be reminded on every page that the king's judges might have been judged by a human court, but were able to justify their actions with the help of God. His insistence on this minor change of the title is significant, as it added weight to the regicides' cause.

Last dying speeches have commonly been considered as reinforcing established authority, since convicts confessed to their deeds and showed remorse for their actions. Thus they acted as a deterrent for other criminals as they faced their just punishment. But the convicts' speeches, prayers and comportment at their scene of execution, in particular the 'discourse of divine judgement', could also be used subversively to challenge secular authority, as was the case with the regicides, who acknowledged 'no King but Jesus'.[57] Republicans frequently drew on the First Book of Samuel from the Old Testament to make this point: God had been angered by the Israelites' request for a king because it constituted a rejection of his authority over them.[58] The regicides' political actions, in contrast, had been guided by God's will. Both the *Speeches and Prayers* and its French translation highlighted the fact that the regicides – in fulfilling God's will – were

---

[53] i.e. 'The judges judged'. Ludlow, 'Voyce', p. 949.   [54] i.e. 'The judges judged and justified'.

[55] i.e. 'The judges judged ... justifying themselves'. The present participle of the verb 'se justifier' (to justify oneself) indicates that the justification process was still in progress.

[56] Ludlow, 'Voyce', pp. 949–50. This is not entirely true, as the full title also appears on the title page, not just on the frontispiece.

[57] *Speeches and Prayers*, p. 11; and McKenzie, 'God's Tribunal', p. 131. For a more traditional view, see J. A. Sharpe, '"Last Dying Speeches": Religion, Ideology and Public Execution in Seventeenth-Century England', *Past and Present*, 107 (1985), 144–67.

[58] I Samuel 8.

not afraid of death. The friends who visited Harrison in prison in the days
before his execution 'found him full of the Joy of the Lord'. He 'parted
with his wife and friends with great joy, and chearfulnesse' as he used to
'when going ... about some service for the Lord'.[59] Likewise, Cook had
been 'preparing himself for his Suffering, with such a chearfulnesse, as an
Astonishment to the spectators'.[60] Contemporaries would have considered
such a 'chearfull countenance' in the anticipation of death to be a sign of
innocence, affirming the belief that God gave the righteous extra strength
in their suffering.[61] Thus Carew noted that his strength was 'in the Lord of
Hosts, who hath helped me from my beginning to this day, and will help
me to the end'. He was equally sure that '[t]hough man have Condemned
yet the Lord hath and doth justifie'.[62] Similarly, Cook told his friends that
'it matters not who condemns, when God justifies'. On being reminded by
some of the '*disaffected*' that '*the Jesuits*' also '*suffered cheerfully and confi-
dently*', meanwhile, Cook is said to have replied that his justification was
'not built upon the merits of Works, but alone upon Grace in the bloud of
Christ'. He thus asserted the Protestant doctrine of justification by faith.[63]
In his 'Speech upon the Ladder', Harrison also showed himself confident,
citing Scripture, that his God, 'the King of Kings, and Lord of Lords',
would 'never leave those that truly trust in him, unto whose Glory I shall
surely go, and shall sit on the right hand of Christ in Heaven, it may be to
Judge those that have Unjustly Judged me'.[64] Harrison here recalls the
words of Christ in his sermon on the mount: 'Judge not, that ye be not
judged', warning his disciples against rash judgement of their neighbours.[65] Harrison meanwhile could die in peace because he had God on
his side. While a worldly court had 'unjustly' found him guilty, God had
reserved his place in heaven.

The same pattern was followed in the execution narratives of Corbet,
Barkstead and Okey added to the French translation. Although these
accounts are much shorter than those of the other martyrs and are patched
together from a variety of other publications, they were fitted into the same
format of events leading up to the execution, 'occasional speeches' and
'dying speeches', including the stage-acting performances.[66] The account

[59] *Speeches and Prayers*, pp. 3–4; and *Les juges*, pp. 11–12.
[60] *Speeches and Prayers*, p. 32 (recte p. 27); and *Les juges*, p. 64.
[61] *Speeches and Prayers*, p. 28, and *Les juges*, p. 67. See McKenzie, 'God's Tribunal', p. 138.
[62] *Speeches and Prayers*, p. 12; *Les juges*, pp. 31–3.   [63] *Speeches and Prayers*, p. 25; *Les juges*, p. 60.
[64] *Speeches and Prayers*, p. 9; *Les juges*, p. 25. Harrison is referring to Matthew 25:33–4 and
     I Corinthians 6:2.
[65] Matthew 7:1.   [66] *Les juges*, pp. 160 ff., 171 ff. and 225 ff.

of Vane's trial and death was slightly different, as his speech was not reported at length. Instead, the printer provided the 'substance' of what Vane said, condensing his final message to the world to just under seven printed pages. The pamphlet's key statement was that if the regicides and Vane were able to walk towards their death with confidence and a cheerful disposition it must be proof of their innocence because God had given them the gift of his grace.[67] The regicides and saints were not just judged by a human court. While being tried and resisting worldly authority through their strength, they were also witnesses to the kingdom of God and his cause, as Carew pointed out in his scaffold speech, saying: 'I desire to bear witness to the true Magistracy, that Magistracy that is in the Word of the Lord. And that true Ministery, which is a Ministery from the anointing; that doth beare witness to the Lord Jesus, and hath his holy Spirit.'[68] Scot's prayer went: 'thy poor and unworthy Creature comes now to bear his Witness in this great Spectacle, before Thee, Angels and Men'.[69] As models of human virtue chosen by their creator to spread his word even in their hour of death, the martyrs had fulfilled their destiny. And their speeches and prayers, immortalised in print, could serve as an evangelisation tool. In this respect, the *Speeches and Prayers* and their French translation resembled other works of Protestant hagiography and martyrology, including exemplary 'lives', that were circulated after the Restoration in print or manuscript form 'for the encouragement of the Saints'.[70]

Despite Ludlow's many criticisms of the translation with its omissions and expansions, its evocative title and its emphasis on justification made the French pamphlet much clearer and more coherent than the various texts on which it was based. Besides, Ludlow himself conceded that the printer was sympathetic to the regicides' cause, even though he remained mindful of his profit.[71] The pamphlet did deliver its message well, as it was 'calling God to witness' and a witness to God.[72] Thus as it was translated, edited and modified for a new audience, the regicides were turned into timeless witnesses of God's cause. And as the need for a translation of their justification indicates, the English or even British context was not wide enough. The translation was intended for a much wider audience, in an attempt to get fellow Protestants in Europe and elsewhere to rally behind

---

[67] References to 'grace' are made in *Speeches and Prayers*, pp. 25, 32, 70 ff.; see *Les juges*, pp. 60, 101 ff.; the reference from p. 32 in *Speeches and Prayers* is omitted on p. 76 of *Les juges*.
[68] *Speeches and Prayers*, p. 19; *Les juges*, pp. 46–7.   [69] *Speeches and Prayers*, p. 69; *Les juges*, p. 101.
[70] See Clarke, 'Re-reading the Exclusion Crisis', p. 150.   [71] Ludlow, 'Voyce', p. 949.
[72] McKenzie, 'God's Tribunal', p. 133.

the regicides for their protection.[73] In particular, Ludlow may have been
thinking of 'the distressed Rochelers and other Protestants in France', who,
he felt, had been betrayed by Charles I in the late 1620s in a similar way
as the dissenters in the British Isles were now, when he initially sent
three different relief missions to the besieged Huguenot stronghold of
La Rochelle in 1627–8, only to withdraw later from the operation and take
the side of the Catholic French king.[74] He may also have been thinking of
the 'the poore distressed Protestants in Piedmont' suffering under the
Duchess of Savoy, their 'great Enemy', and others in similar circumstances.[75] As we have seen above, a wider European network of Calvinists
and other Reformed Protestants had been built up from the mid-sixteenth
century, with Geneva at its spiritual and geographical centre. While this
city was now struggling to maintain its central position under pressure
from neighbouring states, its language still connected Protestants all over
Europe, first of all the Huguenots in France, but also a great number of
Huguenot refugees and their descendants all over Europe. Over the course
of the seventeenth century, French also came to rival Latin – the language
associated with Rome and the papacy – as the new European *lingua franca*
in scholarly discourse.[76] For the work's distribution, we have to turn to its
printer.

According to Ludlow, the man who produced the pamphlet was not
primarily a printer by trade but 'practised physick' at Yverdon.[77] This
description points towards Dominique Chabrey, a Genevan physician who
had established himself in Yverdon in 1648 and bought a disused printing
press in order to produce a work on botany.[78] He subsequently took on
other jobs to supplement his income, but never built up a bigger printing
business, although he remained the only printer in the town for a long

---

[73] I owe this point to Andrew McKenzie-McHarg.
[74] Ludlow, *Voyce*, ed. Worden, p. 130 (764–5).   [75] Ludlow, 'Voyce', p. 1004.
[76] Lorraine Daston, 'The Ideal and Reality of the Republic of Letters in the Enlightenment', *Science in Context*, 4 (1991), 367–86, at p. 376; Margaret C. Jacob, 'The Mental Landscape of the Public Sphere: A European Perspective', *Eighteenth-Century Studies*, 28 (1994), 95–113, at p. 98.
[77] Ludlow, 'Voyce', p. 949. *Les juges* is also not listed in any of the catalogues of the established printers in Yverdon at the time. See the 'Catalogue' of works printed or published at Yverdon in the seventeenth and eighteenth centuries, attached to Jean-Pierre Perret, *Les imprimeries d'Yverdon au xviie et au xviiie siècle* (Lausanne: F. Roth, 1945), pp. 375 ff. Yverdon did not get a printing press until the seventeenth century, and because of strict censorship from Bern, printing remained very constrained even then. Such an environment would have encouraged the establishment of illegal presses.
[78] The work had been planned by the previous printer of Yverdon, Pyrame de Candolle, and the manuscript, herbarium and plates were still kept in the town. See Perret, *Les imprimeries d'Yverdon*, pp 49–54.

time. As the son of a Protestant minister from Geneva, Chabrey was sympathetic to Ludlow's cause, but he also needed the money.[79] Hence he may have tried to turn *Les juges* into a viable commercial venture. The printers of Yverdon produced their works not just for the Swiss, but primarily for the French market, so most of the works coming off the press there in the seventeenth century would have been sold in the bookshops of Lyon and elsewhere in France.[80] Yet print runs were still comparatively small. While Chabrey's predecessor in Yverdon, Pyrame de Candolle, usually produced between 1,000 and 3,000 copies at a time, the average print run now was closer to 500,[81] and there is no evidence that *Les juges* should have been an exception. Presumably, a work like this would be particularly attractive for the Huguenot market across the border and possibly the French-speaking parts of the Netherlands. After all, exporting their works to France and elsewhere had been common among the printers dotted along the Franco-Swiss border since the sixteenth century.[82] While surviving copies of the work are very rare in the United Kingdom, however, a number of copies of *Les juges* can be located in France as well as Germany.[83] The target audience for the French translation of the *Speeches and Prayers* of the regicides, with its additional material on other saints and martyrs, thus may have been Protestant Europe, and the text of *Les juges* an appeal to solidarity among Protestants, in particular for their persecuted English brothers and sisters (either living in fear at home or being exiled across Europe and the American colonies). The publication may also have been an attempt by Ludlow to improve his own security by turning to popular sentiment and reminding fellow Protestants of their duty to rally behind their co-religionists in times of trouble – just as his own safety had been put at risk.

Probably for that very reason, Ludlow's translation project caused considerable consternation among the English authorities, to whose attention it had come. The city of Geneva too was keen to distance itself from the undertaking as well as from the exiles themselves in an attempt to keep the peace with the English monarchy. The Council of Geneva had only

---

[79] According to Perret, Chabrey applied to the Council of Yverdon in August 1656 for an increase in his salary because he had a large family to support. Ibid., p. 52 and n.
[80] Ibid., pp. 46–7. It was only later that the market expanded towards northern Europe.
[81] Ibid., pp. 45–6. [82] Darnton, *The Business of Enlightenment*, p. 39.
[83] In England, copies can be found in the Bodleian Library in Oxford at Vet.L3.f.8, and in the British Library in London at 8122.aa.14. In France, at least two copies of *Les juges* are available in the BNF. The work can also be found in Germany, at the Anna Amalia Bibliothek in Weimar at Saal-SLS:22, 5:31.

three years previously offered a prayer on the Stuarts' restoration, and the city-state was currently on good terms with its French neighbours. So it seemed only reasonable that it would want to maintain those good relations, and this meant that it could not be seen to be harbouring regicides.[84] The extent to which the pamphlet threatened to upset diplomatic relations between England and Geneva is evidenced by Ludlow's personal account. According to Ludlow, his friend Labadie had heard that the English ambassador in Paris, Denzil Hollis, had complained to his Genevan counterpart, Jean Lullin, about it, assuming the pamphlet had been printed in Geneva.[85] Following this incident, it may well have been the case that some on the Council of Geneva thought it might be better to withdraw protection from the regicides, or at least not make them feel too comfortable. Whether or not the councillors had dropped a hint we do not know, but in any case, the incident raised the exiles' fear that Geneva would extradite them to appease the English and French monarchies. In response to their enquiries about their refugee status, the exiles got verbal reassurances, but nothing formal or official from the council, and decided to move on to the safer and quieter Pays de Vaud – first to Lausanne and later to Vevey – under the control of the Bern authorities.[86]

Ludlow must have been deeply disappointed in the Genevan authorities for letting him and his fellow sufferers down. All the stronger was his gratitude to the townspeople of Vevey. They were committed to the exiles on account of their shared religious beliefs and the advocacy of Labadie, Hummel and the authorities of Bern. As we have seen above, the personal links of the English exiles to their Swiss brethren went back via their Civil War networks to the Marian exiles of the Counter-Reformation period; and the survival of Ludlow and his friends was evidence of the strong Protestant networks across Europe and the solidarity that arose from them. Far from being a group of isolated English exiles in a foreign country, the regicides who had settled in Switzerland during the Restoration were part of a wider European network of radical Protestants who contributed to a discourse of faith and persecution through their translation and publication of the *Speeches and Prayers* of the English republican martyrs. If "'A Voyce from the Watch Tower" was clearly written with a nonconformist

---

[84] See AEG, Registres du Conseil, RC 160 (1660), entry for 23 May 1660, fol. 80r. According to Ludlow, the Duchess of Orléans had offered 2,500 pounds 'for the betraying of us into our Enemyes hands' ('Voyce', p. 951).
[85] See Ludlow, *Memoirs*, ed. Firth, ii, p. 359; and Ludlow, 'Voyce', p. 993. On the Genevan ambassador in Paris, see 'Lullin, Jean', *HLS*.
[86] See Chapter 1.

audience in mind' and intended 'to fortify and unite the godly in England', as Blair Worden contends, then *Les juges* was published for the godly in Europe.[87]

However, the distribution of their narratives of suffering in Protestant Europe was only the beginning. Ultimately, the exiled regicides wanted the story of their friends' fate to travel much further. After all, the exiles saw themselves as members of God's invisible church around the world, and the *Speeches and Prayers* could be used as a tool in their evangelical mission. Thus Ludlow agreed with the regicide and martyr John Carew that the last words of those who died for the 'good old cause' would not just be useful to Protestants at home and across Europe, but also 'to the Churches of Christ beyond the Seaes'.[88] Given that the words of the republican martyrs were now available both in English and in French, this might include English Puritans as well as French Huguenots in the Americas.[89] This international nature of Ludlow's republicanism and his faith in the church of all true believers around the world was also confirmed by his motto *Omne solum forti patria quia patris*', which roughly translates as: 'To the brave every land is a fatherland because it is of the father.'[90] Persecution to Ludlow was part of a greater divine plan, in which he willingly played his part because he was prepared to go wherever providence would take him. It may have been the project of remembering the regicides and their actions that incited Ludlow to write down his own version of events. Thus the regicides' attempt to give meaning to their own history and preserve it for subsequent generations was already there before the radical Whigs of the later seventeenth and early eighteenth centuries decided to employ it for their own purpose.[91]

Exile as a Spiritual Journey in the 'Voyce'

Both the 'Voyce from the Watch Tower' and *Les juges* can be seen as Ludlow's way of promoting the Lord's cause by writing and publishing. He is setting the official record straight by drawing up his own version of events through the lens of a republican activist and observer on the one hand, and as a witness and servant of the Lord on the other. Early on in the 'Voyce' we hear from Ludlow that he had been destined by God to follow

---

[87] Worden, 'Introduction' to Ludlow, *Voyce*, p. 10.   [88] Ludlow, 'Voyce', p. 948.
[89] There were Huguenot settlements in Canada, Florida and Brazil.   [90] See Chapter 2.
[91] On the history factory of the radical Whigs, see Worden, *Roundhead Reputations*, and Goldie, *Roger Morrice and the Puritan Whigs*, i, chapter 5.

a particular path in life, through an event he remembered as he was escaping the authorities for the first time in the spring of 1660.

When Ludlow heard of the re-admission of the secluded members and the plans for the election of a convention Parliament that would most probably restore the monarchy, he knew he was in danger. And before he could be summoned to swear an engagement oath to the present power, he had left London on the urging of his wife to go to Wiltshire and stand in the upcoming elections. Through this move, Ludlow says, 'the Lord at this tyme delivered me out of the Denne, and Lyon's Mouth'. Yet he still took the precaution of arriving for the elections with a party to protect him against any potential violence from his royalist enemies.[92] As he reached the parish of Maiden Bradly, where he owned property and intended to raise money among his tenants, Ludlow was reminded of a childhood dream he had had when he was about ten years old, and which he had perceived as a vision or a message from God. In this dream, he had heard a noise from a house and on looking in had seen two blood-stained people lying on their backs on the floor opposite each other, then rising to fight each other in the air before turning on Ludlow himself. Since the God of the Old Testament used dreams as a way of communicating with individuals, Ludlow thought that God had here been trying to communicate with him and shown him a vision of the Civil War, from which he understood that 'the Lord hath engaged me in a cause wherein his glory and the good of his people is concerned'. The dream left such a deep and lasting impression on the republican that he had 'dreemed of the same dreame often since, and spoken of it to many persons'.[93] This sense of being engaged in God's cause would accompany him throughout his life and exile, as is documented in the 'Voyce'.

On his arrival in Wiltshire, Ludlow raised as much money from his tenants as he could – probably knowing he would need it later if he had to make a quick escape – and then went into hiding, so 'that I might not fall into the hands of my enemyes, but be at liberty to improve what opportunity the Lord should give me for the serving of my generation, which in all probability would either suddenly be, or else to wayt the Lord's tyme'.[94] After the general elections and Lambert's escape from the Tower and the latter's recapture following an attempted plot, Ludlow nevertheless decided

---

[92] Ludlow, *Voyce*, ed. Worden, p. 105 (741).

[93] Ibid., pp. 105–6 (741–2). On the meaning of dreams for pious Protestants, see Alec Ryrie, 'Sleep, Waking and Dreaming in Protestant Piety', in Jessica Martin and Alec Ryrie (eds), *Private and Domestic Devotion in Early Modern Britain* (Farnham: Ashgate, 2012), pp. 73–92, at pp. 74, 87.

[94] Ludlow, *Voyce*, ed. Worden, p. 108 (744).

to leave his hideout in Wiltshire to go to London 'and there to wayte what the pleasure of the Lord should be, in relation either to my doing or suffering for him'. This he did, eventually arriving to stay at a friend's house in Holborn.[95] However, London did not remain a safe place for Ludlow for long, for in the meantime the Convention had voted for a return of the king and the Council of State had issued an order for his capture.[96] Nevertheless, Ludlow decided to take his seat as the Committee of Privileges had confirmed his election, 'knowing that without breach of priviledge none could seize me (being a member of parlament)'. Yet his position was far from secure, as he heard that certain members of the House had taken a resolution to accuse him of high treason and sent him to the Tower for his involvement in the trial and execution of Charles I; and with actions already being taken against some of his fellow regicides, his fears for his life did not seem unreasonable.[97] In the event, he cast his own escape and survival as a matter of divine providence as he reflected on his destiny in relation to that of the other regicides who had been less fortunate than himself.

Ludlow had heard how in the spring of 1660 Chief Justice Cook was seized in Ireland and how Major General Thomas Harrison was captured in Stafford without offering any resistance, 'being so fully satisfyed in the justice of the cause which the Lord had honoured him to be an instrument in, and of his duty to seale the trueth thereof with his blood'.[98] These were people he had been collaborating with closely during the Civil War and Interregnum years, and he could easily have shared their fate. Yet Ludlow had escaped capture and needed to rationalise his actions. While he respected and admired the executed regicides for being prepared to die for their convictions, he had also been agonising over his own escape and survival and justified it to himself by citing the words and the example of Christ. Referring among others to the Gospel of Matthew, Ludlow argued that it was 'the duty of the people of God when persecuted in one citty to flee to another' and that it was not to deny the cause if 'we seeke to save our lives to promote God's cause'.[99] After all, David had been 'flying from the fury of Saul', and Christ himself had withdrawn himself 'from the people when they attempted several tymes to kill him'.[100] Similarly,

---

[95] Ibid., pp. 113–14 (749–50). [96] Ibid., pp. 117–18 (753).
[97] Ibid., pp. 119, 123–4 (754, 759). [98] Ibid., p. 126 (761).
[99] Ibid. He is referring to Matthew 10:23: 'But when they persecute you in this city, flee ye into another: for verily I say unto you, Ye shall not have gone over the cities of Israel, till the Son of man be come.'
[100] Ludlow, *Voyce*, ed. Worden, p. 126 (761). He conveniently omits that Christ would later die on the cross.

Ludlow decided to make his way abroad when he felt that his safety could no longer be guaranteed in England. Throughout the different stages of his flight and exile, Ludlow came to rationalise his actions with reference to God's will, the authority of Scripture and the example of Christ.

When it was resolved in May 1660 that all signatories to the king's death warrant – as well as some associated with that act – were to be taken into custody, some such as the High Court clerk John Phelps decided to go abroad, while the regicides Thomas Scott and Ludlow initially decide to hide in England until the situation became clearer.[101] Yet, as time went on, the indemnity bill was drafted and exceptions were being made, Ludlow found that the climate was growing more and more dangerous, with Colonel John Jones and Gregory Clement already captured and taken to the Tower, while a number of other regicides were beginning to make their way across the Channel to Holland or to 'other partes beyond sea'.[102] So he finally decided to leave the country himself and increasingly had to rely on the help of others, such as that of a gentlewoman in London who concealed him in her house and looked after him 'as if she had bin my sister' even though she was a 'well-wissher[ ] to the King', in all of which Ludlow 'desired to see . . . the overruling hand of the Lord'.[103]

When the time had come, Ludlow made his way out of London in the dusk and first travelled to Lewes in Sussex, across the Downs and to the harbour to the vessel that was to take him to France. Here he was lucky that he changed the boat he intended to travel on, because searchers checked the first boat, but not his new vessel, which he considered 'a providence as to my preservation'. The master of his ship also asked him for Lieutenant General Ludlow, 'desiring to know if he were in hold', to which Ludlow replied he 'thought not', which clearly was another sign of God's favour. Then, on his journey to France, he stated that the 'Lord blessed us with so favourable a wynd' that they reached Dieppe harbour 'before the gates of the towne were shut'. And, as he did not speak French, 'providence so ordered it' that an English-speaking apprentice of Madame de Caux became 'my interpreter upon all occasions'.[104] Thus much of his journey was guided by providence and the people God sent to help him along the way.

When he reached France, Ludlow received a letter from his relations informing him about a proclamation for his capture. Concerned that he was still close enough to England to be captured, he decided to move

[101] Ibid., pp. 149–50 (781).   [102] Ibid., pp. 153–4 (785).   [103] Ibid., p. 189 (815).
[104] Ibid., pp. 190–1 (816–17).

further away. He was given the option to take a vessel to Holland with his host's son-in-law; but he neither liked the idea of another sea journey nor wished to move to a country that depended so much on England for its trade: 'And therefore looking into the mapp for some inland Commonwealth, judging such an ayre most suitable to my constitution, the Lord was pleased to direct me to the consideration of Geneve, a citty very renowned for liberty and religion'.[105] When Ludlow finally arrived in the territory of Geneva, he rejoiced both because he felt safer and because he 'had a great love and inclynation to the ayre of a Commonwealth', but also because he 'hoped to enjoy the society of mankind, and above all the servants, and ordinances, of Christ'.[106] He considered it 'a great mercey' that he had been conveyed safely through France by the 'overruling hand of God', and he was convinced that 'the Lord hid me in the hollow of his hand', so that he would be 'so affected therewith as to sacrifice the remainder of my life entirely to his praise and service'.[107] As we have seen above, Ludlow did not only choose Geneva because he received a sign from God, but also because he had acquaintances there whom he could rely on for help. But he also had a sense of being guided by God in his decisions.

Sufferers for the Lord's Sake

Once he is out of immediate danger to his life and settling into his exile community, the focus of Ludlow's writing shifts to his new situation and status. He considers himself a religious refugee, part of the 'people of God',[108] one of the 'sufferers for the Cause of Christ, & the Libertyes of our Country'[109] or 'sufferers, for the Lords sake',[110] and one of the 'exiles for the sake, & worke of the Lord'.[111] In this suffering role, he remains connected to the persecuted dissenters in England, whose situation he observes throughout his time abroad by following new laws being made and executed against them.[112] The main thing that distinguished the regicides from the other faithful in England was the leading role they had taken during the Interregnum period, which now made them prime targets of the king's wrath, but they still belonged to the same community

---

[105] Ibid., p. 192 (818).   [106] Ibid., p. 195 (821–2).
[107] Ludlow refers to Isaiah 49:2, which reads: 'And he hath made my mouth like a sharp sword; in the shadow of his hand hath he hid me, and made me a polished shaft; in his quiver hath he hid me.' *Voyce*, ed. Worden, p. 195 (822).
[108] Ludlow, 'Voyce', p. 939.   [109] Ibid., p. 966.   [110] Ibid., pp. 985, 1363.
[111] Ibid., p. 1378.   [112] Ibid., pp. 1043, 1063, 1079.

of believers and were persecuted for having followed their religious conviction in removing the usurper and tyrant Charles I. Time and again, Ludlow describes the regicides as 'the faithfull witnesses of Christ'[113] persecuted for their beliefs, and he ascribes to them a special duty 'that by suffering we may be fitted for the doing of his will'.[114] The title Ludlow gave to his memoir, 'A Voyce from the Watch Tower' – itself taken from the Book of Isaiah – perfectly encapsulates this obligation to be ready when the Lord calls,[115] for 'being on our Watch Tower, and living by faith, we may see our duty so plainly, that when the Lord's tyme is come we may up and be doing, and the Lord may appear to be with us and to owne us'. At a time when sleeping for the godly was often associated with self-indulgence, and being awake was seen as 'a spiritual discipline' and an 'ascetic practice akin to fasting', Ludlow figured himself as the watchman waiting for signs from God 'to know when to goe forward and when to stand still, that by making hast we may not strengthen the hand of the enemy, nor by standing still neglect the opportunity he puts in our hands'.[116] While he was spending a lot of time watching out for his enemies, he was also watching out for signs from heaven. As his fellow regicides in England had been martyred for their faith, Ludlow had found safety among his co-religionists in Europe, where he was waiting for his time to come. Naturally, the community that was becoming increasingly important to him was that of the Reformed Protestants in Geneva and later in the Vaud under the administration of Bern, especially in Vevey, 'where the Lord enclyned the hearts of the Majestrates, Mynisters & people to receive us with all Expressions of affection & kindness'. Overall, Ludlow was more than grateful for the friendly welcome he and his friends received from their fellow Protestants, 'which layd a great Obligation on us to bless the Lord, who had raysed up so many to favour us & our righteous Cause in a forreigne & strandge Land'.[117] However, this friendly welcome was not just kindness or luck, but also a sign of God's favour and the result of belonging to 'the communion of saints, who endeavoring to keepe the unity of the Spirit in the bond of peace have a sympathy with each other, as being members of the same body whereof Christ is the head'.[118] Throughout the 'Voyce' Ludlow stresses his Protestant identity and the destiny attached to it.

[113] Ludlow, *Voyce*, ed. Worden, p. 298 (918).   [114] Ibid., p. 309 (928).
[115] The passage in Isaiah 21:8 reads: 'And he cried, A lion: My lord, I stand continually upon the watch tower in the daytime, and I am set in my ward whole nights.'
[116] Ludlow, *Voyce*, ed. Worden, p. 309 (928); Ryrie, 'Sleep, Waking and Dreaming', pp. 74, 76.
[117] Ludlow, 'Voyce', pp. 965–6.   [118] Ibid., p. 1378.

Thus he had originally set out for Geneva because he considered it 'a citty very renowned for liberty and religion' and a place where he was hoping 'to enjoy the society of mankind, and above all the servants, and ordinances, of Christ'.[119] Yet it is only in Lausanne – under the jurisdiction of Bern – that the regicides finally receive official recognition as Englishmen persecuted for their faith and they are issued with papers allowing them to live under the protection of the local authorities as members of the Reformed Church professing the evangelical religion, which Ludlow considers a sign 'of their [the local authorities'] couradge and faithfulness to the cause of God and his people, in that they so openly owned his poore persecuted witnesses'.[120] Throughout his memoir, Ludlow stresses that he desired to make the Lord's 'will revealed in his word' the rule of his actions as 'one who wissheth well to the prosperity of Zion', while he also judges other people according to their faith and public conduct.[121] He has high expectations of others and scorn for those who compromise their principles out of self-interest, such as the Council of Geneva when refusing to give formal protection to the regicides or the Dutch when extraditing the regicides 'contrary to their owne principles and publique interest'.[122] Likewise, his resolution not to join the plotters in Rotterdam in their planned military action against the English government was based on his unwillingness to collaborate with the Dutch – as traitors who 'prefer their Trade before the honour of God & Christ'.[123] He regarded the Dutch magistrates as 'guilty of that blood' of the three regicides in Delft and anyone collaborating with them as a 'partaker of their sin', and thus he was unable to join Sidney's scheme because he was unwilling 'to act against my faith', although he left it to the other exiles 'to act according to their Consciences'.[124] He was simply not willing to follow any but his 'owne Light' or 'to yield active Obedience to the absolute Commands of any, save the Lord Christ'.[125] Overall, he did not display any of the pragmatic opportunism we find in Sidney, who was willing to collaborate with both the Dutch and the French to achieve his goals, or in Neville, who even accepted the protection of a royalist patron in the form of Clarendon, whom Ludlow considered to be one of the dissenters' chief enemies.[126]

---

[119] Ludlow, *Voyce*, ed. Worden, pp. 192, 195, (818, 821–2).
[120] StAB, A II 454, Raths-Manual der Stadt Bern, vol. 143 (27 January–7 June 1662), p. 317; ACV, BA 33-4, Weltsch Spruch-Buch der Statt Bern, Décrets Romands Nr. 4, p. 66; and Ludlow, *Voyce*, ed. Worden, p. 305 (924).
[121] Ludlow, 'Voyce', pp. 1081, 1082.   [122] Ludlow, *Voyce*, ed. Worden, pp. 304, 297 (923, 917).
[123] Ludlow, 'Voyce', p. 1057.   [124] Ibid., p. 1056.   [125] Ibid., p. 1081.
[126] Ibid., pp. 1019, 1098.

Frequently, Ludlow based his decisions on whether or not to associate with someone on the quality of their faith, even to a degree that he might appear arrogant or superior, as he did with his neighbours in Vevey, where the exiles were hesitant to take communion with the locals, Ludlow arguing that they did not have 'a freedome to communicate with any in that holy Ordinance of the Lords Supper' if they did not have 'particular satisfaction of a worke of grace in their hearts'.[127] Ludlow appears principled and uncompromising, though his choices were never entirely his own. They are always presented as the Lord's will.

Matters of life and death to him too were in the hands of God, whether a life was threatened by illness or by more sinister machinations. Thus when the regicide Cornelius Holland arrived in Lausanne severely ill, he managed to survive 'with the blessing of the Lord on the diligence of the Physitian, the care of those in the Howse, and the kindness of his Countrymen, who one or more watched with him every night for about a month together'. And while he remained very weak, 'the Lord was pleased not to add affliction to our affliction, and will I trust yet reserve him to be Imployed further in his service'.[128] When the Lord reclaimed the life of a friend, Ludlow was sad, but took the news with relative equanimity, because he knew that they had fulfilled their purpose on earth. When both Hummel and Labadie died in short succession in early 1674, Ludlow remarked that it had 'pleased the Lord to put a period to the Pilgrimage of his eminent, & faythfull witnesse Mr John De Labadie' and to take Hummel 'more immediately to himselfe, to glorify his name in heaven'.[129] Like the executed regicides, these men had fulfilled their purpose on earth and could look forward to returning to their heavenly father.

Yet the Lord also kept reminding Ludlow of his own mortality and put him through his trials, so that he would not forget his duty. Thus Ludlow states that 'the Lord knowing how apt we were to grow wanton with prosperity' did not suffer 'this sun shyne to continue long without the Interposition of a Clowd which truly was darke & thick, threatning our distruction by Vyolence or by deceit', when the lives of the exiles are for the first time threatened by a hired assassin – a mysterious Irishman – in the service of the Duchess of Orléans. Ludlow considered himself to be the prime target, while the exiles looked 'unto the Lord … for direction

<hr/>

[127] Ibid., pp. 1184–5.   [128] Ibid., p. 964.
[129] Jean de Labadie died on 13 February, and Johann Heinrich Hummel on 2 March 1674. Ibid., p. 1376.

herein' and secretly changed their lodging during a fair in the town.[130] When the assassins arrived in the town of Vevey, 'the Lord was pleased in much mercey to prevent them' through his 'Instrument' in the form of Samson Dubois, the exiles' 'Watchfull Host', who had spotted the men in time to alert his guests.[131] Ludlow's life had thus been endangered and was spared by God's will. So when he was advised by Labadie to relocate for his own safety, he 'resolved not to move from the place where I looked upon my selfe . . . called to by the Lord'.[132] Likewise, another time, when there were new rumours about assassins being sent from England, Ludlow was pleased to state that the Lord had not left them 'altogether in the darke, as to the Course they steere against us', as the exiles had their own informers both in England and in Switzerland, so that they were able to prepare for all eventualities.[133] Moreover, while Ludlow believed that the devil was 'ready to assist his Instruments' as much as he could, he was also comforted by the thought that the devil could not 'exceed his Chaine, which is always in the hand of our father'.[134] Thus Ludlow felt he was spared by the providence of God and because he had a purpose to fulfil.

His interpretation of life's meaning thus followed a Puritan tradition of thought, according to which 'there has been unfolding from the beginning of time the grand design of God's miraculous providence, a divine scheme, directing, conditioning, and controlling each and every event in history'.[135] This perspective had been shared since the early seventeenth century by the Puritan migrants to the American colonies, who also had left England to escape persecution by the authorities of their mother country and seek religious freedom abroad. However, while the Puritan migrants to New England had left their home country because the English Church had failed to complete the Reformation and they aimed to build the New Jerusalem across the Atlantic, Ludlow was not looking to establish anything new where he went. On the contrary, he moved to the Continent because he knew that a community of Reformed Protestants already existed and that he would be welcome there among his brothers and sisters as a member of God's invisible Church.

Ludlow's Critique of Monarchy

As much as Ludlow's exile was a spiritual journey to him, it was also a flight from the rule of powers that he considered illegitimate – the usurpers

---

[130] Ibid., pp. 994–5.   [131] Ibid., p. 998.   [132] Ibid., p. 1002.   [133] Ibid., p. 1021.
[134] Ibid., p. 1023.   [135] Zakai, *Exile and Kingdom*, p. 6.

of God's role on earth. To Ludlow, the only legitimate earthly authority in England still remained the Long Parliament because it had been elected by the people and, at least as he saw it, had not been dissolved by the consent of its own members, because not all of them were present when the decision to part was made.[136] He therefore considered the newly elected Convention illegitimate and refused to use the description of 'Parliament' for any of the post-Restoration assemblies, including the Cavalier Parliament, because he resented 'those bloody Conventions, who have taken upon them the title of Parliament since the Usurpers retorne'.[137] Charles Stuart to him was a 'mocke king', a 'tyrant' and a 'usurper' of the Lord's power.[138] The life of the 'faithfull witnesses of Christ' under King Charles II was thus constantly threatened by his arbitrary interference with their political and religious liberties.[139] While Ludlow's language is overall more strongly religious than that of Sidney and Neville and is scattered with scriptural citations and imagery, his constitutional aims were similar to those of both men, as is apparent in his critique of kingship and his Protestant vision of government.

Like Sidney's *Court Maxims* and Neville's *Isle of Pines*, Ludlow's 'Voyce' rejects patriarchal hereditary monarchy by divine right. It is notable that throughout his work Ludlow refers to both Charles I and his son Charles II as 'Charles Steward'.[140] That is, he does not recognise them as divinely appointed monarchs, but simply as private individuals and office-holders who had usurped a power that could belong only to God or Christ on earth.[141] For a Reformed Protestant like Ludlow, the only legitimate king was the Lord, as he made clear by citing the Bible passages commonly used by republicans to reinforce their case.[142] Thus Ludlow on several occasions refers to I Samuel 8, in which the Israelites ask the Lord for a king after the

---

[136] Ludlow argued that while the secluded members had been re-admitted by Monk before the dissolution of the Long Parliament in 1660, only a small number of the Lords who had been sitting 'upon the election of the people' after the establishment of the Commonwealth were present at the time and were therefore not able to give their consent. Therefore, the members 'of that Convention who take upon them the title of Parlament, are to be looked upon but as private persons'. See *Voyce*, ed. Worden, p. 206 (831).

[137] Ludlow, 'Voyce', pp. 1026, 1079. Ludlow is inconsistent here as he had stood for a seat in the Convention.

[138] Ludlow, *Voyce*, ed. Worden, p. 286 (907); Ludlow, 'Voyce', pp. 1009, 1072, 1082; and ibid., pp. 945, 997, 1021, 1026, 1049, 1077, 1102, etc.

[139] Ludlow, *Voyce*, ed. Worden, pp. 297–8 (917–18).

[140] Ibid., pp. 777, 936–47, 951–8, 961–77, etc.

[141] See Gaby Mahlberg, 'Charles Stuart as Office-Holder: On Regicides and Monarchical Republicans', in Anette Pankratz and Claus-Ulrich Viol (eds), *(Un)making the Monarchy* (Heidelberg: Winter, 2017), pp. 177–200.

[142] Ludlow, 'Voyce', pp. 1132, 1103, 1104.

manner of those that heathen nations were ruled by, and God responds by sending them a brutal tyrant. Ludlow insists that this passage could not be used to legitimise the rule of monarchs, as was done by royalists, but instead illustrated that the children of Israel had rejected the Lord, who ruled via Samuel, in favour of a force of evil. Every magistrate, according to Ludlow, had a duty 'to decree justice, either as directed by the light of nature, or the word of God'. To think that God would support 'magistrates (who are his vicegerants) to commit murders, and therein to destroy his owne image in man' would be sheer 'blasphemy'.[143] For Ludlow, it was thus a fact 'that Israel in choosing a King had rejected him (the Lord)', and that 'by their owne confession it was an addition to all their other wickedness'.[144]

Likewise, Ludlow objects to the royalists' use of the phrase 'Touch not mine anoynted, and doe my prophets no harme' to justify the inviolability of the monarch. He sees in this use a malicious attempt 'to wrest the scripture itselfe to a contrary sense to what the spirit of the Lord intended it', perpetuated by the practice of 'anoynting ... kings at their coronation, in allusion to the anoynting of old the kings of Judah'. Instead, he argues, the phrase was applied in the Bible to 'the children of Israel, as they passed from Egipt, till possessed of Canaan; at which tyme they had no king'. Therefore the 'anoynted' were not monarchs, but in actual fact 'the people of God'.[145] These and many other examples are given by Ludlow in a lengthy passage defending the regicide and thus his own actions in the aftermath of the English Civil War and casting doubt on the legitimacy of monarchical rule. Any means to strengthen or maintain the monarchy were therefore fraudulent to him, as was the professed motive of the Second Anglo-Dutch War.

Ludlow on the Anglo-Dutch War

To Ludlow, the Second Anglo-Dutch War (1665–7) had never been the great opportunity that Sidney and other exiles on the Continent saw in it. For him, it was first and foremost a pretext used by the English government to strengthen the monarchy and advance the interests of Charles II's royal relations in Europe – that of his nephew the Prince of Orange in the United Provinces and of his cousin the King of France.[146] Thus Ludlow presented the conflict as one between the monarchical and the republican

---

[143] Ludlow, *Voyce*, ed. Worden, p. 134 (768).   [144] Ludlow, 'Voyce', p. 1104.
[145] Ludlow, *Voyce*, ed. Worden, p. 139 (773).   [146] Ludlow, 'Voyce', pp. 1013, 1098.

interests in Europe, disregarding any animosities that might have existed between the respective princes themselves. The greatest threat was posed by France as a Catholic power, but, to Ludlow, all monarchy was popish, and 'the great popish designe' was 'to destroy all Comonwealths, especially such as are Reformed'.[147] This also led to a conflict of interest within the United Provinces, where monarchical and republican forces coexisted.

Ludlow always had doubts about the loyalty of Dutch republicans to a common Protestant cause, and he was fully aware of tensions within Dutch society between Orangists and supporters of the republic. He did not believe at any stage that Dutch republicans would be willing to jeopardise their peaceful coexistence with the House of Orange through a firm commitment to the English dissenters, nor did he think that they would be prepared to endanger a peace treaty with Charles II for their sake. Thus he was highly sceptical of an alliance between the Protestants in the United Provinces and the English republican exiles scattered across the Continent because he distrusted the motives of the Dutch, and all the more so because he considered them responsible for the extraordinary rendition of Barkstead, Corbet and Okey and their subsequent deaths, and because they relied so heavily on Britain for their trade.[148] In fact, while Ludlow saw the main reasons for war in the Stuart desire to strengthen the monarchy, he felt that trade was being put forward as its public justification and that English merchants were being used to mask this fact. As he argued, the monarchy was intent on making the war look as if it had been called for by Parliament 'upon the Request of the Merchands'.[149] These merchants would then be 'Encouraged by the Court Instruments to make their Complaints against the Hollanders for the Losses they have susteyned by them', and the House would then present them to the king 'with their desire, that he will see satisfaction may be made', while they would in turn promise 'that in Case the Hollanders doe not give satisfaction for the Indignityes done to the Crowne, & wrong to the Merchants, they will stand by him with their Lives & fortunes in making warr upon them'. The Dutch, in contrast, had 'a desire to suppress the Commonwealth' Interest and to advance the Prince of Orange as the absolute Soveraigne of those Countryes'. Some even said, Ludlow reported, 'that a Considerable party of the states themselves being of the Orange party' had 'given Orders and Encouradgement to their owne people' to abuse English merchants in India and 'affront the English flagg, to bring those matters to pass'.[150]

---

[147] Ibid., p. 1043.   [148] Ibid., pp. 1017, 818, 1057.   [149] Ibid., p. 1014.
[150] Ibid., pp. 1016–17.

Naturally, Ludlow's rhetoric was strong, but he was biased in his views. His hatred of Charles II and of the Stuart monarchy led him to exaggerate ideological issues and overlook more practical concerns. It is true that De Witt had been concerned to establish good relations with Charles II on the Restoration, and, as a result of his uncle's changing fortunes, support for the Prince of Orange had been growing in the United Provinces.[151] Yet the tensions within the United Provinces should not be overrated, and De Witt remained firmly in control of the situation. Far from seeing the Second Anglo-Dutch War as a conflict between monarchical and republican powers, the Dutch perceived it primarily as an English attack on their trading advantage. Soon after the restoration of the Stuart monarchy, Charles had revived the 1651 Navigation Act and claimed sovereignty over adjacent waters to secure English trade and fishing rights at the expense of the United Provinces.[152] The Dutch, in turn, responded in 1664 with the reconquest of territories and trade on the coast of Guinea, before the English formally declared war on 4 March 1665 – a conflict that after more than two years was to end in an embarrassing defeat for the English at home.[153]

Nevertheless, despite his distrust of the Dutch and internal disagreements among the plotters, Ludlow had been aware that a second Anglo-Dutch war could also be seen as an opportunity for the dissenters in England to rise, not just by the dissenters themselves, but also by the war's royalist critics, who 'thinke it may be dangerous to engage in a Warr abroad, whilst so considerable a parte of the Nation is discontented at home; who may rise when their Enemyes are Imployed elsewhere'.[154] The English authorities therefore feared that while they were engaged in a foreign war, 'the dissatisfyed at home' might take the opportunity to throw off their yoke.[155] This also became an issue when the English were looking to recruit 'some of the old [Commonwealth] Commanders to serve in the fleete'. The Duke of York was warned that 'it would be dangerous to Intrust the Phanaticques in Command, least they should set up for themselves when they had beaten the Dutch'. But he reportedly replied only that 'when they had done their worke with them, they would pull their skinnes over their Eares; Which harsh & plaine languadge made the Phanaticques the more Wary to Engage', as did their unwillingness 'to

---

[151] Rowen, *John de Witt*, pp. 80, 90–2, 107.   [152] Ibid., pp. 93, 127.
[153] Ibid., p. 113; and Jonathan Israel, *The Dutch Republic: Its Rise, Greatness, and Fall 1477–1806* (Oxford: Clarendon Press, 1995), pp. 766–76.
[154] Ludlow, 'Voyce', p. 1014.   [155] Ibid., p. 1017.

conforme to the English Liturgy', as they would not have been allowed to choose their own chaplains.[156] Those former commonwealthmen who had joined the English fleet, meanwhile, were considered as apostates and turncoats by Ludlow. In his opinion they deserved to die 'for the supporting of Tirrany, & suppressing of Liberty, yea, for the upholding of those Montaynes that are in the way of the Lord'.[157] Some former Parliamentarians did in turn serve on the Dutch side.[158] Yet neither their number nor their influence appears to have been great enough to turn the Anglo-Dutch war into a success for the English republican cause.

Conclusion

Ludlow's life was strongly determined by his faith, and this faith steered his political and military action. After the restoration of the monarchy, his faith also determined his exile – from his decision to go abroad and seek his purpose in the promotion of the Lord's cause on the Continent to his considerations of concrete political action. One way to fulfil his duty as a true follower of the Lord for Ludlow was to look after the translation and publication of the stories of martyrdom experienced by his fellow regicides and republicans. Another was to set the historical record straight by putting to paper his own version of events surrounding the English Civil War and regicide and the political events that followed. Life in exile gave him a unique opportunity to do so, both because it provided the enforced leisure necessary to pursue these projects and because it opened up a new perspective on the events in the British Isles through geographical distance. The experiences relating to life as a refugee also brought into focus the sense of community created by transnational networks of Reformed Protestants across Europe and the role of England and English republicans within this community. While Ludlow clearly saw himself as a republican and an Englishman, he also considered himself to be a follower of the Lord belonging to a community of true believers scattered across the earth and as such not a national, but rather a transnational or international agent.

---

[156] Ibid., pp. 1023, 1025.
[157] As was the case with Admiral John Lawson, who had initially served under the Commonwealth, but later collaborated with Monck in the Restoration process and headed an English squadron in the Second Anglo-Dutch War. Ibid., p. 1071. See J. Binns, 'Lawson, Sir John (c. 1615–1665)', *ODNB*.
[158] Ludlow, 'Voyce', p. 1127.

CHAPTER 6

Sidney's Rebellious Vision

They that may bind kings in chains may also lay the sword to their throat.

... there is no evil in absolute monarchy which is not increased by rendering it hereditary.

We promise ourselves peace, but there will be, can be, no true peace till by the blood of the wicked murderers a propitiation be made for the blood of the righteous that has been shed by them.[1]

Algernon Sidney, *Court Maxims* (c. 1664–5)

Introduction: The *Court Maxims* as Sidney's Call to Arms

Like Ludlow's 'Voyce from the Watch Tower', Sidney's major exile work, *Court Maxims*, was not published during his lifetime. The reason for this is all too obvious. The piece openly condemns the Restoration monarchy in England as tyrannical and calls for rebellion against the Stuarts. With the tightening of pre-publication censorship in England under Sir Roger L'Estrange such a project would have seemed unthinkable.[2] But even anonymous publication in the United Provinces would have been risky. Sidney was a persecuted man. By the mid-1660s he had already escaped several assassination plots, first in Rome, then in Augsburg.[3] Yet this does not mean that Sidney's work, probably written in 1664–5, after the English defeat off Guinea in late 1664 but before the official declaration of the Second Anglo-Dutch war in March 1665, could not have circulated in manuscript among the exile community in Holland, for whom it may

---

[1] Sidney, *Court Maxims*, pp. 56, 28, 198.

[2] See L'Estrange, *Considerations and Proposals*; and Annabel Patterson, *Censorship and Interpretation: The Conditions of Writing and Reading in Early Modern England* (Madison: University of Wisconsin Press, 1984, repr. 1992). On possible publication plans in the 1660s, see Carswell, 'Algernon Sidney's "Court Maxims"'.

[3] Sidney, 'The Apology of Algernone Sydney, in the Day of his Death', in *Discourses* (1751), p. xxxi; and Ludlow, 'Voyce', p. 1063.

first and foremost have been produced as a call to arms for an invasion of England.[4] As we have seen in Chapter 4, Sidney's aim at the time had been to gather money and troops to restore republican government in his home country with Dutch and French backing. The *Court Maxims* thus reveal Sidney's political concerns in the years immediately following the Restoration, while also giving an insight into his exile life.

What marks out the *Court Maxims* as a work of exile was Sidney's increasing preoccupation with the balance of power in Europe – an issue he had been interested in throughout his years in the diplomatic service of the Commonwealth, but which he now came to see from another perspective as he was lobbying foreign governments to support his cause. As we will see below, Sidney (despite what he might have been telling Turenne) had always been wary of the growing influence of France, which had replaced Spain as Europe's most powerful country, while attempting to foster a closer relationship with Protestant neighbours such as the United Provinces and the Lutheran and Reformed territories of Germany. The Protestant cantons of Switzerland and their associated cities, such as Geneva, were also considered potential partners against the Catholic monarchy in Paris, which was worryingly close to the Stuart court, while the Huguenot regions in the south of France were another important source of support. For English republicans, meanwhile, the United Provinces remained the strongest potential partner both as a country of exile for many displaced former commonwealthmen and as an ally against the French and English monarchies. Sidney's debt to the political thought of Dutch authors such as Johan and Pieter de la Court and the Grand Pensionary Johan de Witt is obvious in that context.[5] The Second Anglo-Dutch War was seen as a major opportunity by English republicans on both sides of the Channel to tip the balance of power in Europe in favour of the Protestant trading powers of the north. At the same time, the United Provinces were also a model for English republicans, thanks both to their form of self-government and to their successful practice of liberty of conscience, which facilitated immigration, trade and economic growth.[6]

---

[4] On the dating of the manuscript, see the Preface to Sidney, *Court Maxims*, pp. vii, xiv; and Carswell, 'Algernon Sidney's "Court Maxims"'.

[5] Scott, *Algernon Sidney and the English Republic*, pp. 207–16; and Weststeijn, *Commercial Republicanism*, p. 352. Sidney draws, for instance, on Johan and Pieter De la Court, *Interest van Holland, ofte gronden van Hollands-Welvaren* (Amsterdam: Joan. Cyprianus vander Gracht, 1662). De Witt is sometimes credited as a co-author of that work.

[6] On the aspect of trade, see in particular Kustaa Multamäki, *Towards Great Britain: Commerce & Conquest in the Thought of Algernon Sidney and Charles Davenant* (Helsinki: Academia Scientiarum Fennica, 1999).

In the secularised historiography of seventeenth-century English republican thought, however, the religious aspect of the struggle for freedom has often been neglected. This is partly due to the focus on the classical Greek and Roman sources of English republicanism. Puritan 'tirades about wicked biblical kings', meanwhile, are not usually considered 'Sidney's normal tone of voice'.[7] However, as we will see below, Sidney's belief in divine providence and his defence of the Protestant cause allied him more closely with Ludlow and a radical Puritan agenda than with the classical constitutionalism of Harrington and Neville.[8] While pursuing a restoration of the Commonwealth in England, he always had the establishment of liberty of conscience on his agenda. This agenda was also influenced and shaped by the people he met along his way – or rather, his choice of acquaintances reflected his own beliefs. As we have seen from Sidney's circles in Rome, these acquaintances were not exclusively Protestant. Christina of Sweden and Cardinal Decio Azzolino, the Prince Pamphilio and other courtiers of Rome were part of his network. Yet Sidney's political interests were always much closer to those of his fellow Protestants, and he was bitterly disappointed by the relative lack of support offered by De Witt, who must have gathered that aiding the English republican cause in the short term would have meant fostering a long-term rival.

Structure and Argument

Sidney's *Court Maxims* are written in the form of fifteen dialogues between the 'Commonwealthsman' Eunomius and the 'moral, honest Courtier' Philalethes, who meet to discuss the situation of England after the recent restoration of the Stuarts as well as broader ideas of government.[9] Philalethes cannot understand 'why the people of England, who within these few years did so passionately desire a king, do seem extremely dissatisfied now that one is established', while Eunomius thinks that the people are

---

[7] Carswell, 'Algernon Sidney's "Court Maxims"', p. 100. However, Blair Worden suggests that Sidney may have tailored his writing to his audience. See his 'The Commonwealth Kidney of Algernon Sidney', pp. 25–6.

[8] On Sidney's religious, especially Protestant and Calvinist, influences, see Winship, 'Algernon Sidney's Calvinist Republicanism'; and Hans-Dieter Metzger, 'David und Saul in Staats- und Widerstandslehren der Frühen Neuzeit', in Walter Dietrich and Hubert Herkommer (eds), *König David – biblische Schlüsselfigur und europäische Leitgestalt* (Freiburg: Universitätsverlag; Stuttgart: W. Kohlhammer, 2003), pp. 437–84.

[9] Sidney, *Court Maxims*, p. 1.

disappointed because they hoped for something better and now find themselves 'unwilling to be oppressed'.[10] Therefore, he thinks, 'nothing is more reasonable than that they should repent of their choice *and endeavour to unmake what they have made*'.[11] So the courtier begins to outline fourteen maxims of government, which the republican goes on to refute and in the process explains Sidney's thinking on the present state of England and Europe and the rights and wrongs of rebellion.

Despite its topicality, the *Court Maxims*, as its title suggests, also engages more generally with the unchanging principles of government, the evils of absolute monarchy and tyranny and the virtues of limited or republican government. These more timeless aspects of Sidney's earlier work would later also find a place in the much more elaborate and substantial *Discourses*, written in response to Sir Robert Filmer's *Patriarcha*, the manuscript of which sent Sidney to the scaffold and earned him a place in the pantheon of republican martyrs after the failure of the Rye House Plot. As the *Court Maxims* remained unpublished during Sidney's lifetime, discussions have arisen over the appropriate order of the manuscript and the format which Sidney may have intended it to take.[12] For the sake of ease, I will be using the modern Cambridge study edition of the *Court Maxims* (edited by Blom, Mulier and Janse), fully aware that it provides only one possible version of the work, while also referring back to the original manuscript located in the Warwickshire County Record Office where appropriate.[13] At the end of this chapter, I will then add some thoughts on what the surviving manuscript might tell us about Sidney's purpose in writing and the evolution of his thought, and how the *Court Maxims* might relate to the *Discourses*. The main issue here is the broader themes and ideas Sidney engaged with during the early years of his exile, when the restoration of the English Commonwealth still appeared like a feasible option to some. The first eight and the final court maxims deal with the domestic power of the English king and the institution of monarchy more widely, the remaining five more specifically with the role of England's monarchy in a wider European context.

---

[10] Ibid., pp. 3–4.   [11] Ibid., p. 8.
[12] Scott, *Algernon Sidney and the English Republic*, pp. 189 ff.; and Sidney, *Court Maxims*, p. ix.
[13] Warwickshire County Record Office, Warwick, MS CR 1886. I would like to thank the staff at the Warwickshire County Record Office, and in particular Robert Pitt, for making the MS available to me in a digitised copy.

The Restoration Monarchy

The *Court Maxims* is an attack on the restored monarchy in England and Charles II's shortcomings as a king. From the beginning, Sidney questions the basis on which the English monarchy is founded as well as the king's legitimacy to rule. Thus he denies that monarchs are appointed by God to rule their people as fathers rule their children, while also rejecting the hereditary principle outright.[14] He similarly rejects the right of conquest, if the conquest is the result of an unjust war and if it only serves to enhance the monarch rather than the nation as a whole.[15] Therefore Sidney distinguishes clearly between a 'monarch' in the literal Greek sense, describing any kind of single-person ruler, and a legitimate 'king': 'For every usurper or thief that gains the chief power over a nation is a monarch, but none deserves the name of a king but he that governs by a right legally conferred on him.' The ultimate test for a government, however, was to him the success of a nation. As many republican governments had achieved great things and expanded their power in recent times, Sidney considered them clearly superior to monarchies. One obvious example for him was 'the English commonwealth' itself, 'which in five years conquered absolutely Scotland and Ireland, and in so many battles broke the Hollanders that they were brought to the utmost weakness'.[16] He was echoing the likes of Sir Arthur Haselrig, who in Parliament in 1659 had praised the strength of the English Commonwealth, observing that 'Trade flourished ... we were the most potent by sea that ever was known in England. Our Navy and Armies were never better.'[17] Sidney argued that, since many successful 'free states by divisions' often fell 'into monarchy', this only showed that monarchy was 'a state as death unto life'. Thus Sidney reasoned, 'as death is *the greatest evil that can befall a person, monarchy is the worst evil that can befall a nation*'.[18] England was therefore threatened by imminent death if it was not soon returned to republican rule.

Sidney's argument anticipates much of his later *Discourses*. Yet his immediate enemy in the 1660s was not Filmer, but the courtiers, bishops and lawyers who had helped Charles II to reclaim the power the republicans had wrested from his father.[19] Sidney argued that monarchy was not divinely ordained, but that the power to set up governments was originally

---

[14] Sidney, *Court Maxims*, pp. 10, 28. [15] Ibid., pp. 13–15. [16] Ibid., p. 18.
[17] *Diary of Thomas Burton*, iii, p. 97. [18] Sidney, *Court Maxims*, p. 20.
[19] Ibid., Eighth and Ninth Dialogues.

in the people. God had given the people the freedom to choose their own government, according to their own specific circumstances and the situation of their country.[20] Governments had not originated from fatherhood, as contemporary patriarchalists suggested, because the power of fathers did not extend beyond the family, and consequently monarchs could not claim obedience from their subjects on the basis of paternal authority.[21] This did not mean that republicans did not respect the authority of fathers in either family or state. On the contrary, republicans did not question that a father was the head of his household and responsible for his wife, children and servants.[22] They were just unwilling to concede that the father's power over his family could be extended to legitimise the rule of kings over their subjects. Kings were not 'God's anointed vicegerents' on earth, and their rule was not natural.[23] And since kingship could not be derived from fatherhood, the title of King could also not be hereditary. As Sidney put it, 'there is no evil in absolute monarchy which is not increased by rendering it hereditary'.[24] Even if the governor was good, no man could be confident their sons would 'inherit their fathers' virtues', and if they did not, what could be 'more extravagant than to give them the power wherewith their fathers were entrusted?'[25] Hereditary power, according to Sidney, could only beget 'hereditary hatred' because 'a virtuous generous people' would always abhor 'an absolute monarch'.[26] High birth was by no means a guarantee for good character or superior abilities. In fact, Sidney argued that there was 'hardly any sort of men' that nature did 'more sparingly impart her most precious endowments of body and mind to'. Therefore, it would be 'contrary to reason and nature' to endow an individual with responsibilities and duties on the basis of 'accidental advantages' such as riches or birth, which could never confer 'any natural privilege'.[27] Despite Sidney's own claims to a leading position in society on account of his noble birth, he strongly condemned inherited privileges that were not warranted by ability. His resentment of the restored Stuart line was mainly based on Charles II's poor performance as a king and the monarch's disregard of the law.

Sidney was thus far from claiming that all forms of monarchy were 'absolutely unlawful' in principle.[28] It was possible to have a constitutional form of monarchy in which a 'freeman governs free men according to law' and in which the 'good of the governed' took priority.[29] A 'wise, virtuous

[20] Ibid., p. 38.   [21] Ibid., p. 12.   [22] Ibid., p. 35.   [23] Ibid., p. 50.   [24] Ibid., p. 28.
[25] Ibid., p. 30.   [26] Ibid., pp. 33, 37.   [27] Ibid., p. 202.   [28] Ibid., p. 193.
[29] Ibid., p. 200.

man' could advance the public good without exalting himself 'above his brethren'.[30] And if a ruler was properly limited by the law, his personal qualities would become negligible. As Sidney puts it: 'The law errs not, the king may be mad or drunk.'[31] Unfortunately, the present king, Charles II, was as bad and as incompetent as his father, and the hereditary principle prevented any proper accountability. Thus his rule was 'despotical' and could be maintained only with the help of the bishops, who preached obedience because their own existence depended on the king, and of corrupt lawyers who made money out of defending the king's law.[32]

The only legitimate form of monarchy for Sidney was one limited by the law and fully accountable to the people. Like the constitutional republicans Harrington and Neville, Sidney held that in a commonwealth 'well-constituted laws govern, not men', and although 'the magistrate be wicked, the constitution is to be such that his exorbitant lusts may be restrained and his crimes punished'.[33] Like his fellow exile Neville, who wrote his major political treatise after the Restoration, Sidney even saw room for a 'legal' or 'constitutional' monarch in his system of government.[34] Such a legal monarchy was created 'when a man of admirable valour, justice, and wisdom' rose up 'amongst a free people, excelling every one and all together', so that they would 'willingly submit to be governed by him'.[35] But a man of such singular merit was rare; sovereignty and the choice of government would always remain with the people, and if necessary this choice could be implemented by force. Neville would not go as far as Sidney in allowing an individual of exceptional talent to emerge as a natural leader, though. He may not even have believed that such an individual could exist. Therefore Neville's emphasis was on accountability throughout. The key to maintaining popular sovereignty was to limit the powers of any monarch, no matter how virtuous he seemed to appear.[36] Sidney meanwhile was more explicit about what could happen to a monarch who did not respect the law and thus the people's will. As a last

---

[30] Ibid., p. 32. [31] Ibid., p. 82.

[32] Ibid., pp. 199 and 21 and the Eighth and Ninth Dialogues on bishops and lawyers.

[33] Ibid., p. 196. The principle that 'good orders' rather than 'good men' make for a stable government was promoted by Harrington in *Oceana* and 'A System of Politics', in *The Commonwealth of Oceana and A System of Politics*, ed. J. G. A. Pocock (Cambridge, UK: Cambridge University Press, 1992), respectively at p. 64 and pp. 267–93, at p. 274; and Neville, *Plato redivivus*, p. 91.

[34] Rachel Hammersley argues that, under certain circumstances, this could even be said of Harrington. See *James Harrington: An Intellectual Biography* (Oxford: Oxford University Press, 2019), chapter 5.

[35] Sidney, *Court Maxims*, p. 203. In the *Discourses*, ed. West, p. 38, Sidney calls such an individual 'a king by nature'. Harrington, however, did see space for a temporary dictator – the Cromwell figure Olphaus Megaletor of his *Oceana*.

[36] Neville, *Plato redivivus*, pp. 186–8.

resort, a monarch could always be deposed – if necessary by force, as had happened in England in 1649.

Sidney considered the absoluteness of kings 'a plain mistake', for 'no man can say he has absolute power who is not king till elected by the people, and is no longer king when the same disapprove him'.[37] This point of the *Court Maxims* may owe something to the *Consideratien van staat ofte politike weegschaal* (1661) by the brothers De la Court, which argues that only the people as a collective can appoint a sovereign ruler and rescind his power when he is no longer able to protect them. It also feeds into the De la Courts' and Sidney's arguments against hereditary monarchy, that the descendants of a ruler cannot be expected to share his ability and virtue.[38] A monarch had to be accountable; if he acted against the people's will set down in the law he was a tyrant, and a tyrant could be removed,[39] for '[t]hey that may bind kings in chains may also lay the sword to their throat'.[40] Sidney strongly advocated the principle of rebellion against unjust rulers, even as he would reject the use of the word 'rebellion' for its negative connotations in the *Discourses*: 'a people resisting oppression, and vindicating their own liberty' could never 'incur either guilt or infamy'.[41] Instead, he insisted that a subject was 'obliged to disobey the king if he commands anything contrary to that law', as, in doing so, the king would break 'the order he should observe' and so oblige his subjects to disobey him.[42] Thus if a tyrant were to force false religion on his subjects, they would be obliged to resist him.[43]

Overall, there were three kinds of monarchy for which Sidney could find scriptural precedents: theocracy, in which a worldly ruler was guided by the spirit of God's will; a limited monarchy, in which the ruler did not depart from the Law of God; and finally 'evil' monarchy, which renounced God and therefore had to be condemned.[44] Sidney clearly thought that the Stuart monarchy was of the latter sort, and that the English people shared in the king's guilt because they had recalled Charles Stuart from exile, thus permitting his ungodly rule. As he put it in rather dramatic biblical language: 'We could never be contented till we returned again into Egypt, the house of our bondage. God had delivered us from slavery and showed us that he would be our king; and we recall from exile one of that detested

---

[37] Sidney, *Court Maxims*, p. 62.
[38] Johan and Pieter de la Court, *Consideratien van staat ofte politike weegschaal* (Amsterdam: Jacob Volckert, 1661), part I, chapter 7.
[39] Sidney, *Court Maxims*, p. 53.   [40] Ibid., p. 56.   [41] Sidney, *Discourses*, ed. West, p. 519.
[42] Ibid., p. 520, and Sidney, *Court Maxims*, p. 82.   [43] Sidney, *Court Maxims*, p. 100.
[44] Ibid., p. 194.

race.'[45] England's unhappiness was its own fault, because the English had acted like the Israelites, who, while Moses was away to receive the Ten Commandments, had set up the golden calf and worshipped it: 'We set up an idol and dance about it, though we know it to be most filthily polluted with innocent blood.' Therefore there could be 'no true peace till by the blood of the wicked murderers a propitiation be made for the blood of the righteous that has been shed by him'.[46] In other words, there would be no 'true peace' in England unless Charles II was removed. This was Sidney's current agenda, the driving force behind his plot.

Religion, Providence and Monarchical Power

While much of Sidney's religious language had faded by the time he wrote the *Discourses* (see Figure 4), his *Court Maxims* were firmly rooted in the Puritan thought we have previously witnessed in Ludlow's writing.[47] Like Ludlow, Sidney frequently compared the English to the Israelites who had lived in bondage under the Egyptian pharaoh; he used stories from the Bible to depict monarchy as tyranny; and he used the authority of Scripture to justify rebellion against unjust rulers. Sidney's change in tone from one work to the other, as Michael Winship points out, was probably due to 'changing times'.[48] While the *Court Maxims* were addressed to those 'Sidney calls the "saints"' in an attempt to 'inspire rebellion against Charles', the *Discourses* were written for 'a society increasingly suspicious of anything resembling religious "enthusiasm" or dogmatic Calvinism'.[49] The *Discourses*, as Blair Worden suggests, may even have been edited with this suspicion in mind to make the work more palatable to a Whig audience 'by removing all taint of a now-archaic religious intensity'.[50] And Hans-Dieter Metzger suggests that such an edition would have been necessary to ensure the work's reception in an increasingly rational Enlightenment environment.[51] More cynically, Alan Houston suspects that the Puritan language 'of Egypt and Canaan' used in the *Court Maxims* was only 'a matter of expedience' – a ploy used by Sidney to bring Ludlow 'over to his side' and convince him of 'the feasibility of fomenting revolution during the Second Dutch War' by adopting 'Ludlow's language'.[52]

---

[45] Ibid., p. 197.   [46] Ibid., p. 198. The scriptural reference is to Exodus 32:4–6.
[47] Winship, 'Algernon Sidney's Calvinist Republicanism', p. 756.   [48] Ibid., p. 765.
[49] Ibid., pp. 756, 765.
[50] Ibid., p. 765, referring to Worden, *Roundhead Reputations*, pp. 13, 101, 131–2.
[51] Metzger, 'David und Saul', pp. 465–6.
[52] Houston, *Algernon Sidney and the Republican Heritage*, p. 130n.

Figure 4   Algernon Sydney, *Discourses Concerning Government* (London: A. Millar, 1763),
image of the author from frontispiece.
© The British Library Board. 687.h.22

However, I would contend that this language was very much Sidney's
own. As Metzger has shown, both Sidney and Ludlow were writing in the
same Protestant tradition as Jean Calvin and Theodore Beza, theologians
they respected and referenced in their works, both implicitly and explicitly.[53] And both Sidney and Ludlow saw the Bible as a guide for political

---

[53] Metzger, 'David und Saul', pp. 455–6.

consideration. As Sidney points out, whether a particular form of monarchy was lawful or unlawful, 'we will examine according to the rules of Scripture, reason, and human authors'.[54] This triad of authorities – 'Scripture' as well as 'reason, and human authors' – needs to be taken seriously in order to understand Sidney's political thought. Scripture and reason for Sidney were not in conflict with each other; rather reason was a guide to Scripture. As Sidney had emphasised when addressing Lantin, religion had primacy above all, and the study of theology and the knowledge of God was of the utmost importance. Like the Spaniard Márquez, he clearly thought that Scripture should be a guide to practical politics.[55] Whatever the reasoning, therefore, behind the different emphasis in tone in the *Discourses*, in the *Court Maxims* Sidney calls on his readers to follow God's guidance in establishing an accountable commonwealth that would also provide liberty of conscience and enable the people to 'serve God without fear'.[56] His providential stance becomes apparent in Sidney's rejection of absolute monarchy.

While the courtier in the *Court Maxims* defends monarchy by divine right and uses it as a legal source of authority, he does not appear to be guided by religious principles or the word of the Lord. On the contrary, it is Sidney's commonwealthman who makes extensive use of the Scriptures to justify accountable government. The commonwealthman thus occupies the moral high ground as the voice of the true believer and follower of Christ. Philalethes meanwhile has to concede that 'at court we little trouble ourselves with the intricacies of the Bible', not least for fear of being 'looked upon as a fanatic'. If courtiers used the Bible at all to justify their actions, he says, they did so through the authority of 'learned and grave men', who were 'better versed in such matters'. The major part of the Fourth Dialogue on the biblical justification of royal power then revolves around the interpretation of I Samuel, chapter 8, and the question of whether or not kings are sacred and should therefore have the right to rule in an arbitrary manner as agents of the Lord. Naturally, Philalethes takes the royalist stance that God originally set up monarchy 'first in the person of Moses, then several judges, and afterwards of Saul and David', and that the Lord's express will subsequently came to be 'a perpetual law to succeeding ages'. God had honoured kings 'to bear his image on earth' and given them 'the name of his anointed, forbidding any to touch him'

---

[54] Sidney, *Court Maxims*, p. 193.
[55] BNF, MS Français 23254, Lantiniana, fol. 101. See also Chapter 4.
[56] Sidney, *Court Maxims*, p. 49.

and 'commanding all to obey him', no matter what the ruler demanded. This, according to the courtier, was confirmed by the words of Samuel describing the kind of king that God would give to the Israelites: a cruel king who would take his people's sons and daughters and all their possessions and 'give them to his servants'. And yet the people would not be allowed to resist him as he was the Lord's anointed.[57] This interpretation of Samuel's speech as justifying the right of kings to act as they pleased had been prevalent in medieval times and was used by seventeenth-century royalists in defence of the royal prerogative and absolute rule.[58]

Eunomius, in contrast, argues in the Calvinist tradition that Moses was not a king in the manner that Philalethes suggests, as he did not give any laws to the people but only 'transmitted to them what he received from God'. He also did not pretend 'to the government by a prerogative of birth, but for the assurance of God's presence with him, demonstrated by miracles'. In any case, Moses' sons 'did not inherit his power', and he therefore did not establish any form of hereditary succession. Thus it was 'a greater crime to reverence as Christ's vicegerent him that is not so, than not to obey Moses who truly was so'.[59] Nor were any of the succeeding judges kings, Eunomius argues, for 'Gideon said: neither I nor my sons will reign over you.' And 'Samuel was no king, for then the Israelites would not have said to him: give us a king.' In fact, the people had rejected God in asking for a king, and God had punished them for their sin by appointing a tyrant 'being of the same nature as plagues and fiery serpents sent to destroy them'.[60] Thus, like Philipp Melanchthon and Jean Calvin in the sixteenth century, Sidney interpreted Samuel's description of the king as a caricature. Israel had been in a state of liberty when it was ruled directly by God via Moses, and it became enslaved under the rule of Saul.[61]

Likewise, the commonwealthman doubts that kings should not be resisted because they are 'sacred' and 'absolute'.[62] Instead, he argues that the text 'touch not mine anointed' had always been abused by 'those who have most endeavoured to deceive and oppress mankind', who 'sought impunity' by applying these words to themselves.[63] In England, Eunomius blames Archbishop Thomas Cranmer for first using ceremony to make Henry VIII 'head of the church' and obliging the people to acknowledge

---

[57] Ibid., p. 39.   [58] Metzger, 'David und Saul', pp. 445–6.
[59] Sidney, *Court Maxims*, pp. 40–1.   [60] Ibid.. pp. 42–3, 47.
[61] Metzger, 'David und Saul', pp. 463, 449; Scott, *Algernon Sidney and the English Republic*, p. 212.
[62] Sidney, *Court Maxims*, p. 43.   [63] Ibid. The reference is to I Chronicles 16:22, Psalm 105:15.

him 'supreme in church as well as state', thus enhancing both the king's power and that of his clergy against Rome. As Sidney puts it: 'This is the idol of their own making that they have set up.' Anyone refusing 'to worship the impure idol', meanwhile, was 'looked on as a fanatic and appointed for destruction'.[64] The true anointed were the prophets, as 'the text explains itself: touch not mine anointed and do my prophets no harm. The same thing is more strongly inculcated under two names: anointed and prophets are the same persons.'[65] Those often taken as the anointed, in contrast, were nothing more than idols of the people's making. As Sidney has Eunomius explain, when the Israelites asked for 'such a king as the nations around about them had', they also decided 'to follow those nations in their beastly idolatry', rejecting 'the civil government of God's own institution' and 'renouncing the liberty of being subject to him only, to make themselves slaves unto a king'.[66]

In Eunomius' opinion, meanwhile, the English monarchy is much worse than the government God threatened to give the Israelites. For 'we find nothing there of the spies, informers, trepanners, and false witnesses, which render every man's house a snare to him', and there is 'no mention of corrupt, obscene, mad favourites, inventions to delude the subjects, pervert the law, sell justice, corrupt manners, and destroy families'. God's appointed ruler Saul instead allowed the people to 'serve God without fear' by giving them liberty of conscience, while among the English 'a praying meeting is looked on as a conspiracy, and the chief in such exercises are haled to prisons, cast into dungeons, and caused to perish with hunger or cold'. Eunomius goes on to complain: 'It is no matter whether a man be an Independent, Presbyterian, or Anabaptist, if he can pray or preach he is a fanatic with them. Our prisons are full of such, our churches empty.'[67] Sidney was clearly recalling Ludlow's complaint that Charles II was 'laying hands on the prophets & people of the Lord for meeting together; to seeke his face, and to speake in his name' in the wake of the new penal legislation included in the so-called Clarendon Code, and that 'the prisons [were] being filled with such' as well as 'some plotters as is given forth'.[68] Like Ludlow, he also bemoaned 'noble [Henry] Vane', who had died a martyr's death bearing 'ample ... testimony' to God's truth and therefore had earned 'a famous victory and a never

[64] Sidney, *Court Maxims*, p. 53.   [65] Ibid., p. 55.   [66] Ibid., p. 47.   [67] Ibid., p. 49.
[68] Ludlow, 'Voyce', p. 1079. The Clarendon Code included the Act of Uniformity (1662), the Conventicle Act (1664) and the Five Mile Act (1665).

perishing crown'.[69] In Sidney's opinion, Vane had to die because the English monarchy feared him as a model of 'virtue, prudence, courage, industry, reputation, and godliness'. The king, he argues, wanted to destroy 'all virtue, wisdom, and godliness, since those, who were eminent in any of those qualities, looked on him as their master, and seemed to have learnt all they knew or practised by his precepts or example'.[70] For Sidney too, the conflict between the dissenters and the king had something of the eschatological struggle between good and evil about it. The 'court fears and hates all good and virtuous men', which showed 'the evil' of its government. English prisons were 'full of the most godly persons in the nation' and the royal 'palace receptacles of the most wicked and vile men in the nation'.[71] The situation had escalated to such an extent that Sidney was convinced that God would not long delay his vengeance for the 'blood of the saints'. Invoking the same biblical passage as Ludlow on the matter, Genesis 15:16, Sidney assured the English government that 'the measure of your iniquity seems to be full, the harvest ripe, and when a separation is made between the wheat and you, you will be fit for the fire'.[72] In the meantime, the saints themselves had to withstand the powers of evil.

As kings were not God's anointed, but idols of the people's making, Sidney argued, they could be held accountable and should be resisted. As Eunomius points out: 'God has several times commanded kings to be slain; therefore, to slay them is not simply evil. God in some cases has approved the slaying of kings; therefore, in some cases to slay kings is not evil.' Thus, for instance, those who are 'wicked idolaters and tyrants' should be punished, and 'They that may bind kings in chains may also lay the sword to their throat.'[73] Overall, the commonwealthman Eunomius states that he acknowledges 'only three original titles' to the crown:

> First, that of those that are made kings by God's immediate command, as Saul, David, etcetera.
>   Secondly, when a man by a free people is freely made king.
>   Thirdly, when a kingdom is acquired by victory in a just war, all depending upon the condition on which a power is given or gained.[74]

But even if a monarch fulfilled those criteria, he still remained accountable because the relationship between ruler and ruled was governed by a contract. Therefore 'no king can be so firmly established by God's designation and the people's choice but that the subjects may justly withdraw

---

[69] Sidney, *Court Maxims*, p. 49. See Ludlow on Vane in 'Voyce', pp. 935, 950, 976, 1063.
[70] Sidney, *Court Maxims*, pp. 185–6.   [71] Ibid., p. 188.   [72] Ibid., p. 191.
[73] Ibid., pp. 55–6.   [74] Ibid., p. 57.

obedience from him and set up to themselves another governor or government if he recede from his duty by governing ill'.[75] In other words, the people or the subjects could lawfully resist a king if he did not fulfil his duty and became a tyrant.

Liberty of Conscience

Part of the tyrannical government in Restoration England was the monarch's supremacy over the Church, his insistence on religious conformity as an indicator of political loyalty and his consequent suppression of religious dissent. Like Ludlow in his 'Voyce from the Watch Tower', Sidney complains about the arrests of 'fanatics' in the aftermath of the Act of Uniformity and depicts the bishops as the dissenters' main enemies. While his spokesman Eunomius concedes that the upholding of order is important in a state, he also claims that the need for order has often been used as a pretext for religious persecution and condemns 'the power of the civil magistrate in spiritual things, ridiculously setting a temporal head upon a spiritual body'.[76] Here too Sidney agreed with the brothers De la Court, who argued that monarchs under the influence of courtiers and clerics were more likely to prescribe religion than republican rulers who feared they might be deposed by the people.[77] Yet religious persecution was not only wrong because a temporal power was meddling in spiritual affairs; it was also wrong because belief could not be forced, Sidney argued, both recalling the De la Court brothers and anticipating Locke, whose ideas on toleration were likewise influenced by a period of exile in the United Provinces:[78] 'if it be true that belief is not the act of the will, it is neither in my power to believe what I please, nor what pleases another man that is stronger than I'.[79] Forcing the people to profess a certain faith did nothing but create hypocrites, Sidney argued, illustrating his case with an example from geometry: 'I believe the three angles of a triangle to be equal to two right angles. Torment may perhaps force me to say they are equal to three right angles or but to one, but all the tyrants in the world can never make me believe they are not equal to two.'[80]

---

[75] Ibid., pp. 58–9.   [76] Ibid., pp. 96, 95.
[77] De la Court, *Consideratien van staat*, part I, chapter 25, pp. 92–3.
[78] See Scott, *Algernon Sidney and the English Republic*, p. 212, and De la Court, *Interest van Holland*, esp. chapters 13 and 17. On the De la Court brothers' stance on religious toleration and the impossibility of forcing belief, see also Weststeijn, *Commercial Republicanism*, p. 326.
[79] Sidney, *Court Maxims*, p. 98.   [80] Ibid.

Locke would come to argue in his *Letter Concerning Toleration* in very similar terms that faith was not a matter of choice and therefore could not be imposed by an external force: 'For no Man can, if he would, conform his Faith to the Dictates, of another. All the Life and Power of true Religion consist in the inward and full perswasion of the mind: And Faith is not Faith without believing.'[81] The conclusion Sidney drew from his conviction was that God was the only authority to be followed. It was 'from God, not the prince or hangman, that we must learn religion', he observed.[82] Conversely, the true faith could never be rooted out, he argued with reference to Hugo Grotius's history of the Dutch revolt, *De rebus belgicis*, which framed 'the struggle against Habsburg Spain as a repetition of the fight of the Batavians against Roman oppression'. Like Grotius, Sidney suggested 'that freedom of conscience was embedded in the character of the Batavian people'.[83] The Spanish had caused much bloodshed in the Low Countries, where the Duke of Alva had boasted of killing many heretics during the Dutch Revolt. Nevertheless, the present state of that region showed 'that the seed of truth sown by God cannot be rooted up by man'. Likewise, '[t]he bishops, imprisoning, banishing, and killing some dissenters' in England would 'not bring the people of God to join in their frivolous profane worship, or associate themselves with the obscene and impure crews that attend it'. Unless a prince followed 'true doctrine and worship' the people had to resist him: 'when the cause of God is in question and I must disobey the king or sin against God, the choice is easy'. As faith was 'the gift of God', no injury to a man could be 'more justly repelled than violence offered to the conscience'.[84] In England, where the bishops prohibited 'all worship of God but what they and their king set up in a Common Prayer Book', the dissenters still followed their

[81] John Locke, *Second Treatise of Government* and *A Letter Concerning Toleration*, ed. Mark Goldie (Oxford: Oxford University Press, 2016), p. 128.
[82] Sidney, *Court Maxims*, p. 98.
[83] See Geert H. Janssen, 'The Republic of the Refugees: Early Modern Migrations and the Dutch Experience', *Historical Journal*, 60:1 (2017), 233–52, at p. 242. Sidney was probably referring to Hugo Grotius, *De rebus belgicis: Or the Annals, and History of the Low-Countrye-Warrs* (London: printed for Henry Twyford in Vine-Court Middle-Temple; and Robert Paulet at the Bible in Chancery-Lane, 1665). Since the work did not appear in English until 1665, Sidney may have worked with the Latin text of 1657: *Hugonis Grotii Annales et historiae de rebus belgicis* (Amsteerdam: Ex Typographejo Joannis Blaev, 1657). On the significance of this work, see Jan Waszink, 'Tacitism in Holland: Hugo Grotius' *Annales et historiae de rebus Belgicis*', in Craig Kallendorf, G. H. Tucker et al. (eds), *Acta Conventus Neo-Latini Bonnensis: Proceedings of the 12th International Congress of Neo-Latin Studies, Bonn, 2003* (Tempe: Arizona State University, Arizona Center for Medieval & Renaissance Studies, 2006), pp. 881–92.
[84] Sidney, *Court Maxims*, pp. 99, 101.

own faith: 'The fanatics yet meet to call upon God, pray and expound the Scriptures, comfort one another in their afflictions, know the mind of God, and humble themselves before him for their sins.' Kings and princes might threaten them, but the fanatics stood firm in their resistance to illegitimate power: 'If the king command them to worship in his way, they will not do it, knowing it to be absurd and profane. If he forbid them to worship God as they know God had commanded them, they desist not from doing it, having his word for their warrant.'[85]

The dissenters in England would continue to follow their consciences because they had the assurance of their faith that they were doing right by God. Besides, Sidney argued, religious persecution had serious political and economic consequences, as it would lead England to 'be dispeopled' as 'the best men in the nation' were 'banished and destroyed' – an argument taken from the De la Court brothers and later recalled by both Slingsby Bethel and Henry Neville in the 1680s.[86] In their 'principled pragmatism', the De la Courts had argued that merchants 'persecuted for their beliefs' would 'simply settle in another country' where they would be able to 'enjoy greater liberty'. Instead, toleration would be 'the most powerful means to maintain in Holland many Residents' as well as to 'attract foreign Inhabitants from the surrounding Countries hither to reside'. Religious freedom was thus 'an essential element of the liberty that defines a true commercial commonwealth'.[87] The political and religious divisions in England, in contrast, as Sidney pointed out, were in danger of leaving the country weak and open to foreign invasion, and England was certainly 'worth conquering'. As Sidney put it in the voice of Eunomius: 'When the people are strong, numerous, valiant, wise, well disciplined, rich, well content with their present condition, a conquest is difficult. If weak, few, cowardly, without discipline, poor, discontented, they are easily subdued; and this is our condition.'[88] The restoration of a strong

---

[85] Ibid., p. 106.

[86] Ibid., p. 103; [Slingsby Bethel], *The Interest of Princes and States* (London: printed for John Wickins at the White-Hart against St Dunstans Church in Fleetstreet, 1680), p. 31; Neville, *Plato redivivus*, p. 157.

[87] Weststeijn, *Commercial Republicanism*, pp. 327–8, referring specifically to Johan and Pieter de la Court's *Aanwysing der heilsame politike gronden en maximen van de Republike van Holland en West-Vriesland* (Leiden and Rotterdam: Hakkens, 1669), I.14, pp. 59, 65–6. The treatise was a revised edition of *Interest van Holland* (1662), which Sidney would have known. Weststeijn (*Commercial Republicanism*, pp. 229–30) also points out that, unlike most English republicans, the De la Court brothers extended this toleration to Catholics. However, the relative openness of both Sidney and Neville towards Catholics suggests that there was more common ground.

[88] Sidney, *Court Maxims*, p. 78.

republican government and civil peace in England therefore was necessary to maintain the balance of power in Europe.

At this point, it might be interjected that liberty of conscience was not just a good reserved for Protestant dissenters. As we have seen in Chapter 2, Sidney could well imagine a peaceful coexistence of Protestants and Catholics if the English government was prepared to grant equal freedoms to both. He had told Turenne that the Protestant dissenters felt 'less hatred for the Catholic religion than for the government of bishops' and that liberty of conscience, broadly conceived, would keep the country quiet and Charles's subjects loyal.[89] Overall, Sidney feared Catholics less than he did High Anglicans or strict Presbyterians, or rather, he 'feared the Prince of Orange more than the Duke of York' because a Catholic king would always have to accommodate religious minorities outside the Church of England.[90] A Protestant monarch, meanwhile, was likely to model the state Church according to his own beliefs and impose one creed and form of worship for all. Besides, Sidney had acquired considerable respect for Catholics during the early years of his exile, not least the many capable cardinals in Rome, whose characters he captured in some detail. In this respect, he resembled Neville, whose stay in Italy would notably affect his views on Catholicism and toleration. Unlike Harrington, Milton or even Bethel, Neville argued in the 1680s that Catholics too should be tolerated and be able to live without fear of persecution.[91]

Anglo-Dutch Relations and the Balance of Power in Europe

According to the five dialogues discussing the ninth to thirteenth court maxims, the European power balance was currently under threat through the growing influence of France and the waning fortunes of England. Sidney's preferred solution to the European power struggles was an Anglo-Dutch alliance against the French that would also promote the Protestant cause against the Catholic forces on the Continent.

The courtier Philalethes argues that Charles II was aiming for a 'union with France' because the country was currently 'the most absolute in these parts of the world' and England endeavoured to model its own government along the same lines. The English king also intended to 'bring in the

---

[89] Louis XIV, St Germain, to Colbert, 29 July 1670, AE, Correspondence Politique, Angleterre, 8CP/99, 1670, Supplément, pp. 270–1.
[90] See Scott, *Algernon Sidney and the English Republic*, pp. 2, 153, referring to NA, Baschet Correspondence 150, fol. 261 (1681).
[91] Mahlberg, *Henry Neville and English Republican Culture*, pp. 200–7.

vices of the French, to corrupt our young nobility, gentry, and people', and seek the protection of the powerful neighbour. The commonwealthman Eunomius in contrast sees Charles's policy as a grave mistake and argues that England should assert its own strength as it has done in the past, so that it will not come to be 'dependent on and subservient to its interest'.[92] For that reason, Eunomius also bemoans the recent sale of Dunkirk across the Channel in northern France, which had been 'one of the best places in the world' for the English as a strategic military point and important trading port on the Continent. Likewise, Ludlow had been angered by the 1662 sale, 'an Action so villanous & unworthy of a man, that none on this side of the sea could be drawne to believe it', not least because the town had been a Protestant sanctuary on the edge of a Catholic nation. It had been occupied by the Protectorate since 1658 and was confirmed as an English possession by the Treaty of the Pyrenees in 1659. The 'acquisition of Dunkirk' stood for the 'continued vigour' of the English government in foreign affairs, whatever republicans might otherwise think of Cromwell as a ruler.[93] The recent transaction, for which Clarendon was frequently blamed, had therefore rendered Charles II 'most Odious & Abominable to all the Protestant interest; that being the only refuge they had in those partes in case of Extreamity'.[94] Sidney feared that any further concessions to French interests could only lead England into dependence and slavery.[95]

At the same time, Philalethes argues that a union of the English court with France would necessitate a breach with Spain as the two countries' interests are in conflict with each other. Eunomius meanwhile contends that England, which has been unable to gain pre-eminence in Europe, should not advance either country and 'rather curb ... the growth of that greatness that is already become formidable to all the states of Europe'.[96] While Philalethes concedes that it might be 'good for England to keep the balance more equal between France and Spain', he nevertheless considers it necessary for England to get support, 'knowing how uncertain all our affairs are at home by people being disaffected, officers corrupt, treasure exhausted, and that we want men, money, commanders, councillors, and everything, except spies, trepanners and bawds'.[97] The English court thus needed money from France if it was to deal with its problems at home. Eunomius meanwhile warns against the strong foreign protector who might turn into a predator in the English sheepfold, for 'being of a nation

[92] Sidney, *Court Maxims*, pp. 153–4.   [93] Davis, *Oliver Cromwell*, p. 42.
[94] Ludlow, 'Voyce', p. 937; and Seaward, *The Cavalier Parliament*, pp. 113, 221.
[95] Sidney, *Court Maxims*, p. 154.   [96] Ibid., pp. 155–6.   [97] Ibid., p. 158.

France was ever a rival and an enemy to, and that has often shaken and sometime enjoyed the crown he now bears, I do extremely fear him, that he expects an occasion of absolutely enslaving us'. If the French king decided to support the Stuarts, it was 'not for love or alliance, but because he expects we shall be sooner destroyed by their fraud and ill government than by his power'. Besides, help from the King of France would not come without a price and might well end in total dependence: 'If the king of France protect he will expect you shall be his servants.' If England wanted to maintain the balance of power in Europe and was torn between Spain and France, it should always support the weaker of the two countries.[98] For Sidney's Eunomius, this may have been a lesson learnt from the Protectorate, which had seen Spain as '*the* national enemy' and ignored 'the latent and nascent power of France'.[99] It was therefore now time to change track regarding France to prevent Louis XIV from becoming a serious threat.

In a similar vein, Sidney's courtier and commonwealthman disagree about the United Provinces' relationship to England, with the courtier seeing them as an enemy and the commonwealthman considering them an ally. Philalethes argues that the United Provinces are enemies not least because the English are jealous of them: 'we ... look in their power and riches, the security, happiness, and prosperity they enjoy in a commonwealth, as a most pernicious example to England'. This model of liberty on England's doorstep was a threat because the people might come to realise that 'the splendour of a court and glory of a king' were not the only path to the happiness of a nation. For this and other reasons, the Stuarts had an interest in ruining the United Provinces and, as Eunomius agrees, would try to establish in power Charles II's nephew William of Orange, who in fact was due to succeed to the office of stadtholder in 1672. What is more, the English court feared that the Dutch would make common cause with the dissenters in England during the impending Anglo-Dutch war, as 'the fanatics are fuller of spirit than formerly, and will not let slip so fair an opportunity of destroying us when engaged in a war with Holland'. Philalethes even suspects that 'France has encouraged us to the war, that we may perish in it', for England was currently 'not in a condition ... to undertake it'.[100]

To avert the threat of an alliance between the Dutch and the dissenters, Philalethes thinks, the English court has to stir up strife between them.

---

[98] Ibid., p. 160.   [99] Davis, *Oliver Cromwell*, p. 42.
[100] Sidney, *Court Maxims*, pp. 161–3, 165–6.

As he points out, there was already some underlying tension between them, as the English Commonwealth had previously declared war on the Dutch in the 1650s, and the dissenters for their part were still annoyed with the Dutch for the extraordinary rendition of the three regicides Barkstead, Corbet and Okey. He also thinks that the English envoy George Downing, who was instrumental in their delivery, could help to advance the Orangist faction in the United Provinces, while internal divisions and jealousies between the weaker provinces and Holland might also come in handy, as 'all those that cannot get, or will not seek a livelihood by honest means, are ready to set up a tyrant who will need such ministers as they are'. By setting up a faction whose interest was separate and different from that of the whole, the English could help to dissolve the union, so that the Dutch would fall into their hands.[101]

Eunomius meanwhile does not think that the schemes of the English court to sow divisions between the Dutch and the dissenters are likely to succeed as '[b]oth parties know their interests as inseparable, as that of the houses of the Stuarts and Orange, the common enemies of both'. The perceived enmity between 'the Hollander and fanatic', according to Sidney's spokesman, was only skin deep, as the English Commonwealth had entered the last war by accident, and both parties had come to see it as a mistake, while 'the delivery of Okey, Corbet, and Barkstead' was 'not to be imputed to the States General, who were surprised and cheated by Downing'.[102] Sidney thus took a rather different view from Ludlow on the case of the three regicides, as documented in previous chapters. Having lived in the United Provinces, and thus being potentially better informed on the actual course of events, he insisted that the nation 'gave from the beginning evident marks of abhorring so barbarous a treachery'. In fact, he was convinced that England and Holland needed to join against the houses of Stuart and Orange: 'The opposition between us and them, their concernment and ours, is universal and irreconcilable. Their safety is our destruction, our safety is their destruction.' As he sums up the republicans' aims: 'We desire to be governed by good laws, possess our goods in safety, with the full enjoyment of our civil and spiritual liberty. We seek to increase our fortunes by honest industry, advance our persons and families by virtue and the service of our country, and by merit gain that which truly deserves the name of honour.' All this ran counter to the interests of tyrants, and therefore the dissenters and commonwealthmen had to 'overthrow ... a few guilty heads' to 'secure a multitude of innocents'.[103]

---

[101] Ibid., pp. 169–70.   [102] Ibid., pp. 171–2.   [103] Ibid., pp. 172, 176.

Sidney held on to his dream of an Anglo-Dutch Protestant republican alliance until the very end, even sending Benjamin Furly a cryptic prophecy that seemed to predict the end of French dominance in Europe and the victory of the Continent's Protestant powers. He sent 'A Prophesy of St Thomas the Martyr' from his exile in the south of France to Furly in Rotterdam, who published it in 1689 in both English and Dutch as the *Copy of a Prophecy Sent to B:F: in the Year 1666 from Montpelliers by the Late Honourable Alguernon Sidney Esqr* (see Figure 5).[104] It refers to an apocalyptic struggle between Catholics and Protestants in Europe, in which the '*Lilly*' (France) will lose its crown to the 'Son of Man' with backing from the 'Land of the *Lion*' (United Provinces), the 'Land of Wool' (England) and the '*Eagle*' (the Empire).

Furly claimed to have found the prophecy by accident after the Glorious Revolution, in which the Protestant William of Orange came to the aid of his English co-religionists to protect religion and liberty in England and the Anglo-Dutch alliance was finally realised, albeit in a slightly different way from what had originally been envisaged. The 'Prophesy' meanwhile was not original to Sidney, but in fact a much older story that 'has been traced back to the early fourteenth century'. It was apparently revived and circulating in the seventeenth century in response to fears of 'a French claim to Universal Monarchy' and found by the republican in Montpellier.[105] Sidney presumably shared it because it fitted the current political situation. Seeming somewhat over-optimistic when it was originally sent, the pamphlet may have taken on a new symbolic meaning in 1689 as the Protestant succession in England hailed the end of French domination in Europe – at least for now.

During the Second Anglo-Dutch War Sidney was still hopeful for a victory of the Dutch, an Anglo-Dutch alliance and a defeat both of the French as well as of their Stuart rivals. This all changed after the Medway disaster with the decisive Dutch victory over the English and the abandoning of the Anglo-Dutch Protestant republican project. The Anglo-Dutch war had come and gone, the attempt to free Major-General John Lambert from prison to lead the invasion of England had failed and cost more English republicans their lives, and the Dutch had turned from a promising ally into a political and economic rival. It may have been due

---

[104] On the manuscript, see Chapter 4, n. 53.

[105] Lionel Laborie, 'Millenarian Portraits of Louis XIV', in Tony Claydon (ed.), *Louis XIV Outside In: Images of the Sun King beyond France, 1661–1715* (Farnham: Ashgate, 2015), pp. 209–28, at pp. 212–13.

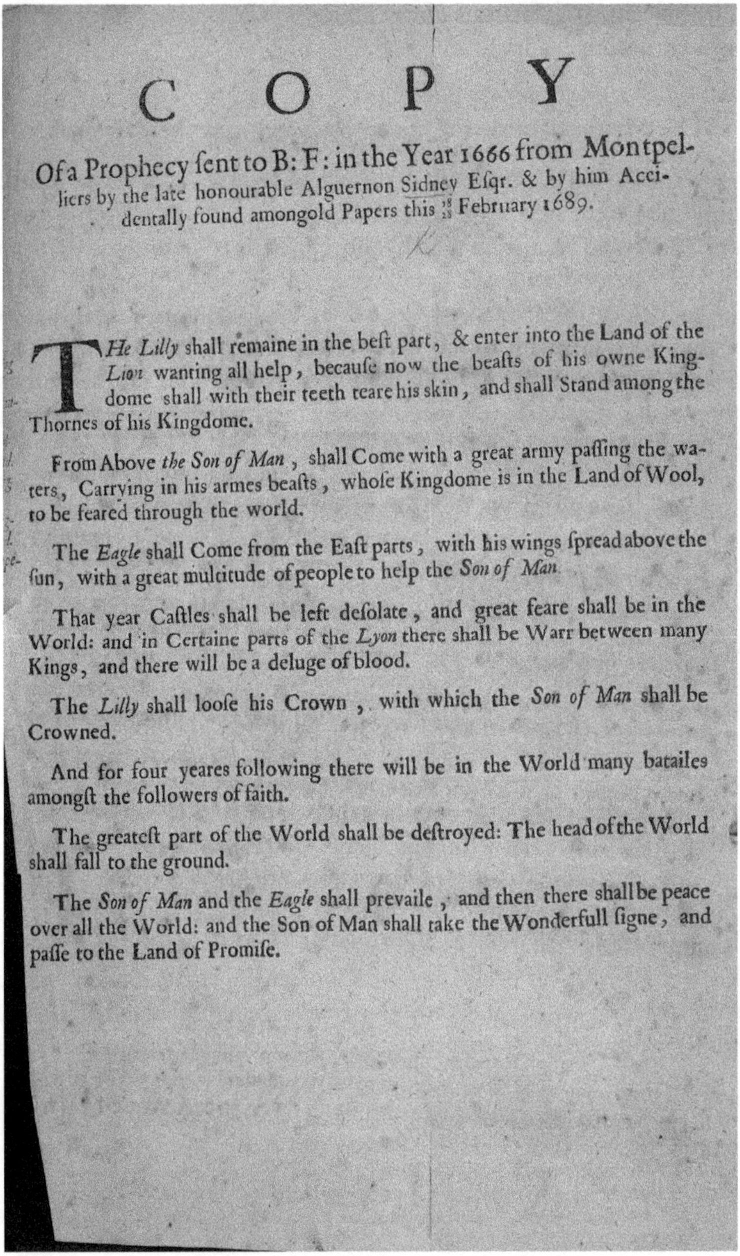

C O P Y

Of a Prophecy sent to B: F: in the Year 1666 from Montpelliers by the late honourable Alguernon Sidney Esqr. & by him Accidentally found amongold Papers this ⅛ February 1689.

THe *Lilly* shall remaine in the best part, & enter into the Land of the *Lion* wanting all help, becaufe now the beasts of his owne King-dome shall with their teeth teare his skin, and shall Stand among the Thornes of his Kingdome.

From Above *the Son of Man*, shall Come with a great army passing the wa-ters, Carrying in his armes beasts, whose Kingdome is in the Land of Wool, to be feared through the world.

The *Eagle* shall Come from the East parts, with his wings spread above the fun, with a great multitude of people to help the *Son of Man*.

That year Castles shall be left desolate, and great feare shall be in the World: and in Certaine parts of the *Lyon* there shall be Warr between many Kings, and there will be a deluge of blood.

The *Lilly* shall loose his Crown, with which the *Son of Man* shall be Crowned.

And for four yeares following there will be in the World many batailes amongst the followers of faith.

The greatest part of the World shall be destroyed: The head of the World shall fall to the ground.

The *Son of Man* and the *Eagle* shall prevaile, and then there shall be peace over all the World: and the Son of Man shall take the Wonderfull signe, and passe to the Land of Promise.

Figure 5 *Copy of a Prophecy Sent to B:F: in the Year 1666 from Montpelliers by the Late Honourable Alguernon Sidney Esqr. & by Him Accidentally Found among Old Papers This 18/28 February 1689.*
© The British Library Board. 1103.f.27.(15.)

to this change of fortunes that Sidney's *Court Maxims* were never published during his lifetime.

The Manuscript of the *Court Maxims* and the *Discourses*

As we saw at the beginning of this chapter, *Court Maxims* remained unpublished until it was rediscovered some three hundred years later by Blair Worden in Warwick Castle and edited for Cambridge University Press by Hans Blom, Eco Haitsma Mulier and Ronald Janse.[106] Nevertheless, as John Carswell has convincingly demonstrated, there had probably been plans for a publication of at least part of the work in the 1660s.[107] Its first eight dialogues had been copied in a late seventeenth-century hand that Carswell takes to be Furly's, and been corrected and annotated by a second contemporary hand that probably belonged to the regicide William Say, who had lived in exile in Switzerland and Germany before moving to the United Provinces to join in Sidney's scheme to invade England.[108] The manuscript layout was arranged in such a way as to 'leave a broad margin on the right of each page for possible amendment and correction', which left an 'impression … of extreme care, as for a manuscript being prepared for the press'.[109] If the corrections were indeed added by Say, the manuscript would date from 1666 at the very latest, as this is the year in which Sidney's fellow plotter disappears from the historical record and is thought to have died.[110] The likely date of the manuscript is also corroborated by other evidence. It was clearly known that Sidney had been working on a manuscript, to judge from one of the dispatches which the government agent Aphra Behn sent from the Low Countries and which Carswell dates around early August 1666. This document written by the double agent William Scott, son of the regicide Thomas Scott, stated that Sidney was 'at present writing a Treatise in defence of a Republique, and against Monarchy' and designed it 'soone or late for the presse'.[111] The project was eventually abandoned. While it seems obvious that the manuscript may have been thought of as too

---

[106] Blom and his team have made very few editorial interventions. One notable change from the original MS is the renaming of Sidney's chapters as 'dialogues'.

[107] Carswell, 'Algernon Sidney's "Court Maxims"'.

[108] Ibid., pp. 99, 101. See Warwickshire County Record Office, MS CR 1886.

[109] Carswell, 'Algernon Sidney's "Court Maxims"', p. 99. See Warwickshire County Record Office, MS CR 1886.

[110] J. T. Peacey, 'Say, William (1604–1666?)', *ODNB*.

[111] SP 29/172, f. 81 ii (109), quoted in Carswell, 'Algernon Sidney's "Court Maxims"', p. 101. For Aphra Behn's complete correspondence, see Cameron, *New Light on Aphra Behn*.

incendiary to publish it in the 1660s, it was hardly forgotten. Indeed, readers of the *Discourses* would have noticed a remarkable consistency and many parallels between the arguments of the two works, and I would even suggest that there is a possibility that Sidney considered publishing *Court Maxims* as late as 1678 or 1679, before it was eventually superseded by the *Discourses*.

As Jonathan Scott has aptly observed, while the *Court Maxims* were written long before Filmer's *Patriarcha* was published, 'Sidney's courtier anticipates most of Filmer's case'.[112] This may be due to the fact that Filmer's argument was hardly original, but summarised much of the mainstream royalist thought of the seventeenth century, which helped to make him such a popular target for critics in the 1680s.[113] In any case, as Scott points out, '[t]he *Discourses* and the *Maxims* cover much of the same ground'.[114] Both the *Court Maxims* and the *Discourses* attack divine right, patriarchalism, absolutism and the hereditary principle. They address the issue of conquest, the people's right to rise against unjust rulers, and the need for the rule of law and for religious liberty – often in very similar language.

In the *Court Maxims*, Sidney denounces the 'folly' of those pretending 'princes are ordained by God', he sees kings as 'plagues' and denies that they are in any way 'sacred and anointed' by God, nor were 'the names of God and the king ... ever joined together in the law of God'.[115] In the *Discourses*, Sidney likewise denounces the 'divine absolute monarchy' put forward by Filmer as a 'folly' and insists that 'the king should be subject to the censure of the people'. He denies that men can be free under the rule of a monarch 'endowed with an unlimited power' and 'restrained by no law'.[116] Sidney also remains consistent in his rejection of patriarchal power at the highest level of government. 'The paternal government extends only to a family', Eunomius insists in the *Court Maxims*. And while 'the head of a family' may need 'to be obeyed', an individual is 'obliged to disobey the king if he commands anything contrary to th[e] law'.[117] In the same vein, he rejects in the *Discourses* the 'whimsey of Adam's kingdom, or that of the

---

[112] Scott, *Algernon Sidney and the English Republic*, p. 191.
[113] Yet Filmer's *Patriarcha* was also much more than that. For an excellent, recent, fully contextualised analysis of Filmer's political thought, see Cesare Cuttica, *Sir Robert Filmer (1588–1653) and the Patriotic Monarch: Patriarchalism in Seventeenth-Century Political Thought* (Manchester: Manchester University Press, 2012).
[114] Scott, *Algernon Sidney and the English Republic*, p. 191.
[115] Sidney, *Court Maxims*, pp. 41, 43, 45, 50, 142.
[116] Sidney, *Discourses*, ed. West, pp. 161, 7, 10, 17.   [117] Sidney, *Court Maxims*, pp. 12, 81–2.

ensuing patriarchs'. Thus Abraham 'pretended to no authority beyond his own family, which consisted only of a wife and slaves'. But it was impossible to derive any claims to political power from this familial rule. Therefore 'it must be confessed this paternal right is a mere whimsical fiction, and that no man by birth hath a right above another, or can have any, unless by the concession of those who are concerned'. In short, 'No man . . . can claim the right of a father over any, except one that is so.'[118]

Sidney also consistently denies the legitimacy of absolute and hereditary rule. Absolutism cannot be justified with reference to either Scripture or to the writings of Aristotle, Sidney argues in the *Discourses*.[119] To him, the subjects of an absolute, unaccountable monarch are 'slaves', and the evils of absolute monarchy are increased through the hereditary principle, which 'creates a hereditary hatred between him and his people' that is destructive to both. And even if the fathers are good men, it cannot be guaranteed that 'their sons will inherit their fathers' virtues'.[120] He also argues in the *Discourses*, in direct response to Filmer, that any hereditary succession would 'necessarily perish' over time, 'since the generations of men are so confused, that no man knows his own original, and consequently this heir is nowhere to be found'. Hereditary right is therefore not just irrational but also impractical, Sidney argues. Even 'if mankind could be brought to believe that such a right of dominion were by the law of God and nature hereditary, a great number of the most destructive and inextricable controversies must thereupon arise', and this 'the wisdom and goodness of God can never enjoin, and nature, which is reason, can never intend'.[121]

In both works, the *Court Maxims* and the *Discourses*, Sidney also denied that monarchs could claim their power by right of conquest. Men could conquer nations only in their role as 'prince, general, or officer employed by another nation', which meant that any conquest would be made on behalf of another country, not as individuals, he argues in the *Court Maxims*. Even William the Conqueror, according to Sidney's logic, enjoyed his power 'by election' because he had in Harold removed 'a pretender to the crown', and a 'good part of the nobles and commons of England did from the first make him their head and leader' under 'certain conditions' that he was not allowed to break.[122] In the *Discourses*, Sidney confirms, 'The rights therefore of kings are not grounded upon conquest;

---

[118] Sidney, *Discourses*, ed. West, pp. 24, 29–30, 34, 319.   [119] Ibid., pp. 26, 452.
[120] Sidney, *Court Maxims*, pp. 28, 33, 53, 30.   [121] Sidney, *Discourses*, ed. West, pp. 39, 58.
[122] Sidney, *Court Maxims*, pp. 14–15.

the liberties of nations do not arise from the grants of their princes.' Moreover, 'the oath of allegiance binds no private man to more than the law directs, and has no influence upon the whole body of every nation'.[123]

If kings overstepped the mark and acted against the law, meanwhile, they could be resisted. For those 'that may bind kings in chains may also lay the sword to their throat', Sidney argues in the *Court Maxims*. If kings turned into tyrants, their subjects could 'justly withdraw obedience' from them. In particular, if rulers obliged their subjects to follow a false doctrine and form of worship, the latter had to resist.[124] In the *Discourses*, Sidney confirms that 'Unjust Commands are not to be obey'd', and that 'The general revolt of a Nation cannot be called a Rebellion.' According to Sidney, it is not possible 'that a people resisting oppression, and vindicating their own liberty, could commit a crime, and incur either guilt or infamy'. In fact, it was 'much better that the irregularities and excesses of a prince should be restrained or suppressed, than that whole nations should perish by them'. The key principle of good government was the rule of law, 'as it is the fundamental right of every nation to be governed by such laws, in such manner, and by such persons as they think most conducing to their own good'.[125] This is why Sidney's Eunomius in the *Court Maxims* defends republican rule, for 'In a commonwealth ... well-constituted laws govern, not men.' And even if 'the magistrate be wicked', he is constrained by the constitution. The same is true for a 'legal' monarchy, in which a 'free man governs free men according to the law' and acts for the 'good of the governed'.[126] In the *Discourses*, Sidney reinforces his point that 'All just Magistratical Power is from the People' and that 'governments are not set up for the advantage, profit, pleasure or glory of one or a few men, but for the good of the society'.[127]

Among the civil liberties to be protected by the rule of law, Sidney counted the free exercise of religion. He therefore considered it problematic that princes or civil magistrates had assumed control over religion in the name of order and that clerics colluded with them to maintain their own position. It was in his opinion ridiculous to set 'a temporal head upon a spiritual body'. Sidney's Eunomius states in the *Court Maxims*, 'If we had a Saul we might serve God without fear.' Instead, in the current climate in England, 'a praying meeting is looked on as a conspiracy' and every

---

[123] Sidney, *Discourses*, ed. West, p. 522.   [124] Sidney, *Court Maxims*, pp. 56, 59, 100, 106.
[125] Sidney, *Discourses*, ed. West, pp. 436, 519–20, 523–4.
[126] Sidney, *Court Maxims*, pp. 196, 200, 203.   [127] Sidney, *Discourses*, ed. West, pp. 69, 91.

dissenter considered a 'fanatic'. This was the result of giving the civil magistrate power in religious matters although it was evident that faith could not be forced, and it was a great injury to compel an individual to worship in a specific way.[128] The matter was less dominant in the *Discourses*, as the persecution of the dissenters had eased by the 1680s, but the separation of church and state was once again under discussion as England faced the succession of a Catholic heir to the throne in James, Duke of York. It was necessary, Sidney argued, to demarcate the secular from the religious world, 'lest we happen preposterously to obey man when we ought to obey God'.[129] Thus in all these points the parallels and continuities between the *Court Maxims* and the *Discourses* are strong. Sidney even uses some of the same examples to illustrate his arguments, such as I Samuel 8, on the evils of monarchy, although this passage from the Bible was of course frequently employed by English as well as continental republicans to make the same point.[130]

The corresponding arguments nevertheless suggest that the two works may have been more closely related than is often assumed and that – with the *Court Maxims* remaining unpublished – the *Discourses* were essentially a rewriting of the earlier work for a new purpose and a new audience. At least, such a possibility is suggested by a letter from Sidney to Furly of 23 March 1678/9, in which he writes

> Yesterday Mr. Foot met me, and desired when I writ next unto you, to minde you of the book, which as was hoped might have been printed before this time. I see he and others are of opinion it might now be done heare, the Act for restraining the presse being expired, and the care he would take to oversee the presse might abate the expence, and thinks the paper that was bought may be put off with littell or noe losse.[131]

Furly's biographer William Hull takes this letter to imply that the Quaker merchant had been trying to get a book published for the republican in Rotterdam and that the plans had already progressed so far that he had obtained the paper for it. Hull assumes the book in question must have been the *Discourses*, because the existence of the *Court Maxims* was still

---

[128] Sidney, *Court Maxims*, pp. 95, 49, 98, 101.   [129] Sidney, *Discourses*, ed. West, p. 437.

[130] e.g. *Court Maxims*, pp. 46–50, and *Discourses*, ed. West, pp. 130–1. The De la Court brothers also employed the argument from I Samuel 8 in *Consideratien van staat*, part I, chapter 31, pp. 121–6.

[131] Algernon Sidney, London, to Benjamin Furly, 23 March 1678/9, in *Original Letters of Locke; Algernon Sidney; and Anthony Lord Shaftesbury, Author of the 'Characteristics.' With an Analytical Sketch of the Writings and Opinions of Locke and Other Metaphysicians, by T. Forster* (London: J. B. Nichols and Son, Parliament Street, 1830), pp. 11–12.

unknown in 1941 when his study of Furly came out.[132] However, it is usually assumed that Sidney did not start writing the *Discourses* until after 1680, when Filmer's *Patriarcha* was first published, as the work contains a blow-by-blow refutation of Filmer's justification of divine-right monarchy.[133] Thus the manuscript referred to in the letter must be a different one, probably the *Court Maxims*. This may also explain why parts of the *Court Maxims* have survived in Furly's handwriting.[134] If he was involved in the publication process, it is likely that he helped prepare the manuscript to be passed on to a printer in the United Provinces. We might even wonder whether the fact that only the first eight dialogues were prepared for publication suggests that the editing was done some time after the Anglo-Dutch war, when Sidney may have changed his mind on the United Provinces and came to collaborate more closely with France. This would have rendered the tenth to fourteenth dialogues, focusing on the European balance of power, obsolete, even counterproductive, although this still leaves the dropping of the ninth dialogue on corrupt lawyers unaccounted for. In any case, what had remained of the original manuscript was Sidney's criticism of the English monarchy. Yet, as Sidney's letter suggests, the plan to publish the work in the United Provinces may have been abandoned after the lapse of the Licensing Act in England in 1679, which opened up the possibility of a publication in London, and this would have allowed him to oversee the editorial process himself. The publication of Filmer's *Patriarcha* may then have made him reconsider the project and led either to an extensive rewriting of the existing manuscript or to the starting of a completely new one – albeit recycling many older ideas – that would eventually become the *Discourses*. Nevertheless, Sidney still did not have the work published by 1683, when its treasonous content eventually led to his conviction and execution. The survival of the remaining five dialogues in a late eighteenth-century hand in the Warwickshire County Record Office meanwhile suggests that at some point a complete version of the work must have made it to England, and this copy taken from it before Sidney's original manuscript was lost or destroyed.[135]

---

[132] William Hull, *Benjamin Furly and Quakerism in Rotterdam* (Lancaster: Lancaster Press, 1941), p. 78. Carswell too assumes that the 'Court Maxims' were never mentioned by Sidney in any surviving records. See 'Algernon Sidney's "Court Maxims"', p. 98.

[133] Sidney, *Discourses*, ed. West, pp. xvi–xvii.

[134] The identification of Furly's handwriting was made by Carswell in 'Algernon Sidney's "Court Maxims"', p. 101.

[135] For several possible explanations, each without much evidence to back it up, see ibid., pp. 102–3.

Conclusion

The *Court Maxims* clearly show how closely Sidney's writing was related to his political activities. The work justifies his project of a republican invasion of England with Dutch support, while drawing on a wealth of ideas that had developed during the English revolutionary period and that were now being adjusted to fit the post-Restoration scenario. Sidney's Restoration work shows no sign of resignation or defeat. While his first reaction to the return of the Stuarts in 1660 had been a reluctant acceptance of the new order paired with an attempt to find a place for himself in the new government, his realisation that the Stuarts had no intention of honouring their promise of forgetting old divisions and accommodating dissent turned him into a violent opponent of the new regime. After several years of retreat in Italy, Sidney resumed his travels across Europe to gather his exiled allies for a revival of the republican cause with the backing of foreign powers, and the Anglo-Dutch war seemed just like the opportunity he had been waiting for.

The influence of his exile was clearly visible in Sidney's writing. The *Court Maxims* might be condemning Stuart aspirations to absolutist rule in England first and foremost, but their outlook is entirely European. For the more religiously inclined English republicans never saw themselves just as inhabitants of England, but as agents in a much wider, universal struggle between the powers of good and evil. The godly people everywhere had to join together to fight oppression and tyranny and establish forms of government in accordance with the Scriptures. The Dutch seemed the ideal ally for this cause, and it must have been a tragedy for Sidney to see this ideal connection between the two northern Protestant trading countries break apart over the course of the Anglo-Dutch war. However, distrust and fear of competition had made the Dutch wary, and a weak country across the Channel was in the end safer to maintain Dutch trading interests and military power than a strong partner and potential rival, especially as the chances of the English republicans for a restoration of the Commonwealth seemed to be waning amid French support for the Stuart monarchy.

On the relationship between the United Provinces and England Sidney anticipated much of Bethel's argument of the 1680s: the shared Protestant heritage, the common trading interest, the desire for free republican government and liberty of conscience all made the English and the Dutch ideal allies. But if the United Provinces could not be a partner at this stage, they could still serve as a model to aspire to, even as they were a neighbour to be closely watched, which is how they were seen from Henry Neville's more sceptical perspective.

CHAPTER 7

Neville's Utopian Vision

Io vo fin ora molto adagio in farmi buon cortegiano di Roma e trovo
che sia cosa molto difficile per uno che ha passato quarant'anni e che
è stato sempre fin adesso satiro, d'imparare bene l'adulatione.

Henry Neville to Bernardino Guasconi, 1 August 1665[1]

Introduction: Exile and Utopia

Henry Neville's *The Isle of Pines* (1668) is the fictional account of a man
and four women who survive shipwreck during Queen Elizabeth's time
and establish a new society on a remote island in the Pacific Ocean.
Their descendants are discovered several generations later, in 1667, by
the crew of a Dutch ship that brings the story of the English Pines back
to Europe for publication. The pamphlet combines elements of the
popular travel narrative, satire and utopia with the aim of promoting
political change.

There is no doubt that Neville's narrative of shipwreck and survival is a
commentary on the Restoration monarchy, Anglo-Dutch relations and in
particular the recent war with the United Provinces. During his Italian
exile (1664–7), Neville had been following 'all the news of the world,
whether true or false' and observing Restoration politics from a distance,
protected by the Earl of Clarendon as his royalist patron. Throughout his
stay abroad he took a keen interest in English affairs, following and
commenting on the news of the Second Anglo-Dutch War in the correspondence with his brother Richard and his friend Bernardino Guasconi,
although there is no evidence that he took an active part in any republican

---

[1] 'I have so far tried very slowly to become a good courtier of Rome and I find that it is very difficult
for someone who has spent forty years and has always been the satyr to learn well how to flatter.'
Henry Neville, Rome, to Bernardino Guasconi, 1 August 1665, in Crinò, 'Lettere inedite', p. 181.

plots between 1665 and 1666, when many of his former allies were hoping for a new opportunity to change the government in England.[2]

Yet Neville had not entirely been staying away from subversive action, which in his case consisted in the authorship of a political satire in the form of a rather spectacular fictitious travel narrative.[3] This narrative would soon be translated into at least five Western European languages to enthral readers across large parts of the Continent, as well as travelling to New England.[4] Thanks to its narrative form, satirical purpose and wide popular appeal, *The Isle of Pines* was long studied more as literature than as political philosophy, with only a few scholars of utopianism giving due attention to its constitutional implications.[5] This has changed in recent years, and renewed interest in the work from both literary critics and historians has contributed to a growing literature on *The Isle* which I will explore below. What follows here is a close reading of *The Isle of Pines* as Neville's assessment of the state of Restoration England and the republican cause in the aftermath of the recent Anglo-Dutch war, but above all as a work of exile.[6] In order to see what makes *The Isle* an exile work, we need to pause and look at the genre in which it was written and

---

[2] Ibid.; and intercepted letter from Richard Neville, Billingbear, to Henry Neville, Rome. 21 June 1667, NA, SP 29/206, fol. 135.

[3] Recent modern editions of *The Isle* include Derek Hughes (ed.), *Versions of Blackness: Key Texts on Slavery from the Seventeenth Century* (Cambridge, UK: Cambridge University Press, 2007); Peter G. Stillman, Gaby Mahlberg and Nat Hardy, *The Isle of Pines*, special issue, *Utopian Studies*, 17:1 (2006); Gregory Claeys (ed.), *Restoration and Augustan British Utopias* (Syracuse, NY: Syracuse University Press, 2000), pp. 115–30; and Susan Bruce (ed.), *Three Renaissance Utopias*: Utopia, New Atlantis, The Isle of Pines (Oxford: Oxford University Press, 1999), pp. 187–242. In order to comment on the different parts comprising *The Isle*, I will here quote from the original seventeenth-century English and, where applicable, foreign-language editions of the work. The English editions, as cited below, are easily accessible via *Early English Books Online*, https://search.proquest.com/eebo.

[4] On the publishing history of *The Isle*, see Worthington Chauncey Ford, The Isle of Pines *1668: An Essay in Bibliography* (Boston: Club of Odd Volumes, 1920); Stillman, Mahlberg and Hardy, *The Isle of Pines*, special issue; and Gaby Mahlberg, 'Authors Losing Control: The European Transformations of Henry Neville's *The Isle of Pines* (1668)', *Book History*, 15 (2012), 1–15. In most cases, only the first part of the story was translated.

[5] e.g. J. C. Davis in his *Utopia and the Ideal Society: A Study of English Utopian Writing 1516–1700* (Cambridge, UK: Cambridge University Press, 1981), pp. 24–6; A. Owen Aldridge, 'Polygamy in Early Fiction: Henry Neville and Denis Veiras', *Proceedings of the Modern Language Association*, 65 (1950), 464–72; and Pierre Lurbe, 'Une utopie inverse: *The Isle of Pines* de Henry Neville (1668)', *Bulletin de la Société d'Études Anglo-Americaines des XVIIe et XVIII Siècles*, 38 (1994), 19–32.

[6] On the Anglo-Dutch perspective see in particular Adam Beach, 'A Profound Pessimism about the Empire: *The Isle of Pines*, English Degeneracy and Dutch Supremacy', *The Eighteenth Century: Theory and Interpretation*, 41 (2000), 21–36; Gaby Mahlberg, 'An Island with Potential: Henry Neville's *The Isle of Pines* (1668)', in J. C. Davis and Miguel A. Ramiro (eds), *Utopian Moments: Micro-Historical Approaches to Modern Literary Utopias* (London: Bloomsbury Academic, 2012), pp. 60–6; also Jonathan Scott, *When the Waves Ruled Britannia: Geography and Political Identities, 1500–1800* (Cambridge, UK: Cambridge University Press, 2011), pp. 100–1.

the way in which Neville addresses key themes such as travel, distance, alienation, loss and a sense of being lost.

On the surface, *The Isle* is a story of shipwreck and survival. As we have seen in the introductory chapter, shipwreck was a powerful metaphor in societies which heavily relied on trade and shipping for their existence. Here, it addresses the state of flux in which Neville found himself as a traveller between England and Italy, and as a survivor of a political experiment that had collapsed several years earlier. His choice of narrative also resonates with the letter his fellow exile Sidney had sent to his father seven years earlier, in which he described himself as 'a broken Limbe of a Ship-wracked Faction', at times feeling desperate or 'naked, alone, and without Help in the open Sea'.[7] Like the other exiles, Neville had left his country to secure his own liberty. Yet the physical distance from his home country also created in him a sense of rejection, as he was 'not only hatted but persecuted at home'.[8] This rejection came with a degree of alienation, as the country he now saw from abroad was no longer the same country in which he had served as a councillor of state only the previous decade. That country had been marked by revolution and constitutional change, in which he had played an active part, whereas the country he was now observing from abroad had fallen back into the old monarchy, with Charles II replacing Charles I. While observing and satirising from afar a country that had fallen back into its old ways, meanwhile, Neville was also toying with the many possibilities the distant island offered to an explorer, coloniser or settler and thus crossed into the territory of political utopia. Just as for the exile England always was 'a very present absence', so for the utopian writer his thoughts were always with England, even if the story was set in Utopia, New Atlantis or Oceana or on the Isle of Pines.[9]

Both travel writers and utopians offer a visitor's view of a country, as the narrator makes new discoveries and observations and reports back to the readers at home.[10] Unlike the travel writer, though, the exile writer is often less concerned with his new environment than with the country he had to leave behind.[11] This links him more closely to the utopian, who tends to create an alternative version of his country in order to be able to discuss

[7] Algernon Sidney, Frascati, to Robert, Earl of Leicester, 23 June/3 July 1661, in Collins (ed.), *Letters*, ii, pp. 720–1, at p. 720.
[8] BRO, D/EN F8/1/11, Henry Neville, Florence, to Richard Neville, London, 20 January 1665.
[9] Quotation from Major, 'A poor exile stranger', p. 166.
[10] J. C. Davis, 'Going Nowhere: Travelling to, through and from Utopia', *Utopian Studies*, 19:1 (2008), 1–23.
[11] Cf. famous exiles from Nazi Germany, like Bertolt Brecht or Thomas Mann.

sensitive issues more freely. One author creates a geographical, the other an imaginary distance to his country. Since both are frequently motivated to write by dissatisfaction with conditions at home, both types of author tend to be concerned with the analysis of systemic defects and the potential for political change.[12] The utopian travel narrative therefore seems an ideal vehicle for Neville's thoughts on Restoration England.

Utopias play with 'the general questioning of the veracity of travellers' tales'.[13] Yet in utopia, there is also often a point at which the author reconnects his imaginary world with reality. In Thomas More's *Utopia*, the harsh poverty and social injustice described in book I is what makes the comparatively egalitarian, if rather constrained, living conditions described in book II so appealing; in *Oceana*, the socio-economic developments the fictional country has undergone, which mirror those of England, necessitate the establishment of a particular form of equal commonwealth; in Neville's *Isle of Pines*, the encounter of the islanders with the Dutch sailors shows why England has to change if it is not to disappear into economic and political insignificance.[14]

The alienation Neville may have experienced in exile is expressed in his choice of a fictional genre over a straight political pamphlet. The realm of fiction gives the author more freedom to explore different possibilities at the same time as acting as a protective measure in the face of political persecution. As other Restoration republican works, such as the *Speeches and Prayers* of the regicides, had drawn the displeasure of Sir Roger L'Estrange, Neville may have preferred the safety of a satirical fiction that did not give the appearance of a political work at first sight. *The Isle*'s entertainment value also ensured its wide distribution and public attention beyond the limits of England and thus could serve as effective political propaganda.[15]

Like Sidney's *Court Maxims*, the *Isle* is a contemporary political commentary as well as a reflection on the nature and failings of patriarchal monarchy. It comments on the Anglo-Dutch war as well as the growing naval and economic power of the United Provinces versus England's perceived decline since the time of Queen Elizabeth I. Moreover, it weighs up the strengths and weaknesses of patriarchal monarchy versus republican rule through an engagement with recent English history, including the

---

[12] Davis, *Utopia and the Ideal Society*, pp. 36–40.   [13] Davis, 'Going Nowhere', p. 3.
[14] Thomas More, *Utopia*, ed. George M. Logan and Robert M. Adams (Cambridge, UK: Cambridge University Press, 1989); Harrington, *Oceana*.
[15] Harrington too experimented with genre to achieve various ends, not just in *Oceana*. See Hammersley, *James Harrington*, chapter 8.

Commonwealth, the rise of Cromwell and godly, republican rule and the Stuart Restoration. It is also notable for its use of Scripture, which shows close familiarity with Old Testament texts – as would be expected from a country gentleman raised in the Protestant tradition – while at the same time dismissing any literal interpretations of the Bible. Neville's *Isle* is thus quite different in character from the radical Puritan writings of Ludlow and Sidney, not least on account of his chosen genre. The *Isle*'s explicit descriptions of the Pines' sexual mores also connect *The Isle* to Neville's bawdy Civil War and Interregnum pamphlets on a Parliament of Ladies that established his reputation as a libertine.[16] While Ludlow's 'Voyce' is half-way between a war memoir and a spiritual diary, and Sidney's *Court Maxims* a highly polemical Platonic dialogue informed by Puritan thought, Neville's *Isle of Pines* is a satirical utopia written with an irreverence for scriptural authority that at times verges on the blasphemous, calling to mind the atheism charge brought against its author in the late 1650s.[17]

Like Sidney's *Court Maxims*, Neville's *Isle of Pines* needs to be read in the context of the Second Anglo-Dutch War. Yet, unlike the *Court Maxims*, the *Isle of Pines* was written after the event, when any hopes for a successful republican rebellion against Charles II and the Restoration monarchy had been dashed. The war had come and gone without much chance for the exiled republicans to turn it in their favour. Although some English republicans and dissenters had fought on the Dutch side, their failure to raise sufficient support for a successful republican invasion, Sidney's foolhardy shot at going it alone, and the failed attempt at freeing Lambert from prison on Guernsey followed by the arrests of several allies, all constituted significant setbacks for the republican cause.[18] The Dutch had crushed the English, and the latter's defeat in the Medway showed clearly who was the dominant naval power in northern Europe. Neville's

---

[16] See [Henry Neville], *The Ladies Parliament* (1647), *The Parliament of Ladies* (1647), *The Ladies, a Second Time, Assembled in Parliament* (1647), and *Newes from the New Exchange* (1650). For a discussion of those pamphlets in connection with *The Isle of Pines*, see Mahlberg, *Henry Neville and English Republican Culture*, chapter 3. On the relationship between libertinism and political disorder, see my chapter '*The Parliament of Women* and the Restoration Crisis', in Cesare Cuttica and Markku Peltonen (eds), *Democracy and Anti-democracy in Early Modern England 1603–1689* (Leiden: Brill, 2019), pp. 279–96.

[17] Mahlberg, *Henry Neville and English Republican Culture*, pp. 198–200.

[18] On English republicans and dissenters allying with the Dutch, see *Colonel Joseph Bampfield's Apology 'Written by Himself and Printed at His Desire' 1685*, ed. John Loftis and Paul H. Hardacre, including John Loftis, 'Bampfield's Later Career: A Biographical Supplement' (London and Toronto: Associated University Presses, 1993), pp. 204–8. Both Englishmen and Scots enlisted in the Dutch navy. In fact, the English dissenters are believed to have helped plan the assault on Chatham. See Pincus, *Protestantism and Patriotism*, pp. 312–13.

Isle of Pines therefore showed a much more ambiguous attitude towards the Dutch, depicting them as both a role model and a potential ally as well as a competitor and therefore likely enemy. Like Sidney, Neville thought that England and the United Provinces shared a common interest as seafaring Protestant trading nations; but, like Ludlow, he also remained highly sceptical of the trustworthiness of England's Dutch neighbour, aware that like-minded nations are also competitors that may not always play a fair game. Nevertheless, despite its negative tenor, *The Isle* carries a message of hope. Even if life in Neville's island society seems far from any utopian ideal, his pamphlet points the reader towards its hidden potential that good laws, industry and an expansionary foreign policy might help to fulfil.

The Isle of Pines I: Scripture and Creation

Neville published his bogus travel narrative in three instalments. The first part, *The Isle of Pines, or, A Late Discovery of a Fourth Island in Terra Australis Incognita* was licensed on 27 June 1668 and printed for Allen Banks and Charles Harper in London.[19] It contains the story of the English bookkeeper George Pine, who is travelling with his merchant master to East India during the reign of Queen Elizabeth to set up a factory when their ship is caught in a storm and destroyed. The survivors are able to rescue themselves and settle on a lonely island near Terra Australis Incognita, where they create a new society.

Pine relates how he and four women, including his master's fourteen-year-old daughter, two maids and a black slave, manage to survive the shipwreck by clinging on to the bowsprit and being washed ashore. They save what they can from the debris and settle on the island, which provides shelter and plenty of food, so that the group 'want[ ] nothing' for a comfortable life.[20] Moreover, they do not experience any threats to their lives as the island is uninhabited and does not have any dangerous beasts. Even the climate is welcoming. The country is 'very pleasant, being always clothed with green, and full of pleasant fruits, and variety of Birds, ever warm, and never colder then in *England* in *September*'. In fact, if the island 'had . . . the culture that skilful people might bestow on it', it 'would prove a *Paradise*'.[21]

---

[19] *The Isle of Pines, or, A Late Discovery of a Fourth Island in Terra Australis, Incognita . . . Licensed June 27. 1668* (London: printed by S.G. for Allen Banks and Charles Harper at the Flower-Deluice near Cripplegate Church, 1668). This pamphlet will hereafter be referred to as *Isle of Pines* I.

[20] Ibid., p. 4.   [21] Ibid., p. 5.

After six months in those paradisiacal conditions, '[i]dleness and fulness of every thing' create in George Pine 'a desire of enjoying the Women', so that he first persuades the two maids and then his master's daughter to have intercourse with him.[22] Finally, the slave woman, condescendingly referred to as 'my *Negro*', also longs for 'her share', so that one after another all four women are pregnant by the man who has made himself their master.[23] Thus the five survivors begin to people the island and together have forty-seven children, before their offspring also start multiplying, so that after several generations, forty years after the shipwreck, the original settlers have produced a total of 565 children, grandchildren and great-grandchildren. George Pine then takes 'the Males of one Family' and marries them to 'the Females of another, not letting any to marry their sisters, as we did formerly out of necessity'. He orders them to 'remember the Christian religion' and 'to admit no other' should anyone come to the island and attempt to convert them, and also charges that the Bible saved from the shipwreck 'should be read once a month at a general meeting'.[24] George Pine also makes his oldest son Henry 'King and Governor of all the rest', thus setting up a hereditary line of succession that passes on patriarchal political power from one generation to the next.

Shortly before his death, 'in or about' the eightieth year of his life, the patriarch George Pine once again gathers his descendants together to be numbered, finding they have grown to 1789 in total, before passing on the account of the island society's origin to his oldest son, 'commanding him to keep it' and to allow any strangers that should chance on the island to see and copy it, 'that our name be not lost from off the earth'.[25] He names his people the 'English Pines' after his own name and that of his master's daughter, which was 'English', and he also names the individual families or tribes after their mothers' surnames, the English, the Sparks, the Trevors and the Phills (after the first name of the black slave who did not have a surname). The narrative then ends with the patriarch's prayer for his offspring 'whom God blesse with the dew of Heaven, and the fat of the Earth, AMEN'.[26]

Neville's borrowings from the Pentateuch, and in particular the Book of Genesis, are easy to spot, even though he condenses and liberally mixes elements of the biblical creation story with the story of Noah and the Ark and that of the Twelve Tribes of Israel, which are said to have descended

---

[22] Ibid., pp. 5–6. [23] Ibid., pp. 6, 3. [24] Ibid., p. 8. [25] Ibid., pp. 8–9. [26] Ibid., p. 9.

from the sons of Jacob.[27] The time it takes for the shipwrecked group to settle on the island – 'the space of a week' – corresponds to the seven days of creation, except that here God does not create, but the settlers *re*create a version of the Old World.[28] The living conditions on the island are akin to those in the Garden of Eden. But while Adam and Eve are tempted by the snake to eat the fruit from the tree of forbidden knowledge, it is the abundance of food, fair weather and rest on the island that leads Pine into temptation and lets him desire the four women, and the five castaways implicitly follow God's call to '[b]e fruitful and multiply'.[29] Like Noah and his family, Pine and the four women are also the only survivors saved from a disaster, starting society anew with their descendants. However, instead of pairs of all the animals, they bring only a few 'Hens and Cocks', which 'bred exceedingly', adding to the 'Fowl', and 'Water-fowl' and other tame beasts and fish native to the island, so that the company do not want any food.[30] The names of the main characters are also references to Scripture. Pine's favourite wife and highest in rank is called Sarah after the wife of Abraham. Impregnated by George, named after the patron saint of England, she gives birth to the tribe of the English.[31] Even the blessing given by the original patriarch to his offspring is directly adapted from the benediction of Isaac for his son Jacob, 'God give thee of the dew of heaven, and the fatness of the earth.'[32]

The resonances with the Old Testament were obvious to contemporary readers. When the story was translated into German, one publisher added to the title 'Vorbild der ersten Welt' ('Model of the first world'), while the letter framing the Leiden edition of *The Isle* notes that, even though it might not be literally true, the narrative was valuable because it was 'so close to what Moses has told us'.[33] Another German commentator in

---

[27] For Noah and the Ark, see Genesis 7–9. In Genesis 35:10–11, God says to Jacob: 'thy name shall not be called any more Jacob, but Israel shall be thy name ... a nation and a company of nations shall be of thee, and kings shall come out of thy loins'. For the Twelve Tribes of Israel, also see Genesis 46:8–34, Deuteronomy 33:6–25 and Judges 5:14–18; for the benediction of Isaac, see Onofrio Nicastro, *Henry Neville e l'isola di Pines, col testo inglese e la traduzione italiana di* The Isle of Pines (Pisa: SEU, 1988), p. 126.
[28] *Isle of Pines* I, p. 5.   [29] Genesis 3:1–6; and Genesis 1:28.   [30] *Isle of Pines* I, pp. 4–5.
[31] Nicastro, *Henry Neville e l'isola di Pines*, p. 124.
[32] Genesis 27:28. See Nicastro, *Henry Neville e l'isola di Pines*, p. 126.
[33] *Vorbild der ersten Welt, das ist: Wahrhafftige Beschreibung eines neu-erfundenen Eylandes genant das Pineser-Eyland welches der vierdte neu-erfundene Eyland im Süden ist* (Hamburg, 1668); *Relation fidelle & veritable de la nouvelle découverte d'une quatrième Isle de la terre Australe, ou Meridionale inconüe, sous le nom d'Isle de Pines* (Leiden: Abraham Gogat, 1668), p. 44. According to tradition, the Pentateuch, containing the books of Genesis, Exodus, Leviticus, Numbers and Deuteronomy, was written by Moses and is alternatively known as the 'Five Books of Moses', although this part of the Old Testament probably had multiple authors.

contrast – unimpressed by any deeper truth within the story – tried to expose the narrative as a fiction, pointing to the unlikely coincidences that had enabled Pine and his company to survive on the island, such as the 'Tinder-box, and Steel, and Flint to strike fire' and the natural abundance of food and shelter, as well as the chronological inconsistencies of the story. He also suspected that the island's name was an invention as it could be read as an anagram of the male reproductive organ.[34]

Neville's pamphlet also has a constitutional dimension, as it tells a version of the creation story that accounts for the origins of societies, tribes and nations as imagined by patriarchalist thinkers who sought to justify the legitimacy of monarchical rule by divine right. The story almost reads like a fictionalised and satirical version of Filmer's *Patriarcha*, which considers Adam, the first father, as the first king over his wife, children and other dependants who passed on his rule from one generation to the next through the principle of primogeniture.[35] But the republican Neville was far from endorsing patriarchal rule, as he would state more explicitly in his *Plato redivivus*, written around the same time as Sidney's *Discourses* during the Exclusion Crisis. Abraham and Isaac to him 'were but ordinary fathers of families, and no question governed their own household as all others do'. But their paternal power did not extend beyond the boundaries of their own home. Therefore political patriarchalism to him was only a 'fancy ... first started, not by the solid judgment of any man, but to flatter some prince; and to assert, for want of better arguments, the divine right of monarchy'.[36] Incidentally, in the *Discourses* Sidney also refers to *The Isle* to prove that monarchs could not claim paternal power over their subjects. The right of a father over his family, Sidney argues, 'cannot relate to that which a king has over his people; unless he, like the man in the Island of Pines ... be also the father of them all'.[37] Thus Sidney states he is not aware of any place 'where this paternal power could have any effect,

[34] *Isle of Pines* I, p. 3; *Das verdächtige Pineser-Eyland* (Hamburg: Johann Naumann, 1668), fols A5r, A7r, A8, B2v, B3r, B1v, B6v, B7r and A5v.

[35] Harold Weber, 'Charles II, George Pines, and Mr. Dorimant: The Politics of Sexual Power in Restoration England', *Criticism*, 32 (1990), 193–219, at p. 202; David Fausett, *Writing the New World: Imaginary Voyages and Utopias of the Great Southern Land* (Syracuse, NY: Syracuse University Press, 1993), p. 83; Susan Wiseman, '"Adam, the Father of All Flesh": Porno-political Rhetoric and Political Theory in and after the Civil War', in James Holstun (ed.), *Pamphlet Wars: Prose in the English Revolution* (London: Frank Cass, 1992), pp. 134–57; and Gaby Mahlberg, 'Republicanism as Anti-patriarchalism in Henry Neville's *The Isle of Pines* (1668)', in Jonathan Scott and John Morrow (eds), *Liberty, Authority, Formality* (Exeter: Imprint Academic, 2008), pp. 131–52.

[36] Neville, *Plato redivivus*, p. 86. On the settlers' hopes of being found, see *Isle of Pines* I, p. 4.

[37] Sidney, *Discourses*, ed. West, chapter 3, section 1, p. 320.

unless in the fabulous Island of Pines'. And even there, 'it must have ceased, when he died, who by the inventor of the story, is said to have seen above ten thousand persons issued of his body'.[38]

The English, we learn from *The Isle*, were not suited to patriarchal monarchy. In fact, to a Puritan audience the blessing of the patriarch might imply that they had quite a different purpose to fulfil. Jacob's sons generated the Twelve Tribes of Israel. Hence the blessing might point to the vision of the English as part of the Elect guided by the Lord on their mission to build the new Jerusalem and prepare the world for the second coming of Christ.[39] It is a society full of promise inhabiting a country with ideal conditions – the right place for utopia. Yet there is something distinctly uncomfortable about Neville's message. What he goes on to describe in the second and third part of his island narrative is not, as might first appear, a well-ordered commonwealth in which the people are happy and free of worries, but a regressive society: the people are naked, lazy, remote from all civilisation, indulging in the pleasures of the flesh with little order or moral guidance beyond a vague reminder to remember the Christian religion; a society still in hope of being found and leaving a record for visitors to copy so that the English Pines might not be forgotten by the rest of the world.[40] It is a story written by a republican exile whose high hopes for English expansion and grandeur fuelled under the Commonwealth had been dashed and who feared that his own country was drifting into insignificance under a self-indulgent King Charles II who appeared to the outside world more interested in his mistresses than in the well-being of his people and his country.[41] The second part of Neville's narrative makes this even clearer, telling the story of the island's discovery in 1667 by a Dutch ship, whose crew find a multitude of naked savages speaking English, yet – weakened by decades of laziness and overindulgence – lacking even the most rudimentary means to maintain a basic civilisation.

---

[38] Ibid., chapter 2, section 4, p. 96.

[39] Neville's pamphlet resonates with John Winthrop's famous sermon 'A Model of Christian Charity', written in 1630 and delivered on board the ship taking him to New England, in particular the 'City upon a Hill' section, in which Winthrop warns his fellow Puritan settlers to avoid 'shipwreck' and not to fail in their cause. The sermon was not published until the nineteenth century. See Zakai, *Exile and Kingdom*, chapter 4. Yet Neville is not advocating emigration here. To him, England has all that is needed for a better society except the right government. Given his scorn for a literal reading of the Scriptures, Neville may be criticising his Puritan friends for having overreached themselves and failed in their ambitions to create a godly commonwealth at home.

[40] Lurbe, 'Une utopie inverse'.

[41] Weber, 'Charles II, George Pines and Mr. Dorimant'; Beach, 'A Profound Pessimism about the Empire'.

The Isle of Pines II: Chaos and Constitutionalism

A New and Further Discovery of the Isle of Pines in a Letter from Cornelius Van Sloetten a Dutch-Man, dated 22 July 1668, is the alleged account of the ship's captain who had struck on the marooned English society on his voyage to the East Indies.[42] In it, Neville relates the encounter of the Dutch with George Pine's grandson William, the current ruler and king of the island. The sea captain's letter assumes that its readers are familiar with the first pamphlet on the Isle and explains how the copy 'being the same Relation which you had Printed with you at *London*' was passed to him by Pine's descendants. Accounting for the intervening years between the death of the island's founder and his arrival, the narrator explains that, after George Pine died, corruption and licentiousness spread on the island.[43] The 'grandest offender', a descendant of the black slave, had been punished by being thrown from a high rock into the sea, before Pine's successor Henry gave a basic code of law to his people.[44] These laws had kept the country orderly to the present day. But just as the Dutch sailors are about to leave the island, a rebellion breaks out instigated by the ruler of the Phills (another descendant of the black woman), who has raped the wife of another tribal leader. Unable to cope with the insurrection by himself, William Pine asks the Dutch for help, and they put down the rebels with a few gun shots before returning to Europe. To add credibility to the captain's story, Neville adds information on the ship's journey home and a postscript using details taken from earlier travel pamphlets, such as an episode from *The Golden Coast* (1665), which he must have read during his exile, in which the natives of Guinea take a bagpipe for a living creature.[45]

In the second instalment of *The Isle*, Neville's criticism of *patriarchal* political power is even more explicit than in the first. While the original father was still alive and ruling directly over his own immediate household

---

[42] *A New and Further Discovery of the Isle of Pines in a Letter from Cornelius Van Sloetten a Dutch-Man (who First Discovered the Same in the Year, 1667.) to a Friend of His in London. With a Relation of His Voyage to the East Indies ... Licensed According to Order* (London: Allen Banks and Charles Harper, 1668), hereafter *Isle of Pines* II.

[43] The narrator refers to George Pine's story as follows: 'Then stepping into a kind of inner room, which as we conceived was his lodging Chamber, he brought forth two sheets of paper fairly written in English, (being the same Relation which you had Printed with you at *London*) and very distinctly read the same over unto us, which we hearkened unto with great delight and admiration, freely proffering us a Copy of the same, which we afterward took and brought away along with us. Then proceeded he on his discourse.' Ibid., p. 6.

[44] Ibid., pp. 11–12. [45] *The Golden Coast; or, A Description of Guinney* (London, 1665), p. 80.

and offspring, all had remained peaceful in his island society. This was due
not least to the basic rules George Pine had instituted shortly before his
death 'in or about the eightieth year of my age, and the fifty ninth of my
coming there', which the attentive reader would calculate as the year 1628,
in which the parliamentary opposition in England had wrested the Petition
of Right from Charles I to protect his subjects from interference with their
liberties.[46] But, like the Petition of Right, these rules soon no longer prove
sufficient on the island.

Just as 'in multitudes disorders will grow, the stronger seeking to
oppress the weaker; no tye of Religion being strong enough to chain up
the depraved nature of mankinde', the next generation of Pines descend
into civil war. Suddenly, what looked like a well-ordered patriarchy has
turned into a Hobbesian state of nature.[47] The isle's inhabitants no longer
listen to the word of God: 'the neglect of hearing the Bible read' and the
loss of 'all other means of Christian instruction' lead to their fall. They lose
their 'sence of sin', falling 'to whoredoms, incests, and adulteries; so that
what my Grand-father was forced to do for necessity, they did for wan-
tonness'.[48] There is rape and violence, to which the island's new ruler and
king, Henry Pine, responds by gathering a company who march against
'their brethren' armed with 'boughs, stones, and such like weapons'.[49] At
the end of the Civil War, 'the grandest offender of them all' – a descendant
of the slave – is captured. Found guilty of 'divers ravishings & tyrannies',
he is executed by being 'thrown down from a high Rock into the Sea'.[50]

The tribal warfare on the island resonates with the history of the English
Civil War or the 'war of the three kingdoms' that Neville had experienced
during the 1640s. Likening the story of the Civil War to that of the fall of
man, *The Isle* plays on the same theme as Milton's *Paradise Lost*, which had
appeared a year earlier.[51] However, the parallels of Neville's work to
English history are more explicit, if also cruder. The four tribes correspond
to the English, Scots, Welsh and Irish, with the Irish being represented by
the offspring of the slave woman.[52] Colonised and subjected by her fellow

---

[46] If Pine, as he says, arrived on the island in 1569, and he is at that point seventy-nine, having lived
there for almost sixty years, the year of his exhortations is 1628. *Isle of Pines* I, p. 8.
[47] *Isle of Pines* II, p. 9; Thomas Hobbes, *Leviathan*, ed. C. B. Macpherson (London: Penguin, 1985),
chapter 14.
[48] *Isle of Pines* II, p. 10.   [49] Ibid.   [50] Ibid.
[51] John Milton, *Paradise Lost*, ed. John Leonard (Harmondsworth: Penguin, 2000).
[52] The descendants of Mary Sparkes, sharing her first name with the Queen of Scots, may represent
the Scots, and the descendants of Elizabeth Trevor, sharing her first name with the Tudor Queen,
the Welsh. Of course, Mary and Elizabeth are also the names of the mothers of Jesus and John the
Baptist.

men, she leaves a race of rebels, who continue to cause problems over the following generations. Their leader John Phill stands for Charles I, who was said to have allied with his presumed co-religionists across the Irish Sea. His punishment by death corresponds to the regicide, after which King Henry institutes a basic code of law to restore order.

Unlike the fictionalised kings and queens of Harrington's *Oceana*, the rulers of Neville's island do not directly represent actual rulers of England: there are only three successive rulers – George, Henry and William – to cover the reigns of Elizabeth, James I and Charles I as well as the Interregnum regimes and the Restoration monarchy of Charles II. Thus Charles I can be found in the trouble-maker John Phill, while King Henry's rule covers part of his reign as well as the period of the Interregnum. Henry's new order and rule of law represents parliamentary government, the Commonwealth and Protectorate; there is even a hint of Puritan law and of Cromwell's Instrument of Government as well as the Mosaic law of the Ten Commandments in his legal code.[53] Henry's first law against blasphemy and his sixth against defaming or speaking evil of the governor both recall the third commandment, not to 'take the name of the Lord thy God in vain'.[54] His second, against the failure to attend the monthly Bible reading, recalls the fourth commandment to 'Remember the sabbath day, to keep it holy.'[55] The third and fourth laws against rape and adultery correspond to God's commandments not to 'commit adultery' or 'covet thy neighbour's wife'.[56] The fifth law against causing injury to one's neighbour or stealing from them is based on the tenth commandment against theft.[57] The Interregnum too saw laws and ordinances against blasphemy and adultery, enforcing sabbath observance and punishing property offences.[58] In most cases, legal provision had existed before, but was either renewed or enforced more strictly by the new rulers.

---

[53] See also Peter G. Stillman, 'Monarchy, Disorder, and Politics in *The Isle of Pines*', in Stillman, Mahlberg and Hardy, *The Isle of Pines*, p. 159; and Bruce (ed.), *Three Renaissance Utopias*, p. 241n. Of course, the godly law of the Interregnum was partly based on religious teaching, so the connection between them is not accidental.

[54] *Isle of Pines* II, pp. 11–12; and Exodus 20:7.   [55] *Isle of Pines* II, p. 11; and Exodus 20:8.

[56] *Isle of Pines* II, p. 11; and Exodus 20:14, 17.   [57] *Isle of Pines* II, p. 11; and Exodus 20:17.

[58] In May 1648 Parliament issued 'An Ordinance for the punishing of Blasphemies and Heresies, with the several penalties therein expressed'; see *Acts and Ordinances of the Interregnum, 1642–1660*, ed. C. H. Firth and R. S. Rait (London: HM Stationery Off., 1911), pp. 1133–6. In May 1650 it passed the 'Act for suppressing the detestable sins of Incest, Adultery, and Fornication', *Acts and Ordinances*, pp. 387–9. As early as April 1644, there was 'An Ordinance for the better observation of the Lords-Day', *Acts and Ordinances*, pp. 420–2.In 1657 Parliament then passed 'An Act for the better observation of the Lords Day', *Acts and Ordinances*, pp. 1162–70. The protection of private property against arbitrary taxation by the monarchy had been a major issue before the Civil War.

In *The Isle*, Henry's godly law code works well until the time of the Restoration, when new trouble looms for Prince William. But this time, the Dutch are on hand to help. They have befriended the English islanders by giving them gifts, listening to their story and attending their 'Religious Exercises', which resemble conventicles where the members of the congregation 'hear the Word read' before the 'Priest' starts 'expounding the most difficult places' for several hours.[59] But as they go on a tour of 'discovery' on the island, they also come to grasp the full extent of the Pines' backwardness, which proves to be their weakness. They live in 'little Cabbins or Huts ... made under Trees'; they are fearful and in awe of the Dutch, and scared of their guns.[60] So the visitors know they have nothing to fear from 'these poor naked unarmed people' who have been so far from civilisation for so long that they are 'wondering at our ship, as if it had been the greatest miracle of Nature in [the] whole World'.[61] As Van Sloetten repeats, the English Pines had 'not, as we could see, any ships or Boats amongst them' and were 'altogether ignorant and meer strangers to ships, or shipping'. In fact, they had likely never seen 'a thing called a Ship'.[62] This is a shameful description of an island nation that could be making a virtue out of its location, abundance of people and fertile soil. It also suggests where Neville might see his own country with regard to shipping and trade in comparison to its competitor for the East India market. The English in his mind were clearly lagging behind.

The friendship between the English Pines and the Dutch thus proves to be unequal and superficial. Once they are sure of the islanders' trust, and realising that they have 'a free and clear passage' on the island, the Dutch take over and explore the place for six whole days, 'setting several marks in our way', determining the exact location of the island, measuring its shape and size and taking note of its natural harbours – all the things the English settlers had failed to do in all their time on the Isle.[63] The Dutch behave like explorers and colonisers, describing the burial rituals and country dancing of the English Pines with a distant anthropological interest, while also trying to make the natives drink alcohol, which Prince William declines.[64] Yet they also assist Pine, building a palace for him and, crucially, putting down an insurrection that would have threatened the

---

On Interregnum law, see among others Nancy L. Matthews, *William Sheppard, Cromwell's Law Reformer* (Cambridge, UK: Cambridge University Press, 2004).

[59] *Isle of Pines* II, pp. 5, 12–13. The Pines address the Dutch as 'Friends (for so your actions declare you to be ...)'.

[60] Ibid., pp. 13–14.   [61] Ibid., pp. 14, 3.   [62] Ibid., pp. 5–6.   [63] Ibid., p. 15.

[64] Ibid., p. 17.

order on the island once again.[65] While William Pine's authority is 'too weak to repress such Disorders', the Dutch need only to arm twelve people and discharge 'three or four Guns' to disperse the rebels – 'for what could nakedness do to encounter with Arms'. The suspected rapist and chief rebel is then sentenced to death and 'thrown off a steep Rock into the Sea' – a scene that for English readers in 1668 would have recalled the impeachment and subsequent banishment of Neville's patron Clarendon, who had been scapegoated for the Second Anglo-Dutch War and the English defeat.[66]

Once the Dutch have seen enough, they continue their journey as planned, stopping at 'Cambaia' (Cambay) and 'Calecute' (Calicut) and many other ports, while leaving the English – whose shipwreck had prevented them from reaching India – behind like any other country they have come to explore and trade with.[67] After the defeat of the English in the Medway during the recent Anglo-Dutch war, this episode in particular shows the superiority of the republican Dutch over the weak patriarchal monarchy of the English Pines. Years later, in *Plato redivivus*, Neville was still agonising over the question of how England, which had 'ever been esteemed ... one of the most considerable people of the world', was 'now of so small regard', signifying 'so little abroad'.[68] And if the humiliation of the English Pines by the capable Dutch explorers and traders was not enough, the report of the Dutch crew's onward journey further ridicules the basis of the English constitution by pointing to a significant weakness in the principle of hereditary succession: the uncertainty of paternity. This is illustrated by the Dutch captain's description of the marriage rituals of Indian rulers, of which he learns on his onward journey: in India, he recounts, the Brahmins have the right of the first night with the king's wife, so that the king cannot be sure about the paternity of his first child. Therefore his sister's sons succeed to the throne, 'as being more certainly known to be of the true Royal blood'.[69] The whole principle of patriarchal rule and hereditary descent is depicted as an absurdity.

---

[65] Ibid., pp. 17, 19.
[66] Ibid., p. 19. On the fall of Clarendon, see Richard Ollard, *Clarendon and His Friends* (Oxford: Oxford University Press, 1988).
[67] *Isle of Pines* II, p. 20; and Bethany Williamson, 'English Republicanism and Global Slavery in Henry Neville's *The Isle of Pines*', *Eighteenth-Century Fiction*, 27:1 (2014), 1–23, at pp. 8–9.
[68] Neville, *Plato redivivus*, p. 79.   [69] *Isle of Pines* II, pp. 20–1.

Figure 6   *The Isle of Pines, or, A Late Discovery of a Fourth Island near Terra Australis, Incognita by Henry Cornelius Van Sloetten* (London: Allen Banks and Charles Harper, 1668), frontispiece.
© The Bodleian Library, University of Oxford. Wood 386 (11)

The Isle of Pines III: Dutch Deception

The two parts of *The Isle* were later combined into one and issued under the title *The Isle of Pines; or, A Late Discovery of a Fourth Island near Terra Australis Incognita by Henry Cornelius Van Sloetten* (see Figures 6 and 7).[70]

---

[70] *The Isle of Pines; or, A Late Discovery of a Fourth Island near Terra Australis Incognita by Henry Cornelius Van Sloetten. . . . Licensed July 27. 1668* (London: printed for Allen Banks and Charles

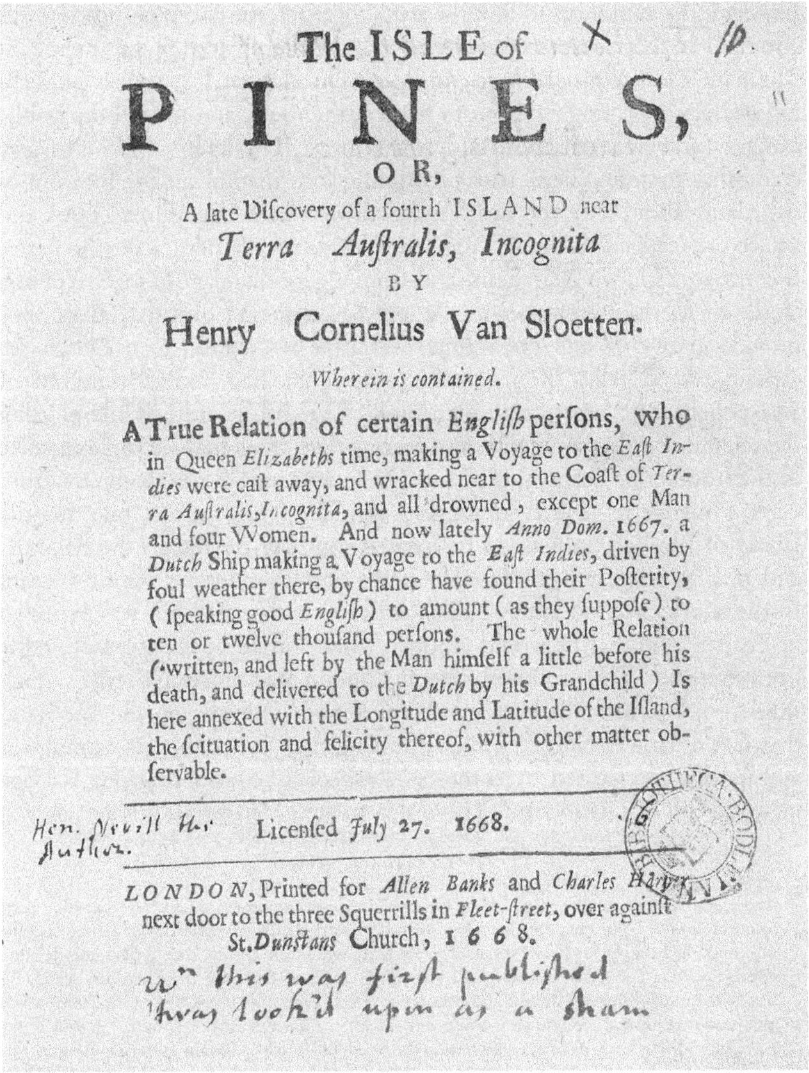

The ISLE of ✕ 𝑙𝑝.

P I N E S,

O R,

A late Difcovery of a fourth ISLAND near

Terra   Auftralis,   Incognita

B Y

Henry   Cornelius   Van   Sloetten.

Wherein is contained.

A True Relation of certain *Englifh* perfons, who in Queen *Elizabeths* time, making a Voyage to the *Eaft In-dies* were caft away, and wracked near to the Coaft of *Ter-ra Auftralis,Incognita*, and all drowned, except one Man and four Women. And now lately *Anno Dom.* 1667. a *Dutch* Ship making a Voyage to the *Eaft Indies*, driven by foul weather there, by chance have found their Pofterity, (fpeaking good *Englifh*) to amount (as they fuppofe) to ten or twelve thoufand perfons. The whole Relation (·written, and left by the Man himfelf a little before his death, and delivered to the *Dutch* by his Grandchild) Is here annexed with the Longitude and Latitude of the Ifland, the fcituation and felicity thereof, with other matter ob-fervable.

Hen. Nevill the Author.   Licenfed *July* 27. 1668.

LONDON, Printed for *Allen Banks* and *Charles Harper*, next door to the three Squerrills in *Fleet-ftreet*, over againft St.*Dunftans* Church, 1 6 6 8.

wᵐ this was firſt publiſhed 'twas lookᵈ upon as a ſham

Figure 7   *The Isle of Pines, or, A Late Discovery of a Fourth Island near Terra Australis, Incognita by Henry Cornelius Van Sloetten* (London: Allen Banks and Charles Harper, 1668), title page.
© The Bodleian Library, University of Oxford. Wood 386 (11)

Harper, 1668), hereafter *Isle of Pines* III. There were two largely identical contemporary editions of the complete version. One was published with and the other without a frontispiece.

Besides a few sentences to link the parts together, the complete edition was also flanked by two letters purported to be written by the Dutch merchant Abraham Keek to a reliable friend in Covent Garden.[71] Neville's publishing strategy was designed both to feign authenticity and to feed the public hunger for news, sensation and adventure.[72] The letters appear to give credibility to a fake news story, including information on the location of the island 'about 2 or 300 Leagues Northwest from Cape Finis Terre', and assure the reader that though the 'story seems very fabulous, yet the Letter is come to a known Merchant, and from a good hand in France'. Yet at a closer look, the accompanying letters cause more confusion than they provide clarity. While the framed narrative is credited to a Dutch sea captain, Keek talks of a 'French ship' that had recently arrived at La Rochelle with news of an island full of English people. While praising the reliability of his source, he also admits that 'there may be some mistake in the number of Leagues, as also of the exact point of the Compass, from Cape Finis Terre'. He even suggests that the island in fact may be 'the Island of Brasile', thought to be located south of Ireland in the Atlantic, and not, as suggested in Van Sloetten's narrative, in the Pacific Ocean. In the shorter second letter, Keek then reports that the ship was expected in Zealand and that he would report further, should he receive more news from France.[73] The promised news is Captain Van Sloetten's letter, which similarly plays with the veracity of its content, claiming on the one hand that it is a 'true Relation', while admitting that 'it is a thing so strange as will hardly be credited by some . . . , especially considering our last age being so full of Discoveries'. He is also aware of 'such Nullifidians as will

---

[71] This edition inserts the core story told by George Pine between pages 7 and 16. The transition parts read as follows: 'Then stepping into a kind of inner room, which as we conceived was his lodging Chamber, he brought forth two sheets of paper fairly written in *English*, (being the same Relation which you had Printed at *London*) and very distinctly read the same over unto us, which we hearkened unto with great delight and admiration, freely proffering us a Copy of the same, which we afterward took and brought away along with us; which Copy hereafter followeth. / A Way to the East *India's* being lately discovered by Sea, to the South of *Affrick* by certain *Portugals*, far more safe and profitable then had been heretofore; . . . whom God bless with the dew of Heaven, and the fat of the Earth, AMEN. – Ater [sic] the reading and delivering unto us a Coppy of this Relation, then proceeded he on in his discourse. My Grandfather when he wrote this. . .'

[72] Andrew Pettegree, *The Invention of News: How the World Came to Know about Itself* (New Haven, CT: Yale University Press, 2014); Joad Raymond (ed.), *News Networks in Seventeenth-Century Britain and Europe* (Routledge: London, 2006); Joad Raymond (ed.), *News, Newspapers, and Society in Early Modern Britain* (London: Frank Cass, 1999); Kate Loveman, *Reading Fictions, 1660–1740: Deception in English Literary and Political Culture* (Aldershot: Ashgate, 2008); and Daniel Carey, 'Henry Neville's *Isle of Pines*: Travel, Forgery, and the Problem of Genre', *Angelaki*, 1 (1993), 23–39.

[73] *Isle of Pines* III, fol. A2v.

believe nothing but what they see, applying that Proverb unto us, That Travelors may lye by authority'. He thus undermines his own account, and yet he warns of 'false Copies' of his narrative 'which might be spread'.[74] The captain's name is also suspect. His first name recalls that of the Dutch admiral Cornelis Tromp or Cornelius van Tromp, while his surname sounds similar to 'slet', the Dutch word for 'slut'. This may be a criticism of the perceived royalist sympathies of the Dutch that questioned their commitment to their nominal republicanism.

Tromp was a supporter of the Prince of Orange, whose Christian name, like that of the current island ruler, was 'William'. And the Dutch, in a rather royalist act, build a palace for the island prince.[75] Maybe Neville chose his character's name to make the connection between the houses of Orange and of Stuart, since the two were related, with William of Orange being the son of Charles II's sister Mary and thus his nephew. Through this family connection, the causes of Stuart and Orange were related too, as were the causes of English and Dutch republicans.[76] Thus the opposition here is not simply between the English and the Dutch, for the Dutch were equally torn. For instance, during the recent war, Tromp had saved the Dutch fleet from complete destruction in the Battle of Lowestoft, but, lacking the trust of the republican Grand Pensionary Johan de Witt, was soon replaced with Michiel de Ruyter, the man credited with the raid in the Medway. These divisions within Dutch society led English commonwealthmen to see the Dutch as bad republicans because they were tainted with their Orangist connection and the coexistence of the Orange dynasty alongside republican rule, while the Dutch likewise saw the English as bad republicans because they never considered the Commonwealth and Oliver Cromwell's centralist government to be a proper constitutional state form, which contributed to their mutual distrust.[77]

[74] *Isle of Pines* II, p. 23; *Isle of Pines* III, p. 30.
[75] Pincus, *Protestantism and Patriotism*, p. 339; Daniel Carey, 'Henry Neville's *The Isle of Pines*: From Sexual Utopia to Political Dystopia', in Chloë Houston (ed.), *New Worlds Reflected: Travel and Utopia in the Early Modern Period* (Farnham: Ashgate, 2010), pp. 203–18, at p. 216; and Daniel Carey, '*The Isle of Pines, 1668: Henry Neville's Uncertain Utopia* by John Scheckter', *Utopian Studies*, 23:2 (2012), 546–50, at p. 549. On the wider conundrum of the royalist leanings of the Dutch, see Helmers, *The Royalist Republic*.
[76] Pincus, *Protestantism and Patriotism*, pp. 108–9, 202, 312. Note, however, Helmers's recent warning against identifying the Stuart and the Orangist causes as identical in *The Royalist Republic*, p. 9.
[77] Pincus, *Protestantism and Patriotism*, p. 14. Weststeijn, *Commercial Republicanism*, p. 253. Ludlow for one thought that the Anglo-Dutch war and the cause of the nation and its merchants was just a

Yet it is the name of the letter-writer that should make us pause.
For Abraham Keek ('Keck' or 'Kick') was also the name of the
Dutchman considered to be responsible for betraying the three regicides
in Delft – Corbet, Barkstead and Okey – whose extraordinary rendition
by the government of the United Provinces had irritated Ludlow so
much that he refused to enter into any negotiations with De Witt, had
contributed to divisions between the exiles and had left plans for a
republican invasion of England doomed to failure for lack of adequate
leadership.[78] Keek was thus a highly contentious figure, and his name
would certainly not inspire great confidence in those in the know.[79] In
short, the message that Neville was trying to convey may simply have
been that the Dutch could not be trusted. Where historians have seen a
narrative of Anglo-Dutch rivalry and missed opportunity, however,
several literary scholars have read *The Isle* from a post-colonial perspective, highlighting its implicit assumptions about freedom of the sea, land
acquisition rights, slavery, male sexual-imperial fantasies, race relations
and kinship.

Colonial Ambitions, Race and Kinship

As an admirer of the 'divine Machiavel', Neville saw England's potential
for territorial expansion, or, in Harrington's terms, he considered his
country a 'commonwealth for increase'.[80] The Commonwealth he had
served as a councillor of state had great ambitions for trade and empire,
and MPs in the 1650s praised the fact that England had never before been
so considerable on the international stage.[81] England expanded close to
home with the invasion of Scotland and Ireland, while the empire was
growing across the Atlantic through its settlements in the American
colonies. To those would later be added schemes in the Caribbean under

---

 pretext to 'advance the absolute soveraignty of the Prince of Orange, the better to support that of
 Charles Stewards over England'. Ludlow, 'Voyce', p. 1013.
[78] See Chapter 4. Another (?) Abraham Keek (or Kick) in the 1680s hosted dissenting exiles, such as
 the Earl of Shaftesbury and Slingsby Bethel, at his house in Amsterdam, and helped the bookseller
 John Starkey obtain the freedom of the city. See BL, Add. MS 41809, fols 100r, 206r; Add. MS
 41813, fol. 107. I owe these references to Mark Knights.
[79] There were other hints in the pamphlet that it was not a true report, for despite George Pine's
 careful accounting, the story does not add up. For example, the first pamphlet wrongly has the year
 of departure as 1589 or '11. or 12. Eliz.' This is later corrected to 1569.
[80] Neville, *Plato redivivus*, p. 92; Machiavelli, *Discourses on Livy*, I:6, p. 22; and Harrington, *Oceana*,
 ed. Pocock, p. 7.
[81] See Chapter 6.

the Protectorate.[82] The Commonwealth also promoted commerce along trading routes to Asia, where the Dutch were prime competitors for the East India market. For that very reason, it has been argued, Neville himself had supported an 'aggressive foreign policy', including the First Anglo-Dutch War.[83]

English expansion of trade in the 1650s was at least in part the result of the 1651 Navigation Act, which had restricted Dutch encroachments on English territorial waters.[84] It followed the 'closed sea' policy put forward in John Selden's *Mare clausum* (1635), opting for protectionism over the freedom of the seas as propagated in Hugo Grotius's *Mare liberum* (1609) that had been employed to justify Dutch overseas trade expansion. In 1660 the Convention Parliament had passed a new Navigation Act to slow Dutch competition, but after the Second Anglo-Dutch War things looked different. Neville's depiction of the de facto situation on the Isle suggests that he may have acknowledged the strength of the Grotian principle, as the English Pines had, through complacency, failed to make the island and its surrounding waters their own, while the Dutch were preparing to take possession of it by charting its territory and defeating a local uprising. The situation also reflects on Grotian property theory, which originally argued for 'the right to use what was not privately owned', and was later developed by Locke to stipulate that land can be acquired simply by applying one's labour to it, while humans who had inhabited the land without claiming or cultivating it could be subjected.[85] In the present case, the English had inhabited the Isle, but not appropriated it, leaving it vulnerable to colonisers and invaders.

On their arrival on the island, the territory is yet uninhabited by humans. This leaves the property question open, but it also means that there is no encounter between the English and a native population. If at all, the meeting between the explorer/coloniser and an 'indigenous culture'

---

[82] Nicole Greenspan, *Selling Cromwell's Wars: Media, Empire and Godly Warfare, 1650–1658* (London: Pickering & Chatto, 2012), esp. chapters 1 and 2; and David Armitage, *The Ideological Origins of the British Empire* (Cambridge, UK: Cambridge University Press, 2000).

[83] Beach, 'A Profound Pessimism about the Empire', p. 22; and Blair Worden, 'Marchamont Nedham and the Beginnings of English Republicanism, 1649–1656', in David Wootton (ed.), *Republicanism, Liberty and Commercial Society, 1649-1776* (Stanford, CA: Stanford University Press, 1994), pp. 45–81, at pp. 48–9.

[84] Thomas Leng, 'Commercial Conflict and Regulation in the Discourse of trade in Seventeenth-Century England', *Historical Journal*, 48:4 (2005), 933–54, at pp. 945, 949, 954.

[85] Marco Barducci, *Hugo Grotius and the Century of Revolution 1613–1718: Transnational Reception in English Political Thought* (Oxford: Oxford University Press, 2017), pp. 143, 149, 151–2, 160, 163–72; and John Locke, *Two Treatises of Government*, ed. Peter Laslett (Cambridge, UK: Cambridge University Press, 1988), Second Treatise, chapter 5, pp. 285–302.

takes place later between the Dutch and the English Pines.[86] However, the issue of race relations is introduced by Neville with reference to the black slave who had travelled with the English merchant family on the ship, simply referred to by Pines as 'my *Negro*'.[87] It is true that the extraordinary circumstances of the shipwreck work as a social leveller to an extent. John Scheckter's recent suggestion that the integration of the black woman into the Pines' emerging society indicates that distinctions of race, gender and class are eroded on the island and that there are 'no outsiders' and 'no otherness', however, does not entirely hold up.[88] The four women who become Pine's companions are classified in a clear hierarchy, with his master's daughter at the top, the two white maid servants – one of whom is only characterised by being 'something fat' – in the middle and the '*Negro*' at the bottom of the pile.[89] In fact, Pine's preference for his master's daughter continues to her death, when she is allocated a burying place closest to where his own human remains would be laid to rest, while the slave is buried furthest away from him.[90] Throughout, the black woman or '*Blackmore*' is described as tough and 'less sensible then the rest', which enables Pine to use her as a key source of labour. Among other things, she is the one who keeps watch outside the tent as the others rest after having exhausted themselves by building a shelter.[91] Her inferior social rank and marginal status are marked by her lack of a surname, so that her descendants are named Phills after her Christian name, Philippa.[92] While she becomes Pine's sexual partner, fulfilling what could be considered a 'male imperial fantasy', relations between her and her master are overshadowed by the perceived stigma of racial difference that reflected

---

[86] John Scheckter, The Isle of Pines, *1668: Henry Neville's Uncertain Utopia* (Farnham: Ashgate, 2011), p. 155.

[87] *Isle of Pines* I, p. 6; *Isle of Pines* III, p. 12. See also Amy Boesky, 'Nation, Miscegenation: Membering Utopia in Henry Neville's *The Isle of Pines*', *Texas Studies in Literature and Language*, 37 (1995), 165–85; Fausett, *Writing the New World*, pp. 81–90; and Hughes (ed.), *Versions of Blackness*.

[88] Scheckter, *The Isle of Pines, 1668*, p. 137. Similarly, Seth Denbo argues that '[d]istinctions of class and status are mostly erased by the shipwreck'. Yet, he continues, 'but there is an unconscious sense that the Black woman is a lesser being, not subject to the same sensitivities and sensibilities as the rest'. See 'Generating Regenerated Generations: Race, Kinship and Sexuality on Henry Neville's *Isle of Pines* (1668)', in Nicole Pohl and Brenda Tooley (eds), *Gender and Utopia in the Eighteenth Century: Essays in English and French Utopian Writing* (Aldershot: Ashgate, 2007), pp. 147–61, at p. 152; also Beach, 'A Profound Pessimism about the Empire', p. 26.

[89] *Isle of Pines* I, p. 6; *Isle of Pines* III, p. 12 (*recte* 13).   [90] *Isle of Pines* I, p. 8; *Isle of Pines* III, p. 15.

[91] *Isle of Pines* I, pp. 3–4; *Isle of Pines* III, p. 9.   [92] *Isle of Pines* I, p. 9; *Isle of Pines* III, pp. 15–16.

seventeenth-century warnings against intermarriage.[93] The slave is marked out as a less desirable sexual partner, who 'longed also for her share' and seduces Pine in the dark in an attempt to deceive him. However, he is willing 'to try the difference' and satisfies himself with her, reducing her to an object of his lust. Pine also stresses that he sleeps with her only in the dark of night as otherwise 'my stomach would not serve me', which suggests that Pine associates a certain degree of shame with the illicit nature of their relationship.[94] As a creature perceived closer to nature than the others, Philippa also enjoys remarkably high fertility. She falls pregnant almost every time George Pine has sex with her, and as he never sleeps with her when she is pregnant, she has the least sexual contact with him.[95] She also does not seem to suffer any great pain in childbirth, which suggests on the one hand that this mother role is natural to her, while on the other hand her lack of pain also rejects the curse of Eve as a consequence of the Fall, showing the relationship between Pine and Philippa at once as both transgressive and pure.[96] This tension between the personal benefit Pine derives from the slave and the element of guilt that overshadows their relationship may be a subtle hint at the moral conundrum that Neville may have seen in slavery: how to justify the liberty and prosperity of one at the expense of another in the acquisition of empire.[97] For if republicans considered liberty as an essential prerequisite for the independent citizen, how could they justify the subjection of others? Philippa's integration into the society of the Pines questioned the common republican, Aristotelian assumption that some people were slaves by nature.[98] In fact, Neville's *Isle* may have been 'prophetic' with regard to the legacy of slavery in reflecting its author's 'anxiety about the management of the colonial space'.[99] While the issue remains unresolved in Neville's narrative, however, slavery is identified as the source of potential conflict awaiting resolution, as underlying problems persist in Pine's society, even though they may not be apparent at first sight.

---

[93] Beach, 'A Profound Pessimism about the Empire', p. 26; Boesky, 'Nation, Miscegenation', pp. 168–9.

[94] *Isle of Pines* I, p. 6; *Isle of Pines* III, p. 12 (*recte* 13).

[95] *Isle of Pines* I, p. 6; *Isle of Pines* III, p. 12 (*recte* 13).

[96] *Isle of Pines* I, p. 6; and *Isle of Pines* III, p. 12 (*recte* 13); Genesis 3:16.

[97] Williamson, 'English Republicanism and Global Slavery', p. 14.

[98] Aristotle, *Politics*, pp. 12, 16–19.

[99] Alison Fanous Cotti-Lowell, 'The Pineapple and Colonial Enterprise in Henry Neville's *The Isle of Pines*', *Texas Studies in Literature and Language*, 59:2 (2017), 209–33, at pp. 212, 229, 225.

Thus the first child that results from the transgressive union between
Pine and Philippa is 'a fine white Girle', and it is presumed that her other
children are white too.[100] The slave's blackness is thus not passed on as a
physical feature, but as a social marker, and her descendants remain – at
least temporarily – a separate tribe. Through her otherness, the black
woman over time becomes the ancestor of many trouble-makers on the
island, including John Phill, who is 'guilty of divers ravishings & tyrannies', as well as '*Henry Phil*, the chief Ruler of the Tribe or Family of the
Phils', who causes a rebellion by raping the wife of another tribal leader,
thus threatening 'a general ruin to the whole State'.[101] In a twist that
reveals contemporary racial prejudice, the slave has created a tribe of rebels
and criminals that needs to be controlled. The fact that Philippa's offspring
remains on the margins of the island society also reflects contemporary
practice to consider the offspring resulting from sexual unions between free
white men and female slaves also as slaves.[102] Over time, an increasing
number of Pines would have become mixed-race through intermarriage,
but the issue is nowhere explicitly acknowledged or addressed.[103]
Miscegenation has proved a Pandora's box, and Philippa's descendants
have become the scapegoats for all social ills. In keeping with the scriptural
theme, Amy Boesky also sees the black slave Philippa as a possible female
version of Cush, whom legend depicts as the father of a black race: Cush
was the result of an act of disobedience by Ham, one of Noah's sons, who
ignored his father's exhortation not to have sex with his wife on the Ark
and for his defiance was punished with this black offspring.[104] Blackness is
thus depicted as an element disruptive to social cohesion throughout, and
Neville's short pamphlet can be read as an observation of and commentary
on the complexities of race relations in colonial societies. Aside from being
a reflection on the Anglo-Dutch relationship and England's role in the
early years of the colonial race, *The Isle of Pines* was also a work of exile and
a reflection on life far away from home.

Distance and Alienation

After having lived away from his home country for three years, Neville
made travel, distance, alienation and a sense of loss or of being lost key

[100] *Isle of Pines* I, p. 6; *Isle of Pines* III, p. 12.
[101] *Isle of Pines* II, pp. 10, 18–19; *Isle of Pines* III, pp.17, 25–6.
[102] Boesky, 'Nation, Miscegenation', pp. 168–9.
[103] Carey, '*The Isle of Pines, 1668: Henry Neville's Uncertain Utopia* by John Scheckter', p. 549.
[104] Boesky, 'Nation, Miscegenation', pp. 165–6.

themes of his writing. His fictional castaways experience some of the same uncertainty he may have felt after his departure from England when their ship is destroyed and the rest of their company perish. In the beginning, they still hope that it might please God 'to send any Ship that way', so that 'we might be transported home'. But it does not happen, 'the place ... being much out of the way'.[105] Over time, as their family begins to grow, the five castaways are becoming 'satisfied' with their condition and no longer have any 'thought of ever returning home'. They even swear to each other 'never to part or leave one another, or the place'.[106] Yet they still continue to live in the expectation that someone may come and 'find them out'.[107] Thus George Pine finds it necessary to admonish his offspring not to admit any other religion besides Christianity, while also leaving a written record of the origins of the island society for any strangers that might pass by to take a copy, 'that our names be not lost from off the earth'.[108] The long-expected visitors eventually do arrive on the island and take a copy of George Pine's story. Yet none of the islanders show any interest in re-establishing contact with the country of their ancestors or of being taken back to England. In many ways, this reflects Neville's own feelings about his exile. He considered Italy as a 'paradise' and vented his frustration with England in the rather defiant remark to his brother that he preferred being 'civilly treated, ... valew'd and esteem'd by princes abroad' to being 'hatted' and 'persecuted at home'.[109] He was also rather unwilling to return home and decided to make his way back to London in 1667 only because he was hoping to recover some papers that had been caught by the Great Fire the previous year.[110]

By locating an island inhabited by English savages out on the open seas, Neville also gives us a new perspective on the state of England in the 1660s. Neville sees England from the outside, from a distance, arguably in a more objective way, taking a more dispassionate view. He may have been able to get the foreign perspective on his home country through the way in which England was being talked about in Italy, especially by the many foreigners he encountered in Rome, or through how affairs regarding

[105] *Isle of Pines* I, p. 5; *Isle of Pines* III, p.11.
[106] *Isle of Pines* I, p. 7; *Isle of Pines* III, p. 12 (*recte* 13).
[107] *Isle of Pines* I, p. 8; *Isle of Pines* III, p. 15.   [108] *Isle of Pines* I, p. 9; *Isle of Pines* III, p. 15.
[109] Henry Neville, Rome, to Bernardino Guasconi, 8 January 1667, in Crinò, 'Lettere inedite', pp. 186–7, at p. 187; Henry Neville, Warfield, to Cosimo III, 27 September/7 October 1680, in Crinò, 'Lettere inedite', pp. 204–6; and BRO, D/EN F8/1/11, Henry Neville, Florence, to Richard Neville, London, 20 January 1665.
[110] Henry Neville, Frascati, to Bernardino Guasconi, 30 October 1666, in Crinò, 'Lettere inedite', p. 184.

England were reported in newsletters and in the press.[111] Yet there is also something very personal about his bogus travel pamphlet, especially in the way in which he makes his own 'Henry-ness' part of the narrative. Neville's relationship to his own country is thus at the centre of *The Isle*: part of him is in (King) Henry, the good republican ruler, part in Henry (Phill), the trouble-maker during the Restoration, and part, finally, in (Dutch) Henry, the discoverer of the savages and the man pulling the English Pines out of oblivion. Notably, the law code eventually established on the island makes an ironic reference to Neville's own situation as a republican rebel and exile. Those who 'should defame or speak evil of the Governour, or refuse to come before him upon Summons' will 'receive a punishment by whipping with Rods, and afterwards be exploded from the society of all the rest of the inhabitants'.[112]

Like Neville, the English Pines are far away from England, yet remain English: they have kept many things they brought from the Old World and keep using them, notably the axe that they rescued from the flotsam and jetsam and that has become blunted over time, but also the Bible as their religious and cultural guide.[113] Only necessity and their specific circumstances lead the settlers to deviate from English customs and turn them into savages in some respects. The first generation of settlers resort to polygamy and over time lose the shame that their society of origin would have associated with behaviour that was commonly considered immoral. They also lack clothes for their children, so that the following generations grow up more or less naked. The children 'out of necessity' enter into incestuous relationships because an entire generation shares the same father, although over time, in the generation of his grand-children, George Pine reinstates a degree of decency by marrying 'the Males of one Family' to 'the Females of another'.[114] He orders his descendants to have the Bible read once a month at a general meeting, they follow a general moral code instituted through a set of laws or commandments, and they conduct marriage and burial ceremonies. Overall, the island's inhabitants degenerate over time, but not so much that the Dutch ship's crew would no longer recognise them as English. This is a devastating commentary on English history written from the distance of exile. While the English had existed in a state of arrested

---

[111] On Rome as a news hub, see Henry Neville, Rome, to Bernardino Guasconi, 1 August 1665, in Crinò, 'Lettere inedite', p. 181.
[112] *Isle of Pines* II, p. 12; *Isle of Pines* III, p. 19.
[113] *Isle of Pines* I, pp. 4, 8; *Isle of Pines* II, pp. 5, 13; *Isle of Pines* III, pp. 10, 5, 14.
[114] *Isle of Pines* I, p. 8.

development since the reign of Elizabeth I, the rest of the world had moved on. But what was the bottom line for republicans?

The Experience of Defeat, or an Island with Potential?

While Christopher Hill has argued that many writings of English republicans after 1660, such as Milton's *Paradise Lost*, were characterised by the experience of defeat, the chapters of this book have shown that the radical underground continued its political activities until well into the 1660s and beyond.[115] Neville was arrested twice for suspected plotting and continued to comment on English affairs in his letters and published writings; Sidney actively attempted to gather an army of exiles to invade England from abroad and wrote a pamphlet to spur his allies into action. And while Ludlow may have decided not to take up arms again, he still continued to see the restored monarchy as a usurpation and aimed to set the record straight, both through his French edition of the regicides' *Speeches and Prayers* and through his memoirs of Civil War and exile set down in his 'Voyce'.

Defeat – in the sense that no further major military action to implement regime change was either considered or feasible – was not acknowledged by many republicans until after the Second Anglo-Dutch War and the republicans' failure to drum up support in Europe for an invasion of England from abroad. 1667 might thus be seen as another setback for English republicans in so far as interest in the republican underground subsided and their hopes for immediate political change were lost. As time passed, more and more Civil War republicans may indeed have come to accommodate themselves to the restored Stuart regime and turned their attention to change from within. But a significant number of republicans also continued with their politics and would resurface as soon as they saw potential opportunities for change, such as the Exclusion Crisis, in which both Sidney and Neville as well as Wildman would once again become influential political actors. Even Ludlow made a renewed attempt at politics after the Glorious Revolution, although he would soon come to realise that he would never be able to overcome his radical past. The activities and writings of the English republican exiles in Europe should therefore not be seen as marred by the experience of defeat, but as 'defiant' works, fuelled by hope for change. This defiance in the face of the Restoration has been identified by a number of literary scholars engaging

---

[115] Hill, *The Experience of Defeat*.

with later seventeenth-century republican texts, in particular with reference to Milton's *Paradise Lost*. This epic did not 'represent a guilty retreat from politics and withdrawal into a quiescent concern with individual spirituality'.[116] Instead, it was a text that continued to attack and criticise the nature and foundation of monarchical power. Laura Knoppers likewise sees Milton's *Paradise Regain'd* and *Samson Agonistes* (both 1671) as 'closely linked with the concerns of dissent and republicanism'. His Restoration poems, she argues, 'can be seen as part of oppositional discourse, fostering hope and fortifying resistance in dissenters and political radicals'.[117] According to Katharine Gillespie, a similar argument can be made for Lucy Hutchinson's biblical epic *Order and Disorder* (1679) and her *Memoirs of the Life of Colonel John Hutchinson*, written during the Restoration, though not published until 1806. 'In these works', the republican's wife and political author in her own right 'recovers her husband and republicans in general from oblivion' as she supplants 'their image as demonic rebels condemned to hell' and replaces it 'with that of virtuous republican men whose dedication to the cause earned them a saint's rest in heaven and the satisfaction of seeing their dream realized on earth'.[118] Similar things could be said of Ludlow's editorial work and his own writing efforts that aimed to keep alive a republican narrative of events just as the Restoration regime was keen to erase all memory of the Interregnum.

The Isle of Pines too is a good example of this defiance. The English may have lost their way during Queen Elizabeth's reign, when the country was in their eyes well governed and respected around the world; they may have suffered Civil War and had recently seen the restoration of monarchical rule. But their country, like Neville's *Isle of Pines*, also had a lot of untapped potential. As the bookkeeper-patriarch George Pine keeps reminding us through the repeated numbering of his offspring, the *Isle/England* had a growing population, which the political arithmeticians of the time from William Petty to Charles Davenant and Gregory King saw as the basis for productivity and wealth.[119] The country also benefited from its fertile soil and good climate for the growing of plants and rearing of animals, while its island location made it suitable for shipping and trade.

[116] Gillespie, *Women Writing the English Republic*, p. 285.
[117] Knoppers, 'Englands Case', pp. 584, 587.
[118] Gillespie, *Women Writing the English Republic*, pp. 285–6.
[119] Ted McCormick, *William Petty and the Ambitions of Political Arithmetic* (Oxford: Oxford University Press, 2010); Paul Slack, *The Invention of Improvement: Information and Material Progress in Seventeenth-Century England* (Oxford: Oxford University Press, 2015).

As the Dutch sea captain points out on surveying the island, not all was lost. In fact, 'had but Nature here the benefit of Art added unto it', the Isle of Pines 'would equal, if not exceed many of our *Europian* Countries'.[120] And the narrator is sure that 'time will make this Island known better to the world' – in part through the pamphlet he himself is taking back to Europe. As he repeats in the postscript, the Isle is 'a place enriched with Natures abundance, deficient in nothing conducible to the sustentation of mans life'. Thus, 'were it Manured by Agri-culture and Gardening, as other of our European Countries are, ... it would equal, if not exceed many which now pass for praise worthy'.[121] In short, England had everything necessary for success, but it had to be cultivated, and a lot of work would have to be done. The pamphlet about the little island society meanwhile travelled across the whole of Europe and spoke to many readers at different levels. Like *Les juges* and the manuscript of the *Court Maxims* it may have spoken to those sympathetic to the English republican cause.

The Leiden Edition of *The Isle*

As we have seen above, Neville's *Isle* was translated into a range of European languages and appeared in many different editions.[122] In the context of exile, the French-language edition published by the Leiden bookseller Abraham Gogat in 1668 is probably the most interesting because its paratexts give us some idea of the environment in which the pamphlet may have been read and passed around. It may be the work of a francophone or Franco-Flemish bilingual sympathiser of the English exiles in the United Provinces, possibly even someone belonging to their wider networks.

The French Leiden edition was entitled *Relation fidelle & veritable de la nouvelle découverte d'une quatrieme isle de la terre Australe, ou Meridionale inconüe, sous le nom d'Isle de Pines* and contained a close literal rendering of the first part of Neville's narrative framed by a letter of the translator to his friend and introduced by an address from the bookseller to the reader.[123] According to the bookseller's address, the letter had been intercepted by the writer's friends together with his translation of *The Isle* into French from a Flemish copy that followed the original English text. The main

---

[120] *Isle of Pines* II, pp. 14–15; *Isle of Pines* III, p. 21.
[121] *Isle of Pines* II, p. 24; *Isle of Pines* III, p. 31. [122] Mahlberg, 'Authors Losing Control'.
[123] *Relation fidelle & veritable de la nouvelle découverte d'une quatrième isle de la terre Australe, ou Meridionale inconüe, sous le nom d'Isle de Pines* (Leiden: Abraham Gogat, 1668).

body of the text was therefore a secondary translation with Flemish as a bridging language between English and French, while the letter was directly written in French and had allegedly reached the bookseller via a third party. While it is impossible to verify the letter's origins on the basis of the evidence available to us, the letter was most probably a fiction employed to draw attention to the pamphlet and guide the reader towards its hidden meaning, while also adding weight and credibility to its purpose, if not its veracity. The question of its authorship is closely connected to its creative environment and its intended audience.

The framing letter is addressed 'from Philogyton to Nicophile', with the two telling names adding more specific characteristics to the otherwise anonymous correspondents. In this case, 'Philogyton', composed of the ancient Greek φίλος (philos/loving) and γείτων (geítōn/neighbour), is someone who loves his neighbour, recommending the enclosed pamphlet for the benefit of his friend. 'Nicophile' meanwhile goes back to the ancient Greek νίκη (nikē/victory) and φίλος, describing someone who likes to win, and for them the pamphlet would consequently be beneficial.[124] The letter is then signed 'V.M.', and we can only speculate about who was behind it as no obvious candidates with these initials stand out among the known contemporary translators. We have already noted above that the story about the letter being intercepted was most probably made up. Such fictional credentials for a fictional story were common literary practice at the time, and, indeed, this letter resembles the two by Abraham Keek flanking the complete version of the English edition. Nevertheless, the French letter may give us a hint at the environment in which Neville's pamphlet was read and passed around. There are various indications that this environment was republican, Calvinist and transnational.

After the usual formulae of friendship and apologies for not having responded to a number of earlier letters, the letter-writer goes on to discuss wider political matters in the aftermath of the Anglo-Dutch war, including 'the great calm, & the perfect repose that today reigns in Holland' as well as the country's extraordinary prosperity under the leadership of its Grand Pensionary De Witt, which he then contrasts with the state of the French monarchy. In fact, Holland had 'never found itself in such a peaceful state, never more flourishing than that in which it finds itself at present'.[125] It had completed the war to its advantage and subsequently 'entered alliances and leagues in good faith with all the considerable powers of the north',

[124] I owe these explanations to Markus Egg, who helped me with the derivations from ancient Greek.
[125] Neville, *Relation fidelle*, p. 6.

giving to its inhabitants 'the sweet and delicious fruits of a sovereign tranquillity'. Thus there were no more murmurings or complaints about 'a government, which is the softest internally, & most vigorous in its defence & for its external preservation'. For this reason, everyone in the country respected 'the great man' De Witt, who 'with a number of other intelligent and well intentioned counsellors' steered 'the body of the state' while also moderating its policy.[126] And De Witt was able to do all this 'without having the elevation' to any royal title, 'having all that is necessary for government' without the 'affectation of monarchy'.[127] De Witt's successful leadership is then contrasted with that of the Pope's friend 'the great King of France', whose friendship the United Provinces 'cherished more than his vicinity'.[128] This alludes to the old adage *Gallus amicus non vicinus* – the Frenchman should be a friend, but not a neighbour (to the United Provinces) – which of course referred to French claims to the Spanish Low Countries.[129] Yet there is also an underlying message that De Witt should be careful not to become an autocratic ruler himself, 'pulling to himself all the authority of command, without sharing it with the colleagues who ordinarily exist in republics'.[130]

Besides its defence of Dutch republicanism and its attack on the French monarchy, the letter also contains several indications that it may have originated in a Calvinist environment. The letter-writer, for instance, refers to an inaugural sermon given at the Leiden faculty of theology in the summer of 1668. Leiden University was the oldest academic institution in the United Provinces and renowned for its scholarship, which attracted many foreign students to the city, especially in the seventeenth century. It was therefore not an unlikely place for a pamphlet being read in one language and translated into another. To have been present at this lecture, the letter-writer would have needed some connection to the university and may even have been a scholar there himself. Given his ability to translate a pamphlet from Flemish into French, he may either have been French or possibly have come from the French-speaking southern part of the Netherlands, which today is Belgium and then was under Habsburg control.[131] In any case, he had sufficient Flemish to undertake the translation. The best hint at the environment from which the pamphlet originated, however, comes from the letter-writer's comments on the

---

[126] Ibid., p. 7.   [127] Ibid. p. 8.   [128] Ibid., p. 6.   [129] Rowen, *John de Witt*, p. 101.
[130] Neville, *Relation fidelle*, p. 8.
[131] Of course, the translator did not have to be a native French speaker at all, although it was more common for translators to translate into their own language than out of it.

sermon, which he praises for its erudition and eloquence. This sermon was given by 'M. Valckenier', who can be identified as Johan Valckenier (1617–70), a Reformed theologian and professor at Leiden University from 1668 to 1670, which indicates that the writer is of a similar persuasion or at least sympathetic to Valckenier's views.[132] That the letter-writer has a broader interest in theology and Bible exegesis is also confirmed by his suggestion that *The Isle* provides a 'perfect copy of the first generation of men, which is so close to what Moses has told us'.[133] Moreover, scriptural scholarship was close to the heart of the bookseller-publisher Gogat himself, whose publications included a French edition of the Calvinist New Testament.[134]

However, the letter-writer also casts doubt on the superficial veracity of the story, suggesting that it was at least as strange, if more pleasing, than 'the imaginary voyages of Lucien in the belly of the whale' or 'those of others to the moon'.[135] But he also hastens to add that its veracity is not necessarily the most interesting thing about the enclosed pamphlet, as it contains a deeper truth that he wants its readers to contemplate and exercise their wits on. Thus he recommends *The Isle* to his friend for the entertainment of 'the men that come and see you in the country', not least 'the illustrious triumvirate' and a certain 'Monsieur de Cottans', yet to be identified.[136] Indeed, the letter-writer finds that the pamphlet and its many questions might provide a few days' entertainment for these men, and he is keen to hear what the addressee and his friends have to say about it. Finally, the translator/letter-writer himself drops a further hint at how the enclosed pamphlet should be read, saying he is currently 'busy compiling memoirs for the history of the recent wars between England and the

---

[132] Neville, *Relation fidelle*, p. 10.   [133] Ibid., p. 44.

[134] *Le Nouveau Testament, contenant, la Nouvelle Alliance de Notre Seigneur Jesus Christ. Revu sur les textes grecs, par les ministres & professeurs de l'Eglise de Geneve. Edition fort correcte & tres-commode, tant pour la grosseur & la beaute du caracter, & l'exactitude des renvois, & de la citation des passage paralleles, que pour les Pseaumes qui y sont joint tout en musique, avec de grands arguments, & la prose en marge* (Leiden: Abraham Gogat, 1669).

[135] The reference on p. 44 is to Lucian's *True History*, another well-known tall tale circulating in early modern Europe. See *Lucian's 'True History'*, trans. Francis Hickes, introduction by Charles Whibley (London: privately printed, 1894), pp. 83 ff.; and Aristoula Georgiadou and David Henry James Larmour, *Lucian's Science Fiction Novel 'True Histories': Interpretation and Commentary* (Leiden: Brill, 1998), pp. 156 ff. On reports of contemporary travels to the moon, see David Cressy, 'Early Modern Space Travel and the English Man in the Moon', *American Historical Review*, 111:4 (2006), 961–82. The author here may have been thinking of the story of the Spanish adventurer Domingo Gonsales, who allegedly travelled to the moon with the help of migrant birds to find 'a kind of paradise with peace and plenty, and lunar creatures instinctively inclined toward Christianity' (ibid.,p. 962).

[136] Neville, *Relation fidelle*, pp. 44–5.

States [General], not least to see if the same England from which this narrative has come to us ... cannot shed more light on the below'. It is safe to say, then, that at least some contemporaries read *The Isle* in this political and religious context. The letter-writer then says that he is hoping to go to England soon, which is another hint that there may be some sort of connection between him and republicans and dissenters in England, if not to the original story's author.[137]

Indeed, we might wonder whether either the letter-writer or the addressee could be in some way connected to the English republican exiles in the United Provinces and whether Neville's pamphlet was known within the exile community as the work of a fellow refugee. Several points may even hint at Sidney as a possible translator of the pamphlet, such as the fact that he had been in the Netherlands on and off for around four to five years and was fluent in French. The address 'De Philogyton à Nicophile' is reminiscent of his naming of the characters 'Philalethes' and 'Eunomius' in the *Court Maxims*, and he too admired De Witt and scorned Louis XIV. Finally, Sidney understood *The Isle* as a coded work that reveals a deeper truth underneath its fictional surface, as we have seen above. Yet by mid-1668 Sidney had already settled in Montpellier, and it is unlikely that he would have translated a pamphlet from Flemish into French when he could have used an English version, unless this part of the letter too was a fiction. Conversely, it might be suggested that the pamphlet was translated by an ally of the English republicans in the Netherlands and sent to Sidney for his entertainment in Montpellier, although Montpellier would hardly qualify as being 'in the country'. In any case, it is likely that *The Isle* was or became known also abroad as the work of an English republican. None of this resolves the question of the mysterious 'V.M.' But the many hints in the paratexts to the Leiden edition of *The Isle* suggest that the work's Dutch editors knew a lot more about the pamphlet than they let on and that they provide a key to the political and religious environment in which the narrative was received.

Conclusion

The evidence suggests that *The Isle of Pines* had a certain impact as a work of exile, albeit in ways that could not always be controlled. But it found an audience in Protestant republican circles beyond England and a much wider European public besides. As a republican text, Neville's *Isle of Pines*,

[137] Ibid., p. 44.

like his later *Plato redivivus*, is highly critical of patriarchal monarchy and the government of Charles II in England. Yet it is also evidence of his ambiguous attitude towards the Dutch, holding them up as model colonisers and traders while also showing them as taking advantage of the naive and backward English Pines, who are unable to develop without their help. Neville's work thus reflects both Sidney's enthusiasm for the Dutch and Ludlow's healthy distrust of the powerful neighbour across the North Sea. However, it also had a broader European and transnational appeal.

As the Gogat edition suggests, Neville's *Isle of Pines*, just like Ludlow's French version of the *Speeches and Prayers* of the regicides, was being used as republican propaganda targeted at, among others, a French-speaking Protestant audience, although in this specific case the English republican cause retreated behind that of the Dutch. Nevertheless, Neville's exile work was being employed on behalf of a wider European Protestant republican interest against the old patriarchal monarchies exemplified by France and Restoration England. It thus had a broader appeal well beyond the confines of the British Isles, once again showing that English republicans were part of much wider European networks.

Epilogue

This book has been an attempt to fill a gap in the historiography of seventeenth-century English republicanism that had left a question mark over the period between the Restoration of the Stuart monarchy in May 1660 and the revival of republican activity during the Exclusion Crisis of the 1670s and 1680s. It has been argued that the cause of the English republicans of the 1640s and 1650s survived the Restoration period, which ended with the Glorious Revolution of 1688, but that much republican activity had been hidden from view because it was conducted either underground or in exile – be it in the American colonies or on the European Continent. As most anglophone readers would be more familiar with the transatlantic narrative that has traced the transmission of English republican ideas to America, this book has aimed to provide several European parts of the jigsaw puzzle. Yet the story of the three English republican exiles discussed here does not end with their time on the Continent. For two of them it continued back home in England after years or even decades abroad. For the third of them, it ended with the realisation that even thirty years abroad could not heal the social and political rift created by the regicide.

Having lost the support of his fallen patron Clarendon, Henry Neville was the first of the three exiles to return to England. He must have left Italy some time after June 1667, when his brother sent him his last recorded letter to Rome, and arrived in England some time before June 1668, when he published *The Isle of Pines* in London.[1] *The Isle*, as I have shown above, was as much the settling of a score with the Restoration government and a critique of monarchy as a book of hope for a better England, open to trade and prosperity through religious liberty and a new foreign policy. Neville spent the next ten years in relative obscurity living

---

[1] NA, SP 29/206, 21 June 1667, fol. 134, Richard Neville, Billingbear, to Henry Neville, Rome, 20 June 1667, sent by James Hicks to Secretary Williamson.

in Berkshire and London before standing, albeit unsuccessfully, for a parliamentary seat again in 1679. He also joined the political debate with 'Nicholas Machiavel's Letter' (1675), attacking plans for a further Test Act that would bar Catholics and dissenters from political office, and *Plato redivivus* (1681), arguing for constitutional limitations to monarchical power as a way out of the so-called Exclusion Crisis, which had been triggered by fears of the succession of the Catholic James, Duke of York, to the English throne.[2]

Both pieces are notable for their anti-clericalism as well as their views on Catholicism as they differentiate between the 'popery' and 'priestcraft' of the Catholic Church as an international political force on the one hand and the Catholic faith as a private devotion on the other. Thus they are a document to Neville's Italian exile and his own experiences of the Catholic faith in a foreign country as well as to his high regard for the Tuscan Grand Duke Ferdinando II and his son Cosimo III, who would remain a life-long correspondent of the republican.[3] In their letters exchanged following Neville's return to England, one of the main topics of conversation was the issue of liberty of conscience for Catholics living under the English monarchy, including the Tuscan merchant community in London.[4] This correspondence got Neville into new trouble during the Exclusion Crisis of the late 1670s, when he was suspected of involvement in a scheme to kill the Earl of Shaftesbury, who played a key role in the Popish Plot revelations, and of having contact with the five Catholic lords imprisoned in the Tower for their alleged involvement in the conspiracy. Sensing that the Popish Plot was an invention, Neville knew the five lords to be innocent and had said so to the agent of the Tuscan grand duke, Francesco Terriesi.[5] As someone who opposed the exclusion of James, Duke of York, from the succession, Neville was clearly thought of as a Catholic sympathiser and potential traitor by Shaftesbury's Whigs, while the government feared him as a republican intent on constitutional change. He probably destroyed at least part of his Italian correspondence to avoid its detection.[6] It may be due to this episode that we do not have a full set of letters to go back to

---

[2] Mahlberg, *Henry Neville and English Republican Culture*, pp. 65–9.
[3] Ibid., chapter 5; Gaby Mahlberg, 'Machiavelli, Neville and the Seventeenth-Century Discourse on Priestcraft'; and Mark Goldie, 'The Civil Religion of James Harrington', in Anthony Pagden (ed.), *The Languages of Political Theory in Early Modern Europe* (Cambridge, UK: Cambridge University Press, 1987), pp. 197–222.
[4] Neville's Italian correspondence can be found at BRO, D/EN F8/2.
[5] BL, Add. MS 25358, fol. 353r, Francesco Terriesi to Apollonio Bassetti, 23 June 1679,.
[6] Mahlberg, *Henry Neville and English Republican Culture*, p. 66.

that could shed more light on the latter part of Neville's life. But a significant number of Italian letters kept at the Berkshire Record Office and their responses at the Archivio di Stato in Florence still await further study.[7]

Algernon Sidney returned from exile a full decade later than Neville, in September 1677, with his zest for political action hardly diminished and making good use of his continental connections.[8] As early as 1678, we find him in negotiations with the French ambassador Paul Barillon to assist the 'French-engineered' fall of the Earl of Danby, and he continued over the following years 'to construct an Anglo-Dutch republican alternative to Stuart–Orange foreign policy' via 'the French ambassadors in England and the United Provinces'.[9] Barely two years after his arrival on English shores, Sidney was also standing in his first of three elections between 1679 and 1681, but he failed to secure a seat in any of them.[10] Neverthe-less, he continued his political activism by campaigning against political corruption, possibly becoming involved in 'treasonous activities' through which he was implicated in the Rye House Plot to kill the king in 1683, and writing the *Discourses*, whose authorship would come to be used as evidence in the trial that sealed his death.[11] Throughout, he continued his work for the cause of political and religious liberty and the promotion of a European Protestant interest.

Another important legacy of his exile consisted of the many personal acquaintances and connections Sidney had established or intensified over this seventeen-year period abroad. Some of these connections remained stable after his return to England. In fact, we can observe a certain mutuality developing, with people who had helped Sidney during his period of exile later being able to rely on him in return. One such mutually beneficial relationship was his friendship with the Huguenot Joseph Ducasse, whom he had met in Nérac and who fled to England in 1680 to escape religious persecution. He subsequently became Sidney's valet in London, although he may have taken this role primarily as a

---

[7] At BRO, D/EN F/8/2, and ASFi, Mediceo del Principato and Miscellanea Medicea.

[8] Scott, *Algernon Sidney and the English Republic*, p. 248.   [9] Scott, 'Sidney, Algernon'.

[10] On his second attempt, he was elected for the borough of Amersham (Buckinghamshire) only to be rejected later by the parliamentary committee of elections and privileges. *House of Commons, Journals* (London: His Majesty's Stationery Office, 1802), ix, pp. 677, 687, 692; Scott, *Algernon Sidney and the Restoration Crisis*, p. 128; and Mahlberg, *Henry Neville and English Republican Culture*, p. 65.

[11] Scott, *Algernon Sidney and the Restoration Crisis*, p. 269 and chapters 12–14.

protective cover as well as to gain a foothold in English society.[12] Ducasse also waited on Sidney during his imprisonment in 1683 and appeared before the Lords' committee investigating his 'murder' in 1690. The records of London's French Huguenot Church in Threadneedle Street in 1685 show him as married to 'Marie' and as the father of several children. This Marie may have been Sidney's daughter, as a letter from James Vernon to the Duke of Shrewsbury of June 1697 describes Ducasse, who had petitioned Algernon's brother Henry, then Earl of Romney, as the Frenchman who 'married Algernon Sydney's daughter'.[13] Much later, in December 1725, Ducasse was apparently himself convicted for having misused Sidney's passport and livery to come into the country.[14]

Neville and Sidney returned from their exile with their horizons broadened and their minds opened towards the possibility of a religious toleration that might extend to Catholics and the realisation that opportunities must be seized to achieve long-term goals, even if it involved political compromise. Ludlow's views, in contrast, rather seem to have hardened over time, to the extent that he was unable or unwilling to consider any political action for years. This may have been due to the fact that, unlike Neville and Sidney, he spent most of his exile in the company of other English republicans and regicides. Even though this little group, which had moved from Geneva via Lausanne to Vevey, had numerous contacts within a wider Protestant network, its world was more confined and more inward-looking, while Ludlow's main concerns during his exile seem to have been religious rather than political.

Ludlow made a last-ditch attempt at returning to a public role in England after the Glorious Revolution. In the summer of 1689 he travelled back to his home country for the first time in almost thirty years, hoping to further the republican cause, but was rejected as a regicide, while a new proclamation was issued for his apprehension. So he returned to Vevey, where he died several years later. He was buried in the church of St Martin in Vevey alongside his fellow exiles Andrew Broughton, William Cawley

---

[12] The year 1680 is given in AD, Lot-et-Garonne, Fonds Lagrange-Ferregues, 11 J 13, Notes sur Nérac (Familles), i, p. 318.

[13] Scott, *Algernon Sidney and the English Republic*, p. 244, referring among others to AD, Lot-et-Garonne, Fonds Lagrange-Ferregues, 11 J 13, Notes sur Nerac (Familles), i, pp. 316–19, and the Registers of the French Church of Threadneedle Street, London, Part III (1685–1714). See also James Vernon to Charles Talbot, Duke of Shrewsbury, 19 June 1697, in G. P. R. James (ed.), *Letters Illustrative of the Reign of William III: From 1696 to 1708*, 3 vols (London: Henry Colburn, 1841), i, pp. 270–7, at p. 273.

[14] AD, Lot-et-Garonne, Fonds Lagrange-Ferregues, 11 J 13, Notes sur Nérac (Familles), i, p. 318.

and Nicholas Love.[15] Ludlow's most significant exile legacy undoubtedly remains his autobiography, first drafted as 'A Voyce from the Watch Tower' and posthumously published in 1698–9 as *Memoirs of Edmund Ludlow*. The work's history is tied up with the history of the republican cause itself and the creation of a canon of Commonwealth writings, not least through its editor John Toland and the philanthropist Thomas Hollis, who not only produced further editions of Ludlow's work, but also aided the distribution of republican ideas throughout the Western world. Hollis is primarily known for his efforts in spreading Commonwealth literature and ideas across the Atlantic in America. However, he also established contact with libraries across Europe through his generous book donations to places like Copenhagen, Groningen, Göttingen, Leipzig, Zurich and, significantly, Bern.[16]

The Burgerbibliothek in Bern, which is now part of the city's university library, holds an extensive collection of works donated by Hollis to the local authorities in the eighteenth century in memory of Ludlow's exile in the canton. A presentation copy of Ludlow's *Memoirs* well preserved in the stacks of the university library comes with a printed dedication by Hollis expressing his thanks to the Bern authorities who had been 'the protectors of the author of these MEMOIRS, during the many years of his exile', as well as three handwritten quotes from Robert Molesworth's preface to his translation of *Franco-Gallia* (1711), the *Memoirs* itself and Richard Glover's poem *London: or, the Progress of Commerce* (1739).[17] While Hollis idealised the Swiss republic as the home of civic liberty and popular sovereignty, the city and canton of Bern had in fact become governed by a relatively close oligarchy of patricians, with the same noble families dominating the Great and Small Councils. The collective ideas of seventeenth-century English regicides and republicans were therefore considered rather dangerous reading, potentially inciting resistance to the status quo and, in the worst case, outright rebellion. The Council of Bern therefore considered long and hard whether or not to accept the generous donation, and

---

[15] Firth, 'Ludlow, Edmund'. A memorial plaque was erected by his widow Elizabeth in the church at Vevey in 1693.

[16] Reimer Eck, 'Königliche und andere schön verzierte englische Bucheinbände in der Göttinger Bibliothek – eine Auswahl und zugleich etwas englische Geschichte', in Elmar Mittler and Silke Glitsch (eds), *Eine Welt allein ist nicht genug': Großbritannien, Hannover und Göttingen 1714–1837* (Göttingen: Göttinger Bibiliotheksschriften, 2005), pp. 358–80, at pp. 368–9. Within Europe, Urs Leu has found evidence of donations in Scotland, Denmark, Germany, Italy, the Netherlands, Russia, Sweden and Switzerland. See Leu, 'The Hollis-Collections in Switzerland'. I would like to thank André Holenstein for providing me with a list of works donated to Bern by Hollis.

[17] The presentation copy is available in the Universitätsbibliothek Bern at Hollis 65.

when it finally did so, the monetary value of the leather-bound folios, quarto and octavo volumes seems to have been one of its main incentives. The pristine condition of many of the volumes indicates that few of the books from England were ever read.[18] The friendly welcome Ludlow and his fellow exiles received in Switzerland after the Stuart restoration meanwhile also helped to pave the way for the reception of many more persecuted Protestants in the country after the revocation of the Edict of Nantes in 1685, when large numbers of French Huguenots came to make their way across the border.[19]

As I hope to have shown in this volume, there is a larger European dimension to the post-Restoration history of seventeenth-century English republicanism, and it consists to a large extent in the wide personal networks of key republican actors and in the distribution of their works and ideas. As I have suggested in my Introduction, scholarship on seventeenth-century English republicanism would benefit from further extending its reach both thematically (into the religious sphere) and geographically (into Europe). Extending our research on seventeenth-century English republicanism to transnational religious and political networks would also provide a crucial link to and shed further light on the emergence and development of a republican legacy in Europe as explored in Blair Worden's *Roundhead Reputations*, Rachel Hammersley's work on the English republican tradition in France and Roland Ludwig's work on the afterlife of the English Revolution in nineteenth-century German historiography and political philosophy.[20] Through a fuller exploration of religious and transnational networks within Europe we might thus be able to piece together a more coherent, if not a grand narrative of Britain and Europe's shared republican heritage. Its literary legacy in the form of translations of English republican works on the Continent produced in the context of the European revolutions of the eighteenth and nineteenth centuries will be the subject of my next project.

[18] Leu, 'The Hollis-Collections in Switzerland'.
[19] I owe this point to André Holenstein. On this continuity also see the excellent collection by Larminie (ed.), *Huguenot Networks, 1560–1780*.
[20] Worden, *Roundhead Reputations*; Hammersley, *The English Republican Tradition and Eighteenth-Century France*; Hammersley, *French Revolutionaries and English Republicans*; Ludwig, *Die Rezeption der Englischen Revolution im deutschen politischen*; and Ludwig, 'Die Englische Revolution als politisches Argument'.

Bibliography

PRIMARY SOURCES

Archival and Manuscript Sources

United Kingdom

Berkshire Record Office, Reading [BRO]
  D/EN F8/1, Neville correspondence (English)
  D/EN F8/2, Neville correspondence (Italian)
Bodleian Library, Oxford
  Clarendon MS 80
  Clarendon MS 84
  Tanner MS 74
  'A Voyce from the Watch Tower', MS Eng. hist. c. 487
British Library, London
  Add. MS 21506
  Add. MS 24850
  Add. MS 25358
  Add. MS 32680
  Add. MS 32093
Essex Record Office, Chelmsford
  D/DBy/Z58, Braybrooke Papers
Kent History and Library Centre, Maidstone
  De L'Isle Manuscripts
National Archives, London [NA]
  PROB 11/265/209
  SP 18/38
  SP 29/26
  SP 29/86
  SP 29/92
  SP 29/101
  SP 29/206
  SP 44/15, Entry Book
  SP 44/16, Entry Book
  SP 46/189, Thurloe Papers
  SP 98/4

Warwickshire County Record Office, Warwick
MS CR 1886, Algernon Sidney's 'Court Maxims'

France

Archives Départementales [AD], Lot-et-Garonne,
  Fonds Lagrange-Ferregues
Archives Municipales, Montpellier
  Église Réformée, Mariages 1658–63
  Table des Mariages de Montpellier
Archives Nationales, Paris [AN]
  R/2/82, Algernon Sidney, Nérac, to M. Bafoyl, Paris, 14 January [1677]
Bibliothèque Nationale de France, Paris [BNF]
  MS Français 23254, Lantiniana
Centre des Archives Diplomatiques du Ministère des Affaires Étrangères, Paris [AE]
  Correspondance Politique, Angleterre, 8CP/82, January–October 1664
  Correspondence Politique, Angleterre, 8CP/99, 1670
  Mémoires et Documents, Angleterre, Lettres de Charles II, 1660–9
  Mémoires et Documents, Angleterre, 7MD/29, Négotiations, 1662–4

Italy

Archivio di Stato, Florence [ASFi]
  Mediceo del Principato is a collection held in the ASFi
  Mediceo del Principato 165, Minute di Lettere e Registri, Ferdinando II, 1664–6
  Mediceo del Principato 4241, 4243, 5538
Archivio Segreto Vaticano, Vatican
  Fondo Pio
  Segreteria di Stato (Inghilterra)
  Segreteria di Stato (Particolari)
Archivio Storico Diocesano, Rome
  Parrochia S. Lorenzo in Lucina, Stati D'Animi 1666.
Biblioteca Apostolica Vaticana, Vatican
  Barberini MS (Barb.lat.)
Biblioteca Nazionale Centrale, Florence
  *The WORKS of the famous Nicolas Machiavel, Citizen and Secretary of FLOR-
  ENCE. Written Originally in ITALIAN, and from thence newly and faithfully
  Translated into ENGLISH* (London: printed for John Starkey at the Miter in
  Fleetstreet, near Temple-Bar, 1675) (MAGL. 19.5.67, containing MS)
Biblioteca Planettiana, Jesi
  L'Archivio Azzolino, Lettere a Decio Azzolino, 1661–3

Netherlands

Gemeentearchief, Rotterdam
  225 Engels-Episcopale St Mary's Church ('Klein Londen', English Church)
  962.01 Schotse Kerk (Scottish Church)

Switzerland

Archives Cantonales et Vaudoises, Lausanne [ACV]
  BA 33-4, Weltsch Spruch-Buch der Statt Bern, Décrets Romands Nr. 4
Archives d'État, Geneva [AEG]
  Archives du Bureau 1962, Travaux Recherches 65
  Registres du Conseil (1660), RC 160
  Registres du Conseil (1662), RC 162
Archives de la Ville, Lausanne
  D 56, Manual du Conseil de Lausanne – registre des décisions concernant les
  affaires particulières du public (8 October 1661–20 September 1666)
Staatsarchiv, Bern [StAB]
  A II 454, Raths-Manual der Stadt Bern, vol. 143 (27 January–7 June 1662).
  A II 460, Raths-Manual der Stadt Bern, vol. 149 (1664)
  B III 63, Epistolae virorum clarorum
  B III 98, Epistolae ad decanos bernenses, 1661–1743

USA

Beinecke Library, Yale University, New Haven
  Joseph Spence Papers MSS 4

PRINTED PRIMARY SOURCES

Acts and Ordinances of the Interregnum, 1642–1660, ed. C. H. Firth and R. S. Rait
  (London: His Majesty's Stationery Office, 1911).
Aristotle, *The Politics* and *The Constitution of Athens*, ed. Stephen Everson (Cam-
  bridge, UK: Cambridge University Press, 1996).
The Armies Dutie (London, 1659).
Bampfield, Joseph, *Colonel Joseph Bampfield's Apology 'Written by Himself and
  Printed at His Desire' 1685*, ed. John Loftis and Paul H. Hardacre, including
  John Loftis, 'Bampfield's Later Career: A Biographical Supplement' (London
  and Toronto: Associated University Presses, 1993).
[Bethel, Slingsby], *The Interest of Princes and States* (London: Printed for John
  Wickins at the White-Hart against St Dunstans Church in Fleetstreet,
  1680).
Blencowe, R. W. (ed.), *Sydney Papers, Consisting of a Journal of the Earl of Leicester,
  and Original Letters of Algernon Sydney* (London: John Murray, Albemarle
  Street, 1825).
Brecht, Bertolt, *Svendborger Gedichte* (London: Malik, 1939).
Bruce, Susan (ed.), *Three Renaissance Utopias: Utopia, New Atlantis, The Isle of
  Pines* (Oxford: Oxford University Press, 1999).
[Burton, Thomas], *Diary of Thomas Burton, Esq. Member in the Parliaments of
  Oliver and Richard Cromwell, from 1656 to 1659*, ed. John Towill Rutt, 4 vols
  (London: H. Colburn, 1828).

[Charles II], *By the King: A Proclamation for the Apprehension of Edmund Ludlow, Commonly Called, Colonel Ludlow* (London: John Bill and Christopher Barker, 1660).

By the King: A Proclamation for Apprehension of Edward Whalley and William Goffe (London: Christopher Barker and John Bill, 1660).

By the King: A Proclamation for Calling in and Suppressing of Two Books Written by John Milton: The One Intituled Johannis Miltone Angli pro populo Anglicano defensio contra Claudii Anonymi, alias Salmasii, defensionem regiam, and the Other in Answer to a Book Intituled The Pourtraicture of His Sacred Majesty in His Solitude and Sufferings, and also a Third Book Intituled The Obstructuors of Justice, Written by John Goodwin (London: Printed by John Bill . . . , 1660).

Cicero, *On Obligations*, trans. P. G. Walsh (Oxford: Oxford University Press, 2001).

A Collection of the Most Remarkable and Interesting Trials, 2 vols (London: R. Snagg, 1775).

Collins, Arthur (ed.), *Letters and Memorials of State in the Reigns of Queen Mary, Queen Elizabeth, King James, King Charles the First, Part of the Reign of King Charles the Second, and Oliver's Usurpation*, 2 vols (London: printed for T. Osborne, in Gray's-Inn, 1746).

Copy of a Prophecy Sent to B:F: in the Year 1666 from Montpelliers by the Late Honourable Alguernon Sidney Esqr. & by Him Accidentally Found among Old Papers This 18/28 February 1689, or *Copie van een oude Prophetie van Montpeliers uyt Vranckrijck in den Jare 1666. In d'Engelsche tale door den Edelen Alguernon Sidney (laast in den jare 1683 in Engeland onthooft) gesonden aan Mr. Benjamin Furly, en van hem na 23 jaren bygeval onder oude papieren den 28 February 1689. Gevonden, en na de eyge hand van den Hr. Sidney getranslateert en gedruckt.*

Crinò, Anna Maria, 'Lettere inedite italiane e inglesi di Sir (sic) Henry Neville', in Anna Maria Crinò (ed.), *Fatti e figure del Seicento anglo-toscano: documenti inediti sui rapporti letterari, diplomatici e culturali fra Toscana e Inghilterra* (Florence: Olschki, 1957), pp. 173–208.

'Un amico inglese del Granduca Cosimo III di Toscana: Sir Henry Neville', *English Miscellany*, 3 (1952), 235–47.

(ed.), *Fatti e figure del Seicento anglo-toscano: documenti inediti sui rapporti letterari, diplomatici e culturali fra Toscana e Inghilterra* (Florence: Olschki, 1957).

Declaration of Breda (1660), in 'The Convention Parliament: First Session – Begins 25/4/1660', in *The History and Proceedings of the House of Commons*, i: *1660–1680* (1742), pp. 2–25, www.british-history.ac.uk/report.aspx?com pid=37614 (accessed 24 April 2014).

De la Court, Johan and Pieter, *Aanwysing der heilsame politike gronden en maximen van de Republike van Holland en West-Vriesland* (Leiden and Rotterdam: Hakkens, 1669).

De la Court, Johan, *Consideratien van staat ofte politike weegschaal* (Amsterdam: Jacob Volckert, 1661).

Interest van Holland, ofte gronden van Hollands-Welvaren (Amsterdam: Joan. Cyprianus vander Gracht, 1662).

Eyre, G. E. B., and Rivington, C. R. (eds), *Transcripts of the Stationers Registers 1640–1708*, 3 vols (repr. Gloucester, MA: Peter Smith, 1967).

[Fanshawe, Ann], *The Memoirs of Ann, Lady Fanshawe, Wife of Sir Richard Fanshawe, Bart., 1600–72*, ed. Herbert Charles Fanshawe (London: J. Lane: 1907).

The Golden Coast; or, A Description of Guinney (London: Printed for S. Speed at the Rain-Bow in Fleet-street, 1665).

Grotius, Hugo, *De rebus belgicis: Or the Annals, and History of the Low-Countrye-Warrs* (London: Printed for Henry Twyford in Vine-Court Middle-Temple; and Robert Paulet at the Bible in Chancery-Lane, 1665).

Hugonis Grotii Annales et historiae de rebus belgicis (Amsterdam: Ex Typographejo Joannis Blaev, 1657).

Harrington, James, *The Commonwealth of Oceana* (London: L. Chapman, 1656).

The Commonwealth of Oceana and *A System of Politics*, ed. J. G. A. Pocock (Cambridge, UK: Cambridge University Press, 1992).

The Oceana of James Harrington, and His Other Works; Som wherof Are Now First Publish'd from His Own Manuscripts. The Whole Collected, Methodiz'd, and Review'd, with an Exact Account of His Life Prefix'd, by John Toland (London: Printed, and are to be sold by the Booksellers of London and Westminster, 1700).

The Political Works of James Harrington, ed. J. G. A. Pocock (Cambridge, UK: Cambridge University Press, 1977).

The Prerogative of Popular Government (London: T. Brewster, 1658).

Hartmann, Cyril Hughes (ed.), *Charles II and Madame* (London: William Heinemann, 1934).

H[eylin], P[eter], *The Stumbling-Block of Disobedience and Rebellion Cunningly Laid by Calvin in the Subjects Way, Discovered, Censured and Removed* (London: Printed by E. Cotes for Henry Seile over against St. Dunstans Church in Fleet street, 1658).

Hobbes, Thomas, *Leviathan*, ed. C. B. Macpherson (London: Penguin, 1985).

House of Commons, Journals (London: His Majesty's Stationery Office, 1802).

Hughes, Derek (ed.), *Versions of Blackness: Key Texts on Slavery from the Seventeenth Century* (Cambridge, UK: Cambridge University Press, 2007).

Humble Petition of Divers Well-Affected Persons ... to the Supreme Authority, the Parliament of the Common-Wealth of England (London: Printed for Thomas Brewster, at the three Bibles in Pauls Church-yard, at the West end, 1659).

Hutchinson, Lucy, *Memoirs of the Life of Colonel Hutchinson, with the Fragment of an Autobiography of Mrs. Hutchinson*, ed. James Sutherland (London: Oxford University Press, 1973).

James, G. P. R. (ed.), *Letters Illustrative of the Reign of William III: From 1696 to 1798*, 3 vols (London: Henry Colburn, 1841).

Les juges jugez, se justifiants. Ou recit de ce qui s'est passé en la condamnation & execution de quelques uns des juges du dernier defunct Roy d'Angleterre, & autres seigneurs du parti du Parlement (n.p., 1663).

L'Estrange, Roger, *Considerations and Proposals in Order to the Regulation of the Press: Together with Diverse Instances of Treasonous, and Seditious Pamphlets, Proving the Neceßity thereof* (London: Printed by A.C., 1663).

Le livre du recteur de l'Académie de Genève (1559–1878), ed. Suzanne Stelling-Michaud, 6 vols (Geneva: Libraire Droz, 1959–80).

Locke, John, *Second Treatise of Government* and *A Letter Concerning Toleration*, ed. Mark Goldie (Oxford: Oxford University Press, 2016).

    Two Treatises of Government, ed. Peter Laslett (Cambridge, UK: Cambridge University Press, 1988).

Loftis, J. (ed.), *The Memoirs of Anne, Lady Halkett and Ann, Lady Fanshawe* (Oxford: Clarendon Press, 1979).

[Louis XIV], *Mémoires de Louis XIV, écrits par lui-même, composés pour le grand dauphin, son fils, et addresses a ce prince; suivis de plusieurs fragmens de mémoires militaires, de l'instruction donnée à Philippe V, de dix-sept lettres adressées à ce monarque sur le gouvernement de ses états, et de diverses autres pieces inédites*, ed. J. L. M. de Gain-Montagnac, 2 vols (Paris: Garnery, 1806).

Lucian's 'True History', trans. Francis Hickes, with an introduction by Charles Whibley (London: Privately printed, 1894).

Ludlow, Edmund, *Memoirs of Edmund Ludlow Esq.*, 3 vols (Vivay [sic], 1698–9).

    A Voyce from the Watch Tower. Part Five: 1660–1662, ed. A. B. Worden, Camden Fourth Series (London: Royal Historical Society, 1987).

    Memoirs of Edmund Ludlow, Esq (London: Printed for A. Millar; D. Browne, both in the Strand; and J. Ward, in Cornhill, 1751).

    Memoirs of Edmund Ludlow. With a Collection of Original Papers, and the Case of King Charles the First (London: Printed for T. Becket and P. A. de Hondt, and T. Cadell, in the Strand; and T. Evans, in King Street, Covent Garden, 1771).

    The Memoirs of Edmund Ludlow, Lieutenant-General of the Horse in the Army of the Commonwealth of England 1625–1672, ed. C. H. Firth, 2 vols (Oxford: Clarendon Press, 1894).

Machiavelli, Niccolò, *The Art of War*, ed. Ellis Farnsworth, trans. Neal Wood (Washington, DC: Da Capo Press, 2001).

    Discourses on Livy, trans. Harvey C. Mansfield and Nathan Tarcov (Chicago: University of Chicago Press, 1996).

    The Prince, trans. Russell Price, ed. Quentin Skinner and Russell Price (Cambridge, UK: Cambridge University Press, 1998).

[Magalotti, Lorenzo], *Travels of Cosmo the Third, Grand Duke of Tuscany, through England, during the Reign of King Charles the Second, 1669* (London: J. Mawman, 1821).

Magna Carta, www.bl.uk/magna-carta/articles/magna-carta-english-translation, accessed 21 August 2016.

Milton, John, *Paradise Lost*, ed. John Leonard (Harmondsworth: Penguin, 2000).

The Readie and Easie Way to Establish a Free Commonwealth; and the Excellence Thereof Compar'd with the Inconveniencies and Dangers of Readmitting Kingship in This Nation, 2nd ed. (London: Printed for the Author, 1660).

The Works of John Milton: In Verse and Prose, ed. John Mitford, 8 vols (London: William Pickering, 1851).

More, Thomas, *Utopia*, ed. George M. Logan and Robert M. Adams (Cambridge, UK: Cambridge University Press, 1989).

Neville, Henry, *Das verdächtige Pineser-Eyland* (Hamburg: Johann Naumann, 1668).

The Isle of Pines, or, A Late Discovery of a Fourth Island in Terra Australis, Incognita. Licensed June 27. 1668 (London: Printed by S.G. for Allen Banks and Charles Harper at the Flower-Deluice near Cripplegate Church, 1668) [*Isle of Pines* I].

The Isle of Pines; or, A Late Discovery of a Fourth Island near Terra Australis Incognita by Henry Cornelius Van Sloetten. . . . Licensed July 27. 1668 (London: Printed for Allen Banks and Charles Harper, 1668) [*Isle of Pines* III].

The Ladies, a Second Time, Assembled in Parliament (1647).

The Ladies Parliament (London, 1647).

A New and Further Discovery of the Isle of Pines in a Letter from Cornelius Van Sloetten a Dutch-Man (who First Discovered the Same in the Year, 1667.) to a Friend of His in London. With a Relation of His Voyage to the East Indies . . . Licensed According to Order (London: Allen Banks and Charles Harper, 1668) [*Isle of Pines* II].

Newes from the New Exchange, or the Commonwealth of Ladies, Drawn to the Life, in Their Severall Characters and Concernments (London, 1650).

The Parliament of Ladies (London, 1647).

The Parliament of Ladies . . . and The Isle of Pines, ed. Thomas Hollis (London, 1768).

Plato redivivus, ed. Thomas Hollis (London, 1763).

Plato redivivus, in *Two English Republican Tracts*, ed. Caroline Robbins (Cambridge, UK: Cambridge University Press, 1969), pp. 61–200.

Relation fidelle & veritable de la nouvelle découverte d'une quatrième isle de la terre Australe, ou Meridionale inconüe, sous le nom d'Isle de Pines (Leiden: Abraham Gogat, 1668).

Vorbild der ersten Welt, das ist: Wahrhafftige Beschreibung eines neu-erfundenen Eylandes genant Das Pineser-Eyland welches das vierdte neu-erfundene Eyland im Süden ist (Hamburg, 1668).

Le Nouveau Testament, contenant, la Nouvelle Alliance de Notre Seigneur Jesus Christ. Revu sur les textes grecs, par les ministres & professeurs de l'Eglise de Geneve. Edition fort correcte & tres-commode, tant pour la grosseur & la beaute du caracter, & l'exactitude des renvois, & de la citation des passage paralleles, que pour les Pseaumes qui y sont joint tout en musique, avec de grands arguments, & la prose en marge (Leiden: Abraham Gogat, 1669).

Original Letters of Locke; Algernon Sidney; and Anthony Lord Shaftesbury, Author of the 'Characteristics.' With an Analytical Sketch of the Writings and Opinions of Locke and Other Metaphysicians, by T. Forster (London: J. B. Nichols and Son, Parliament Street, 1830).

[Ovidius Naso, Publius], *Publii Ovidii Nasonis, Fasti*, rev. from the text of J. B. Krebs (London: John W. Parker and Son, 1854).

'Petition of Roman Catholics, about Them', *Journal of the House of Lords*, xi: *1660–1666* (London: His Majesty's Stationery Office, 1767–1830), pp. 275–7, 10 June 1661, www.british-history.ac.uk/lords-jrnl/vol11/pp275-277, accessed 5 January 2015.

Philanax Anglicus: Or a Christian Caveat for All Kings, Princes & Prelates, How They Entrust a Sort of Pretended Protestants of Integrity, or Suffer Them to Commix with Their Respective Governments. Shewing Plainly from the Principles of All Their Predecessours, That It Is Impossible to Be at the Same Time Presbyterians, and not Rebells. . . . Faithfully Published by T.B. Gent. (London: for Theo: Sadler, 1663).

Polybius, *The Rise of the Roman Empire*, trans. Ian Scott-Kilvert, selected with an introduction by F. W. Walbank (Harmondsworth: Penguin, 1979).

Ray, John, *Observations Topographical, Moral, & Physiological; Made in a Journey Through Part of the Low-Countries, Germany, Italy, and France: With a Catalogue of Plants Not Native of England, Found Spontaneously Growing in Those Parts, and Their Virtues* (London: Printed for John Martyn, Printer to the Royal Society, at the Bell in St. Paul's Church-yard, 1673).

Report on the Manuscripts of the Right Honourable Viscount de L'Isle, V.C. Preserved at Penshurst Place, Kent, ed. G. Dyfnallit Owen, vi (London: Her Majesty's Stationery Office, 1966).

Robbins, Caroline (ed.), *Two English Republican Tracts* (Cambridge, UK: Cambridge University Press, 1969).

Sidney, Algernon, *Court Maxims*, ed. Hans W. Blom, Eco Haitsma Mulier and Ronald Janse (Cambridge, UK: Cambridge University Press, 1996).

  Discourses Concerning Government, ed. Thomas G. West (Indianapolis, IN: Liberty Fund, 1996).

  Discourses Concerning Government (London: Printed and are to be sold by the Booksellers of London and Westminster, 1698).

  Discourses Concerning Government, ed. Thomas Hollis (London: I. Littlebury, 1763).

  Discourses Concerning Government. By Algernon Sidney, Esq; To Which Are Added, Memoirs of his Life, and an Apology for Himself, Both Now First Published, and the Latter from His Original Manuscript. The Third Edition. With an Alphabetical Index of the Principal Matters (London: Printed for A. Millar, opposite Catharine's-street in the Strand. 1751).

The Speeches and Prayers of Some of the Late King's Judges, viz. Major General Harison, Octob. 13. . . . Together with Severall Occasionall Speeches and Passages in Their Imprisonment till They Came to the Place of Execution.

Faithfully and Impartially Collected for Further Satisfaction. Heb. 11.4 And by it he being dead, yet speaketh (n.p., 1660).

Statutes of the Realm, v: *1628–80*, ed. John Raithby (n.p., 1819).

Stern, Alfred (ed.), *Briefe englischer Flüchtlinge in der Schweiz. Aus einer Handschrift des Berner Staats-Archivs* (Göttingen: Peppmüller, 1874).

Vane, Henry, *A Healing Question* (London: Printed for T. Brewster, 1656).

SECONDARY WORKS

Abbott, Wilbur C., 'English Conspiracy and Dissent, 1660–1674', *American Historical Review*, 14 (1909), 503–28, 696–722.

Aldridge, A. Owen, 'Polygamy in Early Fiction: Henry Neville and Denis Veiras', *Proceedings of the Modern Language Association*, 65 (1950), 464–72.

Amezúa Amezúa, Luis Carlos, 'La soberanía en "El gobernador cristiano" (1612), de Juan Márquez', *Anuario de filosofía del derecho*, 21 (2004), 75–106.

Appleby, Joyce, *Inheriting the Revolution: The First Generation of Americans* (Cambridge, MA: Belknap Press, 2000).

Armitage, David, *The Ideological Origins of the British Empire* (Cambridge, UK: Cambridge University Press, 2000).

Barber, Sarah, 'Marten, Henry (1601/2–1680)', *ODNB*.

A Revolutionary Rogue: Henry Marten and the English Republic (Stroud: Sutton Publishing, 2000).

Barbour, Reid, 'Recent Studies in Seventeenth-Century Literary Republicanism', *English Literary Renaissance*, 1:3 (2004), 387–417.

Barducci, Marco, *Anthony Ascham ed il pensiero politico inglese (1648–1650)* (Florence: Centro Editoriale Toscano, 2008).

Hugo Grotius and the Century of Revolution 1613–1718: Transnational Reception in English Political Thought (Oxford: Oxford University Press, 2017).

Battigelli, Anna, *Margaret Cavendish and the Exiles of the Mind* (Lexington: University Press of Kentucky, 1998).

Beach, Adam, 'A Profound Pessimism about the Empire: *The Isle of Pines*, English Degeneracy and Dutch Supremacy', *The Eighteenth Century: Theory and Interpretation*, 41 (2000), 21–36.

Berlin, Isaiah, *Four Essays on Liberty* (Oxford: Oxford University Press, 1969).

Binns, J., 'Lawson, Sir John (c. 1615–1665)', *ODNB*.

Black, Jeremy, *The British Abroad: The Grand Tour in the Eighteenth Century* (New York: Alan Sutton, 1992).

Boesky, Amy, 'Nation, Miscegenation: Membering Utopia in Henry Neville's *The Isle of Pines*', *Texas Studies in Literature and Language*, 37 (1995), 165–85.

Bond, William H., *'From the Great Desire of Promoting Learning': Thomas Hollis's Gifts to the Harvard College Library*, introduction by Allen Reddick, preface by William P. Stoneman, special issue, *Harvard Library Bulletin*, 19:1–2 (2010).

Borot, Luc, 'Religion in Harrington's Political System: The Central Concepts and Methods of Harrington's Religious Solutions', in Dirk Wiemann and Gaby Mahlberg (eds), *Perspectives on English Revolutionary Republicanism* (Farnham: Ashgate, 2014), pp. 149–64.

'Subject and Citizen: The Ambiguity of the Political Self in the Early Modern English Commonwealth', *Revue française de civilisation britannique*, 20:1 (2016), 1–15.

Bourrachot, L[ucile], 'Des Écossais en Agenais au XVe siècle', *Revue de l'Agenais*, 106:4 (1979), 283–91.

Brady, David, '1666: The Year of the Beast', *Bulletin of the John Rylands University Library of Manchester*, 61 (1979), 314–36.

Braun, Harald E., 'The Bible, Reason of State, and the Royal Conscience: Juan Márquez's *El governador christiano*', in Harald E. Braun and Edward Vallance (eds), *The Renaissance Conscience* (Oxford: Wiley-Blackwell, 2011), pp. 118–33.

Bruening, Michael W., *Calvinism's First Battleground: Conflict and Reform in the Pays de Vaud, 1528–1559* (Dordrecht: Springer, 2005).

Burgess, Glenn, and Matthew Festenstein (eds), *English Radicalism 1550–1850* (Cambridge, UK: Cambridge University Press, 2007).

Cameron, W. J., *New Light on Aphra Behn: An Investigation into the Facts and Fictions Surrounding Her Journey to Surinam in 1663 and Her Activities as a Spy in Flanders in 1666* (Auckland: University of Auckland Press, 1961).

Campos Boralevi, Lea, 'Classical Foundational Myths of European Republicanism: The Jewish Commonwealth', in Quentin Skinner and Martin van Gelderen (eds), *Republicanism: A Shared European Heritage*, 2 vols (Cambridge, UK: Cambridge University Press, 2002), i, pp. 247–61.

Campos Boralevi, Lea, and Paschalis Kitromilides (eds), *Athenian Legacies: European Debates on Citizenship* (Florence: Olschki, 2013).

Carey, Daniel, 'Henry Neville's *Isle of Pines*: Travel, Forgery, and the Problem of Genre', *Angelaki*, 1 (1993), 23–39.

'Henry Neville's *The Isle of Pines*: From Sexual Utopia to Political Dystopia', in Chloë Houston (ed.), *New Worlds Reflected: Travel and Utopia in the Early Modern Period* (Farnham: Ashgate, 2010), pp. 203–18.

'*The Isle of Pines*, 1668: *Henry Neville's Uncertain Utopia* by John Scheckter', *Utopian Studies*, 23:2 (2012), 546–50.

Carlin, Norah, 'Toleration for Catholics in the Puritan Revolution', in Ole Peter Grell and Robert W. Scribner (eds), *Tolerance and Intolerance in the European Reformation* (Cambridge, UK: Cambridge University Press, 1996), pp. 216–30.

Carswell, John, 'Algernon Sidney's "Court Maxims": The Biographical Importance of a Transcript', *Historical Research*, 62:147 (1989), 98–103.

The Porcupine: The Life of Algernon Sidney (London: John Murray, 1989).

Catterall, Douglas, *Community without Borders: Scots Migrants and the Changing Face of Power in the Dutch Republic, c. 1600–1700* (Leiden: Brill, 2002).

'Fortress Rotterdam? Rotterdam's Scots Community and the Covenanter Cause, 1638–1688', in David Worthington (ed.), *British and Irish Emigrants and Exiles in Europe, 1603–1688* (Leiden and Boston: Brill, 2010), pp. 87–105.

Catterall, Ralph C. H., 'Sir George Downing and the Regicides', *American Historical Review*, 17:2 (1912), 268–89.

Cellérier, M. J.-E., 'Charles Perrot, pasteur Genevois au seizième siècle: notice biographique', in *Mémoires et documents publiés par la Société d'Histoire et d'Archéologie de Genève*, xi (Geneva: Jullien Frères, 1859), pp. 1–68.

Champion, J. A. I., *The Pillars of Priestcraft Shaken: The Church of England and Its Enemies, 1660–1730* (Cambridge, UK: Cambridge University Press, 1992).

Chaney, Edward, *The Evolution of the Grand Tour: Anglo-Italian Cultural Relations since the Renaissance* (London: Frank Cass, 1998).

Choisy, Albert, *Généalogies Genevoises: familles admises à la Bourgeoisie avant la Réformation* (Geneva: Kundig, 1947).

Claeys, Gregory (ed.), *Restoration and Augustan British Utopias* (Syracuse, NY: Syracuse University Press, 2000), pp. 115–30.

Clark, Ruth, *Strangers and Sojouners at Port Royal: Being an Account of the Connections between the British Isles and the Jansenists of France and Holland* (Cambridge, UK: Cambridge University Press, 1932).

Clarke, Elizabeth, 'Re-reading the Exclusion Crisis', *Seventeenth Century*, 21 (2006), 141–59.

Coffey, John, 'Puritanism and Liberty Revisited: The Case for Toleration in the English Revolution', *Historical Journal*, 41:4 (1998), 961–85.

'Quentin Skinner and the Religious Dimension of Early Modern Political Thought', in Alister Chapman, John Coffey and Brad S. Gregory (eds), *Seeing Things Their Way: Intellectual History and the Return of Religion* (Notre Dame, IN: University of Notre Dame Press, 2009), pp. 46–74.

Collinson, Patrick, *De Republica Anglorum: or, History with the Politics Put Back* (Cambridge, UK: Cambridge University Press, 1990).

'The Monarchical Republic of Queen Elizabeth I', *Bulletin of the John Rylands University Library of Manchester*, 69 (1987), 394–424.

Cotti-Lowell, Alison Fanous, 'The Pineapple and Colonial Enterprise in Henry Neville's *The Isle of Pines*', *Texas Studies in Literature and Language*, 59:2 (2017), 209–233.

Cressy, David, 'Early Modern Space Travel and the English Man in the Moon', *American Historical Review*, 111:4 (2006), 961–82.

Crinò, Anna Maria, *Il Popish Plot nelle relazioni inedite dei residenti granducali alle corte di Londra (1678–1681)* (Rome: Edizioni di Storia e Letteratura, 1954).

Curelly, Laurent, '"Do look on the other side of the water": de la politique étrangère de Cromwell à l'égard de la France', *E-rea*, 11:2 (2014), http://journals.openedition.org/erea/3751, accessed 1 January 2019.

Cuttica, Cesare, *Sir Robert Filmer (1588–1653) and the Patriotic Monarch: Patriarchalism in Seventeenth-Century Political Thought* (Manchester: Manchester University Press, 2012).

D'Aprile, Iwan, 'Prussian Republicanism? Friedrich Buchholz's Reception of James Harrington', in Gaby Mahlberg and Dirk Wiemann(eds), *European Contexts for English Republicanism* (Farnham: Ashgate, 2013), pp. 225–36.

Darnton, Robert, *The Business of Enlightenment: A Publishing History of the Encyclopédie 1775–1800* (Cambridge, MA: Harvard University Press, 1979).

Daston, Lorraine, 'The Ideal and Reality of the Republic of Letters in the Enlightenment', *Science in Context*, 4 (1991), 367–86.

Davis, J. C., 'Against Formality: One Aspect of the English Revolution', *Transactions of the Royal Historical Society*, 6th ser., 3 (1993), 265–88.

'Cromwell's Religion', in John Morrill (ed.), *Oliver Cromwell and the English Revolution* (London: Longman, 1990), pp. 181–208.

'Going Nowhere: Travelling to, through and from Utopia', *Utopian Studies*, 19:1 (2008), 1–23.

Oliver Cromwell (London: Arnold, 2001).

'Religion and the Struggle for Freedom in the English Revolution', *Historical Journal*, 35:3 (1992), 507–30.

Utopia and the Ideal Society: A Study of English Utopian Writing 1516–1700 (Cambridge, UK: Cambridge University Press, 1981).

De Beer, G. R., 'Anglais au Pays de Vaud', *Revue historique Vaudoise*, 59 (1951), 56–78.

De Krey, Gary S., 'Bethel, Slingsby (bap. 1617, d. 1697)', *ODNB*.

Denbo, Seth, 'Generating Regenerated Generations: Race, Kinship and Sexuality on Henry Neville's *Isle of Pines* (1668)', in Nicole Pohl and Brenda Tooley (eds), *Gender and Utopia in the Eighteenth Century: Essays in English and French Utopian Writing* (Aldershot: Ashgate, 2007), pp. 147–61.

Ducommin, Marie-Jeanne, and Dominique Quadroni, *Le refuge protestant dans le pays de Vaud (fin XVIIe – début XVIIIe s.): aspects d'une migration* (Geneva: Droz, 1991).

Dulieu, Louis, *La pharmacie à Montpellier, de ses origines à nos jours* (Avignon: Les Presses Universelles, 1973).

Durston, Christopher, *Cromwell's Major-Generals: Godly Government during the English Revolution* (Manchester: Manchester University Press, 2001).

'The Fall of Cromwell's Major-Generals', *English Historical Review*, 113 (1999), 18–37.

'Hesilrige, Sir Arthur, second baronet (1601–1661)', *ODNB*.

'"Settling the hearts and quieting the minds of all good people": The Major-Generals and the Puritan Minorities of Interregnum England', *History*, 85 (2000), 247–67.

Dzelzainis, Martin, 'Harrington and the Oligarchs: Milton, Vane, and Stubbe', in Dirk Wiemann and Gaby Mahlberg (eds), *Perspectives on English Revolutionary Republicanism* (Farnham: Ashgate, 2014), pp. 15–33.

Eck, Reimer, 'Königliche und andere schön verzierte englische Bucheinbände in der Göttinger Bibliothek – eine Auswahl und zugleich etwas englische Geschichte', in Elmar Mittler and Silke Glitsch (eds), *'Eine Welt allein ist nicht genug*': *Großbritannien, Hannover und Göttingen 1714–1837* (Göttingen: Göttinger Bibiliotheksschriften, 2005), pp. 358–80.

Ehrensperger, Alfred, *Der Gottesdienst in Stadt und Landschaft Bern im 16. und 17. Jahrhundert* (Zurich: Theologischer Verlag, 2011).

Farr, D. N., 'Lambert, John (*bap.* 1619, *d.* 1684)', *ODNB*.

Fausett, David, *Writing the New World: Imaginary Voyages and Utopias of the Great Southern Land* (Syracuse, NY: Syracuse University Press, 1993).

Fink, Zera S., *The Classical Republicans: An Essay in the Recovery of a Pattern of Thought in Seventeenth-Century England* (Evanston, IL: Northwestern University Press, 1945).

Firth, C. H. 'Ludlow, Edmund (1616/17–1692)', rev. Blair Worden, *ODNB*.

'Phelps, John (*b.* 1618/19)', rev. Timothy Venning, *ODNB*.

Ford, Worthington Chauncey, *The Isle of Pines 1668: An Essay in Bibliography* (Boston: Club of Odd Volumes, 1920).

Forsdyke, Sara, *Exile, Ostracism, and Democracy: The Politics of Expulsion in Ancient Greece* (Princeton, NJ, and Woodstock: Princeton University Press, 2005).

Fraser, Peter, *The Intelligence of the Secretaries of State and Their monopoly of Licensed News 1660–1688* (Cambridge, UK: Cambridge University Press, 1956).

Freeman, Thomas S., and Sarah Elizabeth Wall, 'Racking the Body, Shaping the Text: The Account of Anne Askew in Foxe's "Book of Martyrs"', *Renaissance Quarterly*, 54 (2001), 1165–96.

Gaertner, Jan Felix (ed.), *Writing Exile: The Discourse of Displacement in Greco-Roman Antiquity and Beyond* (Leiden: Brill, 2007).

Galluzzi, Paolo, 'Nel "teatro" dell'Accademia', in Paolo Galluzzi (ed.), *Scienziati a corte: l'arte della sperimentazione nell'Accademia Galileiana del Cimento (1657–1667)* (Livorno: Sillabe, 2001), pp. 12–25.

Georgiadou, Aristoula, and David Henry James Larmour, *Lucian's Science Fiction Novel 'True Histories': Interpretation and Commentary* (Leiden: Brill, 1998).

Gillespie, Katherine, *Women Writing the English Republic, 1625–1681* (Cambridge, UK: Cambridge University Press, 2017).

Goldie, Mark, 'The Civil Religion of James Harrington', in Anthony Pagden (ed.), *The Languages of Political Theory in Early Modern Europe* (Cambridge, UK: Cambridge University Press, 1987), pp. 197–222.

Roger Morrice and the Puritan Whigs: The Entering Book of Roger Morrice 1677–1691 (Woodbridge: Boydell, 2007).

'The Unacknowledged Republic: Officeholding in Early Modern England', in Tim Harris (ed.), *The Politics of the Excluded, c. 1500–1850* (Basingstoke: Palgrave, 2001), pp. 153–94.

Greaves, Richard L., *Deliver Us from Evil: The Radical Underground in Britain, 1660–1663* (Oxford: Oxford University Press, 1986).

Enemies under His Feet: Radicals and Nonconformists in Britain, 1664–1677 (Stanford, CA: Stanford University Press, 1990).

Secrets of the Kingdom: British Radicals from the Popish Plot to the Revolution of 1688–1689 (Stanford, CA: Stanford University Press, 1992).

Greengrass, Mark, et al. (eds), *Samuel Hartlib and Universal Reformation: Studies in Intellectual Communication* (Cambridge, UK: Cambridge University Press, 1994).

Greenspan, Nicole, *Selling Cromwell's Wars: Media, Empire and Godly Warfare, 1650–1658* (London: Pickering & Chatto, 2012).

Grell, Ole Peter, *Brethren in Christ: A Calvinist Network in Reformation Europe* (Cambridge, UK: Cambridge University Press, 2011).

Calvinist Exiles in Tudor and Stuart England (Aldershot: Ashgate, 1996).

Haley, K. H. D., *An English Diplomat in the Low Countries: Sir William Temple and John de Witt, 1665–1672* (Oxford: Clarendon Press, 1986).

Hammersley, Rachel, *The English Republican Tradition and Eighteenth-Century France: Between the Ancients and the Moderns* (Manchester: Manchester University Press, 2010).

French Revolutionaries and English Republicans: The Cordeliers Club, 1790–1794 (Woodbridge: Boydell and Brewer, 2005, paperback ed. 2011).

James Harrington: An Intellectual Biography (Oxford: Oxford University Press, 2019).

Hankins, James, 'Exclusivist Republicanism and the Non-monarchical Republic', *Political Theory*, 38 (2010), 452–82.

Hanneman, Robert A., and Mark Riddle, *Introduction to Social Network Methods* (Riverside, CA: University of California, Riverside, 2005), www.faculty.ucr.edu/~hanneman/nettext/, accessed 9 August 2015.

Hardacre, Paul H., *The Royalists during the Puritan Revolution* (The Hague: Nijhoff, 1956).

Harris, Tim, *Restoration: Charles II and His Kingdoms, 1660–1685* (London: Allen Lane, 2005).

Held, David, 'Cosmopolitanism, Democracy and the Global Order', in Maria Roviso and Magdalena Nowicka (eds), *The Ashgate Research Companion to Cosmopolitanism* (Farnham: Ashgate, 2011), pp. 163–77.

Helmers, Helmer J., *The Royalist Republic: Literature, Politics, and Religion in the Anglo-Dutch Public Sphere, 1639–1660* (Cambridge, UK: Cambridge University Press, 2015).

Herszenhorn, Borys, 'John Ray, botaniste anglais, à Montpellier en 1665–1666', *Bulletin historique de la ville de Montpellier*, 13:1 (1990), 21–5.

Hill, Christopher, *The Experience of Defeat: Milton and Some Contemporaries* (London: Faber, 1984).

Himy, Armand, '*Paradise Lost* as a Republican "tractatus theologico-politicus"', in David Armitage, Armand Himy and Quentin Skinner (eds), *Milton and Republicanism* (Cambridge, UK: Cambridge University Press, 1995), pp. 118–34.

Hindle, Steve, 'Hierarchy and Community in the Elizabethan Parish: The Swallowfield Articles of 1596', *Historical Journal*, 42 (1999), 835–51.

Holmes, Clive, 'John Lisle, Lord Commissioner of the Great Seal, and the Last Months of the Cromwellian Protectorate', *English Historical Review*, 122 (2007), 918–36.

Houston, Alan C., *Algernon Sidney and the Republican Heritage in England and America* (Princeton, NJ: Princeton University Press, 1991).

Hull, William, *Benjamin Furly and Quakerism in Rotterdam* (Lancaster: Lancaster Press, 1941).

Hunter, Michael, 'The Problem of "Atheism" in Early Modern England', *Transactions of the Royal Historical Society*, 35 (1985), 135–57.

Hutton, Ronald, *The Restoration: A Political and Religious History of England and Wales 1658–1667* (Oxford: Clarendon Press, 1985).

Hutton, Sarah (ed.), *Benjamin Furly 1646–1714: A Quaker Merchant and His Milieu* (Florence: Olschki, 2007).

Israel, Jonathan, *The Dutch Republic: Its Rise, Greatness, and Fall 1477–1806* (Oxford: Clarendon Press, 1995).

Jacob, Margaret C., 'The Mental Landscape of the Public Sphere: A European Perspective', *Eighteenth-Century Studies*, 28 (1994), 95–113.

Jallais, Thérèse-Marie, 'English Harringtonian Republicanism in France and Italy: Changing Perspectives', in Gaby Mahlberg and Dirk Wiemann (eds), *European Contexts for English Republicanism* (Farnham: Ashgate, 2013) pp. 179–93.

Janssen, Geert H., 'The Republic of the Refugees: Early Modern Migrations and the Dutch Experience', *Historical Journal*, 60:1 (2017), 233–52.

Jenkinson, Matthew, *Charles I's Killers in America: The Lives and Afterlives of Edward Whalley and William Goffe* (Oxford: Oxford University Press, 2019).

Culture and Politics at the Court of Charles II: 1660–1685 (Woodbridge: Boydell, 2010).

Johnston, Warren, *Revelation Restored: The Apocalypse in Later Seventeenth-Century England* (Woodbridge: Boydell, 2011).

Jones, Colin, 'The Organization of Conspiracy and Revolt in the *Mémoires* of the Cardinal de Retz', *European Studies Review*, 11 (1981), 125–50.

Kaplan, Yosef (ed.), *Early Modern Ethnic and Religious Communities in Exile* (Newcastle upon Tyne: Cambridge Scholars Publishing, 2017).

Keeble, N. H., *The Restoration: England in the 1660s* (Oxford: Wiley-Blackwell, 2007).

Kenyon, John, *The Popish Plot* (London: St Martin's Press, 1972).

Knachel, Philip A., *England and the Fronde: The Impact of the English Civil War and Revolution on France* (Ithaca, NY: Cornell University Press, 1967).

Knights, Mark, 'John Starkey and Ideological Networks in Late Seventeenth-Century England', *Media History*, 11 (2005), 127–45.

Politics and Opinion in Crisis, 1678–81 (Cambridge, UK: Cambridge University Press, 1994).

Knoppers, Laura Lunger, '"Englands Case": Contexts of the 1671 Poems', in Nicholas McDowell and Nigel Smith (eds), *The Oxford Handbook of Milton* (Oxford: Oxford University Press, 2009), pp. 571–88.

Kraus, Hans-Christof, *Englische Verfassung und politisches Denken im Ancien Régime 1689 bis 1789* (Munich: Oldenbourg, 2006).

Kumar, Krishan, *The Making of English National Identity* (Cambridge, UK: Cambridge University Press, 2003).

Laborie, Lionel, 'Millenarian Portraits of Louis XIV', in Tony Claydon (ed.), *Louis XIV Outside In: Images of the Sun King beyond France, 1661–1715* (Farnham: Ashgate, 2015), pp. 209–28.

Lagrange-Ferregues, G. de, 'Présence des ducs de Bouillon à Nérac', *Revue de l'Agenais*, 90:1 (1964), 29–35.

'Un régicide anglais à Nérac', *Revue de l'Agenais*, 91: 3(1965), 173–8.

Lake, Peter, 'Anti-popery: The Structure of a Prejudice', in Richard Cust and Ann Hughes (eds), *The English Civil War* (London: Arnold, 1997), pp. 181–210.

Larminie, Vivienne, 'The Herbert Connection, the French Church and Westminster Politics, 1643–1661', in Vivienne Larminie (ed.), *Huguenot Networks, 1560–1780: The Interactions and Impact of a Protestant Minority in Europe* (New York: Routledge, 2018), pp. 41–60.

'Johann Heinrich Hummel, the Peningtons and the London Godly Community: Anglo-Swiss Relations 1634–1674', *Journal for the History of Reformed Pietism*, 2:2 (2016), 1–26.

(ed.), *Huguenot Networks, 1560–1780: The Interactions and Impact of a Protestant Minority in Europe* (New York: Routledge, 2018).

Laurence, Anne, *Parliamentary Army Chaplains, 1642–1651* (Woodbridge: Boydell, 1990).

Leng, Thomas, 'Commercial Conflict and Regulation in the Discourse of Trade in Seventeenth-Century England', *Historical Journal*, 48:4 (2005), 933–54.

Leu, Urs, 'The Hollis-Collection in Switzerland: An Attempt to Disseminate Political and Religious Freedom through Books in the 18th Century', *Zwingliana*, 38 (2011), 153–73.

Lewalski, Barbara Kiefer, *The Life of John Milton: A Critical Biography* (Oxford: Blackwell, 2000).

'*Paradise Lost* and Milton's Politics', *Milton Studies*, 38 (2000), 141–68.

Lister, T. H., *Life and Administration of Edward, First Earl of Clarendon; with Original Correspondence, and Authentic Papers Never before Published*, 3 vols (London: Longman et al., 1837–8).

Loveman, Kate, *Reading Fictions, 1660–1740: Deception in English Literary and Political Culture* (Aldershot: Ashgate, 2008).

Ludwig, Roland, 'Die Englische Revolution als politisches Argument in einer Zeit des gesellschaftlichen Umbruchs in Deutschland', in Heiner Timmermann (ed.), *1848: Revolution in Europa: Verlauf, politische Programme, Folgen und Wirkungen* (Berlin: Duncker & Humblot, 1999), pp. 481–504.

Die Rezeption der Englischen Revolution im deutschen politischen Denken und in der deutschen Historiographie im 18. und 19. Jahrhundert (Leipzig: Leipziger Universitätsverlag, 2003).

Lurbe, Pierre, 'Lost in (French) Translation: Sidney's Elusive Republicanism', in Gaby Mahlberg and Dirk Wiemann (eds), *European Contexts for English Republicanism* (Farnham: Ashgate, 2013), pp. 211–23.

'Une utopie inverse: *The Isle of Pines* de Henry Neville (1668)', *Bulletin de la Société d'Études Anglo-Americaines des XVIIe et XVIII Siècles*, 38 (1994), 19–32.

Lutaud, Olivier, *Cromwell, les Niveleurs et la République* (Paris: Aubier, 1978).

Maag, Albert, 'Die Republik Bern als Beschützerin englischer Flüchtlinge während und nach der englischen Revolution', *Berner Zeitschrift für Geschichte und Heimatkunde*, 2:3 (1957), 93–118.

Mahlberg, Gaby, '"All the conscientious and honest papists": Exile and Belief Formation of an English Republican: Henry Neville (1619–94)', in Barbara Schaff (ed.), *Exiles, Émigrés and Intermediaries: Anglo-Italian Cultural Transactions* (Amsterdam and New York: Rodopi, 2010), pp. 61–76.

'Authors Losing Control: The European Transformations of Henry Neville's *The Isle of Pines* (1668)', *Book History*, 15 (2012), 1–15.

'Charles Stuart as Office-Holder: On regicides and Monarchical Republicans', in Anette Pankratz and Claus-Ulrich Viol (eds), *(Un)making the Monarchy* (Heidelberg: Winter, 2017), pp. 177–200.

Henry Neville and English Republican Culture in the Seventeenth Century: Dreaming of Another Game (Manchester: Manchester University Press, 2009).

'Henry Neville and the Toleration of Catholics during the Exclusion Crisis', *Historical Research*, 83 (2010), 617–34.

'An Island with Potential: Henry Neville's *The Isle of Pines* (1668)', in J. C. Davis and Miguel A. Ramiro (eds), *Utopian Moments: Micro-Historical Approaches to Modern Literary Utopias* (London: Bloomsbury Academic, 2012), pp. 60–6.

'Le républicanisme anglais et le mythe de l'anticatholicisme', in Nathalie Caron and Guillaume Marche (eds), *La politisation du religieux en modernité* (Rennes: Presses Universitaires de Rennes, 2015), pp. 17–29.

'*Les juges jugez, se justifiants* (1663) and Edmund Ludlow's Protestant Network in Seventeenth-Century Switzerland', *Historical Journal*, 57 (2014), 369–96.

'Machiavelli, Neville and the Seventeenth-Century Discourse on Priestcraft', *Intellectual History Review*, 28:1 (2018), 79–99.

'*The Parliament of Women* and the Restoration Crisis', in Cesare Cuttica and Markku Peltonen (eds), *Anti-democracy in Early Modern England 1603–1689* (Leiden: Brill, 2019), pp. 279–96.

'The Republican Discourse on Religious Liberty during the Exclusion Crisis', *History of European Ideas*, 38 (2012), 1–18.

'Republicanism as Anti-patriarchalism in Henry Neville's *The Isle of Pines* (1668)', in Jonathan Scott and John Morrow (eds), *Liberty, Authority, Formality* (Exeter: Imprint Academic, 2008), pp. 131–52.

'Wansleben's Harrington, or "The Fundations & Modell of a Perfect Commonwealth"', in Gaby Mahlberg and Dirk Wiemann (eds), *European Contexts for English Republicanism* (Farnham: Ashgate, 2013), pp. 145–61.

Mahlberg, Gaby, and Dirk Wiemann (eds), *European Contexts for English Republicanism* (Farnham: Ashgate, 2013).

Major, Philip, '"A poor exile stranger": William Goffe in New England', in Philip Major (ed.), *Literatures of Exile in the English Revolution and Its Aftermath 1640–1690* (Farnham: Ashgate, 2010), pp. 153–66.

Writings of Exile in the English Revolution and Restoration (Farnham: Ashgate, 2013).

(ed.), *Literatures of Exile in the English Revolution and Its Aftermath 1640–1690* (Farnham: Ashgate, 2010).

Maltzahn, Nicholas von, 'Neville, Henry (1620–1694)', *ODNB*.

Marshall, Alan, *The Age of Faction: Court Politics, 1660–1702* (Manchester: Manchester University Press, 1999).

'Bampfield, Joseph (1622–1685)', *ODNB*.

Intelligence and Espionage in the Reign of Charles II, 1660–1685 (Cambridge, UK: Cambridge University Press, 1994).

'Sexby, Edward (c. 1616–1658)', *ODNB*.

Martelli, Francesco, '"Nec spes nec metus": Ferrante Capponi, giurista ed alto funzionario nella Toscana di Cosimo III', in Franco Angiolini, Vieri Becagli and Marcello Verga (eds), *La Toscana nell'età di Cosimo III* (Florence: Edifir, 1993), pp. 137–63.

Matt, Luigi, 'Magalotti, Lorenzo', *DBI*.

Matthews, Nancy L., *William Sheppard, Cromwell's Law Reformer* (Cambridge, UK: Cambridge University Press, 2004).

Mayers, Ruth E., 'Vane, Sir Henry, the Younger (1613–1662)', *ODNB*.

McCoog, Thomas M., 'Leedes, Edward (1599–1677)', *ODNB*.

McCormick, Ted, *William Petty and the Ambitions of Political Arithmetic* (Oxford: Oxford University Press, 2010).

McDiarmid, John F. (ed.), *The Monarchical Republic of Early Modern England: Essays in Response to Patrick Collinson* (Aldershot: Ashgate, 2007).

McIntosh, A. W., 'The Numbers of the English Regicides', *History*, 67 (1982), 195–216.

McKenzie, Andrea, 'God's Tribunal: Guilt, Innocence, and Execution in England, 1675–1775', *Cultural and Social History*, 3 (2006), 121–44.

Metzger, Hans-Dieter, 'David und Saul in Staats- und Widerstandslehren der Frühen Neuzeit', in Walter Dietrich and Hubert Herkommer (eds), *König David – biblische Schlüsselfigur und europäische Leitgestalt* (Freiburg: Universitätsverlag; Stuttgart: W. Kohlhammer, 2003), pp. 437–84.

Milton, Anthony, 'Puritanism and the Continental Reformed Churches', in John Coffey and Paul C. H. Lim (eds), *The Cambridge Companion to Puritanism* (Cambridge, UK: Cambridge University Press, 2008), pp. 109–26.

Morrill, John, 'England's Wars of Religion', in John Morrill (ed.), *The Nature of the English Revolution* (London: Longman, 1993), pp. 33–44.

'The English Civil War', *Transactions of the Royal Historical Society*, 5th ser., 34 (1984), 155–78.

Mortimer, Sarah, *Reason and Religion in the English Revolution: The Challenge of Socinianism* (Cambridge, UK: Cambridge University Press, 2010).

Multamäki, Kustaa, *Towards Great Britain: Commerce & Conquest in the Thought of Algernon Sidney and Charles Davenant* (Helsinki: Academia Scientiarum Fennica, 1999).

Nelson, Eric, *The Hebrew Republic: Jewish Sources and the Transformation of European Political Thought* (Cambridge, MA: Harvard University Press, 2010).

'"Talmudical Commonwealthsmen" and the Rise of Republican Exclusivism', *Historical Journal*, 50:4 (2007), 809–35.

Nicastro, Onofrio, *Henry Neville e l'isola di Pines, col testo inglese e la traduzione italiana* di 'The Isle of Pines' (Pisa: SEU, 1988).

Nicollier, Béatrice, 'Beza, Theodor', *HLS*.

Norbrook, David, *Writing the English Republic: Poetry, Rhetoric, and Politics, 1627–1660* (Oxford: Blackwell, 2001).

Ó Cuív, Brian, 'James Cotter, a Seventeenth-Century Agent of the Crown', *Journal of the Royal Society of Antiquaries of Ireland*, 89:2 (1959), 135–59.

Ogg, David, *England in the Reign of Charles II*, 2nd ed. (Oxford: Oxford University Press, 1984).

Ó hAnnracháin, Tadhg, 'Bellings, Richard (c. 1603–1677)', *ODNB*.

Ollard, Richard, *Clarendon and His Friends* (Oxford: Oxford University Press, 1988).

Ouditt, Sharon (ed.), *Displaced Persons: Conditions of Exile in European Culture* (Aldershot: Ashgate, 2002).

Pagano de Divitiis, Gigliola, *English Merchants in Seventeenth-Century Italy*, trans. Stephen Parkin (Cambridge, UK: Cambridge University Press, 1997).

Palmer, William, 'St John, Oliver (c. 1598–1673)', *ODNB*.

Parker, William R., *Milton: A Biography*, 2 vols (Oxford: Clarendon Press, 1968).

Patterson, Annabel, *Censorship and Interpretation: The Conditions of Writing and Reading in Early Modern England* (Madison: University of Wisconsin Press, 1984, repr. 1992).

Peacey, Jason, '"The Good Old Cause for Which I Suffer": The Life of a Regicide in Exile', in Philip Major (ed.), *Literatures of Exile in the English Revolution and Its Aftermath 1640–1690* (Farnham: Ashgate, 2010), pp. 167–80.

'Holland, Cornelius (1600–1671?), *ODNB*.

'Order and Disorder in Europe: Parliamentary Agents and Royalist Thugs 1649–1650', *Historical Journal*, 40:4 (1997), 953–76.

'Say, William (1604–1666?)', *ODNB*.

Peltonen, Markku, *Classical Humanism and Republicanism in English Political Thought, 1570–1640* (Cambridge, UK: Cambridge University Press, 1997).

Perret, Jean-Pierre, *Les imprimeries d'Yverdon au xviie et au xviiie siècle* (Lausanne: F. Roth, 1945).

Pettegree, Andrew, *The Invention of News: How the World Came to Know about Itself* (New Haven, CT: Yale University Press, 2014).

Picavet, Camille-Georges, *Les dernières années de Turenne (1660–1675)* (Paris: Calmann-Lévy, 1919).

Pincus, Steven C. A., *Protestantism and Patriotism: Ideologies and the Making of English Foreign Policy, 1650–1668* (Cambridge, UK: Cambridge University Press, 1996).

Pocock, J. G. A., *The Ancient Constitution and the Feudal Law: A Study of English Historical Thought in the Seventeenth Century* (New York: Cambridge University Press, 1957, repr. 1967).

'The Concept of a Language and the *métier d'historien*: Some Considerations on Practice', in Anthony Pagden (ed.), *The Languages of Political Theory in Early-Modern Europe* (Cambridge, UK: Cambridge University Press, 1987), pp. 20–5.

The Machiavellian Moment: Florentine Political Thought and the Atlantic Republican Tradition (Princeton, NJ: Princeton University Press, 1975).

'Machiavelli, Harrington, and English Political Ideologies in the Eighteenth Century', *William and Mary Quarterly*, 22 (1965), 549–83.

Prior, Charles W. A., and Glenn Burgess (eds), *England's Wars of Religion, Revisited* (Farnham and Burlington, VT: Ashgate, 2011).

Raab, Felix, *The English Face of Machiavelli: A Changing Interpretation 1500–1700* (London and Toronto: University of Toronto Press, 1964).

Rahe, Paul, *Republics Ancient and Modern: The Ancient Regime in Classical Greece*, 3 vols (Chapel Hill: University of North Carolina Press, 1992–4).

Raymond, Joad (ed.), *News Networks in Seventeenth-Century Britain and Europe* (London: Routledge, 2006).

(ed.), *News, Newspapers, and Society in Early Modern Britain* (London: Frank Cass, 1999).

Rees, Emma, *Margaret Cavendish: Gender, Genre, Exile* (Manchester: Manchester University Press, 2003).

Robbins, Caroline, *The Eighteenth-Century Commonwealthman: Studies in the Transmission, Development and Circumstance of English Liberal Thought from the Restoration of Charles II until the War with the Thirteen Colonies* (Cambridge, UK: Cambridge University Press, 1959).

'The Strenuous Whig: Thomas Hollis of Lincoln's Inn', *William and Mary Quarterly*, 7:3 (1950), 406–53.

Rodén, Marie-Luise, 'Cardinal Decio Azzolino and the Problem of Papal Nepotism', *Archivum historiae pontificiae*, 34 (1996), 127–57.

Church Politics in Seventeenth-Century Rome: Cardinal Decio Azzolino, Queen Christina of Sweden, and the Squadrone Volante (Stockholm: Almquist & Wiksell International, 2000).

Rood, Wilhelmus, *Comenius and the Low Countries: Some Aspects of Life and Work of a Czech Exile in the Seventeenth Century* (Amsterdam: Van Gendt and Co., 1970).

Rowen, Herbert H., *John de Witt: Statesman of the 'True Freedom'* (Cambridge, UK: Cambridge University Press, 1986).

Ryrie, Alec, 'Sleep, Waking and Dreaming in Protestant Piety', in Jessica Martin and Alec Ryrie (eds), *Private and Domestic Devotion in Early Modern Britain* (Farnham: Ashgate, 2012), pp. 73–92.

Said, Edward W., *Reflections on Exile and Other Literary and Cultural Essays* (London: Granta, 2012).

Sambrook, James, 'Spence, Joseph (1699–1768)', *ODNB*.

Saxby, T[revor] J., *The Quest for the New Jerusalem: Jean de Labadie and the Labadists, 1610–1744* (Dordrecht, Boston and Lancaster: Martinus Nijhoff, 1987).

Scheckter, John, *The Isle of Pines, 1668: Henry Neville's Uncertain Utopia* (Farnham: Ashgate, 2011).

Schochet, Gordon, Fania Oz-Salzberger and Meirav Jones (eds), *Political Hebraism: Judaic Sources in Early Modern Political Thought* (Jerusalem: Shalem Press, 2008).

Schwoerer, Lois, *No Standing Armies* (Baltimore: Johns Hopkins University Press, 1974).

Scott, Jonathan, *Algernon Sidney and the English Republic* (Cambridge, UK: Cambridge University Press, 1988).

Algernon Sidney and the Restoration Crisis, 1677–1683 (Cambridge, UK: Cambridge University Press, 1991).

Commonwealth Principles: Republican Writing of the English Revolution (Cambridge, UK: Cambridge University Press, 2004).

England's Troubles: Seventeenth-Century English Political Instability in European Context (Cambridge, UK: Cambridge University Press, 2000).

'"Good Night Amsterdam": Sir George Downing and Anglo-Dutch Statebuilding', *English Historical Review*, 118:476 (2003), 334–56.

'Patriarchy, Primogeniture and Prescription: Algernon Sidney's *Discourses Concerning Government* (1698)', in Cesare Cuttica and Gaby Mahlberg (eds), *Patriarchal Moments* (London: Bloomsbury Academic, 2016), pp. 73–9.

'Radicalism and Restoration: The Shape of the Stuart Experience', *Historical Journal*, 31 (1988), 453–67.

'Sidney, Algernon (1623–1683)', *ODNB*.

'What Were Commonwealth Principles?', *Historical Journal*, 47 (2004), 591–613.

When the Waves Ruled Britannia: Geography and Political Identities, 1500–1800 (Cambridge, UK: Cambridge University Press, 2011).

Scriba, Christoph J., 'Pell, John (1611–1685)', *ODNB*.

Seaward, Paul, *The Cavalier Parliament and the reconstruction of the Old Regime, 1661-1667* (Cambridge, UK: Cambridge University Press, 1989).

Seddon, P. R., 'Hutchinson, John (*bap.* 1615, *d.* 1664)', *ODNB*.

Sharpe, J. A., '"Last Dying Speeches": Religion, Ideology and Public Execution in Seventeenth-Century England', *Past and Present*, 107 (1985), 144–67.

Shepard, Alex, and Phil Withington, 'Introduction: Communities in Early Modern England', in Alex Shepard and Phil Withington (eds), *Communities in Early Modern England: Networks, Place, Rhetoric* (Manchester: Manchester University Press, 2000), pp. 1–15.

Simonutti, Luisa, 'English Guests at "De Lantaarn". Sidney, Penn, Locke, Toland and Shaftesbury', in Sarah Hutton (ed.), *Benjamin Furly 1646–1714: A Quaker Merchant and His Milieu* (Florence: Olschki, 2007), pp. 31–66.

Skinner, Quentin, *The Foundations of Modern Political Thought*, 2 vols (Cambridge, UK: Cambridge University Press, 1978).

    Liberty before Liberalism (Cambridge, UK: Cambridge University Press, 1998).

    'Meaning and Understanding in the History of Ideas', *History and Theory*, 8 (1969), 3–53.

    'The Republican Ideal of Political Liberty', in Gisela Bock, Quentin Skinner and Maurizio Viroli (eds), *Machiavelli and Republicanism* (Cambridge, UK: Cambridge University Press, 1990), pp. 293–309.

    'A Third Concept of Liberty', *Proceedings of the British Academy*, 117 (2002), 237–68.

Slack, Paul, *The Invention of Improvement: Information and Material Progress in Seventeenth-Century England* (Oxford: Oxford University Press, 2015).

Smith, Geoffrey, *The Cavaliers in Exile, 1640–1660* (Basingstoke: Palgrave Macmillan, 2003).

Spalding, Ruth, *Contemporaries of Bulstrode Whitelocke 1605–1675: Biographies, Illustrated by Letters and Other Documents* (Oxford: Oxford University Press, 1990).

Stark, Werner, *The Sociology of Religion: A Study of Christendom*, 5 vols (New York: Fordham University Press, 1966–72).

Stern, Alfred, *Milton und seine Zeit*, 2 vols (Leipzig: Duncker & Humblot, 1877–9).

Stillman, Peter G., 'Monarchy, Disorder, and Politics in The Isle of Pines', in Peter G. Stillman, Gaby Mahlberg and Nat Hardy, *The Isle of Pines*, special issue, *Utopian Studies*, 17:1 (2006), 147–75.

Stillman, Peter G., Gaby Mahlberg and Nat Hardy, *The Isle of Pines*, special issue, *Utopian Studies*, 17:1 (2006).

Sullivan, Vickie B., *Machiavelli, Hobbes, and the Foundations of a Liberal Republicanism in England* (Cambridge, UK: Cambridge University Press, 2004).

Terpstra, Nicholas, *Religious Refugees in the Early Modern World: An Alternative History of the Reformation* (Cambridge, UK: Cambridge University Press, 2015).

Thiersch, Heinrich W.J., *Edmund Ludlow und seine Unglücksgefährten als Flüchtlinge an dem gastlichen Herde der Schweiz* (Basel: Felix Schneider, 1881).

Trevor-Roper, Hugh, 'The General Crisis of the 17th Century', *Past and Present*, 16:1 (1959), 31–64.

Trim, David J. B., 'The Huguenots and the European Wars of Religion, c. 1560–1697: Soldiering in National and Transnational Context', in

David J. B. Trim (ed.), *The Huguenots: History and Memory in Transnational Context. Essays in Honour and Memory of Walter C. Utt* (Leiden and Boston: Brill, 2011), pp. 154–92.

(ed.), *The Huguenots: History and Memory in Transnational Context. Essays in Honour and Memory of Walter C. Utt* (Leiden and Boston: Brill, 2011).

Turnbull, George H., *Hartlib, Dury and Comenius: Gleanings from Hartlib's Papers* (Liverpool: University Press of Liverpool, 1947).

Tutino, Stefania, 'The Catholic Church and the English Civil War: The Case of Thomas White', *Journal of Ecclesiastical History*, 58:2 (2007), 232–55.

Thomas White and the Blackloists: Between Politics and Theology during the English Civil War (Aldershot: Ashgate, 2008).

Utz, Hans, *Die Hollis Sammlung in Bern: Ein Beitrag zu den englisch-schweizerischen Beziehungen in der Zeit der Aufklärung* (Bern: Lang & Cie, 1959).

Vallance, Edward, '"The insane Enthusiasm of the Time": Remembering the Regicides in Eighteenth- and Nineteenth-Century Britain and North America', in Laurent Curelly and Nigel Smith (eds), *Radical Voices, Radical Ways: Articulating and Disseminating Radicalism in Seventeenth- and Eighteenth-Century Britain* (Manchester: Manchester University Press, 2016), pp. 229–50.

Van Gelderen, Martin, and Quentin Skinner (eds), *Republicanism: A Shared European Heritage*, 2 vols (Cambridge, UK: Cambridge University Press, 2002).

Van Kley, Dale, 'The Jansenist Constitutional Legacy in the French Prerevolution 1750–1789', *Historical Reflections/Réflexions hjistoriques*, 13:2–3 (1986), 393–453.

Van Santvoord, George, *Life of Algernon Sidney: With Sketches of Some of His Contemporaries and Extracts from His Correspondence and Political Writings*, 3rd ed. (New York: Scribner, 1854).

Vernon, E. C., 'Lockyer, Nicholas (1611–1685)', *ODNB*.

Villani, Stefano, 'Britain and the Papacy: Diplomacy and Conflict in the Sixteenth and Seventeenth Century', in Maria Antonietta Visceglia (ed.), *Papato e politica internazionale nella prima età moderna* (Rome: Viella, 2013), pp. 301–22.

'Guasconi (Gascoigne), Bernardo', *DBI*.

'Protestanti a Livorno nella prima età moderna', in Uwe Israel and Michael Matheus (eds), *Protestanten zwischen Venedig und Rom in der Frühen Neuzeit* (Berlin: Akademie Verlag, 2013), pp. 129–42.

'Unintentional Dissent: Eating Meat and Religious Identity among British Residents in Early Modern Livorno', in Katherine Aron-Beller and Christopher Black (eds), *The Roman Inquisition: Centre versus Peripheries* (Leiden: Brill, 2018), pp. 373–94.

Walker, Roger M., 'Sir Richard Fanshawe's *Lusiad* and Manuel de Faria e Sousa's *Lusíadas comentadas*: New Documentary Evidence', *Portuguese Studies*, 10 (1994), 44–64.

Waszink, Jan, 'Tacitism in Holland: Hugo Grotius' *Annales et historiae de rebus Belgicis*', in Craig Kallendorf, G. H. Tucker et al. (eds), *Acta Conventus Neo-Latini Bonnensis: Proceedings of the 12th International Congress of Neo-Latin Studies, Bonn, 2003* (Tempe: Arizona State University, Arizona Center for Medieval & Renaissance Studies, 2006), pp. 881–92.

Weber, Harold, 'Charles II, George Pines, and Mr. Dorimant: The Politics of Sexual Power in Restoration England', *Criticism*, 32 (1990), 193–219.

Westrich, Sal Alexander, *The Ormée of Bordeaux: A Revolution during the Fronde* (Baltimore: Johns Hopkins University Press, 1972).

Weststeijn, Arthur, *Commercial Republicanism in the Dutch Golden Age: The Political Thought of Johan & Pieter de la Court* (Leiden: Brill, 2012).

'Why the Dutch Didn't Read Harrington: Anglo-Dutch Republican Exchanges, c. 1650–1670', in Gaby Mahlberg and Dirk Wiemann(eds), *European Contexts for English Republicanism* (Farnham: Ashgate, 2013), pp. 105–20.

Whatmore, Richard, *Against War and Empire: Geneva, Britain and France in the Eighteenth Century* (New Haven, CT, and London: Yale University Press, 2012).

Wiegandt, Jürgen, *Die Merchant Adventurers' Company auf dem Kontinent zur Zeit der Tudors und Stuarts* (Kiel: Mühlau, 1972).

Wiemann, Dirk, 'Spectacles of Astonishment: Tragedy and the Regicide in England and Germany, 1649-1663', in Gaby Mahlberg and Dirk Wiemann (eds), *European Contexts for English Republicanism* (Farnham: Ashgate, 2013), pp. 33–48.

Exilliteratur in Großbritannien 1933–1945 (Opladen and Wiesbaden: Springer, 1998).

Wiemann, Dirk, and Gaby Mahlberg (eds), *Perspectives on English Revolutionary Republicanism* (Farnham: Ashgate, 2014).

Willenberg, Jennifer, *Distribution und Übersetzung englischen Schrifttums im Deutschland des 18. Jahrhunderts* (Munich: Saur, 2008).

Williams, J. B. [J. G. Muddiman], 'The Forged "Speeches and Prayers" of the Regicides', *Notes and Queries*, 11th ser., 7 (1913), 301–2.

Williamson, Bethany, 'English Republicanism and Global Slavery in Henry Neville's *The Isle of Pines*', *Eighteenth-Century Fiction*, 27:1 (2014), 1–23.

Wilson, Douglas C., 'Web of Secrecy: Goffe, Whalley, and the Legend of Hadley', *New England Quarterly*, 60 (1987), 515–48.

Winship, Michael, 'Algernon Sidney's Calvinist Republicanism', *Journal of British Studies*, 49:4 (2010), 753–73.

Wiseman, Susan, '"Adam, the Father of All Flesh": Porno-political Rhetoric and Political Theory in and after the Civil War', in James Holstun (ed.), *Pamphlet Wars: Prose in the English Revolution* (London: Frank Cass, 1992), pp. 134–57.

Wootton, David, 'The True Origins of Republicanism: The Disciples of Baron and the Counter-Example of Venturi', in Manuela Albertone (ed.), *Il repubblicanesimo moderno: l'idea di repubblica nella riflessione storica di Franco Venturi* (Naples: Bibliopolis, 2006), pp. 271–304.

Worden, Blair, 'Classical Republicanism and the Puritan Revolution', in Hugh Lloyd-Jones, Valerie Pearl and Blair Worden (eds), *History and Imagination: Essays in Honour of H. R. Trevor-Roper* (Duckworth: Holmes & Meier, 1981), pp. 182–200.

'The Commonwealth Kidney of Algernon Sidney', *Journal of British Studies*, 24 (1985), 1–40.

God's Instruments: Political Conduct in the England of Oliver Cromwell (Oxford: Oxford University Press, 2012).

'Marchamont Nedham and the Beginnings of English Republicanism, 1649–1656', in David Wootton (ed.), *Republicanism, Liberty and Commercial Society, 1649–1776* (Stanford, CA: Stanford University Press, 1994), pp. 45–81.

'Providence and Politics in Cromwellian England', *Past and Present*, 109 (1985), 55–99.

'The Question of Secularisation', in Alan Houston and Steve Pincus (eds), *A Nation Transformed: England after the Restoration* (Cambridge, UK: Cambridge University Press, 2001), pp. 20–40.

'Republicanism and Restoration, 1660–1683', in David Wootton (ed.), *Republicanism, Liberty and Commercial Society* (Stanford, CA: Stanford University Press, 1994), pp. 139–93.

'Republicanism, Regicide and Republic: The English Experience', in Martin van Gelderen and Quentin Skinner (eds), *Republicanism: A Shared European Heritage*, 2 vols (Cambridge, UK: Cambridge University Press, 2002), i, pp. 307–27.

Roundhead Reputations: The English Civil Wars and the Passions of Posterity (London: Penguin, 2002).

'Whig History and Puritan Politics: The *Memoirs* of Edmund Ludlow Revisited', *Historical Research*, 75 (2002), 209–37.

Worthington, David (ed.), *British and Irish Emigrants and Exiles in Europe, 1603–1688* (Leiden and Boston: Brill, 2010).

Zagorin, Perez, *Rebels and Rulers 1500–1660*, 2 vols (Cambridge, UK: Cambridge University Press, 1982).

Zakai, Avihu, *Exile and Kingdom: History and Apocalypse in the Puritan Migration to America* (Cambridge, UK: Cambridge University Press, 1992).

Zuckert, Michael P., *Natural Rights and the New Republicanism* (Princeton, NJ: Princeton University Press, 1994).

UNPUBLISHED THESES

Michel, Henri, 'Montpellier du milieu du XVIIe siècle à la fin du XVIIIe siècle', thèse d'état, Université de Paris I, Panthéon-Sorbonne (1993).

POPULAR HISTORY AND FICTIONAL ACCOUNTS

Jordan, Don, and Michael Walsh, *The King's Revenge: Charles II and the Greatest Manhunt in British History* (London: Abacus, 2013).
Treichler, Hans Peter, *Die Brigantin: Oder Cromwells Königsrichter* (Zurich: Verlag Neue Zürcher Zeitung, 2002).

TELEVISION SHOWS

New Worlds, scripted by Peter Flannery and Martine Brant, broadcast on Channel 4, April 2014, www.channel4.com/programmes/new-worlds, accessed 18 May 2014.

REFERENCE WORKS

Dictionnaire de biographie héraultaise, des origines à nos jours: anciens diocèses de Maguelone-Montpellier, Béziers, Agde, Lodève et Saint-Pons, ed. Pierre Clerc et al. (Montpellier: Librairie/Édition Pierre Clerc, Les Nouvelles Presses du Languedoc Éditeur, 2006).
Dictionnaire de la noblesse: contenant les généalogies, l'histoire et la chronologie des familles nobles de France, ed. Aubert de la Chesnaye Des Bois and Jacques Badier, 19 vols in 4 (Paris: Schlesinger, 1863–76).
Eigen's Political & Historical Quotations, http://politicalquotes.org/node/19094, accessed 25 October 2015.
Greaves, Richard L., and Robert Zaller (eds), *Biographical Dictionary of British Radicals in the Seventeenth Century*, 3 vols (Brighton: Harvester Press, 1982–4).
Oxford English Dictionary, www.oed.com.

Index

For EU product safety concerns, contact us at Calle de José Abascal, 56–1°, 28003 Madrid, Spain or eugpsr@cambridge.org.

www.ingramcontent.com/pod-product-compliance
Ingram Content Group UK Ltd.
Pitfield, Milton Keynes, MK11 3LW, UK
UKHW020358140625
459647UK00020B/2543